Reader Response in Secondary and College Classrooms

Second Edition

Dear Reader:

Read, Reread, Regift!
Here's our regift to you from...

Reader Response in Secondary and College Classrooms

Second Edition

Edited by

Nicholas J. Karolides
University of Wisconsin-River Falls

2000

LAWRENCE ERLBAUM ASSOCIATES, PUBLISHERS

Mahwah, New Jersey   London

Lawrence Erlbaum Associates, Inc., Publishers
10 Industrial Avenue
Mahwah, NJ   07430

Cover design by Inga Karolides

Library of Congress Cataloging-in-Publication Data

Reader response in secondary and college classrooms / edited by Nicholas J. Karolides — 2nd ed.
    p.   cm.
Includes bibliographical references and index.
ISBN 0-8058-3024-3 (pbk : alk. paper)
1. Reader-response criticism. 2. Literature—Study and teaching.   I. Karolides, Nicholas J.
PN98.R38R42   1999
801'.95'071—dc21   99-28305
                                                                      CIP

Books published by Lawrence Erlbaum Associates are printed on acid-free paper, and their bindings are chosen for strength and durability.

Printed in the United States of America
10   9   8   7   6   5   4   3   2   1

To Louise M. Rosenblatt
Teacher, Mentor, Friend

Contents

        to Native American Literature
          David W. Furniss

17 Cultivating Understandings Through Reader Response: 269
        Dawn's Responses to *The Things They Carried* and *When*
        Heaven and Earth Changed Places
          Arlette Ingram Willis

18 Teacher Learning in Response to Autobiographical Literature 287
          Jocelyn Glazier, Mary McVee, Susan Wallace-Cowell, Bette
          Shellhorn, Susan Florio-Ruane, and Taffy E. Raphael

19 Calypso, Jazz, Reggae, Salsa: Literature, Response,   311
        and the African Diaspora
          Linda A. Spears-Bunton

20 Reader Responses to Roethke's "My Papa's Waltz":   327
        Exploring Different Perspectives
          Jean E. Brown and Louise Garcia Harrison

        Glossary: Key Concepts and Strategies   339

        Bibliography   345

        Author Index   361

        Subject Index   365

Preface

The recent upsurge of reader-response criticism has caught the attention of many teachers at all levels of instruction. This consciousness has been fomented by an array of books on response-centered critical theory as well as numerous journal articles and conference presentations (see bibliography). Thus the words *reader response* (which are generally applied to a range of theoretical positions) have moved into the mainstream, in effect rocking the boat of traditional literary thinking and instruction. Yet, practice and, perhaps, full understanding of the pedagogical implications of reader-response theory, have not followed principle.

The focus of these writers has been primarily theory—deciphering and clarifying the reading process, determining the role of the reader in relation to the text, exploring how meaning is made, defining the nature of the interpretive act, and assessing the influence of reading communities and literature conventions. In these analyses, there is evident a continuum of reader-response thinking, a range of attitudes with considerable disagreement among theorists (see Mailloux, Suleiman and Crosman, and Tompkins). However, each acknowledges the significant and active role of the reader, an assumption that runs counter to the premises of traditional theories.

This volume is based on the transactional model of literature asserted by Louise M. Rosenblatt. Soundly expressive of each aspect of response-centered critical theory, it is pedagogically the most meaningful for teachers. As detailed within this text, her approach insists on the reader's role in conjunction with the text, the reader's individuality affecting and being affected by the text. In contrast, other theoretical positions give prominence to the reader, the text, or the context. However, this volume is not specifically concerned with close scrutiny of these variations and emphases. Rather, it focuses on the application of the transactional theory of literature, activating it in the classroom, and the theory being expressed as background.

Frequent requests for teaching suggestions from both secondary school and college teachers—how to put theory into practice—establish the need for this book. Furthermore, some teachers seem to believe that reader response somehow refers to helping students relate to the texts they have been assigned to read—a motivational lesson, perhaps to hook them. Once accomplished, the next step is to revert to a traditional analysis of structure and techniques or a search for the author's presumed meaning. Teachers and prospective teachers now seem ready to learn more about the transactional reader-response approach in the classroom.

OVERVIEW

To facilitate understanding of classroom processes, the chapters of this book are organized in four sections. The first, "The Transactional Theory of Literature," establishes the theory that informs the teaching approaches expressed in this volume.

1. The transactional theory: significant features and understandings; differentiation from other theories.
2. Action comparison of a traditionally oriented lesson and a response-oriented lesson—"A Bird Came Down the Walk" by Emily Dickinson.
3. Principles of reader-response teaching—"Breakings" by Henry Taylor, "Those Winter Sundays" by Robert Hayden, and "Black Walnuts" by Neal Bowers.
4. Modes of response writing, expressive and imaginative—"The Goodnight" by Louis Simpson and "Sign for My Father, Who Stressed the Bunt" by David Bottoms.

The second section, "Initiating Readers' Response: Classroom Processes," spotlights strategies for getting started.

5. Teaching film as literature—*Shane* by Jack Shafer.
6. Introducing poetry to resistant readers—"Mending Wall" by Robert Frost.
7. Using Readers Theatre—"Words" by Sylvia Plath.
8. Introducing a novel—*Ordinary People* by Judith Guest.

"Developing Readers' Responses: Classroom Processes," the third section, focuses on exploring, expanding, and reconsidering responses in relation to a text. The six chapters extend the array of genre and situations:

9. Short story—"Petrified Man" by Eudora Welty.
10. Drama—*The Crucible* and *Death of a Salesman* by Arthur Miller.
11. Nonfiction—*Walden* by Henry David Thoreau.

12. Multiple novels—World War II, United States setting.
13. Multiple genre—Using role-play experiences.
14. Classical drama—*Antigone*; writing-to-learn principles exemplified.

The concluding section, "Exploring Differences: Gender, Race, and Culture," concentrates on the exploration of differences among readers in responding to texts, particularly those that are outside the canon.

15. Gendered reading—*Trifles* by Susan Glaspell.
16. Native American literature—*Laughing Boy* by Oliver LaFarge and *When the Legends Die* by Hal Borland.
17. Vietnam War novels—*The Things They Carried* by Tim O'Brien and *When Heaven and Earth Changed Places* by LeLy Hayslip.
18. Autobiography—*I Know Why the Caged Bird Sings* and *Gather Together in My Name* by Maya Angelou.
19. The African Diaspora—*Krik? Krak!* by Edwidge Danticat.
20. Psychological-social reading—"My Papa's Waltz" by Theodore Roethke.

NEW IN THE SECOND EDITION

This revised edition provides six new chapters, each offering a fresh perspective.

In recognition of the roles film as literature plays in the English classroom. "Reader Response at the Movies" (chap. 5) provides understanding of these roles and the application of reader-response instruction. In similar vein, "Reader Response to Drama: Prospecting for Human Understandings and Connections" (chap. 10) relates a teacher's interior shift from traditional pedagogical thinking to reader-response recognitions and activities, and "Role-Playing Experiences: Expanding Readers' Responses to Literature" (chap. 13) focuses on oral and written "presentations" that immerse students within the situations of the characters.

Three chapters enhance multicultural understanding. "Cultivating Understandings through Reader Response: Dawn's Responses to *The Things They Carried* and *When Heaven and Earth Changed Places*" (chap. 17) provides access to a single student's response development through two readings of a novel as affected by other experiences, particularly a multicultural autobiography. This latter genre is also featured in "Teacher Learning in Response to Autobiographical Literature" (chap 18), which reveals the difficulties encountered in discussing race and sexuality and the growth reflected through the medium of book clubs. Arguing that the acquisition of cultural literacy necessitates reading broadly the literature of the diverse people of the African Diaspora, "Calypso, Jazz, Reggae, Salsa: Literature, Response, and the African Diaspora," (chap. 19) demonstrates how engaging a text can move readers toward understanding the complexity and richness of diverse cultural perspectives.

In addition to these new chapters, several chapters from the first edition have been revised. Also, "invitations," an accessory pedagogical feature, have been inserted in the text of each chapter to focus and expand readers' thinking.

STRATEGIES

This volume is not simply a what-should-I-do-on-Monday cookbook, but an expression of the practice of theory in college and secondary school classrooms. The chapters portray a spectrum of strategies, ranging from biopoems, expressive and imaginative writing, journal writing, Readers Theatre, and role playing to unsent letters, using as examples individual works from the several genres. Although a chapter may focus on a particular technique, other procedures or processes are often conjoined with it to illustrate developmental patterns in a lesson or sequence of lessons.

The authors of these chapters are cognizant that teachers who might have been trained in other theories and methodologies may not be ready for their quite different role and expectations in the reader-centered classroom. The spontaneity and unpredictability may be discomforting, indeed, unnerving, at the outset. Students, too, may not be ready to take on primary reactive roles. They may already have been trained that literature study involves recall of data, definition of forms and techniques, and learning of codified interpretations prescribed by teachers. Recognizing these attributes, the authors have provided stepping stones to develop readiness and confidence and suggestions and insights to ease the passage into the transactional model of teaching and learning.

PEDAGOGICAL FEATURES

In addition to an explanatory introduction to each section, defining its orientation and describing content and direction of the included chapters, this volume provides invitations, a glossary, and an extensive bibliography. The invitations elicit engagement of readers with concepts, attitudes, or strategies expressed in the chapters. As individuals or members of a small group, they are asked to consider ideas, and to practice a strategy, among other activities, in order to enhance understandings. The glossary defines key concepts and strategies that are presented in the text; the bibliography provides an extensive list of resources—books and journal articles—both theoretical and applicatory.

ACKNOWLEDGMENTS

The genesis of this book may be traced back to my undergraduate and graduate study at New York University. I am particularly indebted to Louise M. Rosenblatt, who imbued me with the essence of the transactional theory of literature both in the discussion and modeling of it. She inspired me to create this book. Moreover, her criticism of and suggestions for the theory chapter were most valuable.

I wish to extend appreciation to the chapter authors for meaningful contributions to this volume and for their cooperative willingness to undertake revisions; the strength of the book in large measure results from this joint effort. My sincere thanks also go to my colleagues David Furniss and Marshall Toman for their readiness to react to chapters or passages as potential readers and critics; their comments were direct, honest, and helpful. In this vein, I also thank Jeffrey T. Rissman, graduate student and high school teacher, whose thoughtful reading of the theory chapter gave me special audience insights; and James C. Anderson, who reacted to the glossary from the same perspective with comparably meaningful insights. With regard to preparing this revised edition, I am indebted to five individuals for their careful reading of the first edition text and their pithy advice about possible alterations: three colleagues—Joanne Golden at the University of Delaware, Robert Small at Radford University, and Ruth Wood at the University of Wisconsin-River Falls; two students—respectively, undergraduate and graduate—Michael J. Comer and Heather M. Schmidt, both of the University of Wisconsin-River Falls. I acknowledge with professional respect my editor, Naomi Silverman, of Lawrence Erlbaum Associates, Publishers, for her insightful advice and editing and her enthusiastic belief in this book.

I am also deeply grateful to Inga Karolides for her consistent support, her sensitive sense of language nuances and meaning in editing the text, and her excitingly elegant cover design.

REFERENCES

Mailloux, Steven. *Interpretive Conventions: The Reader in the Study of American Fiction*. Ithaca, NY: Cornell University Press, 1982.

Rosenblatt, Louise M. *Literature as Exploration*. 5th ed. New York: Modern Language Association, 1995.

___ *The Reader, the Text, the Poem: The Transactional Theory of the Literary Work*. Carbondale: Southern Illinois Press, 1978.

Suleiman, Susan R., and Inge Crosman, eds. *The Reader in the Text: Essays on Audience and Interpretation*. Princeton, NJ: Princeton University Press, 1980.

Tompkins, Jane P., ed. *Reader Response Criticism: From Formalist to Post-Structuralism*. Baltimore: Johns Hopkins University Press, 1980.

—Nicholas J. Karolides
University of Wisconsin - River Falls

Contributors

Deborah Appleman is Associate Professor of Educational Studies and director of the Summer Writing Program at Carleton College, Minnesota. She has published articles and book chapters on adolescent response to literature, and has coedited *Braided Lives*, a multicultural literature anthology. She is currently cochair of NCTE's Commission on English and English Studies, a member of the executive committee of the Conference on English Education, and NCTE's Standing Committee on Research; she has served as president of the Minnesota Council of Teachers of English. She was a high school English teacher for 9 years.

Joy Gould Boyum is Professor of Humanities and Director of the Program in Arts and Humanities Education at New York University. Formerly the film critic for *The Wall Street Journal*, she has also reviewed movies for *Glamour* magazine and National Public Radio's *All Things Considered* and has served as both Chair and Vice-Chair of the New York Film Critics Circle. The author of a study of adaptations, *Double Exposure: Fiction Into Film*, she has also contributed essays on film and literature to numerous periodicals, anthologies, and encyclopedias.

Jean E. Brown, Professor at Rhode Island College, Providence, is a former high school English teacher and department chair. She served on the SLATE steering committee of the NCTE and chaired NCTE's Conference on English Education's Commission on Intellectual Freedom. She has coauthored with Elaine Stephens 10 books, including *Young Adult Literature in the Classroom: Sharing the Connections, United in Diversity: Using Multicultural Young Adult Literature,* and *Learning About ... the Civil War Literature and Other Resources for Young People.*

Leila Christenbury is Professor of English Education at Virginia Commonwealth University. She is the immediate past editor of *English Journal* and the author of *Making the Journey: Being and Becoming a Teacher of English Language Arts.*

Susan Florio-Ruane is Professor of Teacher Education at Michigan State University. Her research and teaching interests include the social organization of teaching and learning, learning to teach literacy and the role of conversation and autobiographical text in teaching and learning about culture. She is also former president of the Council on Anthropology and Education and associate editor of the *Anthropology and Education Quarterly*.

David W. Furniss, Professor of English at the University of Wisconsin-River Falls, serves as Director of Freshman English. Prior to this, he taught high school English in Connecticut and Minnesota. His courses include Literature for Adolescents, Composition Theory, and Freshman English. He has written about Vietnam War literature, baseball literature, and composition teaching.

Jocelyn Glazier is a doctoral candidate in the Department of Teacher Education at Michigan State University. Her research interests, prompted in large part by her experience as a high school English teacher, include critical pedagogy, multiculturalism, and literacy. Ms. Glazier currently teaches courses in literacy and in teaching methodology to preservice teachers.

Louise Garcia Harrison teaches English and creative writing at Heritage High School (Saginaw Township, Michigan). In 1991 she was honored with the All Area Arts Award for Saginaw County, and the following year she was named the Michigan Creative Writing Teacher of the Year. She is a member of the Michigan Council of Teachers of English Executive Committee and Creative Writing Chair of the Michigan Youth Arts Festival. Most recently she wrote a chapter in *United in Diversity* from NCTE.

Nicholas J. Karolides, Professor of English and Associate Dean, College of Arts and Sciences, at the University of Wisconsin-River Falls, has served on the Conference of English Education executive board and as editor of the *Wisconsin English Journal*. His major publications include: *The Pioneer in the American Novel*, *Focus on Physical Impairments*, *Focus on Fitness* (coauthor with daughter Melissa), *Censored Books: Critical Viewpoints* (coeditor), *Banned Books: Literature Suppressed on Political Grounds*, *Reader Response in Elementary Classrooms: Quest and Discovery*, and *Reader Response in Secondary and College Classrooms, First Edition*. He was honored with the Regents Teaching Excellence Award for the University of Wisconsin System.

Patricia P. Kelly, formerly a high school English teacher, is Professor of English Education and Director of the Center for Teacher Education at Virginia Tech. She also directs the Southwest Virginia Writing Project. She is past chair of the Assembly on Literature for Adolescents of NCTE and the past vice-chair of the Conference on English Education. She has served as editor of *SIGNAL* and *Virginia English Bulletin*, and coeditor of the *ALAN Review*. She coauthored *Questioning: A Path to Critical Thinking*.

Ron Luce is currently Director of Professional and Organizational Development at Hocking College in Nelsonville, Ohio. He has published numerous articles on innovative techniques for the teaching of writing as well as other education-related issues, edited several publications of *Focus: Teaching English Language Arts*, and published poems. He has served in various roles in NCTE, the Ohio Council of Teachers of English Language Arts, and the Southeastern Ohio Council of Teachers of English.

Mary McVee is a doctoral candidate in the Department of Teacher Education at Michigan State University. Her research interests include issues of culture, language, and narrative. Before coming to Michigan State, she taught in the People's Republic of China and Hong Kong. More recently, she has taught literacy courses to both preservice and in-service teachers.

Elizabeth Ann Poe, a high school English teacher for 13 years, is Assistant Professor of English Education at West Virginia University, where she teaches courses in instructional methods and young adult literature. A former president of the Assembly on Literature for Adolescents of NCTE (ALAN) and book review editor for *The ALAN Review*, she currently serves as editor for *SIGNAL Journal*, the young adult literature publication of the International Reading Association (IRA) and as chair of IRA's Young Adult Literature Committee. She is the author of *Focus on Sexuality*, *Focus on Relationships,* and *Presenting Barbara Wersba*.

Robert E. Probst is Professor of English Education at Georgia State University. A former secondary school teacher and supervisor of English, he is the author of *Response and Analysis: Teaching Literature in Junior and Senior High School* and senior author of *Elements of Literature*, a literature, composition, and language program for Grades 6–12, as well as numerous articles on the teaching of literature and composition. He has served on the NCTE Committee on Research, the Commission on Reading, and on the board of directors of the Adolescent Literature Assembly.

Laura Quinn is Associate Professor of English and Women's Studies at Allegheny College, Pennsylvania. She taught English for 8 years at the University of Wisconsin-River Falls and also coordinated the Women's Studies Program. Her main research interests are Africa American literature and the intersection of politics and literature. She has published articles on James Baldwin and Langston Hughes.

Taffy E. Raphael, Professor in the Department of Reading and Language Arts at Oakland University, Michigan, was honored with the Outstanding Teacher Educator in Reading Award from the International Reading Association in 1997. She has published her research work on the Book Club Project—a literature-based reading curriculum centered around student-led literature discussion groups—in journals such as *Reading Research Quarterly, Research in the Teaching of English,* and *Language Arts.* Raphael is vice-president-elect of the National Reading Conference, taking office in 1999.

Duane H. Roen is Professor of English and formerly Director of Composition at Arizona State University. Before pursuing his PhD degree, he taught high school English in Wisconsin for 5 years. His research interests include gender and written language, collaboration, audience, and writing across the curriculum. He has published five books: *A Sense of Audience in Written Communication* (with Gesa Kirsch), *Richness in Writing: Empowering ESL Students* (with Donna M. Johnson), *Becoming Expert: Writing and Thinking in the Disciplines* (with Stuart Brown and Robert Mittan), *The Writer's Toolbox* (with Stuart Brown and Robert Mittan), and *Living Rhetoric and Composition: Stories of the Discipline* (with Theresa Enos and Stuart Brown). He has also written more than 130 book chapters, articles, and conference papers.

Mary Jo Schaars, now retired, taught at Stevens Point Area Senior High School in Wisconsin. Her professional publications include articles on teaching *My Antonia*, Thoreau, and the writing of poetry to high school students.

Bette Shellhorn is an advanced doctoral student and instructor in the Department of Teacher Education at Michigan State University. She teaches courses in literacy instruction to undergraduates with a focus on reading and writing methods. She also coordinates work with a group of classroom teachers for the CIERA research project at Michigan State University, working with classroom teachers to develop literacy curriculum for at-risk students.

Robert C. Small, Jr. is past chair of both the Assembly on Literature for Adolescents of NCTE and the Conference on English Education. He is currently coeditor of *The ALAN Review* and chair of the Intellectual Freedom Committee of the International Reading Association. He is Dean of the College of Education at Radford University in Virginia.

Linda A. Spears-Bunton is Associate Professor and Program Director of English Education at Florida International University. Her most recent publications include a chapter in *Teaching Multicultural Literature: Grades 9–12, Books and Beyond,* and *Transforming Curriculum for a Culturally Diverse*

Society, as well as articles in several journals and monographs. Actively engaged in the education of U.S. students for more than two decades, Spears-Bunton has taught elementary, middle, and high school, and has taught in community colleges and in corporations. She is the recipient of numerous awards for excellence in teaching and scholarship.

Marshall Toman, Professor of English at the University of Wisconsin-River Falls, has previously published on various U.S. authors. Recently, he was a Fulbright senior lecturer at Palacky University and Masaryk University in the Czech Republic.

Linda Varvel has taught English in public high schools in Minnesota for 8 years, most recently teaching and developing curricula for the American Literature portion of the American Studies course at Henry Sibley High School in St. Paul. She is currently on leave to teach acting and direct drama productions at the Minnesota State Arts High School in Golden Valley, Minnesota.

Susan Wallace-Cowell is a doctoral candidate in education psychology at Michigan State University. Her research interests are in the area of adolescent identity development and gender. She is currently completing her dissertation on girls' identity development in a book club discussion group.

Arlette Ingram Willis is Associate Professor at the University of Illinois at Urbana-Champaign. Her published works include: "Reading the World of School Literacy" in *Harvard Educational Review*, "Expanding the Boundaries: A Reaction to the First Grade Reading Studies," *Reading Research Quarterly*; "A Conversation with Gloria Ladson-Billings" (with Karla Lewis) in *Language Arts;* and *Teaching and Multicultural Literature in Grades 9–12: Moving Beyond the Canon.*

Part I

The Transactional Theory
of Literature

The theoretical base for the teaching strategies exhibited in this book is represented in this section. The active, central role of the reader in concert with the text is expressed; in conjunction, the role of the teacher in the instructional setting is clarified. The authors provide discussion of theory and explanation of methodological principles.

Two chapters focus more directly on explanation of reader-response theory, but the authors include appropriate illustrations to entice the pedagogical imagination. The other chapters provide experiences of response-based instruction, providing transcripts of class discussions to illustrate pedagogical practice. Embedded in all the presentations are examples of teaching approaches and suggestions that may be usefully applied to other learning situations.

In chapter 1, I express the dynamics of the reading act as a transactional process. I discuss the reader's active, central role and the factors that influence the preliminary and ongoing responses to the text. The reading process is explained with special attention to the concept of selective attention and the stances the reader may take on the aesthetic–efferent continuum. The role of the author in relation to the text is discussed, as is the validity of readers' responses. The spectrum of reader-response criticism is defined and contrasted with traditional criticism. Classroom pedagogy, illustrated with an initial lesson to introduce *Hiroshima*, expresses the nature and direction of classroom pedagogy.

What role does the teacher play in the response-oriented classroom? What goals are sought? In chapter 2, Robert C. Small, Jr., compares the attitudes and questioning procedures of two teachers, one with a traditional orientation and the other with a response orientation. A transcript of both classes discussing "A Bird Came Down the Walk" by Emily Dickinson provides a meaningful contrast of processes and learnings. He clarifies the goals implicit in these strategies and in the planning conducted by the teachers. Small establishes the active experiences of the readers, in contrast to the carefully orchestrated hunt for the traditional teacher's predetermined answers. This chapter invites comparative analysis.

Leila Christenbury builds her discussion in chapter 3 of reader-response methodology on the dual premises that selected literature must have some connection with students' lives and the teaching approach must be inductive. She identifies five guiding principles: encouraging extensive student talk, making a community of meaning, asking not telling, linking to personal experience, and affirming students' responses. These are illustrated in the teaching of three poems in two classrooms. The apparent understandings generated in these discussions affirm that students can make meaning out of their responses. Moreover, they affirm that student discussion need not be limited to a question–short-answer format with the teacher spoon-feeding the "correct" interpretation.

In chapter 4, Robert E. Probst relates two concepts that inform current English teaching: the unique relationship of reader to text, reflecting the individuality of response to literature; and the broadened range of written discourse to accommodate the variety of perceptions and needs of students. He proposes alternatives to the standard analysis paper, illustrating three types: the personal response growing from the text, focusing on feelings, memories, and conceptions; the creation of imaginative texts, building, perhaps, on a powerfully evoked image; and assertions about the text. His central thesis states that there is more than one perspective to bring to those responses. He argues that "we should invite students to engage in those other ways of experiencing literature and in those other modes of writing."

The Transactional Theory of Literature

Nicholas J. Karolides

"What story are you reading anyway?" My teaching colleague flung that remark at me in the heat of a discussion of John Steinbeck's "The Chrysanthemums." The class of seniors and graduate students laughed, as did she, the tone of the class being relaxed as well as honest. However, despite the humor of the retort to something that I had said, it expressed emphatically the disparity between our interpretations.

We were team teaching a course focusing on literature by and about women. The discussion had moved from introductory responses about the character's behavior to the apparent alienation of Elissa Allen from her husband and her separation from his world of ranch management. Students had offered their perceptions of her feelings and of what had affected her. The view that Elissa is a victim of social attitudes that prevent her from realizing her full potential led to the idea that she is victimizing herself in response to these attitudes. Her childlessness as a key factor in her self-victimization was asserted.

Disagreement of interpretation bubbled up, with my colleague and me on different "sides" of the response; she had perceived Elissa as self-victimizing, blaming herself because she was childless. I sensed Elissa's frustration as resulting from the socially enforced limitations of her role and freedom, given her evident capability and power, thus the earlier remark. Curiously, the factor of childlessness had not occurred to any of the several men in the class; those to whom it was evident were women, although a few of the younger ones hadn't considered this idea. Scrutiny of the text and class reflections about these responses found support for both interpretations.

Proponents of the childlessness view pointed to Elissa's unfulfillment as expressed in her manner—her overeagerness in caring for her mums that were seen as child substitutes, in the fact that there were no children, and the story not specifically placing blame on her husband or society for her condition. They found further support in the several symbols of fertility and Elissa's subdued passion. Contrasting responses focused on the societal constraints on women alluded to in the text—what they can do, where they can go—and the noncommunicative relationship of wife and husband; childlessness is not mentioned in the text. Steinbeck does not state precisely the factors involved in the character's condition or conditioning.

How much each reader contributes is clearly signified in this class's exchange. All readers do not come away from reading a text with the same impressions. Even when those readers are trained and experienced, their felt emotions and ideas will vary from the subtle to the affectively and intellectually significant. Revelations of these differences expand the meaningful potential of the text and of the readers' transactions with it.

The classroom experience briefly summarized here illustrates theoretical issues surrounding the evoking and interpreting of literature and the role that readers play. In recent decades, theories of literature, collectively termed *reader-response criticism,* have signaled a central role for readers as active agents in the reading process. Because the reader's activity had been minimized or rejected by previous theoretical approaches, reader-response criticism has effected a major shift away from "traditional" critical systems and instructional practice.

Although they each reflect the role of the reader, reader-response approaches are not identical in their emphases. They range, as categorized by Richard Beach, from the textual, orientation toward the text; the experiential, a focus on the reader's engagement with text; the psychological, the concern with cognitive and subconscious forces; to the social and the cultural, the recognition of the social and cultural features that affect meaning. (These and the contrasting foci of the traditional theoretical approaches are briefly summarized later in this chapter.[1])

Within the experiential model, the transactional theory of literature, the core of this volume, gives equal voice to the reader and the text and acknowledges the conpenetration of a reader and a text, each conditioning the other. Meaning evolves from the fusion of the author's text and the reader's personality and experience. By thus promoting the reader to an equal partnership in the reading process, the transactional theory necessar-

---

[1]Richard Beach establishes a fuller range and detailed discussion of reader-response theories in *A Teacher's Introduction to Reader Response Theories.* At the conclusion of the presentation of each category, he provides a discussion of the perceived limitation of each.

ily recognizes the inclusion of psychological, social, and cultural contexts of the reader's life. This theoretical focus was first promulgated by Louise M. Rosenblatt in *Literature as Exploration* in 1938 and expounded in *The Reader, the Text, the Poem* in 1978.

READING AS A TRANSACTIONAL PROCESS

Consider reading, the act of reading. It necessarily involves a reader and a text. (The word *text* signifies the marks—i.e., the words as symbols—on the page, as differentiated from "literary work" or "poem," which, as I explain in more detail, evolves from the transaction of a reader with the text.) Everyone would agree that a friend or teacher telling you about a book is not an act of reading for you. Others can no more read and experience a book for you than they can relieve your hunger pangs by eating your dinner. Similarly, reading a synopsis of a book does not substitute for reading it. You may learn something *about* the book, but you will not have experienced it. Further, without a reader, text does not come into existence—does not have meaning or invoke feelings and sensations—but instead is just squiggles on a page.

This focus on the reader and the text grows out of an understanding of what happens during the process of reading; it recognizes that readers, rather than being passive recipients of text, like empty vessels being filled, are active during the process. They are not spectators of the text but performers *with* the text.

According to the central premise, the literary work exists in the transaction between the reader and the text. The term *transaction* is meaningful in expressing the reader–text relationship during the reading event. It signals the connection between them and the nature of the connection. Transaction denotes a situation of mutuality. During the reading activity, the reader and text mutually act on each other, each affecting and conditioning the other.

> In discussion of the reading process, as in other disciplines undergoing revision, we need to free ourselves from unscrutinized assumptions implicit in the usual terminology and in the very structure of our language. The usual phrasing makes it difficult to attempt to do justice to the nature of the actual reading event. The reader, we can say, interprets the text. (The reader acts on the text.) Or we can say, the text produces a response in the reader. (The text acts on the reader.) Each of these phrasings, because it implies a single line of action by one separate element on another separate element, distorts the actual reading process. The relation between reader and text is not linear. It is a situation, an event at a particular time and place in which each element conditions the other. (Rosenblatt, *Reader* 16)

The reader's persona infuses the text; the text impresses the reader. From this blending, an experience is evoked, a meaning is understood for each particular reader.

Several prerequisites are necessary before the reading transaction can take place. The reading act begins with the assumption that the marks on the page are decipherable as words. For more to occur, not only must the text be understandable, within the grasp of the reader, but the reader must also be an active participant. The former may be self-evident, but it merits comment as it applies to the selection of materials for classroom use.

The language of a text, the situation, the characters, or the expressed issues can dissuade a reader from comprehension of the text and thus inhibit involvement with it. In effect, if the reader has insufficient linguistic or experiential background to allow participation, the reader cannot relate to the text, and the reading act will be short-circuited.

The reader's willingness to engage with the text is another necessary ingredient for the fulfillment of the reading act. Distraction or indifference can similarly cause a short circuit. In such meager encounters, the reader may read words, but inattention blocks response. There may be varying degrees of comprehension, but a literary work will not be evoked. Engagement with the text, both emotional and intellectual—although not necessarily immediate or concurrent—is necessary for the evolution of a literary work.

THE READER AND THE READING PROCESS

What influences a reader's responses to a text? Given the text's understandability and the reader's active participation, what happens during the reading process? The relationship between reader and text is dynamic. The reader responding is also dynamic, alive to stimulus and response. Further, what a reader makes of a text will reflect the reader's state of being at a particular time and place and in a particular situation, as well as the reader's relationship to the text.

Presumably, the text is the same for all readers; that is, the marks on the page—the words and the structures—appear the same. Individual readers, however, approach these words and structures with a particular frame of mind formed by their own personal milieu. Indeed, readers' responses to individual words may well vary in connotation, expression, and interpretation; shades of meaning, experientially induced, differing from one reader to the next, may be affective. Over time and region, words may even vary in denotation. Readers, influenced by past experiences or lack of them and current circumstances, regional origins and upbringing, gender, age, and past and present readings, will vary in their responses from those of others. Even readers of the same age, similar background, and circle of relationships will express differences in general impression and nuances of feelings. The reading event for each reader is unique.

> Through the medium of words, the text brings into the reader's consciousness certain concepts, certain sensuous experiences, certain images of things, people, actions, scenes. The special meanings and, more particularly, the submerged associations that the words and images have for the individual reader will largely determine what the work communicates. . . . The reader brings to the work personality traits, memories of past events, present needs and preoccupations, a particular mood of the moment, and a particular physical condition. These and many other elements in a never-to-be-duplicated combination enter into the reader's relationship with the text. (Rosenblatt, *Literature* 30–31)

The reading situation is another dynamic factor. A particular stimulus, mood or preoccupation, context or reason for reading (perhaps, teacher's directions), and the *stance* taken toward the reading, each may influence the reading transaction. These factors suggest not only that the reading transaction is particular to each reader, but also that it is an *event in time* (Rosenblatt's term). Thus, considering the breadth of experiences among readers at any one time and over time (as well as the same reader over time), the range of possible readings of a single text is potentially infinite.

The *reading event* initiates the literary experience, the first formation of the literary work. It should not be construed, however, that this constitutes an immediate flash of insight or meaning comparable to Athena emerging full grown from the head of Zeus. Rather, the process is more evolutionary. The reader reacts to words and situations and the interplay of one word or situation with another. Expectations of the text are projected; later features —words, events, or information—may solidify these impressions or may bring about a revision. Clues of context are perceived and integrated. The reader constructs a constantly adjusted scaffold of understandings attempting to account for the text's many features. A second reading, if there is one, can reveal additional or revised nuances. Depending on the reader's involvement and reading maturity, as well as the text itself, the reading process is reflective and demanding.

The reading is not linear; comparable to the writing process, it is recursive, a backward-and-forward exploration of what is being evoked in relation to the text. Recursiveness may be an actual turning back of pages—immediate glances back or returns many pages later, provocation by another passage to reread a segment to confirm or reconsider an impression, the implication of a behavior or a situation. Recursiveness may be thoughtful reflection on previous scenes, events, or behaviors to savor the images or sensations or to consider the import of a particular dialogue or event. Such explorations, conscious or subconscious, immediate or prolonged, can reveal additional nuances and developmental understandings.

The reader makes choices, both conscious and subconscious; the concept of *selective attention* (attributed to William James, Rosenblatt, *Reader*) operates. One semantic nuance may be selected over another; one feeling state may be heightened in the interplay among the text, the individual's emotional attitudes, and the surrounding situation. From the array of meanings and feelings that are conjured up, the reader selects those that fit with what has already been evoked, or if necessary, reviews and revises the choices or syntheses that have been made (Rosenblatt, Writing 11–12). A dominant perception or purpose in the reader may activate or emphasize certain features or language over others, may skew the reading event to conform to the current circumstances. Close identification with characters or events may intensify the response. Implicit in this situation is the continuous, dynamic interplay between reader and text during which meaning evolves. The created response is the realized experience of the reader.

Social and cultural contextual differences are reflected in these choices. Involvement and interest are conditioned by perceived identity with or distance from the culture and characters, issues, and events. Markers are connected with and understood or given scant attention and, perhaps, misunderstood. What may be a rich experience for the cultural insider may be a poor one for the outsider. Certain historical texts can present comparable selective attention alternatives.

Invitation 1.1

Select a text featuring a culture different from your own. Read it with you mind's eye focused on your responses to cultural features: situations, attitudes, and language. Try to determine, through conversations with others inside and outside the represented culture, what would or would not likely be responded to by individuals in either group. If this isn't feasible, try gender depiction and response.

Thus a range of responses results from the dynamic relationship between readers and text, from differences among readers, and from aspects of the text that are ambiguous or undefined. Each transaction by a reader, given different reading occasions—particular times and circumstances—will be unique as the reader's frame of mind, situation, and experiences change.

STANCE

How—in what frame of mind, with what purpose or expectation—a reader approaches a text depends in part on the text, in part on the reader, and certainly, the two of them together. Consciously or unconsciously, the reader adopts a *stance* toward the reading of a text. The same text may be approached with different purposes or attitudes by different readers or by the same reader at different times.

A reader's approach to a text, that is, the focus of attention or purpose, may be internally motivated or externally assigned, in part or wholly. Thus, a student in a biology class concentrating on a text, especially when preparing for an examination, reads with a quite different stance than one who is engrossed in Jack London's *The Call of the Wild*. When reading, the stance taken may be *predominantly efferent* (nonliterary/informational) or *predominantly aesthetic* (literary) on a continuum of response possibilities somewhere between the two extremes. Depending on the occasion of the reading event, readers may adopt a focus along a continuum, adapting their stance accordingly. Rosenblatt explains:

> The term "efferent" (from the Latin *efferre*, to carry away) designates the kind of reading in which attention is centered predominantly on what is to be extracted and retained after the reading event. An extreme example is the man who has accidentally swallowed a poisonous liquid, and who is rapidly reading the label on the bottle to learn the antidote. Here, surely, we see an illustration of [William] James' point about "selective attention" and our capacity to push into the periphery of awareness those elements that do not serve our present interests. The man's attention is focused on learning what is to be done as soon as the reading ends. He concentrates on what the words point to, their barest public referents, and on constructing the directions for future action. Reading a newspaper, a textbook, or a legal brief would usually provide a similar, though less extreme, instance of the predominantly efferent stance.
>
> The predominantly aesthetic stance covers the other half of the continuum. The term "aesthetic" is used because its Greek source involved perception through the senses, feelings, and intuitions. In this kind of reading, the reader adopts an attitude of readiness to focus attention on what is being lived through *during* the reading event. Welcomed into the awareness are not only the public referents of the verbal signs but also the ideas that are the residue of past psychological events involving those words and their referents. Attention may include the sounds and rhythms of the words themselves, heard in "the inner ear." (Writing 12–13)

The usual explanation of these differences in reading stance is to cite differences in the texts themselves. Some are seen as basically informational, whereas others are literary, suggesting that the differences in the reading of a text arise out of the nature of the content or the structure and style, leading to the reader's approach. For example, a psychology textbook is different from *Crime and Punishment*, often termed a psychological novel.

On the surface, there is some validity to this position. A reader's stance often is adopted in concert with the perceived substance and language of texts, an efferent stance matching the nature of textbooks, baseball cards, and hard news stories, whereas an aesthetic stance relates to folktales, novels, plays, and poems. Authors have intentions and provide guidance to promote or invite a stance appropriate to their purposes and material. For an efferent stance, to project an informational direction, the language choices will essentially be denotative or public—the dictionary definitions—eschewing the images and sensation-laden, connotative, personally associative words favored to create an aesthetic stance. The word *heart* will be presented differently in the context of a science or health fitness text in contrast to its expression in Conrad's *Heart of Darkness*. Structure and content are likewise adapted to signal one stance or the other. Some authors seem to consciously seek a blended response as conveyed by their choices of language, style, and content. Other texts are more deliberately either informational or affective.

The nature of the text is influential but not entirely determinate. The idea that the text fixes the reading purpose, assumed in the past, denies the dynamics of the reading process and belies the role of the reader who is neither passive nor neutral. It assumes a given text is always read the same way. In fact, the reader determines, consciously or unconsciously, the purpose of the reading; the reader is influenced by many factors—the particular reading occasion, present needs, personal concerns—and decides what clues, practical effects, or feeling states to attend to and what results to expect or desire.

The nature of the reader's activity—the stance taken before and during the processing of the text—determines how a response is generated and what response is evoked. The cautionary word *often* used previously is deliberate. It is quite possible to read information-oriented texts with an aesthetic or partially aesthetic stance and, in reverse, to read aesthetic-oriented texts with an efferent or partially efferent stance. Readers are more likely to adopt an aesthetic stance toward a novel that explores a character's reactions to a death, identifying with the loss and emotional travail. However, if the novel is read to ascertain and analyze coping strategies, perhaps because that is the basis of an assignment, then the reading may be limited to the gleaning of information parallel to a reading of the Elizabeth Kubler-Ross analysis of the stages of grief in *On Death and Dying*. Another example: The first question, "What is the color of the bride's dress?" asked in a college reader at the end of Stephen Crane's short story "The Bride Comes to Yellow Sky," certainly projects an efferent/informational stance for the reader. Similarly, despite the aesthetic stance suggested by the structure of a poem, the directions for a classroom assignment and the discussion questions may induce an efferent reading. (Of course, the reader's aesthetic sensibilities may be engaged but the assignment would lead to their neglect.) In contrast, an essentially informative text—about, for example, destruction of the rain forests or child abuse—may well evoke feeling states during the reading that take precedence over the efferent stance for a reader. For example, Rachel Carsons's *Silent Spring*, which discusses the destructive effects of chemicals on the environment, has engendered reactions across the stance continuum from efferent to aesthetic. Newspaper accounts of a baseball game and even a baseball card of an esteemed athlete may call forth vivid emotions from the wellsprings of memory. As indicated earlier, one text may elicit different stances among readers or one reader from one reading event to another.

Invitation 1.2

Select a literary text that you have recently read. List several questions that would tend to provoke an efferent response and several that would promote an aesthetic response. Exchange questions with a peer for comparison and evaluation.

A dualistic view of stance is inappropriate. Potentially, there are readings at either extreme end of the aesthetic–efferent continuum. However, as the words *predominantly* and *partially* suggest, along with the previous examples, readings are more apt to be a blend of the two stances. Despite an efferent orientation, personal experiences, visions, or wishful thoughts may intrude. Similarly, an aesthetic response may be modified, at least subliminally acknowledged, by informational features. The degree of blending that occurs is variable from reader to reader and situation to situation, and it is changeable over time. At the theoretical middle of the stance continuum, the reader would be applying an equal measure of expectations, attitudes, and reading behaviors of the two stances.

The dynamics of the reader's stance are particularly significant in a classroom situation. Indirectly or directly, the teacher can markedly affect the stance that predominates in the transactions of student readers with texts through classroom atmosphere, questions, and assignments.

THE AUTHOR'S ROLES

Authors create the written text. As already noted, they process the language and select the moments in time and the characters to convey feelings, sensations, concepts, and attitudes to readers. Their expectation is to lead readers to share their insights. In a meaningful way, they, too, live through the experience of the text in initiating and incubating it, processing and reading it until it reaches final form. Writers create out of their experience and imagination.

However, a text, once removed, once published, is no longer in the author's control. In a very real sense, the author is outside the immediate, intimate reading circle. A body of words exists, the author's feelings and intentions threaded within them, waiting for a reader to respond to them, to enliven them. The words, in effect, have no symbolic meaning—are only marks on the page—until the reading event occurs, until the literary work has been lived through by the reader. To what extent this is a replication of the author's intention cannot be established. Even if authors have identified their intention, we cannot be sure that the text fulfills it, that there are, further, no unbidden, unconscious elements reflected in the text. As composition theory establishes—and writers themselves often attest—composing is not altogether conscious; the subconscious also operates during the composing process. Composing research also indicates that the pattern of intention and understanding of the writer shifts as the text evolves, adapts as the writer discovers meanings. Indeed, the author may not be altogether aware of revealed meanings.

In real terms, we can imagine the author's work as an intricately designed, multicolored tapestry; the multilayered symbols, figured in the author's design, are perceived by readers through their individual consciousness. Under the stimulus of the author's text, through its guidance and direction, readers create (or re-create) out of their experience and imagination a literary work.

THE TEXT

The discussion up to this point has concentrated on the reader, who has long been the neglected performer of the reading act. However, the transactional theory of literature by no means ignores the text. It is a necessary component of the reading transaction within which the literary work comes into being. It is the catalyst for the reading experience. In addition, the text acts as a mechanism of control or constraint, providing guidance for the reader. Its words, images, and structures propose stance, influence response, and promote meaning.

As has been herein expressed, however, the text does not stand alone. A reader is required to activate the marks on the page. The emerging response, "'the poem' cannot be equated solely with *either* the text *or* the experience of the reader" (Rosenblatt, *Reader* 105) but to a dynamic relationship between the two, each affecting and conditioning the other. The text plays a vital role, neither predominant nor submissive.

The transactional nature of the reading process demonstrates the dynamic nature of the text, as differentiated from the traditional view of the text as unchanging, static, with a single meaning. Although the words on the page appear the same, the text is variable. What the reader makes of the verbal signs reflects shifts in the denotation and connotation of words as well as differences in their perception of images and issues. These are subject to the social and psychological attitudes and behaviors of readers. The effect of such language flexibility is to shift the pattern of response. Thus, although an author may have carefully chosen language and incident with quite specific references and impressions—perhaps readily understood by the author's immediate contemporaries (although this is unlikely to be universal) —responses of audiences with variant experiences, especially those of another time and place, are subject to other environmental forces.

The changing dynamics of a text's issues, characters, relationships, and structures are illustrated by some examples from my classes. During the late 1960s and 1970s when the civil rights movement was at its peak, student readers readily perceived the racial factor as critical to Othello's self-doubt and disintegrating self-control, and easily empathized with his psychological loss. Before and after this period, however, this aspect of Othello's character has emerged less forcefully in discussion and is only minimally explored. During the height of the Vietnam War, some readers of Stephen Crane's *The Red Badge of Courage*—particularly those with antiwar sentiments—acknowledged the possibility that the soldier's leaving the battle was his "red badge of courage"; such responses echoed support for Americans who resisted the call to arms. Readers of John Knowles's *A Separate Peace* tend to identify with either the protagonist Gene, who is a good student but personally uncertain, or with Finny, the carefree, exuberant athlete. This choice, a reflection of the reader's personal sense and maturity, alters the shape and sense of the novel. Responses to Charlotte Gilman's "The Yellow Wallpaper" have moved from seeing it as a horror story to seeing it as feminist protest, reflecting the late 20th-century angles of vision, influenced by feminist criticism, and increased understanding of the situation of women.

VALIDITY OF READERS' RESPONSES

Questions are frequently asked about the validity of individual reader's responses. If a range of responses is recognized as probable and acceptable, is this akin to encouraging an "anything goes" idea? How can one response be more or less valid than another? How can validity be measured?

> What each reader makes of the text is, indeed, *for him* the poem, in the sense that this is his only direct perception of it. No one else can read it for him. He may learn indirectly about others' experiences with the text; he may come to see that his own was confused or impoverished, and he may then be stimulated to attempt to call forth from the text a better poem. But this he must do himself, and only what he himself experiences in relation to the text is—again let us underline—*for him,* the work. (Rosenblatt, *Reader* 105)

This often-quoted passage establishes the significant idea that readers make meaning—create the poem for themselves. It also suggests some of the re-

vision stimuli outside and within the text that may bring about a reexperi-
encing of the text to re-create a fuller meaning. Additionally, it affirms, in
the context of transactional theory, that a text can call forth different experiences, one reader from another, and in addition, not only different, but
"better."

To some critics, theorists, and teachers, this may sound like license—an
"anything goes" premise. In the paragraph immediately preceding the
quoted one, Rosenblatt unequivocally rejects this notion: "Something en-
capsuled in the reader's mind without relevance to the text may be a wonderful fantasy, but the term 'poem' or 'literary work,' in transactional terminology, would not be applicable to such a mental experience any more
than to an entity apart from a reader" (*Reader* 105). Thus, whereas a range of
responses is recognized as probable and acceptable, some may be irrelevant
to the text. Such a response may be valued by and valuable to the reader; it
may reflect a heightened personal experience triggered by a feature of the
text, but it has taken the reader far afield from the text. It may be "confused
or impoverished," invalid or less valid than other responses in relation to the
total text.

Invitation 1.3

Consider the distinction posed between the assertions "valuable for
the reader" and "invalid or less valid transactions with the text."
What are the implications for classroom instruction?

Resisting the idea of an anything goes response does not, however, en-
force the position of a single, identifiable meaning of a text, one interpretation for the literary work. Such arguments are usually made in relation to
the author's intention (discussed by Crosman, in "Do Readers Make Meaning"[2]) and suggested by such questions as "What is the author's purpose?
What does the author mean by . . . ?" Even if the idea of a fully visualized
purpose were not contestable by what we have learned about the composing
process and what authors themselves have to say (along with the near
impossibility of absolutely establishing an author's purpose), it should be
understood that most expert-identified purposes and meanings of texts are

---

[2]In "Do Readers Make Meaning?" Crosman argued that any word or text has meaning only
when it is placed into a larger context, the context of the author's intentions being only one
possible way of understanding a text. The difficulty is that for most texts, there is no author's
stated intention and if there is it is "ambiguous or contradictory, and it must be subjected to the
same process of reader interpretation" (161). Further, Crosman examines and refutes the assumption of one meaning, implied by the author's intention concept.

established by individual readers; that is, readers with "authority." It is not uncommon for one individual authority to promote an interpretation different from another's. This further belies the one-interpretation attitude.

The notion of correctness is based on the belief that the text holds the answers—that a careful scrutiny of all the evidence within the text (aided by supporting data outside the text) will lead to a particular result. The classroom situation described at the beginning of this chapter, as do numerous other examples in this book, exemplifies the fallacy of this position.

The transactional nature of the reading act recognizes the mutuality of reader and text. Validity of a reading is identified in relation to a consistent set of criteria, implicit or explicit. Adequacy of interpretation can be measured against the constraints of the text: to what degree does the individual response include the various features of the text—situations and events, character behaviors and attitudes—and the nuances of language; to what degree does it include aspects that do not reflect the text; to what extent have personal memories or images derailed the response; to what degree has the reading evoked a coherent work? Thus, the out-of-context response —a memory or experience triggered by something in the text—takes the reader far afield or the strongly skewed response leads to the neglect of features of the text. As noted earlier, these may be valuable responses for the reader but, given the criteria, invalid or less valid transactions with the text.

An example of such a valuable but invalid response can be seen in a college student's transaction with Robert Frost's poem, "Stopping by Woods on a Snowy Evening." She asserted that the poem is set on Christmas Eve, the coldest and stillest night of the year, and that the speaker is Santa Claus. She used several lines—"promises to keep, and miles to go before I sleep"—to support her view, but ignored others that do not fit.

A pattern measuring the degree of validity is suggested by Robert Probst: "The reader's experience falls somewhere on a continuum—at one extreme is a reading highly responsive to and closely controlled by the text, and at the other a reading triggered by the text but otherwise responsive to and controlled by the psyche of the reader" (17).

Validity may also be construed as age or maturity-skill related. Naturally, the responses of younger children or less mature readers are influenced by their maturational and chronological age, reading experiences, and interpretive skills. Comparable to the continuum suggested by Probst, a developmental response continuum may be imagined: Third-grade children responding to Frost's poem (it is actually labeled a third-grade poem in a college children's literature anthology) are likely to envision the scene—the falling snow, the questioning horse in midjourney, the magic of the woods; middle schoolers (at least many of those I have taught have so responded) will probably relate to the sense of responsibility and the need to accomplish things as suggested in the closing lines, although they usually also maintain an orientation to the scene. College students (the poem is also anthologized in college textbooks) often go beyond this, arguing whether the repetition of sleep in the closing stanza refers to a much-needed rest after and before a day full of responsibilities or to impending death. Each response is appropriate and valid for each group of readers.

LITERARY THEORIES AND
CLASSROOM IMPLICATIONS

The transactional theory of literature explored here is "central to the experiential theories of response" (Beach 49). Beach's definition is process oriented: "Experiential theorists focus on the nature of readers' engagement or experiences with texts—the ways in which, for example, readers identify with characters, visualize images, relate personal experiences to the text, or construct the world of the text" (8). A related orientation, subjective criticism, identified with David Bleich, promotes the value of the emotional in readers' responses: "Readers enter into an inner dialogue between their experience with the text and their own conceptual framework, creating a dialectical tension between private experience and shared public knowledge which leads to a change in perceptions" (Beach 53). Bleich asserts that subjective response leads to cognitive understanding.

In contrast, "textual theorists focus on how readers draw on and deploy their knowledge of text or genre conventions to respond to specific text features" (Beach 8). Readers familiar with these conventions may respond differently from those who lack knowledge, which, according to Peter Rabinowitz, is acquired primarily from the experience of reading. Kenneth Burke, reflecting a rhetorical theory of response, notes, "Form in literature is an arousing and fulfillment of desires. A work has form in so far as one part leads a reader to anticipate another part, to be gratified by the sequence" (quoted in Beach 33). Phenomenological response theorists focus on how the text shapes meaning. Wolfgang Iser recognizes that a text is a set of incomplete instructions; that is, having gaps or blanks in the text. These unwritten aspects—background, unspoken dialogue, unstated relationships —are filled in by the reader, who reacts to the suggestion of the situations. It is a dynamic process in which the text imposes limits and the reader's imagination, activated by the text, works out the details. Nevertheless, despite this active role for the reader, the text is perceived to be an independent entity and the role of subjective experiences in shaping meaning is underconsidered. The pedagogical debate about applying the textual theory of response is between direct instruction and experiential learning, or between "knowing-that" and "knowing-how" knowledge.

"Psychological theorists focus on readers' cognitive or subconscious processes and how those processes vary according to both unique individual personality and developmental level" (Beach 8). Such response theorists reflect a variety of psychology disciplines, among them being developmental—relating the changes in responses to readers' developmental levels (see J. A. Appleyard); cognitive processing—understanding the thinking processes readers use as they respond to texts (see Robert J. Marzano); and psychoanalytic—considering the application of readers' subconscious fantasy themes to shaping meaning (see Norman Holland). This group of theorists express more attention to what happens to the reader. Developmental psychology theories are helpful to teachers in predicting and assessing readiness for and nature of response.

The influence of the social context on the reader–text transaction is the basis for *social theories of response.* "A social theorist finds meaning as inherent in the social dynamics of sharing responses" (Beach 9). The range of approaches within this context is inclusive of social constructivist theory, advocated by Stanley Fish, who argues that a text's meaning for a reader emerges from the *interpretive community;* that is, the interpretive strategies and conventions operating in specific social situations. Another approach, dialogic theory, promoted by Mikhail Bakhtin, distinguishes between internal intrapersonal dialogue and external dialogue, the former being "intimately related to the social and ideological meanings of the external social context" (Beach 111).

"How readers' cultural roles, attitudes, and values, as well as the larger cultural, historical context, shape responses" (Beach 9) is the focus of cultural theories of response. In contrast to the structuralism of many textual approaches, the poststructuralist cultural theorists examine the ways readers are socialized to respond in keeping with ideological positions of social institutions and cultural forces. David Buckingham notes in his analysis of a group of television viewers' responses, "They are also positioned in society and history, and will therefore bring different kinds of prior knowledge to the text" (quoted in Beach 129). Responses reflect membership in cultural communities.

The classroom application of social and cultural theories suggests pedagogical concerns. On the one hand, the teacher's pedagogical agenda, based on his or her pedagogical and sociocultural perspective, may be at odds with social or cultural orientation of the students, perhaps leading to resistance. The teacher's posture, expressed in presentation format and attitude, may preclude students' explorations of their own responses. On the other hand, should it be valuable and valid to bridge the social and cultural constraints, strategies for building bridges and crossing them need to be developed.

Whereas reader-response theories represent the roles of the reader in relation to the text, other "traditional" approaches focus on the text through emphasis on the author, the society of the author, or the text itself. When these approaches inform instruction, the tendency is for the teacher to teach about literature.

Traditional approaches are based on several underlying assumptions: (a) the author's intention is the key to ascertaining what the work means and this meaning can be identified; (b) the text is an object that has a determinate meaning of its own; and (c) the text can be analyzed through objective, close scrutiny of its formal structure and techniques to establish the meaning. Furthermore, it is often assumed that there is but one meaning. In these approaches, the reader's role is neglected or omitted entirely.

Teaching of literature, from the biographical–historical vantage point, has focused on literary biography, the life and times of the authors— including, perhaps, personal influences such as psychological and social factors, literary relationships, literary periods, and movements. Often, the author's identified themes and attitudes are used as a preliminary framework and applied to texts, sometimes within a literary history or a cultural– philosophical framework. Critics of this approach, including the New Critics (see later), argue that focusing on the author's role in shaping meaning constitutes an *intentional fallacy*. As noted earlier (see Author's Roles section) the author's intention is difficult if not impossible to discern.

The study of texts in isolation of the author and the reader, in accordance with the tenets of New Criticism, rejects biographical and social factors and also rejects the reader's emotional response in shaping meaning—termed the *affective fallacy*. New Critics focus on what is *in* the text; that is, the objective analysis of the language of the text: form, the nature of genre, structural features, figurative language and images, and symbols. These elements are analyzed and explicated in relation to literary effects.

According to the literary–pedagogical basis for these approaches, such knowledge prepares or supports the readers so that they can more adequately read and understand. Presumably, with such background knowledge they can understand what the author is saying and what the text is doing. At times such visions are helpful. However, they tend to predispose or misdirect the specific reading, especially if introduced prior to reading or at the outset of discussion, and if they are proposed directively; they have the effect of derailing the response experience. Furthermore, by focusing on content and form and on knowledge *about* literature, these approaches diminish the capacity of literature to portray and enliven the human experience for readers.

The transactional theory of literature does not reject the relevance of such biographical, historical, cultural, or formal considerations in the process of developing and enhancing insights to literature. Recognizably, such data can provide necessary background for understanding textual situations or for exploring alternative viewpoints. The issue is *when* these should be introduced and *how* they should be projected. The central question: Are such studies ends in themselves or are they used to enhance and develop the reader's transaction?

TRANSACTIONAL THEORY IN ACTION

The class sat in an uneven two-tiered semicircle with their teacher, Linda Larson. I, an observer, joined the circle at its outer edge. After glancing at me momentarily, the students turned their attention back to her; she had just introduced the book *Hiroshima* by John Hersey. Random muttering about the difficulties of the assigned first chapter surfaced around the circle. These high school juniors (in the lowest level of the school's three achievement tracks) had found the shifting array of "characters," and the details of the text too complicated. Linda acknowledged their comments, indicating that she would be helping them with the reading.

Moving away from direct discussion of the text or their reaction to it, she asked them instead to imagine they had just heard that Minneapolis–St. Paul, a metropolis some 40 miles away, had been targeted for a nuclear attack, expected in about an hour or two. They, in their windowless classroom, were relatively safe. She paused and asked, "How would you react? What would you do?"

Their reactions came slowly, but gradually a buzz of talk filled the room as the students exchanged reactions of surprise and fear, as they offered ideas about what they would try, what they would do: Warn others, find their families, organize emergency stations, amass provisions. Then, a girl, previously silent, who, head down, had been filing her nails, interrupted the buzz. "Oh, you wouldn't do that!" she said abruptly. She glanced around the circle. "*You* wouldn't do that. *I* wouldn't do that. You know what I'd do? I'd run and run and run and run." Just as abruptly, she bent her head down again. The students were still for a few moments; when they took up the discussion again, it had taken a new turn.

On this initial day of her literature unit, Linda Larson had accomplished a great deal: She had created involvement among her students and, more important, had raised feelings and issues that could be applied to their primary text, *Hiroshima*. This introductory discussion had set the stage for bringing about their sense of relatedness to the text, helping to bring the work into being, and, furthermore, for developing their thinking about the issues in the book and about themselves. Indeed, given the involvement she had established, she had probably created access into the text and had made it easier for them to engage and understand it.

Discussions of readers' transactions with the text—what they would make of it—would come in subsequent lessons. Linda, by invoking directly her students' transactions—experience—with the text, would encourage them to relate to and reflect on those experiences with the events and people. She would draw from them their emotions and understandings, eliciting their attitudes and concerns. Thus, she would focus on helping her students understand the experience they were living through in the reading of *Hiroshima* and understand the literary work they were evoking.

The students would not all respond with the same impressions. As in the introductory session, their felt emotions, ideas, and experiences would vary. She would help them to interact with each other to comprehend the varying responses; perhaps they would modify or expand their impressions. Generally, they would find commonalities among their responses to the text. However, their developing interpretations of the text would also remain, at least in some measure, individualized.

The text was both springboard and resource; the readers' responses were stimuli for discussion. Through these discussions, along with a survival newsletter and projects, the students' interpretations would be honed and their attitudes clarified. Historical information, structural underpinnings, and language features would be introduced in the discussions, as appropriate, as catalysts for deeper understandings or explanations to help students comprehend a feature of the text. In addition, this reader-oriented process of building the literary work would help students to develop their interpretation ability. Furthermore, by reflecting on their thinking, the readers would come to understand what triggered their own responses, how these affected the developing impressions, and how they might be affected by the insights of others.

TEACHING PRINCIPLES AND STRATEGIES

Embedded in this scenario are significant teaching principles and strategies. Cognizance of and developing the readers' transactions with the text is at the center of the classroom instruction. Class dialogue starts where the student readers are (not where the teacher is), focusing on their initial reactions and understandings. This discussion functions as an initial expression, a comparative unfolding, of what they are making of the text, what feelings are induced, and what attitudes and ideas are emerging. Through shared responses, readers will discern a range of reactions to a text. Such interactive processes, encouraging personal review and revision, have the effect of building and developing the literary work, of clarifying the reader's "poem." Readers may discover and acknowledge more than one valid interpretation, each supported by the text. Often, given the nature of human existence, the shared personal experiences and feelings of readers and the author's selected words and situations, there may emerge a core of common response, a convergence of feelings and understanding among readers.

Teachers should avoid conferring on such converged responses the sense of correctness, in effect, automatically dismissing the individual variations among readers.

By inhibiting their impulses to direct or establish the "correct" interpretation of a text, teachers promote personal growth and allow readers to maintain ownership of their reading. Reader-dependent interpretive skills are developed. Teachers, focusing on the readers' experiences with the text, provide opportunities for them to identify and reflect on their reactions and invite them to compare reactions by questioning themselves and others. They will provide guidance—thoughtful questions, personal responses, and compelling information—so as to encourage a deep consideration, a clarification, of the literary work being evoked by the students.

Through this process, students will have been led to support their statements by referring to the text, thus exploring their responses more deeply. Such classroom discourse promotes cross-fertilization of ideas among students. In the weighing and balancing of class exchanges, the students gain insight into the angles of vision of others. In an atmosphere of acceptance and honesty, students will sense an appropriate, expressive reading or a limited or misdirected reading; they will measure and receive the ideas of others, incorporating them in their own, revising and building their interpretation of the literary work. There is internal growth of response to the text, not merely the noting and organizing of the teacher's knowledge.

By maintaining the reader orientation, students are disposed to acknowledge their own perceptions, as differentiated from those of others, and their responsibilities as readers. They begin to recognize the role of their backgrounds, beliefs, and personalities in the reading act; that is, how each of them shapes their reaction and each is shaped by the text. By maintaining reference to the text, invoking it in relation to interpretive reactions, its role as stimulant and guide is acknowledged and processed; the students begin to recognize the need to support and validate a reading.

Beyond applying these strategies to the immediate literary work, students potentially adopt them for subsequent readings. They gain confidence to approach a text on their own. In contrast, the teacher-directed interpretation has the effect of curtailing these learnings. The interpretive distance between the readers' initial reactions and the teacher's "solution" is not bridged; understanding is minimized. Becoming dependent on teacher and critic, students learn to mistrust or reject their own readings.

Various strategies may serve to clarify and enrich the readers' perceptions. Oral discussions of literary transactions are a mainstay of literature instruction—as a class but also in small groups of various numbers. Small groups can function as preliminary sounding boards or, all the way to the other end of the spectrum, as a culminating means of pulling together ideas. Small-group activities have the merit of encouraging interchange from all class members, too many of whom get lost in the large-group activities. Various types of writing—journals, logs, free responses—similarly encourage active reflection by individual students. These are especially valuable at the outset of a discussion to provide a preliminary outlet prior to the influence of assertive students, or at other times to allow for self-clarification or personal consideration of issues under discussion. Other oral and writing activities—role playing, situation expanding, and dramatizations—can inspire personal involvement with characters and events to bring about thoughtful consciousness among the readers. (These strategies are elaborated elsewhere in this book.)

THE DEMOCRACY CONNECTION

There is no surprise in connecting literature to the humanities. It has long been acknowledged to be at the very heart of humanistic studies. Literature reveals the human condition, the foibles, struggles, and achievements of humankind. Focusing on individuals' reactions to challenges, literature expresses the triumphs and defeats of the human spirit. In tragedy, for example, humans are pitted against gods or social forces larger than themselves; brought to ruin, they struggle to emerge from under the yoke and express an indomitable will to prevail and control their own lives.

An embedded promise of the humanities—thus, of literature—is the promotion of a democratic ideal. We need look no further, perhaps, than the current pedagogical emphasis on multicultural education that meaningfully centers on the use of literary texts. There is explicit recognition that the reading of such novels as *Ceremony* by Silko and *Scorpions* by Myers will enlarge the perspectives of readers who may be limited by a restricted culture. Potentially, these readers will gain understanding, become more accepting of differences, and recognize human similarities. Literary texts, of course, provide a vast array of people, concerns, situations, and places across the human spectrum. Experiencing this array enriches readers, bringing them closer to the lives of others; indeed, when the transaction is strong, they may exchange lives with characters. Such possibilities are effected by the living-through experiences of literature, in contrast, for example, with the efferent-dominated responses to social studies texts.

The democratic impulse arises not only from the array of literary texts and from readers' growth to democratic attitudes through their responses to them; it also emanates from the reading process itself. The recognition of the role of the reader in making meaning, supported by classroom strategies that promote active reader behavior, encourages another democratic attitude. While transacting with the text, as has been explained, active readers relate to the evolving evidence in the text: They weigh the import of language nuances, of character behaviors and traits; they shift the direction of their responses in keeping with these evolutions. These dynamics stimulate the expression and recognition of multiple viewpoints: They must be considered and reconsidered, measured, and tested against the text. Later, when considering their total experience, such recursive weighing and balancing of details is a natural reaction in the process of sorting out their understandings and confusions, in reflecting on the resolution (or irresolution) of the stream of events, and their sense of reality. This pattern of weighing and questioning contains a democratic aspect, for it discourages automatic adherence to a presented idea.

The process of interacting with others is comparable. The reader-oriented discussion creates an atmosphere of empowerment for the students. They need not adhere to the authority of critic or teacher; he or she becomes instead a partner participant, providing an individual perspective. Students reacting to shared-response discussions comment on their feelings of being equal, that everyone's response is equally welcomed. In this regard, significant in a democratic sense as well as in reading interpretation, are the differences in social contexts—culture, race, ethnicity, and gender—that the readers bring to the text and the discussion. The various perspectives within an open, equalizing forum promote acceptance of and insights about the reader-speaker, in addition to enriching and enhancing textual understanding.

The nature of these discussions, the implicit challenge of varied responses or direct disagreement with a stated view, ideally causes students to think through their responses and to find support or clarification for their assertions. This may provide the seeds for a habit of mind that is provocatively thoughtful: less willing to accept surface comments, more assertive in expressing informed opinion, more critical and evaluative of language and ideas. Such processing of thought, reminiscent of the ideal of the town meeting, is at the heart of the democratic process: giving equal voice to all sides and testing these voices against our own.

REFERENCES

Appleyard, J. A. *Becoming a Reader: The Experience of Fiction From Adolescence to Adulthood.* New York: Cambridge University Press, 1990.

Bakhtin, Mikhail. *The Dialogic Imagination: Four Essays by M. M. Bakhtin.* Trans. Caryl Emerson and Michael Holquist. Ed. Michael Holquist. Austin: University of Texas Press, 1981.

Beach, Richard. *A Teacher's Introduction to Reader Response Theories.* Urbana, IL: National Council of Teachers of English, 1993.

Bleich, David. *Subjective Criticism.* Baltimore: Johns Hopkins University Press, 1978.

Buckingham, David. *Public Secrets: "Eastenders" and Its Audience.* London: British Film Institute, 1987.

Burke, Kenneth. *Counter-Statement*. Berkeley: University of California Press, 1931.

Carson, Rachel. *Silent Spring*. Greenwich, CT: Fawcett Publications, 1964.

Conrad, Joseph. *Heart of Darkness*. New York: New American Library, 1950.

Crane, Stephen. "The Bride Comes to Yellow Sky." In *The Western Writings of Stephen Crane*. New York: New American Library, 1979. 86–96.

———. *The Red Badge of Courage*. New York: Norton, 1982.

Crosman, R. "Do Readers Make Meaning?" *The Reader in the Text: Essays on Audience and Interpretation*, Eds. S. R. Sulleman and I. Crosman. Princeton, NJ: Princeton University Press, 1980. 149–164.

Dostoyevsky, Fyodor. *Crime and Punishment*. 2nd ed. New York: Norton, 1975.

Fish, Stanley. *Is There a Text in This Class? The Authority of Interpretive Communities*. Cambridge, MA: Harvard University Press, 1980.

Frost, Robert. "Stopping by Woods on a Snowy Evening." *Quarto of Modern Literature*, Ed. Leonard Brown. 5th ed. New York: Charles Scribner's Sons, 1964. 426.

Gilman, Charlotte. "The Yellow Wallpaper." *The Riverside Anthology of Literature*, Ed. Douglas Hunt. Boston: Houghton Mifflin Company, 1988. 171–183.

Hersey, John. *Hiroshima*. New York: Bantam Books, 1959.

Holland, Norman. *The Dynamics of Literary Response*. New York: Oxford University Press, 1968.

Iser, Wolfgang. *The Act of Reading: A Theory of Aesthetic Response*. Baltimore: Johns Hopkins University Press, 1978.

Knowles, John. *A Separate Peace*. New York: Dell Publishing, 1961.

Kubler-Ross, Elizabeth. *On Death and Dying*. New York: Macmillan, 1970.

London, Jack. *The Call of the Wild*. New York: Dutton, 1968.

Marzano, Robert J. *Cultivating Thinking in English and the Language Arts*. Urbana, IL: National Council of Teachers of English, 1991.

Myers, Walter Dean. *Scorpions*. New York: Harper & Row, Publishers, 1988.

Probst, Robert E. *Response and Analysis: Teaching Literature in Junior and Senior High School*. Portsmouth, NH: Heinemann, 1981.

Rabinowitz, Peter. *Before Reading: Narrative Conventions and the Politics of Interpretation*. Ithaca, NY: Cornell University Press, 1987.

Rosenblatt, Louise M. *Literature as Exploration*. 5th ed. New York: Modern Language Association, 1995.

———. *The Reader, the Text, the Poem: The Transactional Theory of the Literary Work*. 2nd ed., Carbondale: Southern Illinois University Press, 1994.

———. "Writing and Reading: The Transactional Theory." *Reader* 20 (Fall 1988): 7–31.

Shakespeare, William. *Othello*, Ed. Mark Eccles. New York: Appleton-Century-Crofts, 1946.

Silko, Leslie. *Ceremony*. New York: Viking/Penguin, 1977.

Steinbeck, John. "The Chrysanthemums." In *The Portable Steinbeck*, Ed. Pascal Convici. Rev. ed. New York: Viking Press, 1946.

2

Connecting Students and Literature
What Do Teachers Do and Why Do They Do It?

Robert C. Small

HELEN JOHNSON'S CLASS

It is a Monday in late February, 10:45 in the morning. Helen Johnson is ready to begin her poetry unit with her third-period, seventh-grade class. She has taught this unit a number of times, and she always looks forward to it, especially because it begins with several poems by Emily Dickinson, one of her favorite poets. Her knowledge of the life, poems, and critical material on Dickinson is rich and extensive, and she enjoys sharing it with her students.

"Today," she begins, "we're going to start our poetry unit with a couple of poems by Emily Dickinson. Does anyone know anything about her?"

The students look at her. Nobody moves.

"Well," Ms. Johnson continues, "has anyone ever read any of her poems?"

After a pause, Martha raises her hand. "Did she write a poem about two toy animals waiting for the dead little boy who owned them? I remember reading that back in elementary school."

"No, Martha, I don't think so." Helen Johnson smiles at her, "But I'm glad you remember that poem." She pauses, "Anyway, because none of you have read any of Emily Dickinson's poems, this'll be a good chance to get to know her. So, first, I'm going to tell you a little bit about her. Then we'll study those poems. She's one of America's finest writers, and, you know, one of my favorites." She smiles at them while sharing this personal insight.

Her students watch her as she stands behind the speaker's stand. A few take notes. Most sit quietly, waiting. Joe and Susan, in the back row, watch each other. Sam, near the back by the window, has his eyes closed.

After a pause, Ms. Johnson begins her lecture on the life of Dickinson. She emphasizes Dickinson's educated family background, the fact that she published almost none of her poems, that she became a recluse, the individuality of her style. "She chose every word very carefully, as I've urged you to do when you write compositions for me. But she also chose unusual words at times, words that make us stop and think about what she means. And sometimes she gives us an example and then leaves it up to us to see what it is an example of."

Having finished the formal part of her lecture, Helen moves to the teacher's desk at the side of the room and leans back against it. "So, I've got to admit her poetry isn't the easiest in the world to read. But I know you can handle it. After all, you're in the seventh grade now. And the ideas are so fresh, the language so perfectly right, you'll find it worth the effort."

The lecture and the period conclude with an assignment: "For tomorrow," she says, "I want you to read the poem on page 23 in your books, 'A Bird Came Down the Walk.' It's one of her easier poems, so you shouldn't have any trouble with it."

She pauses for the class to write the assignment in their notebooks. "Before you read it, be sure to read the biographical sketch of Dickinson in the back of the book on page 403. And don't forget to read what the textbook tells you about the poem in the headnote. It seems to me like a very good introduction to the poem.

"And remember how we read poetry. Robin, can you remind us how we read poetry?"

Robin frowns with the effort to remember. "Uh, we read through it all the way without trying to stop to figure things out." She stops. "Is that right?"

"Right. And then?"

Robin smiles. "Then we read through it again, stopping to worry . . ."

"Think about."

"Think about the ideas and words."

"Very good, Robin. And don't forget to use the notes in the margin. They'll help you understand hard words and some references you might not know. And watch for the metaphors that Dickinson uses at the end of this poem. Like most poets, she's writing about something more than the poem may seem to be about." The bell rings.

A day has passed, and it is third period again.

"Today," says Helen Johnson, "we're going to discuss the Emily Dickinson poem you were assigned to read last night, 'A Bird Came Down the Walk.' Open your books to page 23."

There is rustle as the students pull their books out from their desks. Sam raises his hand.

"Yes, Sam."

"I forgot my book, Miss Johnson."

"Again. Well, don't forget, that's two points off. Now, look on with Dana. And no talking, either one of you."

Sam smirks. Dana looks annoyed.

"Now, is everyone looking at 'A Bird Came Down the Walk'? Okay. It's a poem about something that all of us have seen, so all of you should be able to say what it means. Dana, will you read it to us first so we can all hear how it sounds and what it says?"

Dana, pale and blond, hunches over her anthology and reads smoothly but nervously:

> A bird came down the walk:
> He did not know I saw;
> He bit an angleworm in halves
> And ate the fellow, raw.
>
> And then he drank a dew
> From a convenient grass,
> And then hopped sidewise to the wall
> To let a beetle pass.
>
> He glanced with rapid eyes
> That hurried all abroad—
> They looked like frightened beads, I thought.
> He stirred his velvet head
>
> Like one in danger. Cautious
> I offered him a crumb,
> And he unrolled his feathers
> And rowed him softer home
>
> Than oars divide the ocean,
> Too silver for a seam,
> Or butterflies, off banks of noon,
> Leap, plashless, as they swim.

Invitation 2. 1

Before continuing with Helen Johnson's class discussion, reread the poem, perhaps aloud, and write your response to it. What do you make of "A Bird Came Down the Walk"? Compare your response with that of a peer.

"Thank you, Dana. Very nice." Ms. Johnson looks around the room. "Mark," she asks, "why do you think the poet included the second line?"

Mark studies the text. "Well, the bird doesn't know he's being watched."

"That's right, of course."

Mark sighs.

"But why is that important?"

Mark has not escaped. He rereads the line. "Well," he stalls.

The class is silent.

"Well, think of it this way: Where does a writer usually tell us the topic of a paragraph? Think of the poem as a theme you're writing for class. Where would you tell me the topic of each paragraph? Mark do you know?"

Mark has been reading through the poem and doesn't seem to have heard. "Well," he says again. "Well, the bird flies away later when he does know that he's being watched."

"So?" Ms. Johnson prompts.

"And, well, the bird wouldn't act natural if it knows the poet's there, right?" He looks at her hopefully.

"Maybe," she says. Her tone of voice and the expression on her face are not encouraging. "So, Michelle, do you think the poem is about flying birds?"

Michelle understands that it isn't. "No, Miss Johnson."

Michelle has also learned to wait.

"Then what might the poem be about?"

"Being afraid?"

"So where in the poem does Dickinson tell us about being afraid?"

"Well," Michelle continues, encouraged by Ms. Johnson's expression, "I'd guess that the worm was afraid of the bird. And the bird's certainly afraid of the poet."

"Let's look at what she says about the bird being afraid." Ms. Johnson reads. "'He glanced with rapid eyes / That hurried all abroad— / They looked like frightened beads, I thought. / He stirred his velvet head / Like one in danger.'" She pauses. "Notice how she describes him. What do you think 'rapid eyes that hurried all abroad' means? Harry?"

Harry is a small, plump boy, who answers in a thin, high voice, "The eyes are moving back and forth rapidly."

"Right, and what does that mean?"

"It's scared it'll miss something."

"Very good, Harry. And isn't the phrase 'rapid eyes that hurried all abroad' a wonderful picture of just how the eyes of a frightened animal look." She pauses. "But now let me ask you, is the poet afraid? Gale?"

"I don't think so. She admires how the bird flies."

"So, what did the poet do when she saw the bird? Henry?"

"Watched it."

"And what else?" Helen Johnson prompts.

"Offered it food," Henry suggests. "At least I guess that's what she means by 'a crumb.'"

"So how did she feel as she offered it the crumb?"

"Cautious," several students shout.

"One at a time, please. Now, Gale, you told us she wasn't afraid of the bird. What does 'cautious' tell us?"

"I just think she didn't want to scare it away. You know, by moving too fast or something."

"Good, and what did the bird do when he came across the worm? Henry?"

Henry is silent.

"He ate it," Karen shouts out.

"Right," Ms. Johnson says. "But please wait to be called on, Karen."

"Now," she continues after a pause, "What is the poet trying to tell us by describing her encounter with the bird? Karen?"

"That poets and birds are different?"

The class laughs.

"Quiet," Ms. Johnson scolds. "And what is the difference between the poet and the bird?" With a frown, she looks at the class. "Sam, you seemed to think Karen's answer was so funny. Can you answer my question?"

"Could you repeat the question?" Sam stalls.

"Certainly. What is the difference between the poet and the bird?"

Sam proposes tentatively, "She can see the bird as beautiful, the way it flew especially."

"Yes, we already said that."

"But the bird only saw the worm as something to eat, right?"

"Right."

"So that's the difference." Sam is clearly frustrated.

"But how did she feel about the bird?"

Dana offers, "She saw it was beautiful, like we've said. And she tried to feed it, so she must have cared about it, or why feed it."

"Right," Ms. Johnson says. "And what does that tell us?"

The class is silent.

"Well, how did the bird feel about her?" Ms. Johnson asks.

"It was afraid of her." several students shout.

"One at a time, please. So we know the poet is sensitive to and aware of the bird, but the bird is self-centered."

Several students write down what Ms. Johnson has just said. Dana raises her hand.

"Yes, Dana?"

"So does the poet look down on the bird because it ate the worm instead of admiring it?"

"No, of course not. Because the poet is sensitive to nature, she knows that the bird is what it is. Notice how she compares the bird's flight to butterflies."

The class is quiet. Martha raises her hand.

"Yes, Martha?"

"Does that mean the bird is like a butterfly?"

"How might they be alike, Martha?"

"They fly."

"And what else?"

Martha shakes her head.

"Does anyone know? Richy?"

Richy, a tall, thin boy who looks older than the other students, speaks in a deep, loud voice. "They're both beautiful too."

"Good. Anything else?"

There are no volunteers. "Well, they're also both a part of nature, aren't they? But what happens then?"

"The bird flies away," several students say.

"And look at how she describes his flying." Helen reads, "'he unrolled his feathers / And rowed him softer home.' Can't you just see the bird rolling out its wings and moving itself into the air. And then she said the bird rowed itself 'softer home / Than oars divide the ocean, / Too silver for a seam.' What do you think she's comparing the bird's flying to?"

After a delay, Martha raises her hand. "Well, she uses the words 'oars' and 'rowed' and 'ocean' so I'd guess she sees the bird as like somebody rowing a boat in the ocean."

"Excellent, Martha. And what do we call that kind of comparison? Anyone remember?"

No one does.

Helen Johnson moves the blackboard and writes "metaphor." "When a poet—or anyone else, even you or me—compares one thing or action to another without saying so, we call it a metaphor. You might write that in your notebooks. And if the poet tells us that she's made a comparison and uses 'like' or 'as' then we call the comparison a 'simile.'" She writes the word *simile* on the board.

"So, what other comparisons does she make the bird's flying to?"

"Butterflies," Mark offers.

"And what about those butterflies?"

"They're swimming."

"And what else? Michelle?"

"Leaping."

"And the word 'plashless,' as your book tells you, means 'without making splashes.' So these butterflies are swimming and leaping without making splashes. How is that like the rowing of the boat?"

No one answers. "Well, look back at line 18. Notice that the oars don't make a seam in the ocean. And the butterflies don't make splashes. Now what does that tell us about the way the bird's wings move through the air?"

Dana raises her hand. "I guess the bird's wings don't disturb the air either."

"Very good. So the bird flies off softly, as softly as oars that don't even leave a mark on the ocean or butterflies move in the air and don't disturb it either as if they were swimming and diving in water. Isn't it wonderful the way she uses water to compare the bird's flying to and then compares its flying to butterflies in the air and describes the butterflies as if they were also in water. Only a great poet can effortlessly build one metaphor on top of another like that."

She pauses to let them think about that. "But let's go back and think about what the poem's about. Let me ask you a question: Who did we say was watching whom?"

Puzzled at this sudden shift, the students look back at the poem. After a moment, several hands go up.

"Sara?"

"We said the bird was watching the worm. And it also says the bird watched a beetle go by."

"Why do you think it just watched the beetle?"

"Oh," Sara says, "it probably wasn't hungry."

"Does anyone have a different answer? Tom?"

"Well, of course, I don't know. But I bet it would have eaten another worm if it'd found one."

"So?" Helen Johnson prompts.

"So, I'd guess the beetle wasn't something the bird ate. I mean it didn't taste good or was too hard or something like that."

"Anyway, it didn't want to eat it, but it did watch it. OK, so who else was watching whom? Sara?"

"The poet watched the bird."

"Right. And."

"The bird watched the poet before it flew away," several students shout out.

"Okay, one at a time. Now, let me ask one last question: Was anyone else watching anyone else?"

The students looked surprised. "But, Miss Johnson, there isn't anyone else in the poem," Michelle says.

Helen Johnson walks to the blackboard at the front of the room. "Okay, let's make a list." She writes "Bird," "Worm," "Beetle," "Bird," and "Poet." "Now, let's draw an arrow from each watcher to each watchee." She laughs. "If there is such a word."

When they have finished, she asks, "Let's see. Did we get them all?"

Sam speaks up, "Well, the beetle may have been watching the bird. Maybe even the poet."

"But we don't know that, do we, Sam? The poet doesn't tell us."

"No," Sam says sullenly.

"We have to be careful to stick with what the poet actually says. So did we miss any?"

"No," several students call out.

"But we did," Ms. Johnson says. "We forgot that the poet was watching herself."

"How do you know that, Miss Johnson?" Sam asks.

"Well, look at that second line I tried to get Mark to study. What does the poet say?"

Sam mumbles, "'He did not know I saw.'"

"But she knows that she saw the bird; so she must have been watching herself, not just the bird. And look at line 11. She says, 'They looked like frightened beads, I thought.' So she's still watching herself watching the bird. And then in line 14 she watches herself try to give the bird a crumb. So I'd say she was watching herself as well as the bird, the beetle and the worm. Does that make sense?"

They watch her.

"And what did we say earlier about the difference between the bird and the poet? Dana?"

"The poet was sensitive but the bird was self-centered."

"And now we know that the poet was the only character in the poem who watched everyone else and also watched herself. What does that tell you?"

"I know," Tony says. "She's human. The others aren't."

"Very good, Tony. And why is that important?"

"Well, the Bible says God made man after His own image, right? And gave man control over the animals. I guess that includes birds and bugs."

"Well, I'm not sure she was thinking of the Bible; but that's close. It seems clear that the poet realizes that only she, the one with intelligence, is able to watch with sensitivity to beauty, to care, and to be aware of her own actions and feelings."

Closing her textbook, Helen Johnson walks back to the speaker's stand. "So much in so few words and such simple words! That's why she's considered one of America's greatest poets. Now, for tomorrow, I want you to read the poem on page 24, 'Success Is Counted Sweetest.' It's a harder poem in some ways, but I'm sure you can deal with it. Just remember what we did today and you won't have any trouble."

The bell rings.

Later, in the teachers' lounge, when we asked Helen Johnson, "How'd it go today?" she told us, "We had a really good discussion of the poem. It took them awhile, but they finally saw the contrast between the poet's sensitivity for nature and the bird's natural self-centeredness."

JANE GRAHAM'S CLASS

Was Helen Johnson right? Well, consider the following episode in which Jane Graham asks her class to consider the same Emily Dickinson poem that Helen taught her class.

It's that same gray February day. The lights are on and the windows firmly closed in Room 202. A sleepy group of seventh-graders sit looking at Ms. Graham, her chair drawn up to their circle.

"Have you ever seen a robin hopping around in your yard?" Ms. Graham asks. She laughs. "They're supposed to be a sign of spring."

Several hands go up.

"You've seen a robin already?" she asks.

"Well, not this year," Karla says. "But we usually have one hoppin' around in March. Sometimes even at the end of February."

"Don't mean a thing around here, does it. I remember a time when we had a dozen robins and then it snowed for two days," Joey says.

The class laughs.

"I remember that year, too, Joey," Ms. Graham says, laughing. "But have you ever watched a robin when he finally did get to your yard?"

"Sure," several students say.

"Well, then, what was that robin doing hopping around?"

"Gettin' worms," the students call out.

"Why, sure," Ms. Graham says. "Did you ever try to save a worm from a bird?"

The class is silent. Ms. Graham waits.

"Why do that, Mrs. Graham?" Salley asks. "I mean a worm's a worm. Who cares!"

"Well," Ms. Graham says, "and a bird's a bird and a person's a person. So?"

They wait. She waits.

"You mean worms are important too?" Jerry asks.

"I don't know, are they?"

"The Bible says God created all living things," Jack says. "I guess that makes worms important too."

"And," Greg says, "my dad told me that some people buy worms to put them in their yards because, well, those worms make the ground better, make the grass grow better."

"Is that right?" Ms. Graham exclaims. "I didn't know that. So suppose you watched a robin looking for worms. What do you think you'd see?"

"A bird hoppin' on the grass," John says.

"Sure, and what do you think the robin would see when he saw you were watching him?"

"Me." Alan says.

"True, but what do you think you look like to a robin?"

"Big, I guess," Alan says.

"Real big, I bet," Ms. Graham agrees. "Most of us said we'd watched a robin. Why do you think we did that?"

"'Cause it was there?" Jack answers doubtfully. "I don't know."

Ms. Graham looks at the class. "What d'ya think? Is that why?"

"Maybe," Salley says.

"We watch lots of things just 'cause they're there," Alan says in a rush. "Lots of things like . . ." He stops.

"Like?"

"Cars."

"TV."

"People."

"Girls," Jack adds with a snicker.

"Well, I'd never watch a boy," Salley adds.

"Sure," Ms. Graham intercedes. "And we look at clouds and rainbows and water running by."

"I'd rather watch a football game," Joe adds.

"So what can you say about us?"

They think about the question. "We like to watch different things?" Salley answers tentatively.

Ms. Graham waits.

"And we watch things for different reasons?" Joe suggests.

"But what do we all do?" Ms. Graham prompts.

"Watch!" the class answers.

"Okay. Now, there's a poem in our book by someone who watched a bird and thought about it just as we've been doing and then wrote down what she thought. It's on page 23. Have you all got your books?"

Harry raises his hand, "I don't, Mrs. Graham."

"Just as I thought. Anyone else?"

Several hands go up.

"Well, just for those of us who are so forgetful, I made some copies of the poem. Here, Jack, you pass them out."

When everyone has a copy, Ms. Graham says, "Okay, let's read it silently all the way through without stopping. Raise your hand when you finish, then read it again. Okay, go."

The class is quiet, heads bent over their books. Ms. Graham watches until the last student has finished. "Great, now I'm going to read it aloud. Follow along in your book if you want or just listen."

When she has finished reading the poem, she pauses, then asks, "So, who'd like to tell us how you felt about what Emily Dickinson said?"

Several hands go up. "Frank, why don't you start us off."

Frank takes a deep breath and speaks in a rush. "Well, she told about what happened okay, I guess. I mean about the bird and it being afraid and flying away and all. But I didn't get that stuff with the beetle and that last part with the butterflies and ocean, well, I just don't see where the ocean came from." He finishes with a gasp.

"That beetle part gave me problems, too, the first time I read it. Anyone have an idea what it means. Salley?"

"Well, I'm not sure, of course," she says cautiously, "but when you were reading it to us, I thought maybe—well, this may sound silly—but maybe the beetle wasn't something the bird would eat, so he just watched it go by."

"But, but, but . . ." Tom is anxiously waving his raised hand in the air.

"Tom," Ms. Graham says quietly.

"But birds eat beetles. I've seen 'em do it."

"So have I," Ms. Graham nods. "What about that?"

"Maybe some beetles, but not all beetles," Harry joins in. "It didn't eat this one."

"Maybe it wasn't hungry," Tom insists.

"Both seem like good reasons to me," Jane Graham says.

"So, if he wasn't gonna eat the beetle, what's it doing in the poem?" Jack asks. "I still don't understand."

"Good question. Anyone got any ideas?"

"Maybe it just really happened, so she put it in," Anne suggests shyly.

"Oh, a poet wouldn't do that," Jack says.

"Could be. Why not," Salley comes to the defense of her friend Anne. "I bet Anne's right."

"Maybe we can find out later, or maybe we'll never know," Ms. Graham intervenes. "Anyway, who else wants to tell us what you thought of the poem? Anyone?"

More hands go in the air. "Anne."

"Well, even if I'm not right about the beetle—and I still think I am—" she says, looking at Jack, "I could see myself watching that bird, you know, to see what it did, just wondering, how did it feel eating a worm. Ugh! I'd rather eat a beetle!"

The class laughs. Jack adds, "I once saw a can of fried ants for sale in the store."

"Oh, Jack, you did not," Karla says.

"I did so. Mrs. Graham haven't you seen 'em?"

"Well, I'm sorry to have to say I have. Chocolate-covered ants, too," she agrees. "But I wanted to ask Anne about what she said."

The class looks at Anne, who blushes.

"You said you wondered how the bird felt eating a worm, didn't you?"

Anne nods.

"So how did you decide the bird felt?"

"Oh, I'd die before I'd eat a worm, but I guess the bird felt good, maybe like I'd feel with a hamburger."

"So maybe it wasn't hungry after eating that worm," Tom insists, going back to defend his earlier contribution.

"Nah," Harry says, "we read in science that animals like birds and mice, little things, have to eat all the time or they die. It's called metabolism."

"So maybe it was an untasty beetle after all," Ms. Graham intervenes again. "Suppose it was, what do you think the bird thought when it 'hopped sideways to the wall / To let a beetle pass'?"

"I'll bet it was thinking 'no food there,'" Jack agrees.

"But mostly it was afraid," Karla said, "hungry and afraid."

"What does Dickinson say, Karla?"

Karla takes a deep breath and reads, "'He glanced with rapid eyes / That hurried all abroad— / They looked like frightened beads, I thought. / He stirred his velvet head / Like one in danger.' See, he was afraid."

"What do you think he was afraid of?" Ms. Graham prompts.

Several hands go up.

"Tom."

"Not getting enough to eat, maybe."

"Maybe a cat," Salley adds. "Our cat catches birds all the time and puts them on the porch. I hate it."

"Maybe that somebody was watching it," Henry says. "After all, somebody was."

They think about that idea for a moment.

"Sure," Tom concludes, "and when she tries to feed it, it flies away, pouff."

"Just what a bird would do," Henry says.

"But she was trying to feed it," Ms. Graham points out. "Why didn't it take the crumb?"

"Oh, it didn't know that," several students say. Then Anne adds, "No, it didn't. Maybe it thought she was going to catch it and eat it like Salley's cat. Remember what we said about how we'd look to a bird."

"Big," several students say.

"If you look big to a bird, then, how does a bird look to you?" Ms. Graham prompts again.

"Small," several students say.

Ms. Graham waits.

"Well," Mike speaks up for the first time, "when we were talking about birds before we read the poem, I wondered if you were going to ask us that."

Ms. Graham laughs. "Saw right through me, did you. Well, I thought I'd wait on that question. So what's the answer, Mike?"

"I was thinking then that it would just look like a robin, you know, nothin' special. But here in the poem, see, she talks about its eyes moving around— 'rapid eyes,' 'frightened beads'—that's how robins do look, nervous, jumpy. Like what my grandpaw calls 'a cat on a hot tin roof.'"

"And then the bird flies away and what does it look like?" she prompts.

"To me, or in the poem?" Mike asks.

"Either. Start with to you."

"Well, if it's a robin, a little clumsy, maybe, at first, and then quick. Wouldn't it be great to be able to fly!"

Ms. Graham nods, then waits.

The class waits. Finally, Jack says, "That's the part of the poem I didn't understand—other than the beetle, and I don't want to get into that again."

"How the flying bird looked to Emily Dickinson," Ms. Graham restates the idea.

"Yeah. All that stuff about oars and oceans and butterflies. How did that get in there?"

"It was my favorite part of the poem," Salley says. "I thought the first part was kinda dull, really. But that last part, it was so pretty."

"Would someone like to read it out loud again?" Ms. Graham asks.

After a long pause, Anne says, "I will" and reads,

> And he unrolled his feathers
> And rowed him softer home
>
> Than oars divide the ocean,
> Too silver for a seam,
> Or butterflies, off banks of noon.
> Leap, plashless, as they swim.

The class is quiet for a moment; then Salley says, "See, isn't that beautiful?"

"Beautiful, maybe," Jack insists, "but what does it mean?"

Ms. Graham waits. When no one volunteers, she says, "Let's take a minute to think about what a flying bird looks like. I'm going to make a list of as many things a flying bird looks like as I can in two minutes. Anyone else who wants to write down a list can, or just try to think of as many as you can."

The class is quiet as Ms. Graham writes. At first only a few seem to be making lists; then a few more start writing. After 5 minutes, Ms. Graham stops, looks up, and says, "Well, I came up with, let's see . . ." She counts silently. "Eight. Did anyone get more than that?"

After a pause, Jack raises his hand. "I got twelve."

When other hands go up, Ms. Graham says, "Wonderful. I'm going to read my favorite one. Then I'd like to hear from anyone else who has a favorite one. Mine is 'A flying bird is like a quiet voice singing in the dark.'"

She waits. Finally, Georgie raises his hand.

"Georgie?"

In a shaking voice, Georgie reads, "A flying bird is like a horse running through a field."

"Ah," Ms. Graham says, "I like that. I really like that."

After a dozen others have read their favorite simile for a flying bird, there is a pause; and Ms. Graham says, "Well, I almost think I could fly. And, Mike, after hearing those comparisons, just like you, I think, Wouldn't it be wonderful to be able to fly!"

She pauses, then says, "Salley, you liked the way Emily Dickinson described flying, and so do I. Would you help us look at what she said?"

Salley sighs, then says, "Okay, but I liked a lot of what we said, too." She waits a minute, then continues, "Well, it seems to me she saw him as like somebody rowing a boat, but so smoothly he didn't even upset the water. And she saw the bird as like butterflies floating in the air so smoothly there aren't any—well—whatever 'plashless' means—I guess no waves in the air."

Ms. Graham says, "I can see that, Salley."

"But," Jack asks, "what's a seam in the ocean?"

"Oh, the boat doesn't leave any mark," Salley says. "Think of a lake with the sun shining on it. A boat moving but not leaving any mark. Can't you see that?"

Jack frowns.

"So," Ms. Graham says quickly, "that's how she saw the bird flying. What do you think of what she said?"

They are quiet. Ms. Graham waits. Then Mike says, "Well, I guess this is wrong, but I liked what I said about a horse better than her butterflies."

"Actually, Mike," Ms. Graham says, "so did I. But I liked the picture of those butterflies swimming in the noon sun, too."

The class murmurs some yeses.

"Okay," Jack asks, "so now I understand. But why write a poem about it?"

Salley, Anne, and some other students, mostly girls, make negative sounds. Ms Graham says, "Anyone have an answer for Jack?"

Mike says, "Well, remember when we were talking about bird watching? Well, somebody said we might watch a bird because it was there. I guess she could write a poem about it because it was there."

"Why not?" Ms. Graham asks. "I guess I started a poem about a bird flying today. And Mike did. And Salley. Well, everybody did."

"But, Mrs. Graham," Salley insists, "this poem is in our textbook. There must be more to it than just a person watching a bird."

"Probably. Anybody got any ideas?"

There is a long silence. Then Anne says, "I don't know. Does there have to be another meaning?"

Ms. Graham waits. Finally Harry says, "Well, I guess she might just've written about something that happened to her. But I bet she thought it meant something more."

"So what more could it mean?" Jane Graham prompts.

"We talked about watching birds. She's watching the bird, right?" Harry says at last.

"Okay."

"And we said the bird was watching the beetle, right?"

"And then the bird sees her. That's watching, right?"

Ms. Graham says, "Could be."

"Oh, I don't know." Harry says.

"Hey, don't stop."

"And then she watches the bird fly away. So is the poem about watching?"

Ms. Graham waits. The students wait. "Well," she says, finally, "is it?"

"Bird watching?" Salley says.

"No," Mike says, "people watching birds, birds watching people."

"And what about birds watching beetles?" Jack asks.

The class groans.

"Sure," Mike says, "and maybe, maybe even worms watching birds. Who knows?"

"Anyone else watching anyone else?" Ms. Graham asks.

They're silent.

"Well, I'm going to make a list of everyone in the poem who watched everyone else. Anyone else who wants to can."

There is a short pause while Ms. Graham and the students make their lists. Then, "Okay, who'll share a list with us?"

After a pause, Tom reads, "Bird watches worm. Worm watches bird, maybe. Bird watches beetle. Beetle watches bird, probably. Emily watches bird hop. Emily watches worm being eaten. Emily watches beetle walk by bird. Bird watches Emily. Emily watches bird fly away. That's it."

"Anyone have anybody else on the list?" Ms. Graham asks.

They look at their lists. "There isn't anyone else," Mike says at last.

Ms. Graham waits. Finally, Anne says, "Can you watch yourself, Mrs. Graham?"

"Well, I've heard of mirrors," Jane Graham says. "Can you?"

"Yes," Anne says, "I watch myself all the time."

Ms. Graham waits.

"Right," Salley says, "we all watch ourselves."

"And," Ms. Graham prompts.

There is silence. Then Mike says, "So, who in the poem was watching itself? The worm? Nah, The beetle? Nah. The bird? Nah. So who else is there?"

Several students shout out, "Emily."

"Ah," Ms. Graham says.

And the bell rings.

"See you tomorrow," Jane Graham says.

Invitation 2.2

Compare the teaching procedures and processes of Helen Johnson and Jane Graham. Then, compare their students' reactions to the lessons and their responses to the poem.

PLANNING

Later, both Helen Johnson and Jane Graham discussed how they planned for these classes. This was Ms. Johnson's reply:

How did I prepare to teach that poem? Well, pretty much the same way I prepare to teach any piece of literature. In a very real way I feel my English major and master's in English took care of that. Then, when I'm going to teach something I haven't taught before, I read it carefully several times. If I need to, I sometimes read about the author. And I always look in the library for any critical articles or analyses in books. I take notes, and then I decide what points I need to be sure my students understand. Then I work up a lecture and a set of questions to ask the class after they've read the work, or, in the case of a novel, after they've read chapters. If I think the students will have real problems with the work, I sometimes give them study questions to use while they're reading.

The final thing I usually do is prepare a quiz for the work, or maybe for a long work some small quizzes and a longer test for the end. If I'm going to have the students do some kind of project with the work, I'll decide what that will be like and prepare some sample topics.

Sometimes, if there is a movie or a record or something like that that's worthwhile, I'll arrange to get it and use it, though I believe that works of literature should be read and valued for themselves.

Of course, I've taught these Emily Dickinson poems several times before, so all I had to do was reread them and my notes and think about the students in this class so I'd be prepared to help any of them who'd have special problems understanding.

Ms. Graham had a somewhat different reply:

Well, I'm afraid preparation for me doesn't have much to do with scholarship. I guess traditionalists would say I'm wrong, but when I prepare, I'm looking for ways to help my students' efforts to understand for themselves. Oh, of course, I read the poem or short story or novel I'm going to teach even if I've taught it a dozen times before. I'm not the same each time, you see, and neither are my students. But I've found I need to read whatever I'm going to teach not just as a person reading it but as a teacher reading it.

I've found, if you're preparing to help another reader be able to respond to the poem or story, then you have to read that work from the point of view of that other reader, my students, I mean. That's not easy, but it's important for me if I'm going to teach literature the way I want to.

Jane Graham explained that, as she read the poem, she tried to think of prereading activities that would be valuable to her students, ways to make the class interaction productive, and possible follow-up activities that would help her students rethink and deepen their insights. She saw it as her job to try to anticipate the areas where her students would be lacking in the knowledge and experience they'd need to begin responding immediately to Dickinson's poem they were about to read and discuss:

I asked myself, Are they likely to have thought about what it's like to be a bird? Have they ever stopped to watch a bird hopping around on the lawn? Have they stopped to think about what they were seeing? I decided, probably they hadn't. So I asked myself, will they have seen how animals and people are similar and different? Again, probably not. But I was pretty sure they'd see the bird catching the worm. But they probably hadn't looked at it from either the perspective of the bird or the worm. So I decided to start with what they could see and work from there.

COMMENTARY

Jane Graham believes that a work of literature only comes to life when readers meet it halfway, bringing to it their unique experiences and insights. She believes that putting a class full of teenagers together in a room to listen to an adult talk about a work of literature is, for most of her students, the worst way to help them interact with that work. At best, they would interact with her lecture; in most cases, they would doze.

There are, of course, times when teachers have information that they want to give to their students. It may well be that the best way to get students interested in the life of Emily Dickinson is to deliver a lively, sensitive lecture on what her life must have been like—if the teacher can be lively and sensitive about that subject. It may be important for students to understand the special qualities of Dickinson's style before reading "A Bird Came Down the Walk." And maybe a lecture on her poetic style is the best way for the teacher to get them ready to understand that style and to cope with its demands. Helen Johnson decided to take that approach.

But whenever she was tempted to lecture, Jane Graham reminded herself of two points she remembered reading some years ago: "Most people learn better when they are looking for answers to important questions than when someone is giving them those answers, and most people—and especially most teenagers—stop listening to someone else talking after about five minutes, at the most."

Also, works of literature like "A Bird Came Down the Walk" are creations that people read, respond to, and then, maybe, discuss with other people. So, a class discussion makes better sense than a lecture, if what happens really is a discussion. But consider Ms. Johnson's class. She believes that her class had discussed the poem, but what happened in Ms. Johnson's class—and very many other English classes—was probably more an oral quiz. As she said later, when she discussed how she planned to teach, she knows what the poem says. She had read the poem several times and thought through it using her training as an English teacher. She had read an analysis of it in the teacher's guide for the text. She had studied Emily Dickinson in more than one class in college. Also, she had taught the poem to more than one class. She had worked out the lesson plan for the poem in advance. She'd gone through it line by line and prepared questions for each phrase and sentence. Where she thought the students might have problems answering her questions, she had worked out simpler questions to lead them to the "big question." She knows what the poem means and what every word, phrase, line, and sentence in it means. She had questions to ask that would help her find out whether or not her students had gotten the correct meaning. If they still didn't get the point, she was prepared to tell them what it means.

But her class was not a discussion in the usual sense of that word. It is probably more accurate to say that Ms. Johnson was fishing for the answers that she had decided in advance were the correct ones. The students—at least those that care to please her or those that want to get the top grades—were trying to guess what she wanted them to say. Emily Dickinson's poem was lost in the game that teacher and students were playing, a game that resembles what Theodore Sizer has called "Horace's Compromise." Here's how Sizer describes that compromise:

> Finally, the students accept the system. As long as school is fun some of the time and rarely humiliating, they go along. They strike their bargains with teachers, and they value the rituals of going to school. For them, school is a rite of passage, and they accept it, even though they may be bored by much of it. The American adolescent is a remarkably tolerant animal. (211)

A discussion of a work of literature among people who have read it is a sharing of different insights. It may be led by someone like Helen Johnson or Jane Graham, but that leader cannot pretend to herself or to her students to have the right answers. In literature classes, we all have the same evidence: the text. As readers, we bring what we bring to it, and then we begin to discuss—not the right and wrong "discussion" that Ms. Johnson conducted, but a real sharing of possibilities.

If a teacher decides to have an entire class read the same selection and discuss that work, it is important to consider what Jane Graham did with "A Bird Came Down the Walk." She carried the discussion from experiences that her students had had with birds and bugs to the experience the poet had and from there to what they learned and what the poet learned. She accepted the students' ideas. She waited for them to decide how they wanted to answer her questions. Most important, her questions were open ones. That is, although she probably had her own answers to her questions, she understood that there were many answers, as many as there were students; and she was willing to look seriously with the class at any serious answer, however different from her own it was. Respect for ideas was the key to her class discussions. Using what they said, she guided her students in the direction of the poem. They shared their responses, but she drew from them elements that would help them understand Emily Dickinson's encounter with the bird.

It took them a while to get to the poem itself—but not more time than Helen Johnson took. When they got there, Jane Graham's students were almost ready to write their own poems and so were ready to consider the poem that Dickinson wrote. Ms. Graham was willing to accept the fact that some of her students might like the Dickinson poem and some might not, but she had created a situation where most of them could judge it from the perspective of informed readers, understanding what the poet was thinking and judging the poem on the basis of how well Dickinson put into words what she had seen and thought.

Invitation 2.3

Consider this question for a journal writing: What does Jane Graham give up and what does she (and her class) gain through her choice of teaching process? Are you comfortable with this teaching style?

CONCLUSIONS

Far too many teachers of literature—and, therefore, readers of literature—believe that reading is a passive act. In that view, the one that Helen Johnson seems to hold, a reader opens a book as one might open a package, reaches down into it, and pulls out what the author put there. Some readers who are careful and perceptive get more from their response to the text. Less attentive and less able readers get less and get it less accurately. But all are mining for the gold that the author has deposited.

In 1938, Louise Rosenblatt published *Literature as Exploration* (4th ed., 1983) in which she presented to teachers of literature a concept that is still not understood by many of them. In that book, Rosenblatt urges teachers and readers not to think of the reading of literature as a passive act. Rather, she points out, when a piece of literature is successful for readers, that success comes from the fact that they bring to the selection all that they are and have experienced. A merger, a mingling of reader and work occurs. From that amalgam comes a new creation that never has been and never will be duplicated because it contains the unique quality of the single reader. As she puts it:

> The process of understanding a work implies a recreation of it, an attempt to grasp completely all the sensations and concepts through which the author seeks to convey the qualities of his sense of life. Each of us must make a new synthesis of these elements with his own nature, but it is essential that he assimilate those elements of experience which the author has actually presented. (133)

When Ms. Graham's students read the Emily Dickinson poem, their responses were uniquely theirs. They brought to their reading everything that they know and everything that they had experienced. As they responded to the poet's words, they were continually creating their own poem. Many students probably had seen birds hopping on a lawn, so they were able to bring to the poem that experience. A few may have stopped to watch birds catch worms. Others may have frightened away the bird, intentionally or without meaning to. On the other hand, other students may have put out food for birds in the winter and watched them flutter around a bird feeder. They may have seen the birds fly away when they noticed a movement through a window. And so they created somewhat different works of their own as they read the poem. That individuality is the real glory of literature and probably the reason why so many people like to discuss literature, even if the only literature they have to discuss is soap operas and movies.

Teachers like Jane Graham, who accept this view of the reader as active creator, do not teach literature to give students the one true interpretation. They accept as fact that such singularity does not exist, although they know that many other teachers believe that it does. Instead of posing as authority, such teachers of literature try to make possible a sharing of their students' personal responses, be they valid, semivalid, or erroneous in relation to the text. In that sharing, their students can learn from each other; reconsider what they found in a poem; keep, modify, or reject parts of their own responses; and go away to rethink their reactions.

Such teachers do not consider it important or even desirable that their students agree with their own view of the work or with that of critics and scholars. It is important that those students share their responses, consider with respect the responses of other students and the teacher, and think seriously about the entire array of reactions they have encountered in the class.

As Rosenblatt cautions, the creation that results from the merger of reader and work should be true to the work, just as it should be true to the reader. The work of literature is not reduced to a trivial part of the interaction. Rosenblatt, for example, uses a musical score as an illustration of valid but individual readings or interpretations: No two violinists play a composition in exactly the same way, yet each of them plays it within the parameters of the score. Being true to the literary work, like being true to the score, is essential to response. Nevertheless, with young readers, although a teacher might help students to correct responses that are not true to the work, as Ms. Johnson did by pointing out those errors, many teachers agree with Jane Graham, who dismissed misreading by saying, "Oh, now and then some of them never do get rid of what is pretty clearly a wrong idea. But, you know, I've found, if they liked what they did make of it, they'll probably go back to it later; and, as more mature readers, they'll discover new meanings."

After one's own discovery, the excitement of literature comes from the very diversity of valid responses. There may be a mild satisfaction in finding that a friend who has read a poem I have just finished agrees in every way with what I say about it, but much more interesting is a discussion with someone who has seen the poem differently.

The joy of Jane Graham's approach to teaching lies in the fact that she is not locked into a boring and repetitious telling of the one right way, an interpretation that she has told her students year after year. Rather, each reading of the work is a new discovery for her, partly because she has changed, but, more important, because this year's students are different from last year's students.

REFERENCES

Dickinson, Emily. "A Bird Came Down the Walk." *Selected Poems of Emily Dickinson*. New York: Random House, 1948, 80–81.

Rosenblatt, Louise. *Literature as Exploration*. 4th ed. New York: Modern Language Association, 1983.

Sizer, Theodore. *Horace's Compromise*. Burlington, MA: Houghton Mifflin, 1984.

3

"The Guy Who Wrote This Poem Seems to Have the Same Feelings as You Have"
Reader-Response Methodology

Leila Christenbury

The title of this chapter comes from a chance remark by one of the teachers represented in this discussion. This student-centered, reader-response-oriented teacher did not praise her student for understanding the poet and sharing his exalted ideas and feelings—she turned the tables and noted that the poet just might have had the same feelings as her ninth-grader. It may seem a small point, but it is a powerful one, a political reversal that underscores a respect for students, even in relation to mature literature and established writers. Through this connection, the teacher insists that the poet and the reader are allied, equal, and in the same human territory. Finally, it has the effect of giving the student intellectual standing and confidence.

Such interchanges can and do happen in classrooms where the reader's response to a text is respected and where a teacher, through both choice of literature that can inspire response and a methodology that allows students to respond, becomes not the knowledge giver or the sole truth teller, but a fellow reader and questioner.

I had a hunch that the primary characteristics of how reader response becomes good classroom practice would be exemplified by gifted high school English teachers who believe in reader response, discussing with their students three poems on a significant, salient topic. I was not wrong. In addition, the discussions represented by the transcripts of these classes also refute two common objections to the implementation of a reader-response

methodology in the classroom; (a) attention to student response to literature will deflect seriously from any literary analysis of the work itself; and
(b) a reader-response approach, in and of itself, takes too much instructional time to be efficient—it is quicker to tell students than to ask them to
explore their own interpretations or reactions to a text. Also, although individual teachers may perceive that large-group discussion involves the majority of the class and that those who participate make extensive comments,
such conclusions may be misleading. Accordingly, based on tapes and transcripts, an effort is made to tally the number of student participants and
their responses and to measure the length of both comments and periods of
silence.

METHODOLOGY AND THEORY

Many teachers reared in New Criticism in undergraduate or graduate training learned to love the close reading of poetry and prose. In this reading we
adhered to a consideration of literature as a relatively isolated object to be
discussed and analyzed—almost as one would turn a hard object such as a
diamond and consider it from all points of view. The diamond itself would
not be altered by the turning and handling; it would retain its entire integrity as an object. Thus New Criticism, as defined in John Crowe Ransom's
1941 book of the same name, was literature without the influence of the
reader, the historical context, or the personal history of the author. Yet for
all its obvious advantages over other forms of literary criticism, many of us
reared in this tradition found, when we became teachers, that the technique
did not often translate well. For many of us, in first period on Wednesday
morning, our tenth-graders were struck dumb at the prospect of close, analytical reading divorced from personal or historical context, and some, we
found, were even repelled. What for us was a celebration of the intricate art
of literature for our students became a repugnant dissection of an already
difficult text, robbing it of joy, making it a task, not a connection to life. We
did not fully realize what Louise Rosenblatt calls the "responsibility to the
students as well as the discipline" (ix).
    I discovered reader response out of my own failure to entice my students
to celebrate what I perceived to be the great craft of literature. I think I had
forgotten that appreciation came to me after, sometimes long after, I had
experienced how a novel or a short story could make me feel, could tell
me about my life, my problems, my capabilities. My reading of Louise Rosenblatt told me, and the transcripts of these classes also show that, first, the literature itself must have some connection to the students' lives. Second, to
capitalize on the students' lives, the approach must be inductive. Third, students must be involved, must be engaged to the point where the discussion

leads them "to raise personally meaningful questions . . . [and] to seek in the text the basis for valid answers" (x).

There is an undergirding principle designating that text is a becoming, or as critic Roland Barthes describes it in *Image-Music-Text* as something that is "held in language, only exists in the movement of discourse . . . *experienced only in an activity of production*" (157). Text is, for Barthes and for many others, "the very plural of meaning . . . [dependent on] the *plurality* of its weave of signifiers" (159). Thus for Barthes and others, *signifiers* are not just readers but those who, in their time and place and with their individual backgrounds, make manifest the meaning of the text. In the two classes discussed in this article, the signifiers are different, their weaves of patterns vary, but their engagement with the literature is real and alive.

The two classes that participated in this discussion are at the secondary level in the Richmond, Virginia area. Elaine Younts's ninth-grade class, considered average to below average academically, is at a suburban middle/lower-middle-class public secondary school. Mary Neary-Rice teaches middle-class tenth-graders, considered average academically, at a private non-denominational school from the metropolitan area. Each class discussed three 20th-century American poems with a common theme of fathers (Henry Taylor's "Breakings," Robert Hayden's "Those Winter Sundays," and Neal Bowers's "Black Walnuts"). Although each teacher's class had some experience with poetry, the students did not prepare for the class beforehand, did not see the poems prior to the class, and were not aware of the project or the taping. All quotations are reproduced virtually verbatim; all names are pseudonyms.

Breakings

Long before I first left home, my father
tried to teach me horses, land, and sky,
to show me how this kind of work was done.
I studied how to be my father's son,
but all I learned was, when the wicked die,
they ride combines through barley forever.

Every summer I hated my father
as I drove hot horses through dusty grass;
and so I broke with him, and left the farm
for other work, where unfamiliar weather
broke on my head an unexpected storm
and things I had not studied came to pass.

So nothing changes, nothing stays the same,
and I have returned from a broken home
alone, to ask for a job breaking horses.
I watch a colt on a long line making

tracks in dust, and think of the kinds of breakings
there are, and the kinds of restraining forces.

—Henry Taylor

Those Winter Sundays

Sundays too my father got up early
and put his clothes on in the blueblack cold
then with cracked hands that ached
from labor in the weekday weather made
banked fires blaze. No one ever thanked him.

I'd wake and hear the cold splintering, breaking.
When the rooms were warm, he'd call,
and slowly I would rise and dress,
fearing the chronic angers of that house.

Speaking indifferently to him,
who had driven out the cold
and polished my good shoes as well.
What did I know, what did I know
of love's austere and lonely offices?

—Robert Hayden

Black Walnuts

The year my father used the car for hulling
was the best. We cobbled the drive
with walnuts gathered in baskets
and cardboard boxes, then rode with him
down that rough lane, forward and backward,
time and again, until the air was bitter to breathe
and the tires spun in the juice.
For years after, every piece of gravel
was dyed brown, and the old Ford
out on the open road would warm up
to a nutty smell, especially in winter
with the windows closed and the heater blowing.

Crouched over hulls mangled green and yellow,
we picked out corrugated shells
even the car's weight couldn't crack
and spread them on the grass to dry.
My father, on his hands and knees, happy
over windfall, talked of how good
the tender meats would taste; and in that moment

> I wished with all my heart that he might live forever,
> as leaves ticked down around us
> and the fresh stain darkened on our hands.

—Neal Bowers

Invitation 3.1

Review the following student responses and exchanges in these two classrooms. How do the students' experiences seem to affect and lead their interpretations?

TEACHERS ENCOURAGE STUDENTS
TO TALK EXTENSIVELY

If engaging in a transaction with literature, having students make the literature their own, is an instructional goal, then students must be able to join in a conversation. This is to be distinguished from a series of responses to a teacher's question, responses that are ultimately regulated, guided, and abbreviated within the class context. If they are to thrive in a reader-response classroom, students must converse: speak at length, pause, argue, question. They should not be confined to one-word, one-phrase answers in response to a teacher's question and in a pattern determined by the teacher. In a reader-response classroom, teachers encourage students to talk extensively.

From the transcripts, the classes of Ms. Younts and Ms. Neary-Rice could be characterized, in general, as highly lively. Whereas the students in Ms. Neary-Rice's class might be described as more sophisticated in their intellectual analysis, repeatedly citing lines from the text in an almost New Critical fashion and speaking more at length than their younger counterparts, the students in Ms. Younts's class also discuss extensively. Students, from the evidence of the tape, remain on task with the three poems during the entire class period, and neither teacher feels compelled to guide students "back to the subject." Ms. Younts does make one comment—virtually to herself—that a topic is off the subject, but she does not correct the student whose comment precipitates her remark.

The longest periods of silence/wait time are a 20-second segment in Ms. Younts's class in response to a question on "Breakings" ("What does he [the poet] say he's learned in the end?") and a 12-second pause in response to a question on "Those Winter Sundays" ("Why [could this poem not take place in modern times]?"). Both periods of silence/wait time are followed by extended, multiple student answers of 15 seconds or more.

In Ms. Neary-Rice's class, students become so heated over their summary discussion of the three poems, particularly in the area of whether the poems are about fathers and daughters or fathers and sons, they are called to order approximately four times ("Try not to talk at the same time because you want to hear each other" is a typical teacher comment in this passage), and much of that portion of the tape is unclear due to the nature of multiple, overlapping student comments to other students on the interpretations of the poems. Ms. Neary-Rice asks a variety of questions ("What makes you think that?" or "Does anyone else think that?" are representative queries), encouraging her students to expand on their answers. In fact, in both classes recorded, student responses are not always one-word or one-phrase answers but extended sentences, largely in clusters of 5 to 7 seconds with a dozen or so 20-second responses. When students do make brief, phrase answers, they occur in the context of a rapid-fire argument/discussion with other students.

TEACHERS HELP STUDENTS
MAKE A COMMUNITY OF MEANING

Because each student's response will draw on individual, even idiosyncratic, personal background and experience, and because exchange and exploration is the goal, reader-response teachers must be patient with factual misunderstanding. Eventually, individual misconceptions are corrected in a community of meaning. In a reader-response classroom, nevertheless, paramount attention is not focused on "right" answers.

Accordingly, Ms. Younts maintains open discussion and explores multiple interpretations. For example, about 5 minutes into the discussion of the first poem, "Breakings," she initiates a discussion on a passage referring to the breaking of a colt. The colt's experience is metaphorically linked to the poem's speaker's own "breaking" by life/reality, but Ms. Younts waits as the students struggle with the meaning. Later, as a whole class, they do agree on their perception of the poem's major point, but it is a journey of interpretation. As in discussions outside of school, meaning is found and lost and found again:

> MS. YOUNTS: What does it ["Breakings"] mean, James?
>
> JAMES: He learned how to be a farmer on his dad's farm and then he left first to find a new job, and he got—he couldn't find nothing better—he couldn't find nothing good—so he had to go back to working on the farm and hopefully . . . (garbled).
>
> KAY: He left his dad and the dad wanted the son to be just like him—so he got tired of it.
>
> MS. YOUNTS: What do you think he's learned at the end [of the poem]?
>
> BILL: I thought he was at a racetrack.

MS. YOUNTS: What made you think that?

JAMAL: Because it said—the colt—he's kicking up dirt. I thought he was at a racetrack.

MS. YOUNTS: What's he doing with the colt on a long line?

JAMES: He's plowing.

KAY: He's breaking.

JAMES: He's plowing . . . he's training.

KAY: He's training.

ANN: He's trying to get it so that he can break the—

MS. YOUNTS: He's trying to break the colt? . . . Ann, you work with horses, don't you? Have you ever seen them when they put them on a long line—what are they trying to do?

ANN: It's a *lunge* line. They're trying to get them to—have them get used to . . .

MS. YOUNTS: Get used to the thing around their head—what do they call that, *halter*?

ANN: Yeah. They call it a halter.

MS. YOUNTS: So what else could they be breaking here?

BILL: Breaking him into a plow . . . getting him used to a plow.

MS. YOUNTS: Breaking on the plow. What does a plow do?

BILL: It plows the field.

JAMES: It breaks up the ground.

MS. YOUNTS: Does it break up anything?

BILL: It breaks up the dirt.

MS. YOUNTS: Okay. What does this guy say about his feelings about his father?

As the discussion goes on, much is said about what the speaker feels about his father and although it would appear the students do not immediately understand the metaphorical significance of *breaking*, they eventually come to the following conclusion:

MS. YOUNTS: What do you think this title, "Breakings," means?

MARY: Breaking of him.

ANN: Breaking the horses.

CURT: Breaking both [of them].

A community of meaning is made.

TEACHERS ASK, DON'T TELL

Teachers who tell students, who talk most of the class time, do not have reader-response classrooms. It must be the students who struggle with the literature, who give the answers, and who make the meaning—their own meaning—of the text.

The major tool in these discussions is the question. Whereas Ms. Neary-Rice does give vocabulary synonyms, and Ms. Younts speaks extensively on the variety of walnuts, both women resist almost all direct instruction. When confronted with a student question, both teachers turn to other students rather than become the answer giver.

Ms. Younts does not provide students with a list of preselected terms but asks twice for words the students do not understand ("Find another word that you don't know what it means"), asks for confirmation regarding terms ("Ann, what do they call that, a *halter?*"), and, when she actually looks up one word for a definition, asks students to give her the spelling of the word. She encourages students to struggle to find meaning themselves and, in a typical exchange, tells a student: "Look at *corrugated* in context . . . have you ever seen corrugated cardboard?" When the student responds. "That word doesn't make sense," Ms. Younts does not correct her or argue but acknowledges the fact and tells the student, "We're going to find out why it doesn't make sense."

When confronted with a 20-second silence regarding the meaning of "Breakings," Ms. Younts gives two prompts but waits for student answers—which do come, from three students. Even when asked for clarification, Ms. Younts turns to her students:

> MS. YOUNTS: What do you think changes in the roles that the dad and the son play? Anything?
>
> ANDRE: What do you mean by the *roles?*
>
> MS. YOUNTS: Does anyone know here what I mean by the roles? [*She receives responses to this question, as she does when she asks for an interpretation in "Those Winter Sundays".*]
>
> MS. YOUNTS: He says in here, let's look down at this bottom line, "speaking *indifferently* to him." What do you think that means?
>
> MIKE: Not any differently than . . .
>
> BOB: Not in a different language.
>
> CURT: Same as everyone, everyone else.
>
> MS. YOUNTS: Why would that be that significant if he's talking to his father the same as everyone else?
>
> ALAN: All fathers are like . . .
>
> CURT: It's probably that same weekend routine.
>
> BILL: Does that mean like *indifferently* to, like, than what he usually does—or just to everybody?
>
> MS. YOUNTS: I don't know . . . what do you think?
>
> BILL: It's everybody—he should be talking to his father differently because his father . . .

Similarly, Ms. Neary-Rice, when asking, "Which of these three [poems] seems to be a *father* poem?," receives two student questions: "What do you mean by that?" and "Which one do you like?—or which poem is a *father* poem?" Ms. Neary-Rice, however, does not answer, letting students argue as to the definition. And the students do subsequently argue in what is the most heated discussion of their particular class (depicted in the "Teachers Affirm Students' Responses" segment).

TEACHERS ASK STUDENTS TO MAKE LINKS
TO PERSONAL EXPERIENCE

Requesting that students make links to personal experience is a paramount activity in reader-response classrooms. In capable hands, however, it becomes more than students simply venting their opinions. While personal experience is shared and cited, the students in both Ms. Younts's and Ms. Neary-Rice's classrooms also pay close attention to the text of the three poems, using it to buttress their points.

Ms. Younts asks students in two separate instances to relate to the anger of the speaker against his father in "Breakings" and receives multiple answers—some students link their assigned household tasks (such as mowing the lawn) to the speaker; some discuss their general anger toward their parents. During the latter instance, three students share responses, one for 22 seconds. Ms. Younts also directly asks, "How many of you think that in 20 years you'll get along a lot better with your father?" Interestingly enough, most students assume they will have an improved relationship, largely because they will be living the same kinds of lives as their fathers.

Fathers and Their Roles

Discussing "Those Winter Sundays," Ms. Younts asks, "What does this dad do that's different from what your dad does?" which leads to a class poll and discussion of weekend sleeping/rising patterns for the students, their fathers, and Ms. Younts. Again, she cycles back to the students' relationships with their fathers, touching on the "chronic angers" aspect of "Those Winter Sundays." Two students responded extensively; one is cited here:

> My dad was like, he started to get—because I knew it wasn't me that my dad was mad at because it was pretty bad you know ever since I was a little kid. It was pretty bad. But once he got to the point where he was losing his job, he started on everything, every little thing—it was getting worse—and I knew it wasn't me.

Ms. Younts, going back to the "speaking indifferently" line of "Those Winter Sundays," asks about students treating their fathers "in a way they shouldn't have"; the request elicits a 3-minute, 8-second response from approximately half a dozen students regarding family disputes with both mothers and fathers. In one instance a student goes back to "Breakings" to buttress his point. At the conclusion of this segment, which Ms. Younts does not interrupt or guide other than to call on students, she makes the point that is used in the title of this chapter, "One good thing about this poem is the guy who wrote this poem seems to have the same feelings as you . . . have."

Ms. Neary-Rice's class, discussing "Sundays," gets into a lively argument about the believability of anybody's father banking a fire or actually polishing their shoes. Although banking fires is agreed on as what Ms. Neary-Rice calls a "father thing to do," in general, there is loud dispute about polishing shoes. Yet two students volunteer, much to the encouragement of some peers, that their fathers perform such tasks. And, in the sharing, John, who had loudly proclaimed that fathers just did not polish shoes, links the comment back to "Those Winter Sundays" ("No one ever thanked him") and, essentially, apologizes to Angela:

ANGELA: Yeah, my dad used to polish my shoes for me when I was little—and I wore those Mary Janes and you'd wear them forever and forever—and they were all scuffed up and my Dad would polish them like every Sunday morning, or right before we went somewhere.

JOHN: Did you thank him?

ANGELA: Did I ever thank him? I don't know. Probably not. I hated those shoes.

JOHN: I stand corrected.

Fathers and Their Children

Almost immediately after this interchange, in response to Ms. Neary-Rice's question about "a father's love being lonely" ("What did I know, what did I know / of love's austere and lonely offices?"), two students make long comments 20- and 30-second responses, respectively). One student literally bursts out:

I saw some kid smack his father down. He was like at a basketball game, and the father was walking around with his kid; he felt real cool, watching these kids out there shoot baskets and everything. And as they're walking off, the kid goes, "I want to ride home with Mommy." And just totally just left the dad.

And the dad said, "Well, why don't you want to go home with me?"

"I just want to go home with Mommy."

And the father just walked off.

Students make a number of astonished and sympathetic noises, which leads to a second student point: "I always felt closer to my Mom than I did to my Dad because my Dad was the one who used to punish me. And my Mom used to say, 'Aw, don't hit him.' "

Later in Ms. Neary-Rice's class, a student says she "can relate" to the poem:

He [my father] does a lot of things for me that I don't think about, and I never thank him for . . . and a lot of times I'll be not very nice to him, and I won't even realize I'm doing it. And then I'll like think about it and realize and then it's kind of too late, kind of like this [in "Those Winter Sundays"].

After this remark, three students add their observations about their fathers and the giving and taking of thanks and praise.

The Walnut Experience

With "Black Walnuts," Ms. Younts asks students about their knowledge of walnuts and walnut trees and, uncharacteristically for this instructor and this class, gives the most extensive background yet on the subject. The disquisition of sorts, lasting about 3 minutes, is almost puzzling. Yet a later conversation with Ms. Younts confirmed what most veteran teachers would assume: The subject matter of the poem, the breaking up of walnuts on the driveway with the family car, is unique enough to worry about. She feared that her students would be hopelessly confused and not understand even the bare surface of "Walnuts," much less the metaphorical significance of the event with regard to the speaker's feelings about his or her father. The discussion of the poem was, also, the last activity of the class period.

Surprisingly, however, not only in Ms. Younts's class, but in Ms. Neary-Rice's class, students had direct experience with a virtually identical event. One of Ms. Younts's students, who grew up in Pakistan, describes how her family used the car to crush black walnuts in their driveway. She tells where her family bought the walnuts, how much they cost, how they broke them open, and so forth. In Ms. Neary-Rice's class a student says she and her family "did this one year" and very briefly describes the procedure.

Certainly the fact that the subjects of the three poems are central to students' lives—parents, if not on-site fathers—makes such an insistence on linkage of personal experience possible. All of the students have stories and opinions and a history in this area; the discussion, as cited here, might not be as rich if the topic were about building highways or going to war. Yet, as the transcripts also show, the students do more than simply link the poetry to their own lives and experiences. Most of the students return to lines, concepts, and ideas in the literature and, while they relate to the text, also do a capable job examining and even analyzing it.

TEACHERS AFFIRM STUDENTS' RESPONSES

In addition, with a reader-response classroom discussion, teachers affirm student response to the literature. They can affirm response by overt praise or agreement, but the transcripts of these two classes show that Ms. Younts and Ms. Neary-Rice reinforce their students' responses through two major instructional methods: (a) by referring to student comments in discussion and (b) by asking other students to respond particularly to those comments. Such actions give powerful confirmation to students that their ideas and responses are legitimate.

Ms. Neary-Rice, specifically prompted by the interchange of two students, directs her class to the "chronic angers" line from "Those Winter Sundays":

CHARLES: Well, it seems like the kid, he feared his father. He doesn't fear him—
he doesn't understand his father it doesn't seems like. It says right there,
"When the rooms were warm, he'd call, / and slowly I would rise and dress, /
fearing the chronic angers." I mean at first it seems like he loves his father for
chasing "out the cold," and then it seems like he fears his father.

KAREN: But does he fear the "chronic angers" of that house or his father? That's
not his father.

CHARLES: It's his father.

MS. NEARY-RICE: Everybody look at this line and let's see how you first thought
about it and see if you think differently on second thought. What are you
thinking the "chronic angers" are?

In answer to this question, approximately seven students respond for a
total of 3 relatively teacher-uninterrupted minutes, taking turns looking at
the phrase. Another student then moves the discussion to the "speaking indifferently" section and talks, without interruption, for almost 1.5 minutes.

Ms. Neary-Rice uses this technique repeatedly, moving students to respond to other student observations some half a dozen times during the
class period. In "Breakings." for instance, she notes: "Jim said you break the
spirit of the colt. If we make an analogy here between the father and son,
does that make the son bitter—as Rick said?"

The technique has the effect of inspiring students to continue to respond
to each other, as in the case of one student who, with no prompting or
teacher-led suggesting, disputes another student's vision of the locale of
"Breakings" as a place of "dying fields and dust and storms." The second
student objects to this characterization and says that the poem is more a
"Kentucky" poem than "Those Winter Sundays," which strikes him as a "New
England" type of piece:

> I think these poems are very geographical. They have two geographical dis-
> tinctions. When I think of horses and breaking horses, I think of Kentucky,
> and the bluegrass, and like the Kentucky Derby and all that. And when I think
> of the "cold" and "austere," I think of New England and the birch trees.

Ms. Neary-Rice's response is both praise and invitation: "Maybe some of
you [students] thought that way, too; that makes sense to me." She encourages students to cite instances supporting the geographical hints/nuances
of the next poem.

In Ms. Neary-Rice's class, the most heated argument is brought to the
fore by the citation of a student's point:

MS. NEARY-RICE: Did you hear what Charles said? "This [poem "Breakings"] is
not about fathers and daughters, this is about fathers and sons." What do you
think of that?

The responses, ranging virtually across the entire class, involve approximately six students, and cover the area of inclusive language ("everybody in

here [this class] is saying *he* anyway") and sex of author ("Neal Bowers wrote this" and, from two other students, "They're [the poems] written by men"; "There's not one woman here—Henry Taylor"). There are personal examples from families (a girl notes, "my father makes me go out and dig ditches and move gravel and stuff like that"; a boy sarcastically says "my mother never takes me by the hand and teaches me how to sew or do the dishes") and a comment on sex roles (How many *daughters* break horses?"). One student cites the archetypal aspect of the poem ("on the surface it could be about fathers and sons, but I think it could be the universal relationship between parents and children"). Another student notes the difference between the relationships between fathers and daughters and mothers and daughters ("You never hear," one student asserts, "about mother/son bonding").

From this very heated, wide-ranging argument there emerges a question of whose poem is it anyway, a discussion that is, essentially, about reader response. Theresa starts the discussion, and her comment is almost lost in the uproar. Neary-Rice does not repeat it for the class, but signals the other students to listen:

MS. NEARY-RICE: Check out Theresa's remark, and let's hear if you agree.

THERESA: I think it [the interpretation of the poem as about fathers and sons or fathers and daughters] is determined by the reader and not the poet.

JOHN: Yeah, it's neutered.

four student voices; garbled. Ms. Neary-Rice calls to order.

MS. NEARY-RICE: Do you agree that there's a different meaning for the reader, that that's possible?

THERESA: Yeah.

RICK: Yeah. Sometimes the poem—you put these allegorical meanings [in it], then it can. But if you just write a straightforward poem, it can't be disputed then. There's, like, no second meaning.

MS. NEARY-RICE: What kind of poem is a "straightforward" poem?

RICK: What the poet wants to write.

ROB: Like a descriptive poem.

KAREN: Like when he says *he*.

ROB: Like a haiku.

KAREN: Yeah.

JOHN: I think you can interpret it however you want—but you may well be *wrong* in your interpretation. Because I think the poet had a set audience in mind and what he was remembering and what he was trying to get out. So if you want to think of it as a father/daughter thing, you may be wrong, but you're welcome to your own opinion.

JIM: The poet's a man.

KAREN: But you don't know the poet.

RICK: But if the author like released what this . . . pamphlet, this book . . . is about, is meant to mean, that would take all the fun out of discussing it.

ROB: Well, you see the poet is writing for the poet himself, and that's how he is interpreting it. But other people can read it, and that's how they interpret it.

And how they interpret it, and the very excitement, the very pleasure of discussing it, is surely at the heart of this reader-response classroom.

Invitation 3.2

Within the context of the five teacher behavior models identified by the author, identify several specific examples of them. Cite the teacher's language and what you believe is the apparent effect of that language on these students.

CONCLUSION

Certainly there is a place for the literary lecture. Certainly the New Critical examination of that well-wrought urn can also be an illuminating and rewarding activity. But as Rosenblatt and Barthes and others remind us, when we consider our middle school and high school and college students and their engagement with literature, the formation of their joy of literature, we must allow them not only the discussion floor itself but the authority of their own thoughts and instincts. In my school history, like the history of many others, virtually no teachers allowed me that authority—only my reader/ guide, my mother, encouraged me to talk of literature in terms of my own experiences and understanding. Certainly no one in English class advanced the opinion that a poet's ideas might be akin to mine or any other student's. Thus, I knew that reading was one thing at home and another in school. This lack of fit should not be the rule in our classrooms, with our students, as we not only take our joy in the words on the page but try to provide an environment where our students can similarly celebrate the text.

The two teachers represented in this article allow their students joy and time, and they honor their ideas. They know and convey that different readers can have different interpretations, and they suggest that poets and young people have similar feelings. What they do is not mysterious or arcane or even terribly difficult. What they do, however, if we care about literature and about developing our students into lifelong readers, is absolutely mandatory.

REFERENCES

Barthes, Roland. *Image-Music-Text*. Trans. Stephen Heath. New York: Hill and Wang, 1977.

Bowers, Neal. "Black Walnuts." *North American Review* 273.2 (June 1988): 19.

Hayden, Robert. "Those Winter Sundays." *I Am the Darker Brother*. Ed. Arnold Adoff. New York: The Macmillan Company, 1968. 10.

Ransom, John Crowe. *The New Criticism*. Norfolk, CT: New Directions, 1941.

Rosenblatt, Louise. *Literature as Exploration*. 3d ed. New York: Noble and Noble, 1976.

Taylor, Henry. "Breakings." *An Afternoon of Pocket Billiards*. Salt Lake City: University of Utah Press, 1975: 3.

4

Writing From, Of, and About Literature

Robert E. Probst

We have, in much of our teaching of literature, emphasized explanatory knowing—knowing that takes the form of propositions and demonstrations, generalizations and evidence, and thus we have privileged the expository, analytical paper in many of our courses. Fort objected to this dogmatism in the English class many years ago:

> If teachers today were to insist that students reach only conclusions that were acceptable to our political establishment, violent protests would erupt. But when students are forced to use only one form, there is little rebellion although this formal tyranny may result in a more basic conformity that content tyranny (629).

He suggests that insisting on argumentative essay amounts to:

> demanding a particular kind of relation between a reader and a work being studied. In broad terms the connection is between understander and thing-to-be-understood; more particularly it is between thesis hunter and source of thesis. In other words, if the only form in which a writer can express himself on literature is one that requires a thesis, then he has to look at literature as a source of theses (633).

There is, of course, nothing *wrong* with such writing—Fort argues simply that there may be something wrong with the academic bias that imposes upon students one form, and one form only, for the literary essay. Such limitations may be unnecessarily confining, restricting students inappropriately, dictating to them the stance they will take to the texts they read when other stances might also be productive or satisfying. The traditional critical essay, valuable though it may be, isn't the only form, and perhaps not necessarily the most appropriate form, for every student with every text.

The work of the past 20 or 30 years in composition has suggested that broadening the range of discourse may be beneficial in the classroom. Britton, Martin, Graves, Murray, Romano, Kirby and Liner, and others, have all argued for a more balanced attention to the various modes.[1] They call especially for more emphasis on expressive writing—writing that explores the perceptions, feelings, attitudes, and values of the students, themselves, in an effort to define who they are.

Similarly, literary theory has for some time shown more interest in the uniqueness of the reader, suggesting that it would be reasonable to respect individuality, to pay attention to what each reader brings to the text and how each goes about making sense of it.[2] Many of these theorists argue that more is involved in reading literature than extracting from texts. Literary experience includes—or might include, if the schools don't discourage it too strongly—recalling previous experience, expressing and exploring emotions and associations evoked by a text, reflecting on the human issues addressed or suggested. It might, in other words, lead to intellectual activity other than analysis, the making and demonstrating of propositions, and thus to writing in forms other than the argumentative critical essay.

Considered together, the work in composition and in literary theory suggest that we should invite students to engage in those other ways of experiencing literature, and in those other modes of writing. The making of meaning can be undertaken in a variety of forms or genres.

WRITING "FROM" LITERATURE

We might, for instance, find that our students are interested in dealing with some issue or event that seems only peripherally related to the text. The reading may awaken a memory or provoke reflections on some issue, question, or problem that seems more significant to the reader at that moment than anything within the literary work itself. Despite its tenuous connection with the text, despite our natural suspicion that it is off the point—a distraction from the work at hand—writing about those reflections might be extremely valuable. It might, first of all, be highly motivated writing, arising

---

[1] See, for instance, Britton et al., *The Development of Writing Abilities (11–18)*; Elbow, *Writing without Teachers;* Graves, *Writing: Teachers and Children at Work;* Murray, *A Writer Teaches Writing.*

[2] See especially Bleich, *Subjective Criticism;* Eco, *The Role of the Reader: Explorations in the Semiotics of Texts;* Holland, *5 Readers Reading;* Iser, *The Act of Reading: A Theory of Aesthetic Response;* Kintgen, *The Perception of Poetry;* Rosenblatt, *Literature as Exploration,* fourth edition, *The Reader, the Text, the Poem: The Transactional Theory of the Literary Work;* Slatoff, *With Respect to Readers;* Tompkins, *Reader-Response Criticism: From Formalism to Post-Structuralism.*

as it does from the student's own life history. And it might intimately connect the literary experience with other experiences, giving the student a
broader base from which to forge understandings of self and world.

Consider several examples: In one class, a teacher, Anne Turner, working
in a high school class with *A Separate Peace,* pointed out the passage describing Gene's inability or unwillingness to tell Finny that he considers Finny
his best friend (Graham and Probst, 30–46). Gene reflects that he should
have told him; that he almost did; but that something stopped him. Inviting students to reflect on moments when they, too, had wanted to speak but
didn't, she led them into writing about those remembered incidents. One
student wrote beautifully about his grandfather who had died several years
—or perhaps it was many years—ago, and in the writing resolved for himself some of the difficult feelings that persist long after someone loved has
died unexpectedly or too soon.

It could be argued that his writing was not about the literature, not about
A Separate Peace, and of course we must grant that it was not about *the text.*
It did not analyze the friendship between Gene and Finny, or Gene's inability to express it; it didn't discuss Knowles's vision or style; it didn't explain
anything about the work itself. But it did deal with *the reader's experience* with
the text. Iser says, of the meaning of literary experience:

> The significance of the work, then, does not lie in the meaning sealed within
> the text, but in the fact that that meaning brings out what had previously been
> sealed within us (157).

Presumably, those memories of his grandfather, and those unresolved issues, whatever they were, had been sealed within that reader until coaxed
into the open by the book and Ms. Turner's skillful questioning. The discussion and subsequent writing gave him an opportunity to deal with the
"significance of the work," which was, if we accept Iser's vision of literary experience, that meaning sealed within him.

The student writing of his grandfather chose the form of the personal
narrative. He had been reassured that his thoughts and feelings, personal as
they may be, were relevant, and he knew that he didn't have to suppress
them in order to produce a five-paragraph theme or a traditional critical
essay. Another student—an adult in another class—also recognized and
accepted the formal freedom his teacher allowed him, and chose the letter
as the appropriate genre for his concerns, writing to his brother, from whom
he had been estranged for about 20 years. The same points could be made
about his writing—it was not about the text, but it was, surely, about the
meaning of the literary experience for him. And, again, it would be difficult
to argue that the experiences of reading and of writing were not significant
for him.

In both of these instance the students were writing, not "about" the literature, but "from" it. The literary work was the catalyst or prompt, but the students, as they pursued their own thoughts, departed from the literary work, writing about their own lives. Clearly, they were not being "responsible to the text" in an new critical way. They were not making and defending propositions about the work. They had no literary thesis to offer and support. They were not purely objective, rational, detached. On the contrary, they were involved, committed, deeply concerned with the statements they had to make. They had assimilated the literary work and the task of writing into the fabric of their lives so that they could understand better their own experience. It would be difficult to argue that they would profit more by writing an analytical/critical/expository essay on some aspect of the text.

Other examples of this involvement with, and subsequent departure from, the text are easy to come by. In "As Best She Could" (Zweigler, 57), a short poem by Donald Jones, an old woman is turned down for welfare support because she lacks the proper documentation. One student who read the poem spoke passionately about her own experiences as a child in a family that survived *only* because of welfare support. The text had evoked a bittersweet memory of pain and comfort, and she, too, was more concerned with that memory than with the diction, the imagery, the tone, the movement of Jones's poem.

Students in yet another class, after reading "So Much Unfairness of Things" (Bryan, 342–367), a short story about a young man expelled from a prep school for cheating on a Latin examination, expressed great concern about the pressures on them to achieve, and the temptation to cheat that faced them all. They, too, might productively have written "from" the literature, had their teacher not directed them conscientiously back to the techniques of characterization employed by the writer. Required to think "about," not allowed to think "from," the literature, they had to forego its potential meaning for them in favor of exercises in analysis, and so went dutifully back to muttering remembered phrases about authors revealing the character's nature through dialogue, in explicit description, and by showing the reactions of others to the character. They had to abandon the curiosity Bryan had awakened in them about loyalty to friends, honor, and the hard choices adolescents sometimes have to make, so that they could parrot definitions from the teacher's manual of literary terminology.

Consider the potential of writing "from," rather than "about," the literary experience offered by this poem—

The Goodnight

He stood still by her bed
Watching his daughter breathe,
The dark and silver head,
The fingers curled beneath,

And thought: Though she may have
Intelligence and charm
And luck, they will not save
Her Life from every harm.

The lives of children are
Dangerous to their parents
With fire, water, air,
And other accidents;
And some, for a child's sake,
Anticipating doom,
Empty the world to make
The world safe as a room.

Who could endure the pain
That was Laocoön's?
Twisting, he saw again
In the same coil his sons.
Plumed in his father's skill,
Young Icarus flew higher
Toward the sun, until
He fell in rings of fire.

A man who cannot stand
Children's perilous play,
With lifted voice and hand
Drives the children away.
Out of sight, out of reach,
The tumbling children pass;
He sits on an empty beach,
Holding an empty glass.

Who said that tenderness
Will turn the heart to stone?
May I endure her weakness
As I endure my own.
Better to say goodnight
To breathing flesh and blood
Each night as though the night
Were always only good.

—Simpson, *A Dream of Governors*, 85–86

What associations, memories, issues might it draw to the surface? To whom might letters be addressed; what might journal entries deal with? If you were to write, not *about* this text, but rather, *from* it, what would you write? who might your audience be? In what genre would you write—letter, essay, poem, journal-entry or memoir, narrative?

The same question might be raised with your students—where would *their* writing take them? What might the reading draw to the surface for them? About what might they write? Obviously, much will depend upon who they are, and where they are in the course of their lives. Readers who have children of their own—and that includes many college students, a fair number of high school students, and some middle-school students—may react differently from those who cannot imagine themselves as parents. How one reads the poem may depend on whether he sees himself as the one fearing, or the one feared for.

How might we encourage students to write "from" this poem? We might ask such questions as the following, both for discussion and writing, to encourage them to attend to their own feelings and thoughts as they read:

- As you read this poem, what thoughts or feelings did it awaken in you? Try to recapture them, and jot them down.
- Perhaps your mind wandered far afield as you read the poem—if so, forget the poem and jot down those digressive thoughts. When you've done so, look closely at them—are there any connections you can see between the text and your own thoughts?
- If you were to be asked to write about your reading of this text, upon what would you focus? Would you write about some association or memory, about some aspect of the text itself, about the author, or about some other matter?
- As you discussed this poem with others in your group, what did you observe about them?

Invitation 4.1

Write a letter or a narrative *from* "The Goodnight," or one of the poems in the previous chapter about fathers. You may stage the writing at any point in your life - when a pertinent event occurred, or in the present retrospectively. Having accomplished this draft, express the effects of this effort on yourself in your journal.

We might also explain, and perhaps demonstrate, various modes appropriate for dealing with the issues likely to arise. We might encourage, for example, brief written responses, hastily prepared for the sake of focussing and stimulating discussion. Such writing is clearly exploratory, not intended to pass as a finished, publishable product. Its purpose is to help students find and articulate the personal significance in the literary experience.

Those brief responses might be extended in the form of journal entries, either brief notes or the more demanding writing of structured journals or commonplace books that ask for longer, more elaborate discussion of responses.[3] It is possible to structure entire papers around responses to the literary work, and the exchange and reading of such essays can sustain much productive discussion in the classroom (Bleich, *Readings and Feelings and Subjective Criticism*).

Writing "from" literature leads the student toward two kinds of knowledge—knowledge of self and knowledge of others. It demonstrates to the student the significance of introspection and reflection on one's own values and beliefs, one's own place in the culture, and one's relationships with others. It seems that a responsible and demanding literature curriculum could be designed to value, and to invite and encourage, such exploration. Such a literature curriculum would not only allow us to learn about ourselves, but it would also serve a socializing function. It would allow students to write about others—friends, family, classmates—and thus might enable them to understand their society and culture as well as the characters or authors of particular texts. Such writing might focus attention on one's self—feelings, associations and memories, thoughts and conceptions, and judgments. It would invite the student to reflect on and write about issues and ideas, ethical questions, and visions of human possibilities. The curriculum should respect the significance of that sort of learning.

WRITING "OF" LITERATURE

It's also possible that a happy experience with a literary work might lead students to writing imaginative literature of their own. Rosenblatt suggests that there may be value not yet examined in that endeavor:

> The potential role of the production of such artifacts in the education of the student of literature or art is another of the many implications of the transactional theory to be explored. (Rosenblatt, "The Aesthetic Transaction," 128)

It seems reasonable to assume that some benefit might accrue from efforts to produce, as well as receive, literary works. If we wish students to understand the structural complexities of literary forms, then efforts to create in those forms should be instructive. More important, the attempt to write literature might teach students something about the mind of the writer, helping them to see how the writer of poetry or fiction sees and thinks.

The task of writing imaginative literature—poems, stories, plays—is, after all, different from that of writing an analytical essay, possibly requiring a different focus for the writer's energy. While the writer of the critical essay is analytical and rational, the writer of the poem is intuitive and receptive. Where the critics seek to articulate and clarify the structures of a text, poets or story

---

[3]See, for example, Price, "A Case for a Modern Commonplace Book," *College Composition and Communication;* Progoff, *At a Journal Workshop;* and Rainer, *The New Diary.*

writers attempt to cultivate a sensitivity to patterns, connections, and links, that they may not fully see or understand. The different genres demand different labors. Little has been done with teaching students to write imaginative literature.[4]

Examples of instruction in writing "of" literature are harder to come upon, restricted as teachers are by curricula that fail to acknowledge the value of imaginative writing. Some teachers, do, however, find ways of luring their students into writing imaginative literature. Dixie Bowden's students, for example, have written brilliant parodies and imitations of Shakespeare's sonnets, and of speeches in his plays. Given the form or the pattern, many students who might otherwise consider poetry beyond their ability have succeeded in producing satisfying poems. Imitation and parody are especially accessible, because they are light, burlesque, and exaggerated, and so excesses and other lapses of judgment are more easily accepted. Excesses in more solemn pieces may turn them into ridiculous caricatures, but excesses in pieces that are already caricatures may simply add to the humor.

Some readers do, however, attempt more serious pieces, and often successfully. A reader of Louis Simpson's "My Father in the Night Commanding No" (Simpson, *Collected Poems*, 152–153), dashed off, within minutes of finishing the reading, a poem of his own, addressed to his son. For him, the reading awakened matters that he needed to deal with, and could deal with best in poetry. To have demanded that he write a critical essay at a time when poetry was surely the more appropriate mode, would only have interfered.

Consider how the following poem might be used to encourage writing poetry—or stories—of one's own. We must keep in mind, of course, that the writing "of" literature may not be appropriate for all students in response to all texts, but we should be alert to the possibilities. What sort of experiences might this poem call to mind that would appropriately be dealt with in poetic form, and how might we invite students to pursue them?

Sign for My Father, Who Stressed the Bunt

On the rough diamond,
the hand-cut field below the dog lot and barn,
we rehearsed the strict technique
of bunting. I watched from the infield,
the mound, the backstop
as your left hand climbed the bat, your legs

---

[4]There are, however, several good texts that might be helpful for anyone who wants to try: Cassill, *Writing Fiction*, second edition; Gardner, *On Becoming a Novelist* and *The Art of Fiction: Notes on Craft for Young Writers*; Grossman, *Writing from Here to There*; *Writing and Reading Poetry*; Jerome, *The Poet's Handbook*; Mearns, *Creative Power: The Education of Youth in the Creative Arts*; Mirrielees, *Story Writing*; Rehder, *The Young Writer at Work*; Riccio, *The Intimate Art of Writing Poetry*; Rilke, *Letters to a Young Poet*; Ueland, *If You Want to Write: A Book about Art, Independence and Spirit*; Tsujimoto, *Teaching Poetry Writing to Adolescents*.

and shoulders squared toward the pitcher.
You could drop it like a seed
down either base line. I admired your style,
but not enough to take my eyes off the bank
that served as our center-field fence.

Years passed, three leagues of organized ball,
no few lives. I could homer
into the garden beyond the bank
into the left-field lot Carmichael Motors,
and still you stressed the same technique,
the crouch and spring, the lead arm absorbing
just enough impact. That whole tiresome pitch
about basics never changing,
and I never learned what you were laying down.

Like a hand brushed across the bill of a cap,
let this be the sign
I'm getting a grip on the sacrifice.

—Bottoms, 22

What questions could we ask of students to encourage the sort of reflection that might lead to imaginative writing of their own? We might first of all ask them to focus on visual images:

> What did you see as you read the poem? Describe the scene briefly. Don't worry about accurately reproducing the scene described in the text if what you saw in your imagination was something else. Perhaps you envisioned some scene in your own past—if so, write about it.

If students are able to recall a powerful image, as this poem about a father and son playing ball together might well evoke, then they might be encouraged to transform it into poetry. They could be asked to get it as clearly as possible in the mind's eye and then to record the details, trying to convey through the picture painted the feelings they recall.

Incidents powerful enough to be remembered for a long time are often the stuff of poetry. Students might be asked, not just for a visual image, but for associations or memories of whatever kind:

> Did the poem call to mind any memory—of people, places, events, sights, smells—or perhaps something more ambiguous, a feeling or attitude? If so, write briefly about it.

Poems are, of course, not the only genre suitable for students to explore. They may be led as well toward personal narratives, invented stories, dialogues (that might become short plays) on issues between real or imagined characters. The point is to make students aware of the possibility that the meaning they create in response to a literary work might take a variety of forms. They should remain open to all of the possibilities, and not assume that the argumentative essay is the only approved, acceptable genre in which to deal with literary experience.

The writing "of" literature might help lead the student toward knowledge of self and of others, and possibly also toward more sophisticated knowledge of texts. It may well teach more about how texts work that any other approach we might consider. We wouldn't teach music without asking students, sooner or later, to try singing or playing an instrument, and we assume that it is everyone's unquestioned right to sing along, if only in the shower. But we often teach literature as if it is virtually unapproachable, something that can be produced only by an artistic elite. That may be hurting us, suggesting as it does that literature is for scholars only, and not for people. Students invited to try their hands at the literary forms might learn to see the writing of poetry, fiction, and drama as ways of thinking about the world, accessible to all, just as music is accessible to all.

Although it is an untested assumption, it seems reasonable to expect that writing poems and stories may enable us to read those genres with more sympathy and insight. We might begin to see and analyze the vision offered by other works with greater clarity and understanding. If so, it would ultimately make us more skillful at the tasks of the reader of literature: examining assumptions and perspectives, evaluating the implications of accepting visions, conceptions, and values offered by works, analyzing how texts work. It might yield sharpened understanding of the potential, the limitations, and the methods of various genres.

The writing "of" literature might also yield greater knowledge of contexts, as well as texts. Literature is written and read in a social and cultural context, and much of literary scholarship is devoted to exploring the effects of that context. Students should be able to examine its shaping effects. Observing how their own works are influenced by their experiences and their surroundings may help them see how the works they study are similarly shaped. They may come to see literature as part of a cultural fabric, both a product and a producer of that culture. Ideally, they would come to see the role of imaginative literature in forming conceptions of human possibilities.

Writing "About" Literature

Finally, there is writing "about" literature, the traditionally emphasized approach. Much that has preceded might, unfortunately, be taken as a rejection of writing in the traditional modes—explicating texts; analyzing structure, movement, diction; speculating about the author's values or assumptions; tracing the influences that might have shaped his work. The expository essay remains, however, an extremely important tool, and it would be foolish for the literature or composition program to ignore it.

Students need to learn something of the processes of making meaning, and the writing of critical essays might lead toward that goal. They should develop an awareness of the strategies of critical thinking, the influence upon thought of personal associations and feelings, the processes of negotiation within a social or academic group, the importance of open-mindedness and flexibility in exploring ideas, and the criteria by which evidence is judged. They need to become aware of the difference between statements about themselves (their feelings and values) and assertions—factual or inferential—about texts and authors, realizing that different kinds of statements require different kinds of evidence or argument. It is important also, however, not to pretend to an unattainable objectivity or purity of reading. Even in the most rigorous analysis, the uniqueness of the reader is apparent, shaping the analysis.

What questions might a teacher raise to invite realistic and valuable writing "about" literary works? Those questions should not imply, as they often do, that there is a right answer, or a single correct interpretation lurking somewhere in the literary woods waiting to be hunted down and shot. They should instead respect the integrity of the individual readers, allowing them to work without embarrassment from their unique perspectives.

We might direct students to the analysis of texts through such questions and prompts as these:

- As you read the text, what word, phrase, image, or idea struck you most powerfully—why? What seems to you to be the most important word or phrase in the text?
- What is there in the text or in your reading that you have the most trouble understanding? did your first reaction to the text raise questions for you that led you to analyze and interpret? How did those first responses guide your thinking?
- What sort of person do you imagine the author of this text to be? Imagine him commenting on or explaining the text to you—what would he say?
- What beliefs does the author seem to hold? How do those views differ from your own, or how are they similar?
- How did your reading of the text differ from the readings of those with whom you discussed it? Do you have vastly different understandings of it, or do you see it in much the same way? What similarities were there in your readings?
- Do you think the text is a good one—why, or why not?

The writing students undertake "about" literary works should, of course, give them practice in inferential reasoning, in the building of demonstrations and arguments. Though it should not ignore response, it should move students from response toward analysis of both readings and texts. Structured assignment sequences, involving a series of questions each building upon the one preceding, may help students learn to build more and more complex arguments.

Invitation 4.2

Following these general response questions, prepare several more specific response questions leading to writing about a particular novel or short story that might be used in teaching it.

The focus of this sort of writing might fall on any of a number of topics: the character's attitudes and values, the ethical positions represented in the text, dilemmas in the plot, the character's problems and choices, stylistic or linguistic elements, the demands, possibilities, and rewards of the various genres, the pleasures in sound, image, emotion, intellectual challenge, the author's ideas or assumptions, character and values, the influences upon his work, and his influence upon others. Writing about and subsequently discussing these issues with others may give students invaluable practice in articulating a position, defending it and modifying it, perhaps even in learning to abandon it in the light of stronger arguments for another view. It is training for the sort of thinking necessary in a democracy, which is a system predicated upon the notion that responsible individuals will value and consider both their own thinking and that of others, and will contribute to the deliberations that will yield the best for all of us.

We should not ignore that in all of this work, a broad objective subsuming all others is pleasure. The literary experience, as all other intellectual and aesthetic experiences, should provide pleasure, whether it is the pleasure of self-expression, as in the personal narrative or the letter, the pleasure of artistic creation, as in the writing of poetry or fiction, or the pleasure of intellectual accomplishment or problem solving, as in the writing of the critical essay.

The purpose of broadening the range of discourse forms students might choose in responding to literary experience is to give them access to all of these pleasures and to enable them to realize their own potential for understanding and shaping themselves and their worlds.

REFERENCES

Bleich, David. *Readings and Feelings: An Introduction to Subjective Criticism.* Urbana, Illinois: National Council of Teachers of English, 1975.

———. *Subjective Criticism.* Baltimore: Johns Hopkins University Press, 1978.

Bottoms, David. "Sign for My Father, Who Stressed the Bunt." *In a U-Haul North of Damascus.* New York: Wm. Morrow and Company, 1983. 22.

Britton, James, Tony Burgess, Nancy Martin, Alex McLeod, and Harold Rosen. *The Development of Writing Abilities (11–18).* London: Macmillan, 1975.

Bryan, C. D. B. "So Much Unfairness of Things." *Literature and Life,* eds. Helen McDonnell et al. Glenview, Ill: Scott, Foresman, 1979. 342–367. (Originally published in *The New Yorker Magazine,* 1962.)

Cassill, R. V. *Writing Fiction,* second edition. Englewood Cliffs: Prentice-Hall, 1975.

Eco, Umberto. *The Role of the Reader: Explorations in the Semiotics of Texts.* Bloomington: Indiana University Press, 1979.

Elbow, Peter. *Writing Without Teachers.* New York: Oxford University Press, 1973.

Fort, Keith. "Form, Authority, and the Critical Essay," *College English* 32.6 (March 1971). 629–639.

Gardner, John. *The Art of Fiction: Notes on Craft for Young Writers.* New York: Vintage Books, 1983.

———. *On Becoming a Novelist.* New York: Harper and Row, 1983.

Graham, Joan and Robert E. Probst. "Eliciting Response to Literature." *Kentucky English Bulletin* 32.1 (Fall 1982). 30–46.

Graves, Donald H. *Writing: Teachers and Children at Work.* London: Heinemann Educational Books, 1983.

Grossman, Florence. *Writing from Here to There: Writing and Reading Poetry.* Portsmouth, N.H.: Boynton/Cook, 1982.

Holland, Norman. *5 Readers Reading.* New Haven: Yale University Pres, 1975.

Iser, Wolfgang. *The Act of Reading: A Theory of Aesthetic Response.* Baltimore: Johns Hopkins University Press, 1978.

Jerome, Judson. *The Poet's Handbook.* Cincinnati, Ohio: Writer's Digest Books, 1980.

Jones, Donald. "As Best She Could." *Man in the Poetic Mode,* volume 6, ed. Joy Zweigler. Evanston, Illinois: McDougal, Littell and Company, 1970. 57.

Kintgen, E. R. *The Perception of Poetry.* Bloomington, Indiana: Indiana University Press, 1983.

Knowles, John. *A Separate Peace.* New York: Bantam Books, 1979.

Mearns, Hughes. *Creative Power: The Education of Youth in the Creative Arts.* New York: Dover Publications, 1958.

Mirrielees, Edith Ronald. *Story Writing.* New York: Viking Press, 1962.

Murray, Donald. *A Writer Teaches Writing,* second edition. Boston: Houghton Mifflin, 1985.

Price, Gayle B. "A Case for a Modern Commonplace Book." *College Composition and Communication* 31.2 (May 1980). 175–182.

Probst, Robert E. "Dialogue with a Text." *English Journal* 77.1 (January 1988). 32–38.

———. *Response and Analysis: Teaching Literature in Junior and Senior High Schools.* Portsmouth, N.H.: Boynton/Cook Publishers, Inc., 1988.

Progoff, Ira. *At a Journal Workshop.* New York: Dialogue House Library, 1975.

Rainer, Tristine. *The New Diary.* Los Angeles, California: J. P. Tarcher, Inc., 1978.

Rehder, Jessie. *The Young Writer at Work.* New York: Odyssey Press, Inc., 1962.

Riccio, Ottone M. *The Intimate Art of Writing Poetry.* Englewood Cliffs: Prentice-Hall, Inc., 1980.

Rilke, Rainer Maria. *Letters to a Young Poet.* New York: W. W. Norton and Company, 1954.

Rosenblatt, Louise M. "The Aesthetic Transaction." *Journal of Aesthetic Education* 20.4 (Winter 1986). 122–128.

———. *Literature as Exploration,* fourth edition. New York: Modern Language Association, 1983.

———. *The Reader, the Text, the Poem: The Transactional Theory of the Literary Work.* Carbondale, Ill.: Southern Illinois University Press, 1978.

Simpson, Louis. "The Goodnight." *A Dream of Governors.* Middletown, Connecticut: Wesleyan University press, 1959. 85–86.

———. "My Father in the Night Commanding No," *Collected Poems.* New York: Paragon Press, 1988. 152–153.

Slatoff, Walter J. *With Respect to Readers.* Ithaca: Cornell University Press, 1970.

Tompkins, Jane. *Reader-Response Criticism: From Formalism to Post-Structuralism.* Baltimore, Maryland: Johns Hopkins University Press, 1980.

Tsujimoto, Joseph. *Teaching Poetry Writing to Adolescents.* Urbana, Illinois: National Council of Teachers of English, 1988.

Ueland, Brenda. *If You Want to Write: A Book about Art, Independence and Spirit.* St. Paul: Greywolf Pres, 1987.

Part II

Initiating Readers' Responses:
Classroom Processes

The chapters in this section focus on beginnings—ways a teacher can draw out in the classroom readers' responses to a text. The authors of these chapters propose strategies through which teachers initially engage students and cause them to explore their responses. They demonstrate how, although the teacher may provide the catalyst to open the discussion, it is the students' responses that are at the heart of the activity. In these chapters we see teachers resist using techniques that have the effect of predicting or directing response —thus limiting responses— such as reference to the writer's turn of mind or critics' understandings of the text.

The chapters offer a variety of approaches for initiating reader response and they illustrate a range of audiences and situations. The strategies described were selected in each case because they fit specific teaching occasions, but they may be adapted to other audiences and situations. Readers are invited to adapt these strategies to their own teaching situations and to think about how they can use them in their future classrooms.

The focus of chapter 5 is film as literature. Joy Gould Boyum positions film in the classroom as the central focus for response, although she acknowledges the value of using film adaptations in concert with teaching novels. She raises the challenge of what to teach about film in the first place, offering choices that follow the conventional paradigms of literature, but she establishes the meaningful appropriateness of a primary reader-response approach. Boyum illustrates this approach through her class's reactions to the western-genre film *Shane*. The students responses are heated and oppositional along gender lines. The developmental stages of the discussion are expressed to reveal the students' emerging understanding, their tentative rapprochement, revealing also her role as catalyst. Follow-up readings are identified in conjunction with the learnings they served to advance the interpretation of the film and the genre.

In chapter 6, Ron Luce reacts to a basic challenge in teaching literature—students who have been turned off, who have lost confidence in themselves as readers. His technical college students groan in dismay at the assignment of a poetry reading. Aiming to reverse their negative attitudes, their concern for "never get[ting] the right meaning," he effects a line-by-line response experience with Robert Frost's "Mending Wall." The students' initial tentative reactions and their developing interpretations are illustrated through their journal entries, which move from initial transaction with the text through a summary response to a connected personal experience. A transcript of a follow-up class discussion demonstrates the dynamics of such group interactions as the students, testing and refining their insights, wrestle with their sense of the poem. Luce offers additional suggested activities to augment his iceberg-breaking strategy.

In chapter 7, Patricia Kelly considers the consequences of two reader-response approaches. Particularly, she explores how the students' perceptions develop in response to Sylvia Plath's "Words," given the stimulus of a prereading experience and that of Readers Theatre. The role of each in focusing or opening the student's responses is examined in relation to the issue of directing or limiting students' transactions with the text. The potential effects of these strategies on the students' interactions are illustrated and discussed. Kelly's representation of these two approaches illustrates reader-response methodology and suggests guidelines for classroom application.

Deborah Appleman, in chapter 8, first makes a case for the suitability of reader-response methodology to "the developmental and intellectual characteristics of adolescents." She then points out features of texts to which these readers respond, using the novel *Ordinary People* as her example. Within this framework, in tune with reader-response theory, she identifies criteria for selecting texts. Furthermore, she argues for the enhancement of students' interpretive abilities by introducing them to "basic tenets of transactional theory" and then asking them to complete a "response diagram" in which they identify features of the reader and the text that affected personal transaction. Appleman discusses the outcomes of these procedures and offers several additional follow-up activities to foster readers' developing responses.

5

Reader Response at the Movies

Joy Gould Boyum

> *There is no such thing as a generic reader or a generic literary work;*
> *there are only the potential millions of individual readers of the potential*
> *millions of individual literary works. A novel or poem or play remains*
> *merely inkspots on paper until a reader transforms them into a set of*
> *meaningful symbols. The literary work exists in the live circuit set up*
> *between reader and text: the reader infuses intellectual and emotional*
> *meanings into the pattern of verbal symbols, and those symbols channel his*
> *thoughts and feelings. Out of this complex process emerges a more or less*
> *organized imaginative experience. When the reader refers to a poem, say*
> *"Byzantium," he is designating such an experience in relation to a text.*
>
> —Louise M. Rosenblatt, *Literature as Exploration*, p. 24

Like Nicholas J. Karolides, the editor of this volume, I had the extraordinary good fortune to have been a student of Louise M. Rosenblatt. It was while I was doing graduate work in English Education at New York University in preparation for a teaching career. Rosenblatt, as anyone who has read her works or heard her speak can imagine, was an enormously persuasive teacher, and I found myself immediately taken by her view of the literary experience—by reader-response theory as it came to be called or transactionalism as she herself later termed her seminal version of it. I like to think, then, my New Critical training in literature and composition at Barnard College notwithstanding, that my teaching from the outset was permeated by Rosenblatt's ideas: her view of the literary work not as objective entity, but as a function of a transaction between a reader and text; her belief in literature as exploration, as a rich source for gaining insight into self and world; and her view of the teacher's role as both privileging the individual reader's responses and fostering growth in that same individual's ability to enter into the literary experience. Moreover, given that I had the further good fortune to begin my teaching as Rosenblatt's colleague and thus, in a teaching training program, I also would like to believe that I inspired these understandings and approaches in others.

No surprise, then, that when I began to incorporate film into my literature classrooms at New York University and ultimately to teach film courses themselves (among these, not insignificantly, a course in the teaching of film), I began to apply reader-response theory to the film experience as well. After all, as a narrative form with enormous storytelling power, film is if not precisely a variety of literature itself[1] at least a close cousin to it. Like the novel to which film bears the greatest family resemblance, it creates settings for us to enter, characters with whom to identify, and conflicts and crises through which to explore and test our values. It also creates meaning through strategies parallel to those of prose fiction: action, imagery, and symbols chief among them. The novel may indeed be as Jean Mitry claims, "a narrative which organizes itself in a world; the film a world which organizes itself in a narrative" (7–8). Nevertheless, in both instances, narrative and world are created. Because of this, film and literature play almost identical roles in our lives. Most of us have always gone to the movies for the very same reasons we read—at least when we are reading, to borrow Rosenblatt's terms, not *efferently* (for information) but *aesthetically* (for the experience itself). We go to movies, that is, for escape and fantasy, for enlarged understanding, for perceptions into other human beings, and a chance to vicariously participate in their lives for awhile.

However, film doesn't simply invite the application of reader response because of its likenesses to literature; it also presents the reader-response classroom with considerable advantages. For one thing, the understanding of the aesthetic transaction that is at the core of reader-response theory applies to the film experience with a startling precision—with even more precision, one might argue, than it does to literature. "A poem . . . must be thought of as an event in time. It is not an object or an ideal entity," writes Rosenblatt (*Reader* 12). Agreed. Still, where it is possible to *think* of a poem as an empirical object existing in time and space and thus to mistake the text—the little black marks on the page—for the poem (or novel) itself, this simply isn't the case with film. A movie is inescapably an "event in time." It is also quite clearly—given that we are unable to hang it on a wall and gaze on it or open it up to read and reread a specific page—something that cannot be considered apart from our perception and recollection of it. To the contrary, the

---

[1] Actually, I believe film is in some sense indeed a variety of literature and I make the case in my text, *Double Exposure: Fiction Into Film*. To explain the position here, however, would take too much time and detract from the discussion at hand.

movie we describe, criticize, praise, and argue about is identical with the movie we have experienced and brought into being. Put another way, it's the movie in our head, even when that movie exists on video.

What is also true is that our students are to a great extent aware of this— conscious, that is, of the intensely personal nature of their experiences and often deeply committed to preserving them. They connect with movies and are at ease with them, often bringing to them, even if gleaned secondhand from television, a strong visual orientation and at least a rudimentary visual literacy. At the primary school level and even earlier, they find themselves able to organize the pattern of lights and darks and sounds projected before them and to connect these patterns to the world out there. Partly, I suspect, because they can do this without our help, they usually feel free very early on to assert their individual views.

Here lies an important distinction between the viewer and the reader and one that has significant implications for practice in the reader-response classroom. Consider that a key tenet of reader-response theory, an argument for it in fact, is the perceived tendency of literary theory (and thus, teaching in turn) to have ignored the role of the reader. As Rosenblatt formulates it, although the critical emphasis has often shifted over the years from a focus on the text to a focus on the author, "the reader has tended to remain in shadow, taken for granted, to all intents and purposes invisible" (*Reader* 1). However, this simply isn't true of the viewer who, somewhat ironically, is nearly always in view. Seated in a darkened movie house, the viewer may be literally "in shadow," but in the figurative sense he or she is brightly lit. Indeed, in no other art form is there so much focus on self, the personal, or the first-person point of view. In no other art form is discussion so run through with autobiography. "Memories of movies are strand over strand with memories of my life," writes philosopher Stanley Cavell in his preface to his otherwise quite heady meditation on the nature and significance of film. "Movies have been my landmarks. My first tragedy was James Dean's death. My first date, to see Danny Kaye in *Merry Andrew*," notes Marjorie Rosen at the outset of her ground-breaking study of women in film. The tendency is unmistakable: In almost all talk about movies, the experiences and role of the viewer are kept vividly before us, not least of all in the classroom. Students may not have confidence in themselves as readers, but they are—if anything—overconfident as viewers and tend to be more than willing to share their individual transactions with films in class discussion.

To bring film into the classroom, then, whatever the level on which we are operating, is to be pretty much released from the problem of initiating student response, just as it also is from the necessity either of offering instruction in basic skills or of generating interest in the first place. This is obviously one of the reasons that film is so often used as motivation. Perhaps the most typical format for bringing film into the classroom—on the secondary level, at least—has been to stimulate reading. Show the students David Lean's *Great Expectations* and then have them read the Dickens classic, screen John Ford's *Grapes of Wrath* for the class and then assign the Steinbeck version. No doubt students will be encouraged to read. When Hollywood brought *Wuthering Heights* and *Pride and Prejudice* to the screen back in the late 1930s and early 1940s, Emily Brönte and Jane Austen both became best-selling authors, giving the lie to contemporary cultural conservatives who claimed movies would destroy reading. Merchant Ivory and their followers have had a similar impact in recent years. Just think of all those paperbacks of *Howard's End* and *A Room With a View* suddenly appearing in your local bookshops or of *The Wings of Dove* with Helena Bonham Carter on the cover or of *Mrs. Dalloway* featuring Vanessa Redgrave. (Why we are impelled to read the books of films we've seen or conversely to see the films of books we've read is another issue. My own sense is that, although we're often curious in the case of the film to see what others have made of a particular text, we're generally driven by the simple desire to relive in another form an experience that in some way mattered to us. After all, we're rarely tempted to see a movie of a book we hated.)

But to use films in this way—as motivation—is pretty much to condemn them to subservience. Put another way, it treats them as little more than a means of moving students from a lesser aesthetic experience to a greater one (even though, one has to admit that where many adaptations are concerned, sadly this is indeed the case). To use films in this way is also to fail to recognize that whatever else it is, an adaptation is also an interpretation that seen prior to reading will frequently, given film's immense power, have a tendency to control the interpretations that follow. Still, when introduced into the classroom with equal sensitivity to the significance and complexity of each medium and the experience it offers, the book–film comparison can be immensely exciting—a process both fascinating in itself and a potentially rich source of insights to students (not least of which are understandings both of the distinctive languages of these two great narrative forms and of the distinctive strategies of viewers and readers in making sense of those languages). It's an especially promising activity for the reader-response classroom. For one thing, if understood as an interpretation of the written text, a film adaptation has a way of allowing students to see vividly before them the process by which others (in this case, directors, scenarists, and actors) bring a text to life. For another, because students' comfort with film in general will tend to spill over into their transactions with even the most challenging of adaptations (*A Clockwork Orange,* let's say, or *Slaughterhouse-Five*), they will tend to feel freer than they would in the context of the novel alone to articulate their responses; put forth their understandings of characters, conflicts, and themes; argue with the explanations of others; and (if they've read the book before seeing the film, which, I'd contend is by and large the preferable sequence) to possibly take issue with the interpretation of the film itself.

However, it isn't only in the context of adaptations that the film serves reader response. Film is, even at this late date in its history, a fairly young and not fully respectable art form. As such, it remains relatively free from tradition and authority, from established criteria and rigid methodology—in sum, from the critical orthodoxy that so frequently stands between students and their personal and direct experiences in other art fields and that frequently hobbles the experiences of their teachers as well. How many literature teachers, for example, intimidated by the literary greats and insecure about their own abilities have allowed the likes of Brooks and Warren to do their reading for them? How many have gone so far as to use such critics' rhetorical questions to fill in the Socratic designs of their lessons? How many, too, have in the process mistaken explication (well-reasoned and well educated as it might be) for the experience of art?

Film's special quality is that there exists neither a well-established community of experts to stand between ourselves and our feelings nor an unassailable canon. (We may tremble before Joyce and Dostoyevsky, Proust and T. S. Eliot, but we tend to stand fearless before even Bergman and Godard, not to mention Hitchcock and Ford, let alone Spielberg and Scorsese.) Besides, there is so much concentration on current releases, which by their very nature remain more open to interpretation than older works, and so little unanimity, in any case, in this present-tense world, that discussion is inevitably spontaneous and free. All the more so, in that relieved of the pressures of cramping and coercive authority, the teacher is also relieved of the need to assert it. In the film classroom, the questions tend to be real ones, questions to which there are no single predetermined answers and surely no single "right" one. While forced to search for their own understandings, teachers are encouraged to listen attentively and sympathetically to the understandings of others. Film, in a very real sense then, affords those of us schooled by Rosenblatt a rare and special opportunity to at long last truly make education discovery, criticism practical, art exploration and experience, and to do all of this, moreover, in an emphatically democratic atmosphere.

However, if film has so much to offer the reader-response classroom, a key problem remains. It is, I contend, the most difficult problem of all that any reader-response classroom faces: how to bring the text into play. The point is that whereas other reader-response theorists such as Stanley Fish might ask, "Is There a Text in This Class?" not so Louise Rosenblatt, for whom the text is an equal partner in any meaningful aesthetic transaction. Encouraging personal response may be a defining activity in the reader-response-oriented classroom, but it's only the beginning of the teacher process and never the end, despite the tendency of many teachers who see themselves as operating in the reader-response mode to make it such. The teacher must ensure that, as Rosenblatt puts it, "[students have] responded to what is actually present in the work," making students aware that their personal understandings, their preoccupations and emotions, must carry with them "a responsibility to the text itself" (*Exploration* 108). The text, that is, is not only stimulus but control—an understanding that should serve to counter another frequent distortion of reader-response theory, which is the belief that anything goes, that any reading is as good as another. To the contrary, reader-response theory may see all responses as equally real and thus to be respected, but it doesn't accept them as equally valid. "(T)he student should be led," Rosenblatt advises, "to discover that some interpretations are more defensible than others" (*Exploration* 108). Ultimately, then, the aim of the reader-response teacher is what one would hope would be the aim of any teacher—fuller understanding of the work at hand, an increase in students' power to make sense of individual encounters with individual texts, and growth in their ability to read works of ever-increasing complexity. The particular challenge for those committed to reader response is how to do this while not violating the integrity of the individual student's transaction.

This is a challenge that film, of course, shares with literature, although film itself faces still another: what, in encouraging such growth, to teach about film in the first place. Should film teaching follow the conventional paradigms of literature? That is, should it focus on teaching about the author (or in this case, *auteur*) as a way of providing entry into or deepening the experience of any given film? (Should a consideration of Scorsese's *Mean Streets* emphasize the film's autobiographical nature? Should it note that Scorsese himself was a sickly and often home-bound youngster raised in New York's Little Italy who found solace in movies, etc.?) Or should film teaching center on the historical background of the work? (Would it be useful in helping a contemporary student make sense of the Fred Astaire–Ginger Rogers fantasies, fantasies not only of romance but of wealth and privilege and elegance, to situate them as escapist products of the Great Depression?) Or should instruction situate the work in relation to its national heritage? (Does the student need to know about Marxist dialectics and the Soviet view of film's revolutionary role in the shaping of the sensibility of the proletariat to appreciate Eisenstein's *Potemkin*?) Or should the emphasis be on the techniques and structures of the medium? (How much will instruction in framing, in shot/reverse-shot patterns, or eyeline matches, increase the student's appreciation of how John Huston controls the viewer's eye and creates sympathy and suspense in *The Maltese Falcon*?) Or should the film teacher attempt to apply the ideological concerns of cultural studies? (Would the student make better sense of Don Siegel's *Dirty Harry* movies, and even of their popularity, were these films to be examined for their political implications—i.e., for the extent to which they express "right-wing

fantasies" and a faith in "vigilante justice," as Pauline Kael claims they do?)
And what about the application of the mythic patterns of genre study? (How
enriched is our view of *Frankenstein* when we relate the driven doctor to *Faust*
and the Faustian archetype?) Or the semiotic approach of structuralism?
(How important is an awareness of social codes and ideological codes to our
understanding of the interplay of characters in John Ford's *Stagecoach*?) Although it may seem I am begging the question, I would—as reader-response
theory in fact suggests I do—allow the particular context to guide me and
bring to bear whatever would be relevant in deepening and enriching the
student–film transaction currently being explored. For, as most of us know,
learning is really only meaningful when it relates to a particular situation;
conversely, divorced from immediate experience, learning generally isn't
meaningful at all. Certainly, one wants to avoid the mere piling up of unex-
amined responses, but one wants to avoid just as much the mere cataloging
of biographical, historical, and technical paraphernalia.

Invitation 5.1

Consider this array of choices for "deepening and enriching the student film transaction" in relation to a film you have seen. Which
option(s) would you select and when and how would you introduce
this aspect to a class that has viewed the film and expressed its initial
responses to it? Share your ideas with a group of peers who may have
seen the same film or developed a parallel set of options for another
film.

So, how to proceed? How to combine respect for individual student response with responsibility to the movie itself, to the art of film, and to the
growth model of learning? One obvious way, in the context of group discussion (which is the foundation for all teaching in the reader-response mode),
is to keep encouraging students to compare their various understandings.
The next step is to lead them, when these understandings conflict (as almost
invariably they will), to the text for evidence and support, and ultimately, to
an awareness of their own particular biases and preconceptions. Following
this, they should be motivated to seek out whatever information about the
film's creators, cultural context, formal qualities, and the like might help
clarify these disagreements.
An example of the process at work is a discussion of the movie *Shane* that
took place fairly recently in a graduate course of mine, The Film Experience. As is true of almost all courses in the Arts and Humanities Education
program in which I teach, the course is addressed chiefly to students who are
potential or actual teachers, few of whom, it's important to note, are or in-

tend to be teachers of film per se. Rather, they are instructors, or at least majors, in media, English, art, music, and humanities who are generally enamored of film and interested in finding ways to bring it into the college or secondary classroom. The Film Experience attempts to address their concerns by illustrating selected approaches to film study (formal, ideological, historical, etc.) and the contexts in which these approaches might be applied. *Shane*, a classic western telling of a mysterious loner (played by Alan Ladd) who comes to the aid of a family of Wyoming homesteaders in their struggle to save their land from gunslinging cattle ranchers, was being used to demonstrate the possible utility of the approach through genre.

For nonfilm majors such as those in this class, all genre films tend to raise problems. As popular works, entertainments if you will, that make use of fixed patterns and recognizable, predetermined themes, genre films are quite distinct from the type of art works traditionally explored in the classroom. The western, however, raises some very exceptional problems of its own in that responses to it tend to break very much along gender lines (the celebratory work of Jane Tompkins notwithstanding). Most women, quite simply, don't like westerns, feeling excluded from the world laid before them, which is, of course, an adamantly masculine one in which men are men and women are either prissy matrons, pleading wives, or prostitutes with hearts of gold. Nonetheless, as America's indigenous form, the western is able to tell us much about our country's values and attitudes. With the help of the genre approach, I hoped to make this very point clear to the class.

As nearly always in my classrooms, our discussion began with free responses to the movie we had all just seen together[2]—a discussion that in this case almost immediately turned into fairly strong argument. One very vocal young woman announced in no uncertain terms that she found the movie trite and absurdly simplistic. The characters were to her mind one-dimensional, the plot overly, annoyingly predictable. "Like the plots of all westerns," she was quick to add. What's more, the view of women was detestable —even out on the range, Jean Arthur's Marion Starrett hardly got out of the kitchen. Another young woman agreed, but her dismay had other grounds. What particularly disturbed her was what she saw as the film's celebration of violence—its glorification of the hero's prowess with his fists and, more important, with his guns. It was movies like this, she went on, that were guilty of encouraging violence in society as a whole. A male student—slightly older than these women, both of whom were in their mid-20s—rose immediately to the film's defense. He loved the movie, he told us, and had in fact seen it many times.

---

[2]Whenever possible, I have students view the film in class, asking that they react to it immediately after the screening either in writing or in discussion to capture that first, unedited response. Of course, I realize such a practice probably has to be adjusted to the high school classroom because it requires a 3-hour session.

To this admission, the young women groaned.

"Have you really? I mean, a movie in which the hero is dressed in white? The villain in black?"

"And what about that dumb dialogue—'Mrs. Starrett, I love your pie. Gee whiz! Oh, Marion, I'd love to have an affair with you but it wouldn't be the gentlemanly thing to do.' Come off it—this guy is totally absurd, totally unbelievable, totally too good to be true."

But of course he was, the older man responded, going on to make clear to these *Shane* novices that they had missed the point. Did they really think director George Stevens wasn't aware that he'd dressed the hero in white and the villain in black?

"I mean, these characters aren't meant to be 'true'," he asserted. "They're symbols."

"Symbols of what?" I asked. "And how do you know? What makes them symbols?"

Although the question was chiefly addressed to the student who had made the claim, it was another student, also male but younger, who in fact answered: "Black and white. Good and bad."

"You got it," said the older man, who went on to elaborate on the movie's use of "archetypes." Of course, this older student was already—without any help from me—making use of generic concepts. A distinctly unusual viewer who brought to bear considerably more sophistication than one ordinarily finds in the classroom, he had already had considerable experience with the film itself—having seen it so many times—but given the terms and concepts he used, he had obviously also had some experience with myth criticism. Shane, the former gunster, was not simply "goodness," he explained, but a figure associated with nature and the great plains, with the American landscape itself, whereas the unredeemed gunfighter (Jack Palance), who had been hired by the cattle rancher to oppose him, was more than "bad"; he was the undermining shadow figure, with the film itself a pure, unmitigated battle between the forces of light and darkness.

"Claptrap," declared the women.

On one level, maybe, said another, younger man, who may not have loved the film quite so much as the first man, but who unlike the women had been deeply touched by it. To him, the movie was fundamentally about coming of age. Neither Shane's story nor that of the Wyoming homesteader, Joe Starrett (Van Hefflin) and his wife, Marion, it was instead the story of their young son, Joey (played by Brandon deWilde).

"What makes it Joey's story?" I asked.

"Well, think how the movie starts," he said. "Right at the outset, Shane talks to Joey about what's involved in being a man. What's the line? Something like 'A man who watches what's going on around him is a real man.'"

"No, 'a man who watches what's going on around him will make his mark,'" corrected another student, interestingly enough, reading from notes. (I should say that I often suggest to students that they take notes during a screening, being careful as they do so not to look away from the movie. As a one-time film critic, I myself learned how to jot down key lines and images without ever taking my eyes off the screen.)

The first student accepted the correction and went on. "And think of what Shane says to Joey at the end: 'A man has to be what he is.' Shane is always talking to Joey about what it takes to be a man."

"So what does it take?" I prodded.

"How to shoot. How to fight. How to pal around with the other guys," one of the two women inserted, to the class's general amusement.

Of course, the young man, the older man, and the two women were not the only students to join in the discussion, nor were their interpretations of the film the only ones voiced at the time. (Another curious one followed from a student's perception that husband and wife were named Joseph and "Mary.") But the examples of these four are sufficient indication, I think, of the conflicting views expressed in the classroom. *Shane* was a modern morality tale; a moving tale of initiation into manhood; a simplistic and chauvinistic offense; an exercise in irresponsible violence. The point now was to lead the students to garner more precise and persuasive evidence for their views —something, interestingly enough, that the defenders of the film were able to do a good deal more skillfully than its detractors. For where both sides could point to elements of the narrative that supported their interpretations, it was only those who loved the film who truly saw it as *film,* who had managed to take careful note, that is, of its cinematography, its imagery, its editing, and its score.

Invitation 5.2

Ideally, you will be able to view *Shane* and join this discussion. What is the nature and direction of your response? Otherwise, select a film for your group to watch, preferably one that might find a place in the secondary school curriculum. Then, conduct a discussion of your responses to this film, parallel to this class's discussion. Write in your journal your response to the film and to the discussion of it.

When asked once again by me, for example, how he was able to read the film as symbolic, the older man summoned up the film's intense stylization —its reliance on strongly contrasting hues and carefully blocked compositions of figures in spacious landscapes that undercut any sense of simple surface realism. Relating the film's look to its use of generic patterns, he was able to make a very strong case for the movie as myth, for Shane as "knight-

errant," for Jack Palance as Shane's *doppelganger,* and for the western itself as
allegorical battleground for the confrontation between good and evil.

Similarly referring to the film's visual texture, the younger man also
made a strong case for his reading of the movie. He noted in particular the
importance of the placement of the camera and, when I encouraged him to
explain, he noted the way in which that placement led us to see things from
Joey's point of view.

"For example," he said, "during the fight between Shane and Starrett and
the Ryker gang, or in the final shoot-out between Shane and Wilson, the
camera is often behind the swinging doors or peeking under them. It's as if
it were looking through Joey's eyes. And not just in these scenes," he went
on. "We often see things with Joey or through him."

"So Joey's point of view is the film's controlling one?" I questioned.

He nodded.

"But that doesn't necessarily make him the central character," another
student commented. "There are lots of instances where the character whose
point of view dominates isn't the central character. *The Great Gatsby,* or *All the
King's Men.*"

"Well, that's open to argument," I inserted. "There are lots of readings of
Gatsby which contend Nick Carraway *is* the main character, or of *All the King's
Men* which see it as Jack Burden's story. But let's stay with *Shane.*"

"Well, here point of view does help tell us whose story it is," the young
man insisted. "We come in with Joey and we leave with Joey and it's his voice
crying 'Shane, come back, Shane,' that stays with us, isn't it?"

No doubt but that the interpretations of both the young man and older
man were very well thought out and argued. This isn't to dismiss the
women's readings entirely, however. It was pretty much in support of their
views that I, myself, entered the fray. Surely, I agreed with the women, the
plot of the movie is formulaic; surely Marion Starrett and the other wives we
meet here are totally bounded by *kinder, küche,* and *kirche;* and no doubt but
that there is glory in Shane's violent defeat of his enemies.

However, I queried, weren't the movie's views on women and violence
perhaps less one-sided than they at first seemed? For example, in the battle
between the all-male world of the ranchers and the familial one of the
homesteaders, consider which side the movie takes.

"The side of the homesteaders, of course," said the first woman.

"And since that's the only side that includes women, doesn't that signify
something?"

Well, yes, the young woman admitted, somewhat irritably.

"Well, what in particular?" I pressed on.

Grudgingly, but finally, she suggested, that women—especially as embodied by the polite likes of Marion Starrett with her fine dishes and good
manners—were civilizing forces; and that without them, there was no way

for the country to develop the values of home and hearth and of family and stability, which the film obviously affirmed.

As to the violence in the film, its macho views of manhood notwithstanding, didn't *Shane* also depict violence as something men must learn to put away? Why, for example, I queried, did Shane so frequently resist using guns? Why was this one-time gunster so melancholy a hero? Did his violent past link somehow with his present mood? Did it relate to his isolation, his exclusion from romance, from home, and from warmth and affection? And if so, how? Why didn't he take Marion in his arms, as he so clearly wanted to? Or, better still, if his resistance to Marion is simply a function of his commitment to honor, why didn't he have a Marion of his own?

The answers here came fast and furious—although not from either of the women. Shane, other students suggested, was a man doomed to loneliness, to melancholy, and precisely by his history as a gunfighter. "'There's no living with a killing,'" one student quoted Shane's remarks to Joey as evidence of his interpretation. "'You can't break the mold. I tried and it didn't work for me."' Shane, then, another student explained, can never be part of the Starretts' world—the world to which he so much wants to belong; thus, his look of sorrow, his "Cain-like destiny," as the student put it.

Why hadn't the two women perceived any of this ambiguity in the film's attitudes? Largely, it emerged in class discussion, because of the power of their feelings—or one might say biases—regarding violent imagery on the screen and the exclusion of women from the world of action. Not that I'm absolutely sure that even after our discussion, they were fully persuaded that the film doesn't celebrate the gunfighter's skills or take a limited, even saccharine view of women. However, the two did own to a greater complexity in the film's vision than they had first perceived and a certain blindness on both their parts to the film's aesthetic. No, oddly, they hadn't noticed the way Shane is associated with nature, either by his framing within a pair of a deer's antlers in the very first shot in which he appears, his imaging as a figure in the film's magnificent landscape, or the costume he appears and exits in—his leather shirt and chaps. And yes, they did have to admit that films that feature men with guns and women as homebodies did have a tendency to set off certain knee-jerk reactions. In short, without sacrificing their ideological positions, they had begun to develop a certain degree of the self-consciousness so critical to the handling of one's own interpretive responses. Partly because I sensed a growing responsiveness on their part and those of others in the class not only to such self-examination but to other possible interpretations of the film at hand, I felt it was time to move on to the next step in our transactions with *Shane*—a further exploration of the concept of genre.

To this end, I assigned some readings—Robert Warshow's classic essay, "Movie Chronicle: The Westerner" and portions of Richard Slotkin's *Gun-*

fighter Nation—that we used in our discussion in a following session. What emerged, first of all, was a sense of how the western in general and *Shane* in particular relate to American history (to the Civil War and its aftermath, to the settling of the wilderness) and how they express key American myths and motifs (the frontier as a field of human possibilities, the hero as loner, women as agents of civilization). In this vein, we spent a good deal of time discussing the problem of violence and the ambivalent attitude of American society toward it that the movie so keenly reflected. What the class also discovered was the way in which placing the movie in the context of genre and seeing its plot and characters in the light of selected archetypes deepened and enriched their individual, personal transactions. Indeed, there was hardly a student in the class (save perhaps the older man, already, as suggested, highly knowledgeable about westerns and myths) who wasn't led by this "broadening of the framework" (to use another of Rosenblatt's phrases) to reexamine his or her original interpretation of the movie.

Invitation 5.3

View two film versions of the same story (e.g., *The Virginian* starring Gary Cooper [1929] or the later version starring Joel McCrea [1946], or two versions of *Romeo and Juliet* or *Death of a Salesman* starring Frederic March [1951] and Dustin Hoffman [1985]). What similarities and differences emerge from these interpretations? How are your responses affected?

Several students were also led to alter their evaluations. Here we encounter still another advantage film offers a reader-response classroom—the opportunity to truly grapple with problems of criticism other than interpretation. Earlier, I suggested that film has no unassailable canon, nor does it operate with any predetermined criteria as to what constitutes film art in the first place (and even less so today than ever when there are no longer any "art films," but only "independent productions" whose defining quality lies not in their aesthetic but in their cost). *Shane* may be rich in mythic motifs and offer much in the way of sensuous enjoyment—an aspect of response that I haven't really touched on here, but that surely is crucial to the living through of any work of art and especially to the living through of movies—but how great a film is it? Robert Warshow finds it overly self-conscious. Pauline Kael doesn't like it much either. And although I myself am a fan of the film, I have to admit I cringe at such scenes as the one in which a dog is shown whining near its master's coffin or where Shane and Starrett form a male bond by taking off their shirts and, together, pulling up the roots of a tree.

The question of what makes for great art, even good art, is one we rarely ask in the context of literature, where the quality of works we are dealing with is usually a given. But it's a question I don't think we can avoid in film, nor should we. Toward the end of our discussion of *Shane,* my class found itself trying to work through meaningful criteria by which to come to some conclusions about the movie's success or failure, noting that the genre approach, although providing strategies of interpretation and analysis, offered little in the way of guiding evaluation.

And what about the film's relationship to the novel on which it is based? Did that offer any clues? Although we hadn't dealt with the film–book conjunction in class, some students wondered about the original text—about the possible challenges it may have presented the filmmaker and about the filmmaker's handling of such literary elements as point of view and tone and symbolism. Was the novel told from Joey's angle of vision? Was its narrative straightforward? What strategies were used in the novel for which the film had to find equivalents and what precisely were these? Was the empathic symbolism of the film generated by that form alone or did it have its source in the novel? We also wondered if, in the case of the western, we weren't confronting a genre more richly fulfilled on the screen than on the page, what with film's epic potential and its marked ability to render landscape and action.

Invitation 5.4

View a film a second or third time (comparable to reading a book again and again). Take notes of what you see, hear, and understand that you missed the first time. Consider, then, the advantages you as a teacher might have over your students watching a film for the first time. How will you handle this without directing their responses?

Regarding the western, we also noted the extent to which such popular forms resisted the application of critical principles traditionally applied to works of art: originality and complexity, for example. Did this make them lesser works or simply different ones? Whatever the answers—and we didn't really come up with very satisfactory ones—such questions still seem crucial, not least of all to the reader-response classroom with aims that of necessity include encouraging the student's ability to develop sound bases for valid judgments and growth in the power of discrimination. What better way, moreover, to encourage such increased sensitivities than in the fresh and fluid context of film? What better way, too, to demonstrate a responsibility to film, itself, in turn? For as anyone who loves movies knows, the movies today couldn't be in more desperate need of the kind of independent, self-aware, and critically awake viewers that the reader-response classroom has a very special capacity to create.

REFERENCES

Boyum, Joy Gould. *Double Exposure: Fiction Into Film.* New York: New American Library, 1985.

Cavell, Stanley. *The World Viewed: Reflections on the Ontology of Film.* New York: Viking Press, 1971.

Fish, Stanley. *Is There a Text in This Class? The Authority of Interpretive Communities.* Cambridge, MA: Harvard University Press, 1980.

Kael, Pauline. "Dirty Harry?" and "Shane." *5001 Nights at the Movies.* New York: Holt, Rinehart and Winston, 1982. 148, 526.

Mitry, Jean. "Remarks on the Problem of Cinematic Adaptation." Trans. Richard Dyer McCann. *MMLA Bulletin* (Spring 1971): 7–8.

Rosen, Marjorie. *Popcorn Venus: Women, Movies, and the American Dream.* New York: Coward, McCann & Georghegan, 1971.

Rosenblatt, Louise M. *Literature as Exploration.* 5th ed. New York: Modern Language Association, 1995.

———. *The Reader, The Text, The Poem: The Transactional Theory of the Literary Work.* Carbondale: Southern Illinois University Press, 1978.

Slotkin, Richard. *Gunfighter Nation: The Myth of the Frontier in Twentieth Century America.* New York: Atheneum, 1993.

Tompkins, Jane. *West of Everything: The Inner Life of Westerns.* New York: Oxford University Press, 1992.

Warshow, Robett. "Movie Chronicle: The Westerner." *The Immediate Experience: Movies, Comics, Theatre and Other Aspects of Popular Culture.* Garden City, NY: Doubleday, 1962. 135–54.

6

Mending Walls
Using a Reader-Response Approach to Teach Poetry

Ron Luce

In his poem "Mending Wall," Robert Frost places two seemingly different men on opposite sides of a stone wall that is in a state of deterioration. Then he sets them about the task of making repairs. One of the men, the speaker of the poem, is ambivalent about whether he truly wishes to repair the wall year after year (although he initiates the activity in this instance) or whether he simply uses mending as a way of sharing time and verbal exchange with his neighbor while sharing a philosophical discussion with those of us who listen in on the poem. He would appear to be motivated by a strong desire to destroy the barriers that inhibit the total enjoining of minds and space. At first, the neighbor appears to serve only as a foil to the insight of the speaker; he is motivated by simpler thought regarding the purpose of mending the wall, stubbornly insisting on maintaining a barrier of stone and minimalist human interaction as the only effective means of getting along in the world.

However, as the poem unfolds, the distinctions between the men, their motives, and their deceptively simplistic dichotomies about the human condition begin to disintegrate; in fact, it is possible, with careful reading, to imagine and support the notion that the neighbor may well be motivated by the same powerful urges to enjoin the human spirit as is the speaker of the poem. He speaks only twice, saying, "Good fences make good neighbours." Admittedly, this is not much to work with. On the surface, it appears that the neighbor is making an attempt to maintain distinct space, to be left alone. However, ironically implicit in the neighbor's statements and *actions* is the

93

suggestion that the eternal *sharing* of the "mending" is as much a part of making good neighbors as is the idea of maintaining separate identities, a perception that is too easily attributed only to the narrator. This ambivalence has come full circle, feeding a paradoxical reading of the title suggesting that the wall gets mended and it does mending; it is both obstacle and source of unification bound by the complexity of human interaction.

Mending Wall

Something there is that doesn't love a wall,
That sends the frozen-ground-swell under it,
And spills the upper boulders in the sun;
And makes gaps even two can pass abreast.
The work of hunters is another thing:
I have come after them and made repair
Where they have left not one stone on a stone,
But they would have the rabbit out of hiding,
To please the yelping dogs. The gaps I mean,
No one has seen them made or heard them made,
But at spring mending-time we find them there.
I let my neighbour know beyond the hill;
And on a day we meet to walk the line
And set the wall between us once again.
We keep the wall between us as we go.
To each the boulders that have fallen to each.
And some are loaves and some so nearly balls
We have to use a spell to make them balance:
'Stay where you are until our backs are turned!'
We wear our fingers rough with handling them.
Oh, just another kind of out-door game,
One on a side. It comes to little more:
There where it is we do not need the wall:
He is all pine and I am apple orchard.
My apple trees will never get across
And eat the cones under his pines, I tell him.
He only says, 'Good fences make good neighbours.'
Spring is the mischief in me, and I wonder
If I could put a notion in his head:
'*Why* do they make good neighbours? Isn't it
Where there are cows? But here there are no cows.
Before I built a wall I'd ask to know
What I was walling in or walling out,
And to whom I was like to give offence.
Something there is that doesn't love a wall,
That wants it down.' I could say 'Elves' to him,
But it's not elves exactly, and I'd rather
He said it for himself. I see him there

Bringing a stone grasped firmly by the top
In each hand, like an old-stone savage armed.
He moves in darkness as it seems to me,
Not of woods only and the shade of trees.
He will not go behind his father's saying,
And he likes having thought of it so well
He says again, 'Good fences make good neighbours.'

In the preceding synopsis of my reading and derived meaning of the central conflict and force in Frost's poem is the essence of the dilemma teachers face in the classroom when we try to teach students literature. In a sense our students are that neighbor of whom Frost's narrator speaks. They, like the neighbor, are called to the task of picking up (analyzing) "loaves and balls" of stone (literature), often handling them savagely; they are called to lift them, grasp them, fix the walls of their assimilated versions of American culture—a culture that has been shaped for them by powerful competing, often unarticulated forces and philosophies. They seem to feel it all differently from teachers; many refuse, like the neighbor, to answer the central question that is asked: Why do good fences make good neighbors?

The teaching of literature has suffered in the past not for a lack of material (loaves and balls) with potential to excite and encourage students. There is more than enough material with which they can become engaged. The teaching of literature has suffered because of teacher perceptions that the written *text* (the wall) is the source of meaning and joy and students must somehow be forced to come to the text to which they are called, not for participating in laying up stones, but for participating in admiring the fence (text), as though this will eventually make them "good neighbours." As the narrator might be doing to the neighbor, some teachers might be misreading the situation created within their classrooms. Insistence on clinging to what a text *says* rather than *does* keeps both their students and them from venturing into the realm of one another's symbolic structures and dealing with the wall between them.

LEARNING HOW TO TEACH POETRY

When I first began teaching, I had no formal training in how to teach. I thought I knew a great deal about writing and reading and that was enough. All I had to do was share all that knowledge with those who had not yet arrived at the place where I was standing (somewhat like the narrator of the poem). I taught subjects. I taught Frost poems, for example. I wasn't teaching students. Fortunately, through the support of a few friends and colleagues and because I was studying the components of effective writing, I came to terms with the idea of "audience" and how I must think about them and their needs—a major revelation to someone who already believed himself to be a most conscientious humanist. I thought I had arrived. I had uncovered the secret. Now I could teach Frost poems *to people.* I just needed to figure out how to get them involved as active participants in the classroom and then they would learn from me. That all seems so arrogant now.

I am not sure of just how it happened; perhaps it was the culmination of many things (not least of which was reading reader-response theory), but somewhere along the way my whole concept of teaching changed. I found myself losing the need to focus on presenting material to students and began to focus more on helping them discover their own thinking processes. As I grew, I had to question what my real objectives for my students were. For example, did I want them to *know* Robert Frost? Or did I want them to know *about* Robert Frost? Or did I want them to know Robert Frost's *poems?* Or did I want them to discover how to think about a poem in general? Or did I want them to learn to read carefully, to feel a powerful emotional response rise up within themselves as a result of reading, to think about what they had read (regardless of what it was), to ask questions, to analyze, to read more, to question more, to explore from numerous perspectives what turned out to be a Robert Frost poem and then share their thinking with others for the purpose of refining their own thinking and feelings? This was an important line of thought, one I was ashamed to say I had not fully contemplated before; up to this point, I had always accepted, without ever effectively articulating it, that the real goal was to help students to come to terms with what I knew to be "true" about literature as I had been taught and as I had learned it through my own reading and interpretations.

Invitation 6.1

Dive into your memory of your poetry "learning" experiences. Given the teaching approaches used, what were the apparent objectives? List a couple. How have these experiences affected your perception of what teaching and learning poetry (and, perhaps, literature) is about? If asked to teach a poem to a group, what are your automatic responses to the task?

Through the presentation of her transactional model—a model that promotes helping students experience literature and create meaning as they transact with a text—Louise Rosenblatt helped me to find my way. Reader-response theory, as Rosenblatt presents it, embraces a level of concern for students that other theories either have not addressed or have misinterpreted to the extent of causing widespread abuse of the student reader.

In this model, meaning emerges from the transaction of reader and text, each affecting the other; it does not reside in the text from which the student gleans meaning as perceived by an author placing words inviolably in a text. Readers bring their experiences and culture to bear on the text; the text serves to isolate and focus the students' realms of meaning.

Rosenblatt's view of literature as part of the fabric of individual lives—all lives (not just an elite few)—provides a great challenge to the way literature is taught. It forces an awareness that many who teach literature or are preparing to teach literature are already good learners and are well-adapted to the limitations imposed by New Critical theory—close, objective analysis to establish the meaning within the text, to discover the "correct" meaning—and most likely have been exceptions to the "norms" in English classes throughout their educational experiences. Reflection on Rosenblatt's theory challenges us to ask what happens to those who do not find literature exciting and interesting and what can be done to keep the English class malaise of previous generations from infecting classrooms. It does not allow teachers to participate in the deliberate perpetuation of the dichotomy between the common reader and the literary elite.

ADAPTING THEORY TO THE CLASSROOM: AN EXAMPLE

What follows is a very brief example of the use of the transactional model to introduce "Mending Wall" to technical college students in a writing course as a way of trying to engender some critical thinking and to promote confidence in themselves as readers. The class, made up of 16 second-year students majoring in diverse areas, including nursing, forestry, medical records, and accounting, had revealed in conversations that they did not feel "smart enough" to work with literature. No one in the group had ever stated (or even joked about) any interest in leaving the technical college to become an English major, and no one expressed a love of writing or reading, although a couple of students admitted to liking to read as long as it was "interesting." Several students expressed downright hatred of any kind of reading except reading purely for escapism (the *National Enquirer* was mentioned as good escapist literature in at least two cases).

Prior to the class where I was to introduce the poem, I had met with the group several times to discuss writing and to work with them on essays they were creating for the class. On one occasion, I had presented them with a well-written student essay from a previous quarter, uncovering it little by little on an overhead screen while they reacted to the language. In that experience, they learned that their own reading and the text are shaped by the interaction of the words and their own interpretation; they perceived and formulated responses that shifted and reorganized themselves as they worked their way down the pages. We took time to share what happened when they visually struck a period or question mark or when their eyes came to the white space at the end of a paragraph. We discussed how they had been trained and had trained themselves over the years to have a visual, emotional, and logical response to the stimuli before them. They were surprised by the experience and impressed by how much they were able to agree on the essence of the essay even though different readers had slightly different interpretations of individual lines and words. Before beginning the Frost poem, I reminded them of the essay project and of the fact that they bring many skills to the reading experience and the goal was to simply react to the new "document" they were about to encounter. (I determined not to refer to the term *poem* until they did.)

HELPING STUDENTS
"EXPERIENCE" THE POEM

I walked around the room, put a sheet of paper face down on each student's desk, and asked them not to look at it until I told them to do so. I had carefully scribbled across all the letters on a copy of the poem, leaving spaces and punctuation intact, so that I ended up with what looked like words that took up the correct amount of line space but had no meaning other than as visual representations:

When the copies were distributed, I asked the students to turn the papers over and react. At first, many seemed somewhat startled, not knowing what the "gibberish" was. I told them I had taken away one of their tools for analyzing: words. Then I asked them to think about what this document might be. How might we analyze it? Does it *do* anything? How might we react without the words to help us? After a pause, a few comments started coming forth. The students began to grasp for meaning. They identified the title because it was bolder and bigger than the rest of the words and because it was centered at the top of the page. They talked about the short line length and capital letters at the beginning of each line. Finally, someone said it looked like a poem. And then I heard the grunts and groans.

I asked them why they reacted as they did. "What does the word *poem* do to you?" I got vague responses, such as "boring stuff" and "I can never get the *right* meaning." They had framed a negative attitude and set themselves up for being inadequate to the task of reading the poem (they wouldn't be able to get the "right meaning") based on previous experiences. We shared the baggage that they were bringing to the task of reading without having read a word as yet, factors that were triggered by visual impressions that ordinarily would be unarticulated but would color every word they were going to read if they did not try to come to terms with their responses. They were surprised at how much they shared a lack of confidence and how much they created stumbling blocks to the potential for meaningful interaction with an, as yet, undisclosed text. I simply stated that this document need not be a revisitation of past experiences and they should try to keep an open mind.

The next step in the process of helping the students to experience the poem involved something with which they were already familiar. I had the poem on a transparency and uncovered the title, "Mending Wall." I asked them to take out a sheet of paper and respond to the words they saw on the screen. I read the title, and stated, "This is not a test. There is no 'correct' meaning; there is only you and the words. What do the words *do* to you?" Then, after a moment, I began to uncover the poem line by line and to read it, giving them a brief period of time to write. At first I uncovered only a line at a time and let them write whatever they wished; then I began uncovering groupings of lines that completed a single image or idea. (The poem contains no stanza breaks.) When they were finished with their notes, I handed them a typed copy of the poem (I had removed Frost's name so that they would not be influenced by recollections of past experiences with his work), reread the entire poem from beginning to end, and asked them to write a very quick summary of their reactions to the poem. After a few moments, I asked them to write down their own mending wall experience. The following notes demonstrate the kinds of responses I received:

Student A: Terry

Notes

Title: I want to know what it means and what the poem is about.
Does it have to do with a type of barrier or is something being fixed?
I'm confused. What doesn't love a wall?
The top of the wall faces upward to the sun.
Two can pass over or around it.
Hunters have gone over the wall and caused stones to fall off.
Come spring you find gaps on the wall.
Two people fix the wall so that it separates two different places.
They had a hard time making the top of the wall level.
The wall separates woods and an orchard.
If they didn't meet to fix the wall they wouldn't be as good neighbors.
It keeps them from crossing each other's paths.
But why do they need the wall?
They can each have their own privacy.

Summary

One neighbor feels that if he doesn't have the wall between them, they wouldn't be such good neighbors. It keeps them from trespassing on each other's territories. One neighbor feels it is just in the way and wants to know why the other one needs and wants it so badly. He feels that it is a waste of time to mend because it will be torn down again. He wants to know what kind of Elf is causing it to fall down. The other one feels his father was right and still abides by that same saying "Good fences make good neighbors."

Personal Mending Wall

I'm the type of person that needs a small wall. Some things I keep to myself and I try to deal with by myself. Although other things I'm willing to share. Usually I'm an open person. For example, if I worked somewhere and was having problems with a certain job or task, I would want to figure it out by myself. But if I was having problems in school with a class or essay, I would want someone to explain to me and tell me what's wrong. It just depends on the problem and how big it is.

Student B: Mark

Notes

Vietnam Vets Memorial.
Resents confinement.
Cold feelings.
Knocking down the wall.
Love.

Doesn't like hunters.
He found holes in his fence.
Fixing the fence between their property—maybe.
How people separate from each other.
Stone fence.
Respect other's things.
Fences only make good neighbors to keep something in, not out.

Summary

Fences or walls are for keeping something in, not out—at least between good neighbors. If there is not a need for the wall, why have it or repair it? The neighbors respect each other's property. By respecting each other's property, you will be good neighbors. Kind of like the saying, "if you never lend it out, you don't have to worry about not getting it back." Friends don't believe that and they don't need walls either. Maybe tearing the wall down will make them better neighbors and better friends. But neither will suggest it or say anything; they'll just leave it be like it has always been and fix it every year.

Personal Mending Wall

When my wife and I were dating, there were parts of me I didn't want to share with her. Even when we were engaged, there were thoughts and ideas that were mine only. As time went on, she showed me that it's ok to be afraid and vulnerable and that brought us much closer together. My fears didn't go away, but someone else knew them. And she cared and was concerned. It helped make our love what it is today. We make it a point to not let a wall get started before it's too big to knock down.

Student C: Mike

Notes

Mending Wall—where you go to reconcile differences.
There are things that don't like barriers.
These things can't get through, so they go around it and break it down.
Slowly tears down the wall?
Breaks through and allows communication to be easily done.
So we have broken this wall/barrier down for petty reasons. The author
    attempts to reconstruct.
No one is aware of this problem until they decide to reconcile.
The holes represent communication, and rocks are blocks in that communi-
    cation.
Some blocks are large, some small.
We get perturbed at this.
People should keep to themselves and not intervene, or get to know peo-
    ple—according to the neighbor.

Are walls good? Should we not get to know one another?
A fence is a means of protecting one's self from others.

Summary

This poem is about how we build walls between ourselves and others, and how
they are torn down by some who want to hurt us, and also by love. The wall is
the barrier between us that doesn't allow us to know each other, for if we do
get to know each other, there is room for love or hurt. The apples won't eat the
cones. This means "I won't hurt you." Why should there be a wall if I'm not
going to do anything to you? The neighbor wants the wall because he/she
does not want to risk being loved or hurt by the other person. They can co-
exist, but there need not be any communication.

Personal Mending Wall

The walls that I have built to keep people out are few. I like to have the freedom to talk personally with people. I hate it when people build them to keep
me out, especially if there is no real reason for the wall. Sometimes people will
instantly put a wall up if they feel that we are getting too close. I try to tear walls
down, to get inside to see what is happening.

It seems to me that some important experiences were articulated here.
For example, notice that the students go through some reactions to the
poem that involve questioning and struggling to answer their own questions. They go through the processes of checking initial responses as the
poem unfolds. Mark, for example, begins with an image of the Vietnam Vet-
erans Memorial, and then has to discard it in light of the evidence he finds.
Terry starts with several questions and then admits confusion about what
doesn't love a wall, and finally comes to terms with her own central question.
"Why do they need the wall?" Many of the notes are simplistic restatements
of the events in the poem. But several go beyond that point. For example,
Mark says, "Fences only make good neighbors to keep something in, not
out." And Mike speaks of reconciliation, and asks, "Are walls good? Should
we not get to know one another?" In each case, it seems to me that these students are struggling with the ambivalence that Frost present in his poems.
    Notice also the desire to find answers to their own questions in their
summary statements. Mark deals with his question, "If there is not a need for
the wall, why have it or repair it?" He responds with "By respecting each
other's property you will be good neighbors. Kind of like the saying, 'if you
never lend it out, you don't have to worry about not getting it back.' Friends
don't believe that and they don't need walls either." And his final "summary"
sentence is a great response restatement of the closing mood of the poem,
"But neither will suggest it or say anything; they'll just leave it be like it has
always been and fix it every year." He seems to be indicating the same kind

of communication gap between the narrator and the neighbor that is articulated by Mike, who focuses on reconciliation: "They can co-exist, but there
need not be any communication."

Notice also in their own "mending wall" statements how the poem begins
to help them articulate and draw on the components of their everyday lives.
Each speaks of needing other people, vulnerability, care and concern, love,
sharing, communication—all universal concerns of human beings. These
are their initial responses to the poem. Not mine. And they have reached
this point without concern for what the poem "means."

Invitation 6.2

Try this exercise with a poem of your choice, challenging enough to
whet the responses of a small group of peers. Compare reactions to
the poem(s) as well as to the exercise after going two or three rounds.

HELPING STUDENTS
SHARE THEIR RESPONSES

After they dealt with their initial responses, the students were then ready to
move on to a closer examination and sharing. I broke them into three
groups and asked each group to discuss different sections of the poem (15
lines each) and prepare to share their perceptions with the whole class. I set
up the session by asking them to look at the lines and ask themselves what
makes the poem work. I asked them to consider what the writer does that
they responded to, that carried them through the poem gracefully, and that
allowed them to feel whatever it was they felt about the poem. I determined
to intervene in the small groups only if the discussion were clearly outside
the poem or related topics or if the groups were clearly unable to proceed
on their own. I spent most of my time walking around the room, listening
and working at not jumping in to explain the poem—an extremely difficult
task. As it turned out, I did not need to intervene, but I had prepared myself
for the possibility: I had predetermined that I could ask the group to summarize their discussion for me and that I could question why they had come
to the conclusions they had, and I could question how they could defend
their responses by pointing to support from the poem or to specific details
from their shared responses.

After the discussion period, I asked students to designate a speaker for
each group, then I brought the class back together and asked speakers to
share their group's perceptions. I planned to allow students to comment
freely after each presentation and to openly discuss their reactions to the responses of their classmates. I planned to intervene only when the discussion

got off track or when their "meaning" needed to be clarified by the text. As it turned out, until close to the end of their presentations and discussions I found myself being involved very little, except to control the potential chaos of several people speaking at once. I expected students would get sidetracked and begin to drift in directions not consistent with the poem or the heart of the discussion. I feared losing momentum. Again, I had a plan: If that happened, I would simply respond with appreciation for the subject matter and ask how the text had inspired the direction of that particular line of thinking or sharing. Sometimes I asked questions like, "Are you saying . . . ?" and then attempted a summary statement to elicit a reaction when it appeared that other students were confused about what a speaker had stated. Other than that, I waited. Essentially, the class agreed on the basic flow of the responses and discussion and seemed to have little difficulty with the poem—up to the point of the last five lines:

> He moves in darkness as it seems to me,
> Not of woods only and the shade of trees.
> He will not go behind his father's saying,
> And he likes having thought of it so well
> He says again, 'Good fences make good neighbours.'

The following is a transcript of the class discussion to demonstrate the basic flow of the ideas raised. In it I have attempted to use my students' own language—taken from audiotape (revising only to the extent of changing pronoun referents, eliminating redundancies, and making transitions between different speakers; my additions to their words and phrases are printed in italics). Several students' comments are grouped together about a particular idea as they occurred:

Whether it is lack of communication or love, something there is that doesn't love a wall. Hunters tear down the wall not out of love or lack of communication. They tear it down to please the yelping dogs. There are these gaps that stay until we take a look in spring. This person [the narrator] says his wall is down and it needs repair. *It is similar to a situation (for example) where* two people get to know each other very well. They break up. They set up a wall between themselves. Then a couple of months later they get together again, but the wall is still there. They don't share. They don't have much in common any more. We all feel this way *sometimes.*

Even though they [the narrator and the neighbor] are two different people, why would they need this wall? That's the way it is in real life. *For example,* cultures may be very different. We need protection. *We are like them* . . . they [the narrator and his neighbor] are never going to be able to get close as long as they have this wall between them. *They remind us of incidents from our own lives.* We made a comparison to these two people. *We* envision these two people trying to put this fence up and then trying to figure out why . . . *mostly saying to themselves,* "You take care of yours and I'll take care of mine." There are parts of *our lives* where *we* don't want anybody in. *What we really* want *are* gates! We can expose too much of *ourselves* to just anybody, *and we need to be able to control it. The neighbor—the "guy on the other side of the fence"—knew this.*

The *neighbor* is not necessarily bad. There's nothing to say that he's not a friendly person or willing to have a friendship with the *narrator.* It's just that he wants his privacy and property respected. *This reminds us of a great* example: *a woman* had these neighbors *with whom she and her husband* were super friends, and they did things together. *But* the neighbors just kept coming over and making themselves at home until they became really annoying. *They didn't know when enough was enough! But it doesn't have to be that way among people who care about one another. For example, a man and his* wife have differences. *His* wife likes to go shopping. *He likes* to go hunting and fishing. *They've* always from the start given each other that *essential* space. Yet *they've* always shared everything about each other. *They* just *know enough to* give each other space. *They* have walls, but they are little . . . *yet* very important *walls. People* should not give *themselves* totally out or *they* won't have anything left.

The poem speaks about darkness. "He moves in darkness, it seems to me." Darkness speaks of loneliness. *The neighbor* can't break the wall down *because he is locked in by tradition.* He won't change or see the light. He feels like he has to do this thing—the wall. What he really wants is to build a gate.

It all gets strange . . . we are looking at the elves thing again. Sometimes we *all* wish someone would take the magic wand and hit someone over the head and get the message across to *him.* The [narrator] is saying, "I could say Elves to him. . . . Little bells go off in the head. . . . *The narrator would* rather this neighbor would see it for himself, *see* that he needs to come out of the darkness *on his own. This is like a true life story in which* for four years *a woman* has been struggling in a marriage where *she* wanted *her* husband to be hit over the head by a magic wand. *She* found after a great deal of time—*after threats of divorce, marital problems, and all-round difficult living*—in some things he *would finally say* it for himself. He [the husband] saw that he needed to change; bells went off in his head.

Darkness probably does represent some kind of *similar* sadness. We tend to associate darkness with sadness. *The neighbor* will not go behind his father's saying. He would like to, but can't do it. Maybe that's the way it is—tradition. Despite what he wants *personally,* the walls will stay. Perhaps it is unsurity. Maybe he could *or should* let this person in. But having the wall makes it safer. *It all comes down to a safety factor,* kind of an "I-can't-get-anything-out-of-it, but-you-won't-hurt-me" attitude.

. . . *But then* . . . on the end of that line about darkness he is not necessarily <u>in</u> darkness . . . this guy [the speaker] is <u>seeing</u> him [the neighbor] in darkness. *We* had been thinking about the guy not being able to change . . . but now *we* see it [the poem] *coming from* this guy who's been talking about this as <u>his</u> feeling . . . he wants to tell this guy [the neighbor] how wrong he is and that he shouldn't be building this fence or wall. In reality this is just his <u>opinion</u>. All this time, he [the narrator] is <u>helping to build</u> the *same* wall he is complaining about.

The last half of the previous transcript is a result of one young woman's follow-up comments to her group's presentation and the subsequent discussion in which the class and I became involved. The last 15 lines of the poem generated the largest percentage of class discussion and interest, so it is worth explaining a bit more about the dynamics of class interaction and how students arrived at what I perceived to be a significant level of sophistication. The young woman began by saying no one in her group really knew what "darkness" meant in the line, "He moves in darkness as it seems to me." The urge to explain almost overwhelmed me. But I was determined to help the class find its own way. I told her to forget what it means and to think about what it does. She then went on to say that she thought it had to do with the fact that the neighbor really wanted to make gates in the wall, but he didn't know how—it equated with sadness. I asked her how she came to that in the poem. She was unable to point to anything that would support her view beyond the statement that she felt it to be so. To help her and her group out, I asked what the class made of the "darkness thing." Responses seemed to evolve into the idea that darkness means the neighbor did not want to get hurt or it shows the neighbor's lack of knowledge. One student got off into a side track about her husband of 4 years who had only begun to communicate recently about his feelings. The discussion screeched to a halt, and I found myself wanting to cut her off and get back to business, but I gave her the time to explain. She became involved in talk about magic wands, and the like, as articulated in the transcription. It was interesting, but seemingly a rehashing of material already discussed. (The class was visually expressing disapproval with the side track.) I let her have her say, thanked her for sharing the experience, and said I wanted to get back to the "darkness" issue because so many people seemed interested in coming to terms with it. The young woman who began the discussion of the meaning of "darkness" asserted once again that the darkness has to do with how the neighbor wanted to make gates. I asked again where she saw this in the poem. Again, she could only say she felt it to be true.

Several more students took a stab at coming to terms with the "darkness" issue, some suggesting that there was something not quite right about the image of darkness hovering over the neighbor. In several instances, students read out loud the line containing "darkness" prior to making their comments. With each statement that was an "I think it means . . ." or an "I feel it means . . ." I kept asking, "Why? Where do you find it in the text? How do you get that from what the text does?" Suddenly, the young woman who initiated the discussion was struck by the repetition of the line and by my insistence on getting at the how and why, and leaped back into the conversation: "He moves in darkness *as it seems to me*. He is not necessarily in darkness. This guy (the narrator) *sees* him in darkness. So he [the neighbor] may not actually be in darkness. He's just *seen* in darkness." I asked, "So what does that do for you?" "Changes it all around," "How?" "Well, I'd been thinking of the guy as wanting to change something and being in sadness. Now I see it where this guy [the narrator] is writing [narrator and author are obviously perceived as one] and talking about this as *his* feeling as if that guy [the neighbor] is in darkness. He [the narrator] wants to tell that guy how wrong he is and he [the neighbor] shouldn't be building this wall. In reality, this is just *his* [the narrator's] opinion."

LEARNING WITHIN THE READER-RESPONSE CLASSROOM

Clearly, these students had come a very long way in the course of an hour. They began with the restatement of lines from the poem. Then they shifted away from the poem toward concrete examples from their own lives that helped them to focus on their initial grasping for meaning and back again to the poem. And then there was the revision process of testing their ideas against what the poem actually says from the perspective of the narrator—a perspective they came to see as being potentially biased, perhaps unintentionally misleading. Here the poet was cast aside as students explored the role of the narrator and his shaping of the initial reading (or misreading). This is, I believe, a sophisticated examination of how to read a poem, one they came to with little more from me than coordinating the division of labor and the means for sharing their responses and creating a forum where revision was possible and where "correct" meaning was set aside for the purpose of finding *legitimate* meanings on which they could grow, meanings that were refined and expanded, readings that were personally varied.

Invitation 6.3

At the outset of this lesson, these students "grunted and groaned." How do their probable anticipations compare with their responses to this lesson and its outcome? What do you think has influenced and informed their attitudes?

Critical to this methodology is tolerance of students' legitimate readings of texts that are given them amidst the texts of their own existence. Analysis of poems requires a vast network of resource experiences on which the reader can draw for comparison. This takes time to develop. The more well read the readers, the more they can draw on memory banks of literary resources, language, and personal successes and sort through the abstractions presented by the shaping of words in new forms and modes. If we do not allow students their honest initial responses, we perpetuate forcing them into an impossible situation of groping through limited resources for the one and only answer the teacher wants and feeling frustrated with the text that will not immediately give up its meaning:

> Such an effort to consider texts always in relation to specific readers and in specific cultural situations, and to honor the role of literary experience in the context of individual lives, has powerful educational implications. . . . At least this can be indicated: a primary concern throughout would be the development of the individual's capacity to adopt and to maintain the aesthetic stance, to live fully and personally in the literary transaction. From this could flow growth in all the kinds of resources needed for transactions with increasingly demanding and increasingly rewarding texts. And from this would flow, also a humanistic concern for the relation of the individual literary event to the continuing life of the reader in all its facets—aesthetic, moral, economic, or social. (Rosenblatt 161)

We must help students learn that meaning lies not in us (the teachers) or in the symbols placed on a page, nor solely in themselves; it is something that happens in the *transaction* of a reader's mind and a writer's recorded symbols. A "web of feelings, sensations, images, ideas," woven as the reader experiences emotional and logical responses to the text, is the all-important beginning place (136–37). That does not mean the first reading should be the only reading or that *any* meaning is acceptable. The notion that any reading is legitimate as a first response is simply a starting point. After that first reading, the readers reflect on what has been read and on what has been experienced as they have read and then revise thinking accordingly, perhaps with enough success to get involved in further study of language and literature. Before students can acquire such zeal, we need to change what we do to them:

> The capacity to participate in verbally complex texts is not widely fostered in our educational system, and desirable habits of reflection, interpretation, and evaluation are not widespread. These are goals that should engender powerful reforms in language training and literary education. But none of these are attainable if good literary works of art are envisioned as the province of only a small, highly trained elite. Once the literary work is seen as part of the fabric of individual lives, the gap may be at least narrowed, without relinquishing recognition of standards of excellence. (Rosenblatt 143)

Instead of passively participating in the learning of literature, students at all grade levels can learn to take responsibility for living in the literature. There are countless ways beyond what has been shown in the previous pages to make opportunities for them to actively engage and reflect. For example, students could read a poem silently to themselves and then frame one or more key questions; then they could be put in groups of three or four and each person could ask a question(s) of the group and attempt to collaboratively sort through their various readings to arrive at some possible meanings. The groups could then choose the best of their three or four questions to pose to the class for collaborative learning. Students could rewrite a poem in light of their own experiences and share the poem with small groups or the class for discussion of similarities and differences between the rewritten poem and the original, looking for whether or not the copy accurately reflects the class's derived meaning of the original. Small groups could put on plays (or create video portrayals) that characterize their collaborative interpretations of a poem; and then the whole class could discuss the interpretations in light of their responses to the original poem. Students could be taken to settings similar to the setting of the poem for the purpose of reenacting it as a living art form and then discuss this *experience* of language — what the poem does as a living thing rather than as a motionless object, ink and paper. Any of these projects could be adapted to individual or group activities. Any of these ideas could be used by small groups for focusing on different poems of one author, group (confessional, imagistic, etc.), or period; then the whole class could discuss the interpretations and make a project of charting similarities and differences among poetic styles and poets, examining texts within larger texts or fields of study. The point of the projects would be to provide opportunities for students first to engage poems without fear of disapproval or being wrong, then to reflect on their assertions, then to test their responses against a collaborative experience and verbal sharing of their derived meanings for further revision and growth.

Helping students develop into readers who can explore the world of literature and its myriad possibilities requires a long-term commitment. Louise Rosenblatt seems to know that it is not something forthcoming in a single poem or a single quarter or semester and she realizes that it requires a concern for each student, regardless of whether the student will be forever an "ordinary" reader or literary scholar. Opportunities for "literary events" to take place are needed, opportunities that will be perceived as representing a meaningful way of being that can be verbally articulated.

Our approaches have too long been limited to taking students to the carefully piled rocks of literature that we place before them each year. We want them to raze the walls. Always we have in mind the making of a way over and through, but what we often get is a pulling—our pulling—of the students, leaving not a stone on a stone of the literary event. For the victims of that approach there is often no tradition, no articulation, and no wall, only the so-called "pleasing." They have heard us say, "Spring is the mischief in us, and we wonder if we could put a notion in their heads," as though they could not possibly have the experience of literature for themselves, as though they are simply empty and waiting to be stuffed by our "greater" perceptions. There are a few—like Louise Rosenblatt—who remind us that "notions" are already there waiting to be made manifest: "We'd rather they said it for themselves." Reader response gives students a way to say it and an ability to move toward the critical perception that perpetuates their desire for more joyful events in the creation of their own texts—their existence within a time and culture—that literature helps them to build. Yes, *good* fences do make good neighbors.

REFERENCES

Frost, Robert. "Mending Wall." *The Poems of Robert Frost.* New York: Random House, 1946. 35–36.
Rosenblatt, Louise M. *The Reader, the Text, the Poem: The Transactional Theory of the Literary Work.* Carbondale: Southern Illinois University Press, 1978.

7

Two Reader-Response Classrooms
Using Prereading Activity and Readers Theatre Approaches

Patricia P. Kelly

I vividly remember several years ago a student, trembling with frustration, standing before me at the end of a class near the beginning of the year, clutching her notebook with pencil poised, and asking intensely: "What was the reason Sammy quit?" after we had discussed multiple possibilities for Sammy, in John Updike's "A & P," quitting his job. Breaking such student expectations for definitive answers to problematic situations in literary texts is not easy, even with a reader-response approach to teaching literature.

To help students learn to reconcile the dissonance caused from multiple views, to see those views as useful, to make sense of a literary selection, and to assume more control for the discussion of literature, I use Readers Theatre. Readers Theatre focuses on "dialogue between two or more delineated characters who, through voice and bodily tension rather than movement, cause the audience to sense imaginatively characterization, setting, and action" (Latrobe and Laughlin 3). This reader-response approach not only provides oral performance possibilities for students but also encourages them to discuss in depth a literary selection to know what "interpretation" they want to get across to an audience. The focus of Readers Theatre is on understanding a literary selection and making others see that interpretation through performance, although, as a classroom strategy, staging and props are usually not emphasized.

When students prepare for a Readers Theatre presentation, their discussion of a text evolves differently from a discussion generated by a prereading

111

activity. What follows is a look into two of Kathryn Atkins's 10th-grade classes when they read and discussed "Words," written by Sylvia Plath in the last weeks before her death. One class discussed the poem using a typical reader-response approach initiated by a prereading activity and one class talked about the poem in small groups while preparing a Readers Theatre performance.

Words

Axes
After whose stroke the wood rings,
And the echoes!
Echoes traveling
Off from the centre like horses.

The sap
Wells like tears, like the
Water striving
To re-establish its mirror
Over the rock

That drops and turns,
A white skull,
Eaten by weedy greens.
Years later I
Encounter them on the road

Words dry and riderless,
The indefatigable hoof-taps.
While
From the bottom of the pool, fixed stars
Govern a life.
                    —Sylvia Plath (85)

Invitation 7.1

Before reading further, establish your own reader response to "Words." If you've already read chapter 6, you may want to use the procedure exemplified to see how it works for you.

PREREADING FOR
READER-RESPONSE DISCUSSION

The first 10th-grade class in Atkins's rural high school, where classes are generally small, had 11 students, which allowed us to use a whole-class discussion model and still provide plenty of opportunity for all students to participate. We taped the class discussion for later analysis. I began the class by asking students to write in their journals about a time when words hurt: When was it? What was the situation? Why do you remember it now? What did you learn? Kathy and I wrote with them, and because these were sensitive remembrances, I began the discussion by telling them of the incident I had written about. Although students did not choose to share their journal entries at that time, in the discussion of the poem that ensued, students referred not only to my experience but also their own.

After this prereading activity, I read the poem aloud to them and initiated the discussion by asking: "Do you see any similarity between your own experience and what Sylvia Plath describes in the poem?" David began by saying, "Well, like us, someone said something she didn't like and it hurt her feelings and made her feel bad."

Immediately students began sharing their personal connections to Sylvia Plath's experience, situations they had written about in their journals. They talked of being called a liar, of being disowned by family members, of comments about having big feet, and being betrayed by friends. The only reason I can offer for students' sharing personally at this point but not earlier is they had connected so strongly with the poem and the depth of hurt feelings that there was safety in a shared experience. Nothing had occurred after their personal journal writing except the reading of the poem.

Throughout the ensuing discussion Kathy and I commented only in ways to keep the interaction going, for example, "Do you want to say more about that? Does anyone else have a different view? Is that idea like anything anyone else has said?" We wanted the students to control the direction and nature of the talk as much as possible.

After the recounted instances of hurtful situations, the discussion shifted to the text of the poem when Michelle said, "Axes sort of cut out your feelings," followed by Susan's tag comment, "Yea, scars your mind," and Kim's observation, "Brings tears."

To which John added. "The tears are like sap out of a tree after you've cut it; someone hurts your feelings so much it makes you cry."

Robert teased, "Would it make you cry?" and John ducked his head and said firmly, "Naw."

After some good-natured laughter, Kim pointed to the poem and read, "Like the water." She looked up puzzled, "Where did they get that from?"

Julie answered, "She's describing a lake like a mirror . . . when you're trying to make yourself feel better."

And Jeanne added, "She's trying to cover up the hurt and hide her feelings."

The discussion of water brought the students naturally to asking about the "white skull, eaten by weedy greens." One student said the skull was a rock; another said it was "old memories; the hurt's still there." At the end of the short silence that then occurred, Mark said, "Like death. . . ." Several students in unison rejected that idea, and it was never brought up again. The reaction was not to Mark himself but to the idea. He continued to contribute to the class discussion. It is my contention that the students felt good about the direction they had taken; their "analysis" was fitting together, and they did not want to entertain as a possibility an idea that would lead them in a different direction.

After that slight diversion, the students went straight to the text again, agreeing that "Years later I encounter them on the road—" referred to meeting the same person or situation again. But they also concurred that she, the persona, might be just remembering the situation and that would have the same effect on her.

Students decided that "dry and riderless" showed that the words didn't affect her any more. And they expressed surprise at "hoof-taps"; Karen said, "Look, she comes back to horses." However, they did not attempt to connect with or to understand that part specifically. Instead they talked about the last stanza in general terms.

For example, Mark said, "She's showing that she can go on with her life . . . but that rock will always be there."

But Robert qualified, "That may depend on how big the pool is."

"Yea, if it's a little pool," Susan began explaining, "like if she's a shallow person and it's a big rock, she'll not get over it. If she's pretty deep or it's a little rock, it won't continue to affect her as much."

Looking at the last line of the poem, "Govern a life," Michelle connected the hurtful experience I had shared with them in her comment: "The hurtful words can make changes in your life; for instance that could have been a beautiful dress," referring to my story about another teacher who had made fun of a dress I was wearing, which I subsequently threw away.

At this point the students had worked their way straight through the poem, making personal connections in some places, and all had participated in some way. To encourage them to take another look at problematic sections of the poem, however, I told them that, although I had read the poem many times, it still puzzled and confused me in places. I then asked them to circle three places in the poem that still confused them a little and then to choose one of the circled places and write about it: why the section was confusing, how the section made them feel, or some possible meanings of the section. The three sections selected most often were "Echoes travelling / Off from the centre, "Eaten by weedy greens," and "fixed stars." No one, however, wrote about or talked about "fixed stars." The discussion of "weedy greens" was similar to their previous conjectures about the line. Students puzzled over "Echoes travelling." Interestingly, they had skipped that section entirely in their earlier class discussion.

Traci finally said, "It's the echo of the wood ringing from the axe; it sounds like it's crying." The boys grinned and shook their heads, good-naturedly disassociating themselves from the consideration of crying.

Michele selected no part that still puzzled her, saying: "She [Plath] puts it in the right words; she knows what she's talking about. It happens to me every day." Kathy said Michelle later chose this poem as her favorite for the year's study.

We then asked each student to select an object, similar to axes, that could also be used as a metaphor for hurtful words. Students compiled quite a list, for example: knives, cactus, razors, thorns, darts, hammer, and stick pins. Kathy suggested they take a favorite metaphor from the list and use it to describe the situation they had written about when someone hurt their feelings, in the way Sylvia Plath had or in any way they chose. After the students wrote—most tried poems—they chose to pass them around the circle to read and compliment each other. One girl's poem began:

> Like darts,
> Propelled by insignificant means,
> Stuck me the same as the voice. . . .

INTERPRETATION OF PREREADING ACTIVITY DISCUSSION

This class discussion was fairly typical of a lesson where a prereading activity helps students connect their personal experiences with literature. The students understood the text, not from a literary stance but from personal associations, and they were pleased with their understanding of the poem. Despite the students' perceived satisfaction, I have two concerns about the class discussion. First, although prereading activities are necessary to provide the bridge between a student's experience and the literature, such activities sometimes can push the discussion in a direction suggested by the prereading to such an extent that students reject contrary views or do not deal with a section of the literature that has them consider a different view. In other words, prereading activities are both a blessing and bane.

Students do need some type of prereading experience, of course, especially with difficult material; however, those prereading activities must be directly, not obliquely, connected to the literature. In a study using simulation games as prereading, a group that played games conceptually unrelated to the stories they read had fewer student responses and slower responses than in either the group using no prereading games or the group using conceptually related prereading games (Kelly 102). Unconnected prereading activities seemed to confuse students, making it more difficult for them to respond to the text. However, we must be cognizant that a prereading activity has the potential to inhibit divergent thinking. For example, the students in

Kathy's class probably cut short Mark's tentative idea about death because the focus on personal hurt of the prereading activity did not include the concept of death.

I am also concerned with this particular discussion because students conducted their discussion of the literary selection as a teacher-led class, even though Kathy and I were managing the student discussion rather than asking text-related questions. Students proceeded through the literary work with the goal of somehow explaining most of it. Although they were actively participating, their preconceived notions of what constituted a discussion of literature were evident, thus limiting their personal exploration of the text.

READERS THEATRE AS READER RESPONSE

What I describe next is another 10th-grade class of Kathy's, in which we used Readers Theatre as the process for discussing Plath's poem. Kathy had engaged these students in creative dramatics activities on many occasions, and they enjoyed performing, although they were not particularly adept at Readers Theatre. We divided the 14 students into a group of five boys, a group of four girls, and a group of five boys and girls. I wanted them to cohere as groups and see the importance of using their voices to convey meaning. I gave each group cards containing the following dialogue:

> Do you know?
> I don't know.
> Well, who does?
> No one knows.

They had 5 minutes to prepare readings of these lines that projected anger, happiness, sadness, and fear. All students in each group had to participate in the performance. Because the groups performed the same dialogue, students also saw different techniques for evoking similar emotions. These miniperformances began the process of their working as a group, reminding them that the purpose of Readers Theatre is to convey with the voice an interpreted meaning to an audience, and got them performing in front of the class to abate any initial self-consciousness. They seemed ready for the poem at this point. (Students who have not worked with drama activities may need more preparation. Latrobe and Laughlin's *Readers Theatre for Young Adults* provides 40 brief scripts from young adult novels and some suggestions for beginning Readers Theatre.)

I then gave them large print copies of the poem, glued to colored paper so that each group had its own color-coded identity when performing. We did not provide any prereading writing or discussion because we wanted the students to wrestle with the meaning of the poem and how they might present that meaning to an audience. Each group discussion was taped, and I took brief notes on my observations.

The group of five boys was initially governed by the task. (I have found this to be true for most groups at any grade level.) Kevin said, "We've got to figure out how to present this poem."

Bobby filled the anxious silence, "Somebody read the poem." Actually two boys read the poem twice.

After listening to the second reading, Kevin asked, "Can we present this in any way we want?" They decided they could do as they wanted with the presentation and immediately got down to the task of understanding the poem when Will, who had been silent thus far, said, "What are the axes? I got it; look at the title!"

At first they thought they might have one person read the title and author and the other four boys read a stanza each. That soon changed as they talked about the emotions in each stanza, for example, Patrick proposed, "Tears should be said softly."

Then Greg said excitedly, "I know; words . . . like sticks and stones will break your bones, but whatever they say, words hurt like anything." They laughed and punched at each other good-naturedly, punctuating their knowledge of the truth of the words just spoken.

With that understanding they discussed how they would read each line, conveying the emotion they wanted: anger, sadness, deep pain, and resignation—or as they put it, "There's nothing she can do about it." They read the poem several times, discussing the effectiveness of their arrangement for communicating their meaning. Their Readers Theatre presentation was a sophisticated blend of choral and individual reading.

The mixed group of boys and girls settled quickly into discussing the poem for developing a presentation with Debbie's first task assessment remark, "We've got to read this to the class. We've got to figure out what it means; what's the emotion?" This group concentrated on the notion of echoes: the sound of the axe echoing and the fact that years later the feelings come back is also an echo. They decided to repeat the last word in each line to provide that "echo effect." Other words, such as "the rock and axes," they saw as important and decided all group members would read them for emphasis.

Their discussion led them to conclude that one line in each stanza carried a lot of meaning (e.g., "To re-establish its mirror" in the second stanza) and those lines would be read by all the group members "to echo and make the ideas echo in your mind," Mark said. Like the other group, they practiced their reading several times. Their presentation was almost musical and certainly projected the echo effect they wanted.

The group of four girls also settled into the task quickly. Melanie read the poem twice before Kari said, "We have to figure out what axes are."

Susan answered, "Words that hurt you."

And Becky, pointing to the poem, said, "Tears."

Melanie explained further, "Something you always remember for years." With that, they ceased dealing with the poem's meaning except indirectly as they worried about presenting it. They experimented with several arrangements, reading the poem multiple times but generally not discussing the meaning they were giving the lines. Only the line "Eaten by weedy greens" generated any further meaning-making attempts. Instead, they treated the task as who would read what; the how and why of the interpretation was not discussed. Ultimately they chose the least imaginative and safest reading arrangement—each of the four girls read a stanza.

After the students had enjoyed each other's Readers Theatre presentations, we asked the groups to spend the last 10 minutes talking about their "readings" and why they had decided to present the poem as they had. Two of the groups shared reasons for their very different emphases, the "echoes" and the "emotions," but they also concluded that the major idea each was presenting was similar: the lasting hurt caused by unkind words. The group of girls reported that they had considered some different ways of presenting the poem but had liked the way each of them could be responsible for a stanza. However, through their body language and facial expressions, I sensed they wished they had risked a more creative approach. The class also talked about a poem they had read earlier by Plath called "Mirrors," remarking on the occurrence of the mirror image in both poems. Throughout this culminating discussion students seemed not only comfortable with differing ideas but also appreciative of the diversity of interpretation. Unlike the whole-class discussion, these students liked having viewed the poem differently.

Invitation 7.2

Along with another group or two, select a poem for a Readers Theatre response. After the groups have performed their readings, discuss the interpretations of each, how they were achieved, and how they expanded the sense of the poem for you.

INTERPRETATION OF
READERS THEATRE APPROACH

These whole-class discussions following Readers Theatre presentations broaden students' understanding of the literary work because they hear the thinking that underlies different interpretations. The discussions are not a "reporting" of the group activity; neither are they like a class discussion of the poem; and therein lies their benefit. They are similar to an "expert" group approach because each group is an expert on its presentation, but the motivation is somewhat different. Each group wants the others, who have appreciated its rendering of the literary piece, to understand the uniqueness of its interpretation. Although they are teaching each other as expert groups do, students do not perceive the discussion in that way; they see it as an informal sharing.

Kathy was surprised by the presentations. The four girls were her best students, but for some reason they did not take the risks necessary to carry out the task creatively. Even their short discussion revealed they had the skills to discuss the poem, but for the presentation they played it safe by assigning stanzas and reading with no evident interpretation. On the other hand, the boys who never shone academically were willing to risk playing with the ideas in the poem because the Readers Theatre process did not resemble any other type of class discussion that might hold them accountable for "knowing" the poem. Furthermore, I have found with other classes that both the small group discussions and Readers Theatre presentations evolving from them improve dramatically in subsequent experiences. I assume, therefore, that with additional exposure to this approach the group of four girls would learn to discuss and perform literature more independently, more freely, and more meaningfully than with this first endeavor.

With Readers Theatre, students read a selection, in this case a poem, many more times than occurs with other discussion arrangements—large group or small group. First they use many readings as a way into meaning; then they practice readings to project their intended meaning to others; and last they listen to readings with the meanings others have derived. I am always amazed that students seem unaware they have read the literary selection half a dozen times or more, for they would most surely resist that many readings in a regular class situation.

In some ways, however, the students in the Readers Theatre class did not "cover" the poem as well as the other class; perhaps the whole-class setting and more familiar structure of the prereading activity influenced them to consider most lines of the poem in a traditional way. The Readers Theatre students did not discuss possible meanings for the more difficult images in the poem, but instead related to the sensory impressions and emphasized those in their interpretations. Like all readers these students made meaning at their own level of literary and personal experiences. Consequently, it is not surprising that they seemed unable to connect with three specific images in the poem, images using sensory language drawn from Plath's own literary and personal experiences. However, the students' choice of relating to the poem from a sensing, emotional approach rather than an explicative one was a useful strategy for them. Their discussions and presentations showed they understood the poem in a holistic way and had personal experiences that connected with the poem. These students were approaching the reading of and talking about difficult text as autonomous learners who accepted and even delighted in varying interpretations. (For this to occur, the Readers Theatre activity must come first, becoming the vehicle of response to and interpretation of the text; if interpretation comes first, then Readers Theatre becomes performance rather than reader response.)

CONCLUSIONS

Whatever the differing surface features of these two classes that used reader-response approaches, there is a common factor in both because students were moving from their "personal responses and interpretations back to the text" (Rosenblatt 282). In the first class the students' personal responses were triggered by an external stimulus, the prereading activity, whereas in the Readers Theatre class something in the text stimulated their personal responses. When Greg said the "sticks and stones" children's rhyme, he was bringing personal experience to explain the poem for him. His addition of "words hurt like anything" was offering personal knowledge to contradict a widely disseminated myth. The reaction of his group members showed they not only understood his connection but also shared feelings about it.

Rosenblatt cautions that in adopting various teaching strategies for literature we must

> be very careful to scrutinize all our procedures to be sure that we are not in actuality substituting other aims—things to do *about* literature—or the experience *of* literature. We can ask of every assignment or method or text, no matter what its short-term effectiveness: Does it get in the way of the live sense of literature? Does it make literature something to be regurgitated, analyzed, categorized, or is it a means toward making literature a more personally meaningful and self-disciplined activity? (279)

Despite the personal connections students made in the whole-class discussion using a prereading activity, they wanted to arrive at conclusions about the poem. Once they derived meanings that satisfied them, they were finished with the poem. It was only then that Kathy and I asked them to write their "metaphor poems." The Readers Theatre class, on the other hand, was left with ambiguity, with many meanings, and with undeveloped ideas; yet students did not seem to be flustered by the lack of closure on interpretations. They controlled the discussions of the poem in a way not possible in a whole-class discussion or even with literature circles, where students have assigned tasks for the group discussions (Daniels). Perhaps because Readers Theatre provided a learning structure different from that usually used for literature, most students felt comfortable exploring the possibilities for interpreting the poem. Because the classroom process was different, then it is possible that students saw the expectations for literary analysis as also different.

Invitation 7.3

In two lists, identify the strengths of each approach represented in this chapter. What learnings were heightened by each? What might be done to offset a potential insufficiency of each approach?

Having students read and discuss literature for Readers Theatre performances is not an activity about literature, but it provides the experience of literature by giving life to literature through performance. This reader-response teaching approach purposefully engages students with literature in a way that encourages the sharing of personal meanings, requires self-discipline to carry out the task, and fosters the diversity of ideas.

REFERENCES

Daniels, Harvey. *Literature Circles.* York, ME: Stenhouse Publishers, 1994,
Kelly, Patricia P. "Can I Know How You Feel If I Haven't Walked in Your Shoes?" *Focus: Teaching English Language Arts* 2 (1983): 98–102.
Latrobe, Kathy Howard, and Mildred Knight Laughlin. *Readers Theatre for Young Adults.* Englewood, CO: Teachers Ideas Press, 1989.
Plath, Sylvia. "Words." *Ariel.* New York: Harper & Row, Publishers, 1961. 85.
Rosenblatt, Louise M. *Literature as Exploration.* 3d ed. New York: Noble and Noble, 1976.

8

"I Understood the Grief"
Theory-Based Introduction
to Ordinary People

Deborah Appleman

> *In the education given the adolescent in America, there is still little*
> *to enlighten him. . . . He will sense needs and curiosities,*
> *and here again, it will often be only from the reflection of life*
> *offered by literature, that he will acquire such insights.*

> —Rosenblatt (88)

> Ordinary People *was about finding your self-identity. It was like a guide*
> *to dealing with people. It showed how people dealt with death and an*
> *attempted suicide. It showed to the reader that ordinary people deal with*
> *these things every day. This means that Joe Average isn't alone in this world.*

> —Chris G., Grade 11

READER-RESPONSE THEORY
AND THE ADOLESCENT READER

For decades, theorists in the field of English education have been heralding reader-response theory as an approach to literature well suited to the developmental and intellectual characteristics of adolescents. Teachers, too, have begun to adjust their teaching styles to acknowledge readers' responses and have selected texts with which adolescents could identify.

Adolescent readers, preoccupied as they are with their own developing identity and the acute need to make some sense of the complex and bewildering world around them, bring their personal experiences to the reading of a literary text and project those experiences onto the textual world, whether or not the teacher encourages or facilitates that process. The very characteristics of adolescence that might prove intrusive to a purely critical reading of the text, leading to what I. A. Richards called a "mnemonic irrelevance," are the very qualities that can enable young readers to respond richly and personally to literature within the theoretical context of reader response. As Probst explains:

> The adolescent, characteristically preoccupied with self, should be an ideal reader. That is not to say that he will read well, or even read at all. He may despise literature, the literature classroom and the literature teacher, and express great pride in his inability to make sense of the written word. But unless he is very unusual, he has the one characteristic essential for a reader—an interest in himself. He is concerned about his relationships with peers and parents and his gradual assumption of responsibility for himself. . . . Preoccupation with self should make adolescents uniquely receptive to literature, for literature invites their participation and judgment. (4–5)

Rosenblatt further reminds us of the importance of consonance between a reader's preoccupations and those that arise in reading a literary text:

> Any insight or clarification the youth derives from the literary work will grow out of its relevance to certain facets of his emotional or intellectual nature. The whole personality tends to become involved in the literary experience. That a literary work may bring into play and be related to profoundly personal needs and preoccupations make it a powerful potential educational force. For it is out of these basic needs and attitudes that behavior springs. Hence, literature can foster the linkage between intellectual perception and emotional drive that is essential to any vital learning process. (182)

By refusing to overlook or ignore the nature of their adolescent readers, teachers can encourage students to bring their personal experiences, values, questions, and concerns to the reading of a literary text, making the "transaction," as Rosenblatt calls it, the very point of the reading experience itself.

ADOLESCENTS AND TEXT SELECTION

> *Ordinary People* is a touching story of male initiation, of a young man who is growing into adulthood against incredible psychological odds. The locale is in the Midwest and the time is the early 1970's, but the novel could be happening anywhere and at any time, which is one of the reasons students respond to it so easily. Conrad Jarrett could be any of us in adolescence; full of awful secrets, trying to gain control of his own world, worried about how other view him, wishing just to become "ordinary." (Peck 43)

The passage from adolescence to adulthood, never an easy trail to blaze, has today become a perilous and stressful journey.

Contemporary American society has struck teenagers a double blow. It has rendered them more vulnerable to stress while at the same time exposing them to new and more powerful stresses than were ever faced by previous generations of adolescents. It is not surprising, then, to find that the number of stress-related problems among teen-agers has more than trebled in the last decade and a half. (Elkind 6)

The contemporary challenges that have created this increase in stress among today's adolescents, in Elkind's terms—the "perils of puberty," "peer shock," and "family permutations"—are precisely those issues that face Judith Guest's adolescent protagonist, Conrad Jarrett, in *Ordinary People*.

Developing an integrated sense of identity is a daunting task, one made even more difficult by our confused and confusing times. That search for self-definition is the focus of Conrad's psychological odyssey as he attempts to derive an "integrated" self-definition after the layers of sibling rivalry, parental expectations, and peer-imposed roles have been pulled away.

Conrad's struggle to define himself within the context of his family, his peers, and his personal history mirror with, remarkable accuracy, the process of self-finding faced by many adolescents. The fact that both Conrad and the adolescent reader are immersed in the same difficult and troubled search for self will facilitate the students' ability to identify with and respond to the text.

But it is not merely the adolescent quest for identity that makes *Ordinary People* a novel with which adolescent readers can easily identify. As Conrad sifts through the details of his life to make some sense of them as well as of himself, he peels back the layers of artifice that have surrounded his life and the life of his family. His mother's preoccupation with appearances and "good taste," the troubled emotional truths that bubble under the smooth facade of his parents' marriage, the falseness of many of his brother's friends and their expectations are all a crucial part of this contemporary coming-of-age story set in the plastic veneer of suburban adolescence. Becoming aware that all is not as it appears is a necessary if painful part of adolescence.

Conrad's suicide attempt, his family's (especially Beth's) reaction to it, and his struggle to recapture a commitment to living are clearly central to the novel and thus will figure significantly in any reader's engagement with the text. Although suicide is a troublesome and potentially dangerous topic for any reader, for adolescents it is an especially difficult topic.

Adolescent suicide has reached nearly epidemic proportions and is currently the leading cause of death among young people, after car accidents. For life's counterparts to Conrad, white males between the ages of 16 and 19, the rate of suicide has nearly tripled since 1960 (*Newsweek* 15).

Recently when I asked a group of 40 high school students if they had personally known anyone who had committed or attempted suicide, 32 responded that they had. Nearly half admitted to having considered suicide at least once, and more than a third said they considered it sometimes or frequently. As one student put it, when asked what experiences she brought to the text that might affect her response, "The fact that I've thought about committing suicide. I know someone who's tried to kill herself and I realize how much she needs to feel liked and normal."

However, some teachers may resist the prospect of discussing suicide with their students. One college student, rereading the novel before he student-taught in a suburban high school English classroom wrote:

> I found myself shocked by the admission in the book about how exactly to slit your wrists. Frankly, I'd be worried about this in the classroom. But you can't not teach this. Just because we have atomic bombs doesn't mean we'll use them. And if we do, the problem runs much deeper than reading to see how they work. If you can't head it off long before it happens, it may already be too late.

But Rosenblatt tells us that "the emotional character of a student's response to literature offers an opportunity to develop the ability *to think rationally within an emotionally colored context*" (228, her italics). By making the discussion of suicide an integral aspect of the response process, then, more than a literary response is enriched; students may, indeed, be able to make sense of a seemingly nonsensical phenomenon.

In addition to the relevance of the issues presented in *Ordinary People*, the style of the book also facilitates a literary response in adolescent readers. Beach and Appleman summarized research that underscores the importance of accessible and realistic, "reader-friendly" language in literary texts. When familiar language is used to convey strong emotions, as it is in *Ordinary People*, engagement with the text is far more likely.

The following passage is representative of the language in the novel as well as Guest's sense of internal dialogue:

> All connections with him result in failure. Loss. Evil. At school it is the same. Everywhere he looks, there is competence and good health. Only he, Conrad Jarrett, outcast, quitter, fuck-up, stands outside the circle of safety, separated by everyone from this aching void of loneliness; but no matter, he deserves it. He does not speak to anyone. He does not dare to look at his classmates in the eye. He does not want to contaminate, does not wish to find further evidence of his lack of worth. (107)

This type of painful self-scrutiny is all too achingly familiar to adolescent readers. Students easily recognize the similarity of Conrad's struggle with self-acceptance with their own struggles. The relevance of the novel's issues to adolescent readers in language that is both real and familiar makes *Ordinary People* a text that will foster an engagement with reading on which the following strategies for teaching can be built.

Invitation 8.1

Some parents and school officials might object to the inclusion of a text such as *Ordinary People,* in some cases for the very reasons that the author recommends it—frank dialogue, realistic situations, relevant social issues such as adolescent suicide. How might you defend the selection of this book against such an objection? Share your response with your peers.

PULLING BACK THE CURTAIN ON LITERARY THEORY: THE READER-RESPONSE DIAGRAMS

What, then happens in the reading of a literary work? Through the medium of words, the text brings into the reader's consciousness certain concepts, certain sensuous experiences, certain images of things, people, actions, scenes. The special meanings, and more particularly, the submerged associations that these words and images have for the individual reader will largely determine what it communicates to *him.* The reader brings to the work personality traits, memories of past events, present needs and preoccupations, a particular mood of the moment and a particular physical condition. These and many other elements in a never-to-be-duplicated combination determine his response to the peculiar contribution of the text. (Rosenblatt 30–31)

Students' interpretive abilities can be enhanced if they are more aware of the theoretical context in which their responses occur. Thus, as teachers discuss specific literary texts with their students using a response-based approach, they should introduce students to the basic tenets of reader-response theory so that the oral and written responses to literature that follow are framed in a theoretical context not only for the teacher, but for the student as well.

What follows is a description of one approach we used with a group of "college-bound" 11th- and 12th-graders. The strategies described, however, are equally appropriate for undergraduate college students.

Before reading *Ordinary People,* the students responded to several poems and short stories that were selected for their ambiguity and openness to a wide variety of interpretations. As a prelude to each whole-class discussion, students wrote brief response papers on each literary work before any teacher or whole-class explication occurred. Students then shared their response papers and were encouraged to listen, not for the most plausible or seemingly "correct" interpretation, but for the diversity represented in their peers' responses. We then discussed some of the general factors that can influence an individual reader's response to a literary text as well as the specific factors that were at play in their own responses. Students were then introduced to the basic tenets of Rosenblatt's transactional theory of reading and were asked to list both the textual and reader characteristics that had influenced their response to the literary texts they had been discussing.

After several prereading activities, including an anonymous suicide survey to elicit and discuss their attitudes about suicide, the students read *Ordinary People*. We then asked them to complete a reader response diagram identifying *Ordinary People* as the "text" and themselves as the "reader."

Reader Response
context

reader (   ) ——→ meaning ◄—— text

Under "reader" and "text," students were then asked to identify specific characteristics of each that might affect the particular nature of their "transaction" with the novel. This information helps to bring to the reader's consciousness the values, assumptions, and beliefs brought to the text; it also helps to inform the teacher of the factors that affect these students' responses to the text.

The resulting diagrams demonstrate the students' remarkable ability to assess their characteristics as readers that were relevant to their reading of *Ordinary People*. Under the "reader" heading, many students mentioned the following factors as influencing their response:

1. Parents' divorce: "Suddenly the family was ripped apart—by choice."

2. Depression: "Get depressed sometimes. Sometimes I close up and won't talk about my feelings."

3. Relationship with parents, specifically, inability to get along with their mothers: "I get along with my Dad better than my Mom," "I know what it's like to have someone act like Beth did," "Don't get along with my mom."

4. Feelings of insecurity: "doubting yourself," "not thinking people will forgive you."

5. Thoughts of suicide: "The fact that I've thought about killing myself," "I though about suicide, what it would do to my family."

6. Experience with close friends or relatives who committed or attempted to commit suicide: "my best friend tried to commit suicide," "my cousin tried to kill himself this year," "my best friend's brother killed himself in April."

7. Sibling rivalry: "older sister/brother who's perfect," "the way I feel I have to be perfect like my brother." "Having to follow a sister's perfection."

8. "Feeling like an outcast."

9. Experience with death: "I understand the grief: I know what it feels like to have someone die in my family."

In terms of text characteristics, the following were the most commonly offered:

1. Realism: "This book was the most realistic book I ever read," "People seemed like real life."
2. Language: "The language was strong. It was written in simple language and not with all these scholarly words." "I liked the swearing."
3. Characteristics of protagonist: "Con's age was close to ours," "Thoughts were some that I've thought."
4. Narrative structure: "Switching from one person to another."
5. Settings: "you could relate it to our time," "It was written in the late 70s rather than hundreds of years ago."

After the students listed both personal and textual characteristics, they were asked to write several statements of meaning that arose from their transaction with *Ordinary People*. The statements ranged from personal insights to general comments about families and society. The following are representative:

1. "Most answers to problems lie within yourself."
2. "Families that look perfect on the outside are not always perfect on the inside."
3. "I have to learn to deal with my feelings and face them better."
4. "Communication is important to keep a family together."
5. "Everybody needs to feel normal, to be accepted."
6. "You can't hide from life and its problems."
7. "How complicated family life is."
8. "Life isn't fair, right or nice, it just is."
9. "Everyone has problems, even 'ordinary people.' The only difference is in the way people deal with their problems."

In addition to making reader-response theory explicit to the students, the reader-response diagrams, especially the reader characteristics listed by the students, helped the teacher gain some additional insight into her students. In the teaching of literature, teachers' knowledge about students is as important as their knowledge of materials. Both are critical to creating the "vital sense of literature" that Rosenblatt celebrates (51).

Through this approach the students saw more clearly that as individuals, they brought salient personal qualities that were not irrelevant or unimportant but were actually critical to the act of reading. They also learned that the self-knowledge they might be gaining from the text was not incidental but central to the literary experience. This notion of self-discovery through literature is clearly explained by Probst:

> Thus, exchange with the text can become for the reader a process of self-creation. The entire process—responding, correcting errors, searching for the sources of the response, speculating about the author's intent and weighing the author's values and ideas against one's own—culminates in a sharpened, heightened sense of self. Some part of the reader's conception of the world is either confirmed, modified, or refuted, and that changes the reader. (21)

The reader-response diagrams help foster the kind of "self-creation" Probst describes. It also encourages personal exchanges with the text that can be built on in whole-class discussions as students develop their responses to a text in both an individual context and the community-of-readers context that a literature classroom can provide. The context of a classroom discussion does not merely provide an outlet for reporting previously constructed responses such as those generated by the reader-response diagrams; it can serve to help the student develop additional responses.

Invitation 8.2

Try the reader-response diagram described on p. 128 with a novel you have recently read and might consider teaching. What personal characteristics were the most relevant to your response to the text? Find a peer who has read the same novel and compare your diagrams.

DEVELOPING READERS' RESPONSES:
ORAL AND WRITTEN STRATEGIES

Steig describes the importance of communicating responses:

> It is also my experience, and that of my students, that attention to one's own or reports of another's reading experiences and associations *does* frequently lead to "dramatic encounters," "surprises," and a sense of "discovery" of something that seems to be in the text. (12)

Ideally, classroom discussions should provide opportunities for readers to express their reactions and their perceptions about the text. The classroom atmosphere should be open and accepting so that these perceptions can unfold and develop. This contrasts from those (often teacher-dominated) discussions that are designed to arrive at a predestined point. These deny response development.

One approach a teacher may use to encourage oral responses to texts that are compatible with the reader-response perspective is described by DeZure. She argues that the structure of a classroom discussion should match the narrative structure of the novel being discussed. Focusing on the

multiple-perspective technique of *Ordinary People* as well as on the theme of
family mythology, she advises using the "jigsaw" technique in the teaching of
Ordinary People. Briefly described, the jigsaw technique involves having students participate in "small groups to discuss a focused problem. Second,
they rotate to other small groups composed of different students to share
their new insights" (17–18). DeZure used the jigsaw technique to explore
the complex family structure of the Jarretts by having preliminary groups focus on individual characters (a Beth group, a Cal group, a Conrad group),
then rotating to secondary groups that were comprised of students who had
analyzed different characters. In the secondary groups students focused on
general questions about the family. Although this procedure is a bit more
complicated than traditional group discussions, as DeZure points out,
"Complex problems often require and deserve complex analytical procedures to solve them. Simple is not always best" (19).

Response journals can help both secondary and college students further
develop and refine their responses to literary texts. For neophyte interpreters who often lack confidence in the validity of their own individual
responses, the private, personal quality of a journal encourages them to explore literary response through writing and to reflect on the nature of their
responses by reviewing what they have written.

These written responses can help students clarify interpretations that
arose in class discussions. They can also be a place to reflect on class discussions, to weigh the results of public discussion about literature against
their own personal responses, and to discover the degree to which their own
responses have been influenced or even altered as a result of classroom
discourse. Thus, the kinds of journal assignments offered here should be
viewed as both extension and support of the responses that will emerge
from the approaches already discussed.

Students can be asked to keep a running response to the novel as they
read it, jotting down almost epigrammatic responses as they occur during
the act of reading. Sometimes called a learning log, students can write on one
side of their notebook, leaving room for the teacher or another student to
comment on their responses. The following are some excerpts from a college
student's reading journal (page numbers refer to Guest's *Ordinary People*):

> p. 3. How important is it to find something that you're good at? Pressure of
> trying to show everybody else that it's all right. Everything will be fine.
> p. 8. What is fatherhood? Not applying pressure, yet talking about what to
> wear? Isn't that pressure?
> p. 20. Uncertainty, the bane of adolescent existence. But Con has experi-
> enced, lived with uncertainty, now back in the real world, he's forced to face
> uncertainty again. His father shows that the adult world is uncertain as well.
> p. 32. The question of obedience has come up a couple of times. Is that
> what makes you a good boy? "Protecting yourself from further grief." That's

the motto, the bumper sticker. Live to avoid problems. This takes us back to the epigram. You can't just live on. Make plans.

p. 87. Being "*Ordinary People,*" that's what's important. Is it? They try and try to be ordinary. The illusion is to make some appear ordinary, happy, unfazed. The reality is individuality, subversion, pain.

p. 207. Here it is. Guest gives the answer. Con lost his direction. Himself when he lost Buck. . . . Keep reading. Berger the wizard sets it down. Social pressures and all. But Con isn't unique. Everyone wants perfect kids. Con just has a legacy.

What is provided here is almost a transcription of the reader's interaction with the text, as it occurs. Some comments react directly to the language or the events presented in the text. Others are more metacognitive in nature, noting the readers' self-reflection on their own response process. The sum effect of this type of journal is to create what Steig calls, after Culler, "stories of reading":

> Associative response papers are not just relevant as evidence of the nature of the process of reading, or of the reader's personality, but can actually become new interpretations—or readings not obtainable through other approaches. (41)

Another type of journal assignment is the dialogue journal. Students write entries about a text in their own journals and then exchange them with another student. Students are then able to read other students' literary responses and receive commentary on their own responses. The following is a dialogue exchange based on *Ordinary People:*

> This book has made me understand more of what my friend is somewhat going through. It has given me hope that things will work out for her just like they have for Conrad. I really didn't like Beth, I thought she was extremely cold and didn't really seem to care about her child. I think she needed help in dealing with her problems. She actually made me more appreciative of my mother because at least I know she cares. I could also relate to Conrad in the way that he had to follow his "perfect brother." That is something I have had to deal with because my brother was extremely smart. It has helped me see that I compare myself to my brother a lot more than other people do. Just like Conrad felt like he had to be so great but no one really expected it from him. He was not really compared like he thought he was. While I was reading this book, I could really get involved with what was happening to Conrad. I would get happy for him when good things would happen or upset if bad things happened. I thought that all the feelings Conrad had were explained well. It gave me the feeling the author knew what Conrad was going through. (Jennifer, Grade 11)
>
> I think it has made me appreciate my mom more, also. When you see such a "bitch" for a mom, you see how much better you have it. I don't know about your friend but maybe this showed you some of the things you should say or not say, for that matter, to her. I can see how you think that you have to com-

pete and be up to the standards of your brother, but obviously no one is exactly alike and no one expects you to be like him. I thought I could really get involved in the book, like I was really there, also. Now I feel I understand what people who commit suicide are somewhat going through and be able to cope with it better. (Teresa, Grade 11)

CONCLUSION

When Louise Rosenblatt first published *Literature as Exploration* in 1938 and described the importance of a transactional approach to literature with adolescents, she could never have imagined the kind of teenagers that inhabit today's high school and college classrooms. Yet, as we have seen, her insight into the nature of adolescents and the qualities that they bring to literature is especially relevant to students today. When such an approach is used with a novel such as *Ordinary People*, students and teachers are likely to be engaged in vital and poignant literary exploration. The responses of many of the students presented in this chapter reveal how deeply they were affected by their reading. By Rosenblatt's standards, the criterion for a successful literary experience has been fulfilled:

> The criterion for judging the success of any educational process must be its effect upon the actual life of the student; its ultimate value depends on its assimilation into the marrow of personality. (p. 182)

Ordinary People found its way into the very marrow of many of the adolescent readers who were quoted throughout this chapter. Perhaps Mark (Grade 12) said it best:

> I read this book in just a few days because it was important to me. I had to find out if Conrad made it. To make sure he didn't kill himself. I really got into it. My life helped me understand the book. The book helped me understand my life.

ACKNOWLEDGMENTS

I wish to thank Martha Cosgrove for her skilled teaching and the Modern Literature students of Henry Sibley Senior High School, Mendota Heights, Minnesota, for their responses to *Ordinary People*.

REFERENCES

Beach, Richard, and Deborah Appleman. "Reading Strategies for Expository and Literary Text Types." *Becoming Readers in a Complex Society: Eighty-Third Yearbook of the NSSE Part I,* Ed. A. C. Purves and O. Niles. Chicago: National Society for the Study of Education, 1984. 115–43.

DeZure, Deborah. "Matching Classroom Structure to Narrative Technique: Using 'Jigsawing' to Teach *Ordinary People,* a Multi-Perspective Novel." *CEA Forum* 19 (1989): 17–20.

Elkind, David. *All Grown Up and No Place to Go: Teenagers in Crisis.* Reading, MA: Addison-Wesley, 1984.

Guest, Judith, *Ordinary People.* New York: Random House, 1976.

Newsweek. spec. ed. Summer/Fall 1990.

Peck, David. *Novels of Initiation: A Guidebook for Teaching Literature to Adolescents.* New York: Teachers College Press, 1989

Probst, Robert E. *Response and Analysis: Teaching Literature in Junior and Senior High School.* Portsmouth, NH: Boynton/Cook, 1988.

Richards, I. A. *Practical Criticism.* New York: Harcourt, Brace, & World, 1929.

Rosenblatt, Louise M. *Literature as Exploration.* 3d ed. New York: Noble and Noble, 1976.

Steig, Michael, *Stories of Reading: Subjectivity and Literary Understanding.* Baltimore: Johns Hopkins University Press, 1989.

Part III

Developing Readers' Responses: Classroom Processes

Going beyond the initial responses to literature is the focus of the chapters in this section. The authors recognize that causing readers to understand a relationship with a character or topic in a text or to express their preliminary feelings or ideas is comparable to only unlocking a door, perhaps opening it slightly. In their chapters they describe and illustrate approaches that cause students to develop and expand their preliminary notions, to consider and reconsider, and to measure and test their evolving understandings against the text. The strategies practiced include writing of several types, oral discussions, activities, and simulations.

There are two pertinent features of the strategies to attend to: the general methodology, the processes by which expansion and refinement of thought and feelings are provoked; and the teaching techniques exemplified that express the nondirective posture of the teacher. Of course, the activities, processes, and questions may readily be reoriented, recombined, and adapted for other literary texts and teaching situations. (Chapters in other sections also present teaching strategies to evoke and develop readers' responses or suggest activities for this purpose.)

In chapter 9, Marshall Toman first acknowledges the evolution of his own perceptions of Eudora Welty's "Petrified Man," using these, particularly his earliest reading, to anticipate his students' responses. In class he reads aloud from his students' preliminary reactions to what they liked or disliked about the story, these comments being a springboard for discussion. He asks open questions that lead students to support and build their understandings with textual evidence. Variant student perceptions and comments by critics are used to expand the framework of responses. Toman considers in detail the nature of transactional discussion: the teacher's avoidance of becoming the dominant reader, which he exemplifies in this classroom processes; and the handling of the types of comments—plausible and implausible and positive and negative—while valuing open expression and using all comments to clarify perceptions.

The nature of drama argues for a specialized teaching approach. It requires active performance, but not necessarily on-stage production or Readers Theatre. Linda Varvel in chapter 10 explores her transition from conventional practices—study guides, background sheets, presentational teaching—to reader-response strategies. The shift is initially cautious, acting out a scene and open-ended questions with the teaching of *The Crucible.* The former generated enthusiasm and involvement, and responses to the questions were dynamic and mind-opening. With the teaching of *Death of a Salesman,* Varvel again uses open-ended questions, followed by a therapy-session role play and a playwriting project. The latter involved rewriting or adding a scene to the play while maintaining character consistency and performing the scene. The details of the students' inventions and the discussion of their apparent learning is enlightening, as is their evaluation. Varvel incorporates in her text her journal writings that convey her thoughts during the processing of these activities, revealing the tension of change in her attitudes about the interpretation of the play.

Two aspects of teaching literature are particularly developed in chapter 11: connecting the students with the text and assuring carryover. Mary Jo Schaars, teaching Thoreau's *Walden,* builds student experiences that connect their lives with Thoreau's concepts to provoke thoughts and feelings. The discussions that emerge are not predictable; as excerpts of two classes' interactions indicate, each class follows its own lead to establish its understandings. The culminating activities turn the students inward to measure Thoreau's values and to compare themselves with him. Samples of students' writing illustrate the personal and intellectual connections that have developed, bearing out the potential for carryover into subsequent readings and students' lives.

Elizabeth A. Poe addresses the concern for individual differences among students by using multiple texts. In chapter 12 she represents her approach with a group of World War II novels. She explains the use of journals as a method of establishing knowledge and feelings about the topic and the use of small-group interaction as a way of exploring and expanding understandings of the texts. Subsequent class discussions develop comparative and contrastive insights that reflect variations among both readers and text. Poe asserts that class exchanges and culminating activities enrich and intensify each student's experiences. She also portrays her active facilitating role and the processing of insights.

The premise of chapter 13 is that role-play situations can activate and enrich response experiences by motivating readers' identification with characters and the issues that confront them. Alternatively, it aids readers in exchanging lives with characters who are socially or culturally distant from them. The essence of the role play is to place students into the text's situations, causing the readers to take on the traits and life of the characters. I provide an explanation of the theoretical base of such activities and illustrate them with examples of several genres—novels, poetry, short stories—at different reading levels. The illustrations use both oral and written formats, presented within the framework of a lesson.

In chapter 14, Duane Roen proposes writing-to-learn strategies as a procedure for responding to literature, strategies that encourage the use of writing as a tool for making sense of the world. He argues that such techniques allow readers to respond individually and privately before public response, thus giving every student the opportunity for self-reflective thought. Roen demonstrates the use of the biopoem, the unsent letter, and the journal or learning log in the teaching of *Antigone*. He notes how these writings can be enhanced by dialogue, leading to broadened interpretations. He also offers a list of topics for classroom discussion and critical essays that correlate with the writing-to-learn model.

9

Teaching Eudora Welty's "Petrified Man"
Expanding Preliminary Insights

Marshall Toman

Eudora Welty sets her 1939 story "Petrified Man" in Leota's western Mississippi beauty parlor. As the story opens, Leota is speaking highly of a new friend, a Mrs. Pike. Mrs. Fletcher, a customer, is irritated to learn that Mrs. Pike is so sharp that she detected from a casual glimpse that Mrs. Fletcher is pregnant. Since the community now knows about the pregnancy through the gossiping of the newcomer, Mrs. Fletcher will certainly have to have the child. Leota, ignoring Mrs. Fletcher's irritation, goes on to tell about her friendship with Mrs. Pike: Leota and her husband Fred have rented rooms to Mr. and Mrs. Pike, Fred and Mr. Pike go fishing together, and Leota and Mrs. Pike have gone to a traveling freak show together. Among other things, they view a man whose joints have supposedly been slowly turning into stone.

One week later, when Mrs. Fletcher returns for her regular appointment, Leota's attitude toward Mrs. Pike has changed. While reading an old copy of *Startling G-Man Tales* that Leota had prettified her lodgers' room with, Mrs. Pike recognized that the petrified man was really Mr. Petrie, a neighbor of the Pikes from New Orleans, and she discovered that there was a $500 reward for information leading to his arrest for raping four women. The Pikes receive the reward and prepare to move out of Leota's rooms. The story ends with Mrs. Fletcher grabbing and holding and Leota vigorously spanking Billy Boy, Mrs. Pike's three-year-old, whom Leota had agreed to watch during business hours so Mrs. Pike could work at Fay's Millinery.

One of my most enlightening pedagogical experiences was witnessing my growth with respect to this story. My encounters with it underwent several revolutions; consequently, the stages were clearly marked. But I think my encounter(s) with "Petrified Man" recapitulates in an obvious way what I experience in any rereading. Being aware of one's own changing responses to a text helps a teacher effectively anticipate and organize various responses of students. Here, then, let me briefly recapitulate my experience.

MY READING EXPERIENCES
OF "PETRIFIED MAN"

In one way, an ideal response to a text, from a pedagogical standpoint, may at first be inadequate. Such a response is likely to reproduce the less expert reading of students. I believe my own first reading of "Petrified Man" was circumscribed. In attempting to capture this first response to the story while my students were once writing down theirs, I came up with the following:

> The description was very realistic and slanted toward the dirty and dingy and morally corrupt (Leota flicking ashes into wet towels). I disliked all the characters. Did Welty want us to dislike them? If so, why? What is the point of the story? There is very little I can relate to here except (as always with Eudora Welty) her portrayal of the small-town life and small-town mind.

I responded to Welty's portrayal and uncharacteristically biting satire of the small-town mind. Let me call this reading the small-town satire perspective.

The first change in my response to the story occurred when it was read and discussed in a graduate seminar on southern women writers. In this discussion the unpleasant characteristics of the men in the story were stressed. Where actions of the women were unworthy, the students tended to excuse them by the circumstances within which the women operated and over which the even more unworthy men shed their unsupportive influence. This interpretation I label the feminist perspective because it was put forward in the context of exploring the aesthetic and political sensibilities manifest in the story as they could be accounted for by the author's gender.

A second revolution in my experience of the story came with the reading of the critical literature, particularly the discussions by Ruth Vande Kieft and William M. Jones. In her study of Welty for the Twayne series, Vande Kieft takes almost an antifeminist stance. In my teaching of the story, I introduce one of her statements as the response of yet another reader to whom the class may respond. The statement, quoted later, encourages students to retrace their steps to a third and more complex response. Jones, in a brief but incisive *Explicator* article, argues for the fruitfulness of viewing the story from what I call the humanist perspective. The women, according to Jones, are smart enough to dominate the men; but money, the final indication of worldly success, is not theirs. Perhaps these women would be slightly smarter if they could train their men toward independent action rather than toward petrified servility. The men are useless as they are now, and so are the women. Each group is less than it ought to be. The result is a misery that finds release in beauty-parlor viciousness for the women and in drugged loafing for the men. (Item 21)

Examining Jones's position after having considered two other comparatively reductive responses permits a coherent ordering of a wide spectrum of student responses.

As if following the spiral of a gyre, I started at the bottom point of the satirist reading and circled 180 degrees around and upward to the feminist reading. The 180-degree oppositional positioning of these two reading represents my seeing the story's ridicule initially as directed at both genders and secondly as directed at only one. The height difference in this metaphor of a coil represents an increased awareness of the story's complexities. With another 180-degree upward turn, I was repositioned by my third reading, also universalist in applying to both sexes, directly over my first but at yet a higher level. Going directly from the first to the third points would have had a linear effect of a standard teaching strategy: presenting a less and more sophisticated response. Traveling through all three points added a three-dimensionality that I could use to better accommodate a range of readers' responses when I taught the story.

These reading revolutions are the background that I bring into the classroom with me. Whereas an individual's reading experience is a transaction between text and reader, what happens in a class, since class time is not spent reading the text, is a transaction between the interpretations of various readers. The participants' interpretations react off one another to produce a reading—a collective, consensus reading specific to that class and that day. How, then, do I allow my reading experiences to mesh with those of other, presumably first-time, readers? I cannot pretend that I do not have the background. I therefore acknowledge it, first of all; second, and most important, I use it to help students organize their responses. Thus I use my three readings of the story (the satirist, the feminist, and the humanist interpretations) to provide a preliminary, tentative organizational pattern for the discussion.

Invitation 9.1

Select a short story, novel, or poem that you have read at least twice, perhaps as part of school requirements. Establish as best you can what the nature and focus of your reactions were with each reading and what influenced these reactions or "revolutions."

KEEPING DISCUSSION TRANSACTIONAL

But before I show how my own background operates on the teaching of the story, one caveat. Pains need to be taken to prevent the teacher's reading from becoming *the* reading. Ordinarily, teachers are the dominant readers, and given their usual greater experience and preparation, there is nothing overly authoritarian about this situation. It is helpful for teachers to be secure in their "final" that is, preclass, interpretation. Acknowledging, however, that their own interpretations were formed through previous interactions with other readings of the story (perhaps, as in the case just sketched, in the context of informal discussions, or graduate seminars or undergraduate or high school classes, or by reading interpretations by other critics) provides an openness to the discussion. Avoidance of presenting an interpretation as though it were both obvious and cast in stone will also permit the possibility that a teacher's own "final" configuration, which could itself be limited, may be modified by student insight.

As with any two-way process, both parties should be changed, and often I find myself reassessing the story. One interesting way of viewing the petrifaction in the story was proposed by a student named Nicole. According to her interpretation, the men are socially petrified and the women are emotionally petrified. The women are cold, as though they are stone. The men, such as Mr. Pike, still acknowledge feeling. The women are able to control the men only because the men care about their wives. But socially the men are kept in straightjackets by their lack of ambition and will. The women, on the other hand, are socially free, out and about, talking, employed, and engaged in a more communal entertainment than the solitude of fishing. Nicole's view can be assimilated into the third part of my paradigm, the humanist perspective that argues that both the men and the women in the story are morally stunted. Her fresh light on the story, however, will help me to integrate other students' comments when they fall along these lines. Being open to fresh insights and either assimilating them or using them as alternative patterns will keep the classroom transactional.

TEACHING "PETRIFIED MAN"

With this as background, let me describe the class on "Petrified Man." Before the discussion of the story begins, I survey students' ability to remember the story's title. This survey initiates a pedagogical "trick" that both makes use of student misreading and fixes the results of a day's discussion of "Petrified Man" in students' minds. Let me defer a complete discussion of the reason behind this survey. Administering it takes about 3 minutes. I ask students to write down the story's title as they remember it (the usual candidates are "The Petrified Man," "A Petrified Man," and "Petrified Man") That's all. Whatever else the exercise does it generates some suspense.

Although it is crucial for students to see that a more experienced reader has deepened his or her response to the text, it is equally crucial that students begin their deepening encounter with a text from their own responses. In *Literature as Exploration,* Louise Rosenblatt offers a number of suggestions for getting students comfortable with their own tentative responses (70–71); one that I use is having students write brief responses to the simple question, "What did you relate to positively in the story and what negatively?" or, even more simply, "What did you like and what did you dislike?" Coming immediately after the students have indulged their instructor's bewildering whim and recorded the story's title to the best of their memory, this request, too, to many students is odd; many teachers of literature consider soliciting the reactions of inexpert readers a waste of time, so students are unlikely to have had much experience of teachers' insisting on the primacy of student responses. Nevertheless, I collect and silently read these responses as the students finish writing, and sort each response into groups, making notes that will later guide my use of their reactions in the class.

I ask them to take "about 10 minutes." As I am reading and sorting the first responses, other students are finishing their paragraphs, adding to them, so that reading these longer paragraphs takes more time. In a class of about 20 students, the writing and my first reading of the reactions takes a little over 20 minutes. After these initial procedures, the discussion proper can begin.

A "SMALL-TOWN SATIRE" RESPONSE

I read aloud either a part of every reaction or else representative examples. As students hear different responses (liking/disliking the story; liking/disliking one of the characters), they begin discussing the differences, or if they don't, I clarify a discrepancy in responses and call on individual students to take a side. Students are uncomfortable with the contradictions and hope to see the story from a unified perspective.[1] I stake out zones on the black-

---

[1] In *The Act of Reading,* Wolfgang Iser discussed this desire for a consistent interpretation, a unified perspective, in his typically sound and cogent fashion (16–19). Since consistency is fundamental for achieving comprehension, when teachers encounter resistance to one of their readings of a story, they may do so because students feel that their accustomed interpretive strategies for building consistency have been disregarded. Until these strategies can be either absorbed into a class interpretation or persuasively shown to be less appropriate to the story at hand than other interpretive strategies, students will continue to feel cheated, stupid, or misguided. An enthusiastic feminist reading of Charlotte Perkins Gilman's "The Yellow Wall-

board and, as they arise, transcribe the students' ideas about the story. Some ideas that I can anticipate from past discussions are notions about the story's small-townishness, gossip, physical harshness and dirtiness, and moral turpitude. I also ask for some textual support for each notion.

From teaching the story over the course of 8 years, I have found many students' written responses to be like my own first response to the story as small-town satire (I have preserved the students' comments typographically intact):

> In petrified man I found I related to the small-town atmosphere as well as the portrayal of these small-town women in their proper characters—not of lawyers and doctors, but of the uneducated, uncultured person in smalltown '40s. (Larry, May 1989)

In the classroom, I reread or call to mind some of the written responses that fit this small-town satire model. I mention that my own first reading of the story was similar, and I describe some of the personal background that led to my small-town satire reading, having spent my summers in a small town and having experienced beauty parlors there. If any student expresses an inability to empathize with any character in the story, I acknowledge that such a response can make the story more difficult to read but that that response may be one that Welty, as a satirist, wished to evoke.

Students have identified one of their responses as a reaction to the portrayal of small-town life, so I ask a question to get them to identify some of the story elements that may have led to this response: "If this story is a satire on small-town life, then the major elements in it that you have identified must be associated with the small town. Is this so?" Students will have responded readily to the element of gossip.

> I can relate to *Petrified Man* in a couple ways. The way the ladies gossiped in Leona's hair salon reminds me of several people I know who have a habit of gossiping. (Christopher, May 1989)
>
> My thoughts on the story were that of hearing two people gossiping. But that doesn't mean the whole story was like that. That was what first popped into my mind in the beginning. (Bob, May 1989)
>
> I didn't like the gossip-like basis. . . (Barb, May 1989)

Can the element of gossip be correlated with the small town? Many of the student responses made the correlation.

> This story reminded myself of two things in which I could relate this too. The first being my small home town and the people in it. That story did an excel-

---

Paper" may afford an example of an approach that could encounter unnecessary resistance if relatively less comprehensive readings of the story as a Poe-esque tale of madness (after all, the traditional interpretation of the story for decades) are not aired *first*. The process outlined here is designed to allow such readings into the debate for students to reach the more encompassing interpretation on their own.

lent job on describing what really goes on in beauty parlor. Beauty parlors are not a place for women to get their hair done, its the home base of all gossip that goes on in town. (Rex, May 1989)

In *Petrified Man* I can relate to the unbelievable amount of gossip throughout the entire story. Being from Ellsworth, a town of less than 2000 people, gossip is spread like wild fire. (Angela, May 1989)

Thus, students feel a connection between small-townishness and the major element of gossip, but because some of the comments tend to view the gossiping as a universal predicament, I ask what textual evidence can be adduced and what arguments constructed to link the gossip to small-town life. A question I use to initiate thinking about this subject is "Is there more gossip in small towns than in large cities, and if so, why?" I wait for students to arrive at various responses. One obvious response points out that the story is set in a small town, and in a small-town community people naturally are more interested in the affairs of their neighbors. This interest develops because it is possible; you know everyone else. This is not true in the city, where the instinct for self-preservation often leads city dwellers to close themselves off from the intimacy of shared knowledge frequently present in a small town.

Students from rural backgrounds are sensitive to the lack of opportunity in the story and may suggest that it is related to the gossiping. There is some evidence that the male characters are innately lazy (Leota believes her husband dreams of floating down the Yazoo river in a houseboat), yet when Leota demands that he seek a job in Vicksburg, Fred doesn't complain that there are jobs closer to home. The inference is that there are no jobs closer to home. Without jobs and many of the opportunities for relaxation supported by jobs, talk becomes a prime means of entertainment.

Lack of education can also be seen as a cause for gossip. Leota's superstitious belief in the fortune teller suggests a small-town lack of education. As one student put it:

If she puts all that faith in something as abstract as fortune telling, she really can't be all that educated or sophisticated. (Bob, May 1989)

If a lack of education leads to a paucity of ideas and vocabulary to discuss them, it is often acquaintances' personal lives that take up the slack. Thus, casual connections and hierarchies can be generated as the separate ideas on the board begin to be ordered. I use outlining, titling, or drawing of arrows to keep track of these relations. For instance, one class might generate "Three Small-Town Causes for the Gossiping Presented in the Story."

When gossip has been linked to Welty's satire of the small-town mentality, I ask the class to evaluate other elements that emerge from the written or oral responses that need to be evaluated as specifically small-townish or not. Asking students about these elements generates textual details that led to their responses. A certain uncouthness is one such element. If students did respond to the uncouthness in the story, then I ask what actions of Leota led to this response. My students have been eager to offer some of the following details. Strong red-nailed fingers press into Mrs. Fletcher's scalp, she is yanked up by the back locks and she is choked until "she paddled her hands in the air" (24). Sometimes students mention that cold fluids trickle down Mrs. Fletcher's neck or that the beautician flicks cigarette ashes into a basket of dirty towels. I can assimilate these details into the pattern of the discussion so far by noting that Leota's inattention to customer amenities and her uncouthness are actions in a business establishment that are more likely to exist in a place where there is less competition than in Manhattan.

At this point I introduce pertinent background materials from Welty's life. Mentioning aspects of an author's life, no matter how pertinent, will usually be remembered better after readers have become engaged with the story. By this point in the discussion of "Petrified Man," students are prepared to hear that despite having lived in Jackson, Mississippi, and having attended Columbia and the University of Wisconsin, Welty was thoroughly familiar with small-town ways. Her first job, which was working for the Works Progress Administration, involved traveling the back roads of Mississippi during the Depression. I use her photographs of rural Mississippi life, published in *One time, One Place: Mississippi in the Depression, A Snapshot Album*, to add visual vividness to her credentials as a small-town satirist.

Finally, a central, although off-stage, element of the story is the freak show. Both the show and Leota and Mrs. Pike's interest in it strike many readers as small-townish. I conclude the discussion of small-town life in the story by ending with (or coming back to) a mention of the freak show. It provides a capping example and a transition to a second way of viewing the story, a perspective that will help organize the responses of students whose reading insights have not been addressed adequately by the small-town satire discussion. A rhetorical question I use to initiate the transition is, "But, do you want to leave it at a story about small-town life, about the meanness connected with it and about people who visit freak shows?" More specifically, "Are there important elements that this view of the story leaves out?" One element that is not specific to small-town life is the element of the battle of the sexes. With these questions we begin to move toward this second perspective.

A "FEMINIST" RESPONSE

The class so far has accomplished a validation of many readers' responses to the story. Other readers, however, have noticed that the men in this story are rather "petrified," and these readers' perceptions need to be addressed. A question I ask to get the class thinking about this petrifaction of the males in the story is "What do the fetuses, the pygmies, and the petrified man have in common?" If this question proves too puzzling, I break it into its parts.

What are pygmies? Notions of what pygmies are circle around the idea that they are people whom we tend to consider as not have reached "normal" height.

What do you think about fetuses? The story's fetuses never mature.

What do we know about what is supposedly wrong with the Petrified Man? Why is he a freak? The Petrified Man is supposedly petrifying in his limbs instead of naturally replenishing his vitality.

What, then, do these three things share? These story details are united by the notion that each has its natural growth checked. Once students see how many elements in the story literally share this trait—suggesting that this is probably not coincidental on the part of the author—their interpretive strategies are usually developed to the point of their searching for figuratively portrayed stunted growth. I ask "Who else in the story has his growth stunted?" Using the masculine pronoun usually means that the men are scrutinized first. When female characters are suggested, I begin a second list on the board (along with, naturally, the textual evidence that the character is indeed stunted).

At this point, I return briefly—before we actually again look at the story closely and begin a list of males who are stunted—to those written reactions that indicate a sense of stunted growth. Such a return to student responses reminds them that some of them had experienced this element in the story.

> I can relate to the way the ladies referred to their husbands as "Petrified Men." Leona says that her husband Fred just lays around the house all day. (Christopher, May 1989)
>
> To me, it seemed as if Leota & Mrs. Fletcher felt their husbands were "above" the petrified man, but they both seemed kind of petrified to me. (Linda, May 1989)

Once the students see the men as petrified, I ask the class about the women: "If the men are unstereotypically passive and weak, are the women unstereotypically active and strong?"

Many of the following aspects of women being in charge will come out in discussion. Mrs. Fletcher claims that Mr. Fletcher "can't do a thing with me. . . . I'll have one of my sick headaches, and then I'm just not fit to live with" (19). She makes him take bending exercises. She pretends to include him in important decisions, but does not tell him of her pregnancy. She only asks his advice about when to get her hair done, and even then, he can only encourage her to do what she wants anyway. Mrs. Mountjoy is another person with whom her husband cannot do a thing; he waits nervously in the car while his wife insists on having her hair done before continuing to the hospital to have her baby. Mr. Pike cannot persuade Mrs. Pike to forego turning over Mr. Petrie to the police. Leota can demand that her husband look for work in Vicksburg. Billy Boy is bossed around by such demands as "mustn't bother nice ladies" (19). Billy Boy is even spanked for his independent action of eating peanuts, as Jones notes, and the women in the beauty parlor gather round to watch.

A "HUMANIST" RESPONSE

Having considered this feminist reading ("feminist," really, only in the sense of the sex-role reversals), further questions can prepare the ground for a humanist perspective. A rhetorical question parallel to the previous one about small-town satire can initiate the discussion of the next perspective: "But, do you want to leave it at a story about women who gain something in our society because they, uncharacteristically, can dominate the men in their lives?" Genuine questions for the class to ponder include: Should the women be in charge? How do the women use their domination? What results from the women's efforts?

A number of readers side with the women. They see admirable traits in Mrs. Pike (her acuity of observation), Mrs. Fletcher (her stubborn striving for dominance), and Leota.

> I felt that Leota was a very talented beautician. (Being able to carry on her duties at the same time as telling dramatic stories to entice Mrs. Fletcher.) (Linda, May 1989)
>
> Their attitude of independence is admirable. (Barb, May 1989)

Those who admire the women have a more difficult time maintaining their admiration in the face of the text; consequently, I try to ensure that the characters of the story's women are thoroughly looked at for their positive traits. If we can accomplish this positive look, I then ask those supporting the feminist perspective to consider Vande Kieft's reaction to Mr. Petrie. I read Vande Kieft's statement out loud, asking the class to ponder whether it is just the men in the story who are petrified: "One is amused at the comically grotesque turn of events, and gratified that at least one man—Mr. Petrie—turned violently, if only briefly, against the collective monstrosity of female sexual action with a comparable male monstrosity of action" (74). If the feminist perspective has been given a thorough hearing, Vande Kieft's response, even if from an established critic, should not be enough to univocally turn the tide. Those students who responded to the story on the feminist level need not feel that they must abandon it. Nevertheless, the quotation is a thorn to deal with from that perspective, a thorn that can modify the feminist reading.

Naturally, other readers disapprove of the women.

> I didn't care for the women's attitudes toward their husbands (Leota esp.) or their pending motherhood (Mrs. Fletcher) although I suppose it is more true to life than anyone cares to admit. . . . Leota didn't seem to truly care about her husband and her life must be pretty dull for all the faith she puts in her fortune teller. The women in the story need to get a life and not worry so much about nothing. They seemed to have nothing better to do than worry what other people think and go to freak shows. (Barb, May 1989—the same student who also acknowledged that there was something admirable about the women's independence)
>
> She [Leota] seemed to have something to say about everything and everybody but where did it get her? (Margarete, July 1989)

Students can explore in an articulated way the story's being antiwoman as much as antiman. The women possess a number of character traits that are not flattering. Leota's quick friendship with Mrs. Pike and her equally quick change of loyalties, Mrs. Mountjoy's ill-timed permanent, and Mrs. Fletcher's belief that only public opinion would hamper her getting an abortion indicate a superficiality. They are back-sniping, referring to another customer as "Old Horse Face" (18). With little true substance to their characters, Leota and Mrs. Fletcher engage in a petty one-upwomanship in regard to what their husbands' heights are (Leota wins) and where they met their husbands (Mrs. Fletcher wins, a library to a rumble seat).

Some students are concerned with what seem to be loose ends in the story, the presence of Billy Boy being one of the most puzzling.

> Some parts of the story didn't seem to need to be present such as the boy in the Saloon. (Erich, May 1989)
>
> What I did not relate to was the use of the little boy in the story—what force was he to represent, so many riddles that one can not help but search for meaning in it all. (Larry, May 1989)

The structure of readings advocated here, particularly the return to a notion of the universality of the satire, can give an answer to the question of Billy Boy's presence. The story closes with the women spanking Billy Boy for insufficient cause. I ask my students why. Some students are good at articulating a reason:

> At the end of 'Petrified Man,' the little boy questions why the women aren't rich if they are so smart. Billy Boy was in the beauty parlor the whole day absorbing every conversation that was going on. He finally deduced that instead of talking about everyone else and chastising them, they could constructively take a careful look at themselves. I get the feeling that when people find problems with everyone else, they often don't find the problems with themselves. I think this was described nicely. (Susan, July 1989)

One student's comment shows that, whether or not one can articulate a reason for Billy Boy's presence, his last words *affect* readers along the lines suggested:

She (Leota) should not have taken her jealousy out on the little kid but he had the last laugh by saying if you are so smart how come you aren't rich. When he said that, it made me smile. (Bob, May 1989)

Students can discuss the idea that Leota and Mrs. Fletcher are taking their frustrations out on the nearest available male. But this male has the last words, literally the last words in the story, and that position grants them a privileged status. His "If you're so smart why ain't you rich" points out that for all the women's domination, their tactics get them no place they really want to go. Billy Boy serves not only to highlight the repression of male assertion (he is continually told to stop one of his actions) but also, and more important, to underscore the women's error, that their tactics are self-defeating.

This third perspective on the story returns us to a satirical reading similar to the satire-on-small-town-life initial reading. However, the process of getting here—via consideration of a second level of the story—like the *process* (rather than the result) *of reading* itself, makes the crucial difference. Viewing the story as a satire *after* discussing the relationship of the sexes is a different, fuller viewpoint than simply understanding the story as a satire, because the third response encompasses the earlier two. The characters are satirized, but the issue is not just small-town mentality. Rather, we can see the issue as the battle of the sexes where both genders are culpable.

Invitation 9.2

Conduct some research on questioning procedures to develop an array of questions and an "automatic" sense of procedure and process. A good place to start is R. Paul's "A Taxonomy of Socratic Questions" in *Critical Thinking: What Every Person Needs to Survive in a Rapidly Changing World.*

"MISREADINGS" CAN CAPTURE
ESSENTIAL ASPECTS OF A TEXT

With these three readings in mind, I refer back to the "titles." I write three titles on the board ("The Petrified Man," "A Petrified Man," and "Petrified Man") and give the number of students who chose each title. I have not kept a record of results for every time I teach the story, but an instructor who asks students for the title is almost assured of two responses, the first and the last.

We discuss the specificity of "The Petrified Man" and the generality of the actual title, with the occasionally misremembered "A Petrified Man" falling between. Students who remembered "The Petrified Man" as the story's title are focusing on the story's literal level of the one side-show freak, *the* petrified man. Such a title suggests a realistic portrayal of small-town people, those who are interested in the minimal entertainments of freak shows and gossiping (hence, one can argue, rural-background students, who tend to remember this title, are especially attuned to the portrayal of small-town life).

Students who chose "A Petrified Man"—and even if none do, that hypothetical title can be discussed—encapsulate the theme of the story at a more general level. "*A* petrified man" can refer to Mr. Petrie, but the phrase is also potentially more generally applicable to a number of "petrified" men, such as the lazy, dominated Mr. Pike or Mr. Fletcher. Such a title would easily mesh with the battle-of-the sexes reading.

Welty's actual title, of course, is the most universal. The ambiguity of "Man" can still refer back to the males in the story, but in the sense of "mankind," humankind, it can apply to the women as well as the men. I believe that the way students remember the title may reflect their experience of the story, which may be the result of focusing their response on one of the story's levels. Pedagogically, at least, a student's remembering an incorrect title can actually be used as a badge of capturing a portion of the story—all, after all, that any reader can be expected to do.

Invitation 9.3

Play with titles. Titles are often a good way to open responses to a text, providing as they do a preliminary key. After each group selects one or two titles of texts, in a round-robin exercise consider the potential lead of each through an initial journal writing and then by oral comparison. Consider the application of the outcomes of this exercise for lesson planning.

LEADING A TRANSACTIONAL DISCUSSION

A main problem in leading a transactional discussion of literature, implied but not addressed in the foregoing outline of my approach, is processing the different responses. Let me categorize, generally, potential responses in two ways: first, intellectually, as plausible (i.e., within the realm of responses that the author probably had hoped to generate) or implausible (outside that realm) and, second, emotionally, as positive about the text or as expressing a negative reaction to some feature. I make these distinctions to illustrate general strategies for dealing with student responses when the discussion in the classroom begins.

First, though, what does plausible mean in a transactional context? Every response produced by the student's confrontation with the text is "accurate" in the sense that a student voices a feeling or an idea engendered by the transaction. The more experienced reader, however, understands some responses as not reasonably within the realm of responses that the author had hoped to arouse. The teacher, while valuing open expression of reactions, seeks to ensure that responses are rooted in the text. Three criteria guide a teacher:

1. *There should be evidence in the text for the reader's contention*. If a teacher sets up the early expectation of some citation of evidence for every expression of reaction, students acquire early the habit of finding some. A general rule should be established stating that an unsupported reaction, although very possibly plausible, cannot count in the arena of the classroom until it is supported.

2. *There should be no evidence that contradicts the reader's contention*. If contradictory evidence obviously exists, the teacher can ask what others think about the proposed idea. When another student offers the contradictory evidence, I turn back to the original student in an effort to get the discussion to bypass me as the teacher. The original student can, disappointingly, simply back down or, on more positive notes, either propose counterevidence or modify the original view. If no one comes up with the contradictory evidence, the teacher can offer it and ask the student what he or she thinks in its light.

3. Finally, *the reader must have taken cognizance of the major elements of the text in their reasonable interpretations*.

POSITIVE AND PLAUSIBLE RESPONSES

The easiest types of responses to process are those that are positive and plausible, particularly those that a teacher can anticipate from previous classroom experience. Although a positive comment may fulfill the three criteria for plausibility, only an agile teacher will recognize it as plausible if, practically speaking, the comment doesn't also fit with the teacher's already organized responses. Granted my structuring of the story, an example of a positive, plausible comment on "Petrified Man" was given in Rex's comment:

> This story reminded myself of two things in which I could relate this too. The first being my small home town and the people in it. That story did an excellent job on describing what really goes on in beauty parlor. Beauty parlors are not a place for woman to get their hair done, its the home base of all gossip that goes on in town. (Rex, May 1989)

For me, this comment gets at two basic elements of the story: the satire of small-town life and the gossip. With positive, plausible comments, I sometimes have to remind myself to ask for—if the student forgets to give—supporting evidence. I separate long comments into components (in this case, gossip and small-town life) and put shorthand titles of these components on the board and list the elicited supporting evidence underneath. This charting of comments on a blackboard will allow for an overall patterning of responses to emerge clearly at the end of the discussion.

Other positive, plausible comments tend to express admiration for Welty's realistic depiction of setting

> I got comfortable with the setting. (Susan, July 1989)

and humorous dialogue/precise dialect

> I liked the characters and their dialogue the best. Welty has a way of making them funny people. (Erin, July 1989)

During discussion of the story, these positive reactions to Welty's setting and characterization can be set against the main negative (although plausible) reaction: frustration over the lack of plot.

NEGATIVE AND PLAUSIBLE RESPONSES

The dominating negative reaction that nonetheless seems a legitimate response to the story is one of frustration.

> I started this story late at night, and by the time I was three-quarters through it, I threw the book across the room. (Dawn, July 1990)

Often there are nods of agreement when a comment like this one is read. A teacher can label such comments with a general expression that will cover many individually phrased responses, and here I point to the "frustration" that Dawn and others experienced. With any negative comment, I probe into its cause by simply asking "Why?"—"Why were you frustrated?" Responses generally split along two lines: the already mentioned intellectual dissatisfaction with the apparent lack of plot ("The story didn't seem to be going anywhere" [Dawn, July 1990] or an empathetic reaction against the unlikability of most of the characters ("I did not really like the story. . . . The characters—the two women in the hair dressers—did not seem good or humane and I guess just dislikeable" [Meena, July 1989]). Once these types of negative reactions are clarified for the class, they can be dealt with by two techniques suggested in *Literature as Exploration:* discussion and presentation of background material.

The plot structure is not that of an O. Henry nor even a Henry James, but discussion can help readers deal with their frustration over this element. Admission that a certain lack of plot is evident in the story can itself be very relieving to insecure readers. From that starting point, two rejoinders are possible: the author was more concerned with other things than with plot; or there exists a type of plot that is latent, and detection of this unobvious thread permits a reader to follow at least a plotlike trail. With respect to the first rejoinder, I can remind students of the positive reactions to the setting and characterization. Sometimes readers must grant an author his or her chosen emphases. Also, however, there is a plotlike element to the story involving the one-up(wo)manship that carries through the narrative. This aspect of a submerged plot will probably best be treated toward the end of discussion when all the story's elements begin to coalesce.

For those readers who are frustrated because they cannot like any of the characters, presentation of the nature of the genre of satire can help. Some readers have a grasp on the story's genre. Meena, quoted earlier, starts out her comment on "Petrified Man" with "I did not really like the story" because the characters were not good or humane, but continues in the same sentence: "and I thought maybe that was the author's intention: (July 1989). If we think of "Petrified Man" as, at least to some degree, a satire, readers are quite correct to dislike the main characters, the objects of the satire. The story's blurring of the boundaries of satire (it also reads like a realistic slice of life) can be offered as a reason for students' not immediately picking up on the conventions that the piece invokes. Discussion here can take several directions, but its most important effect is in allaying the frustration of some readers: Frustration, rightly understood, is part of the point, and feeling it is a response encouraged by the text.

It is important to note that such negative comments, as much as positive comments, help elucidate the text and should be equally encouraged. With "Petrified Man," students who would be lost to further discussion because of frustration have a chance to put aside their negative reactions, at least temporarily, to more fully participate in the text.

NEGATIVE AND IMPLAUSIBLE RESPONSES

But every teacher knows that merely positive and negative comments are not the only ones to deal with; are implausible comments helpful to elucidating the text? Implausible comments can derail discussion whose fruitfulness under most educational systems is subject to time constraints. Such comments, however, must be dealt with tactfully and, ideally, productively if the openness of discussion that is essential to a transactional pedagogical approach is to be maintained.

The *implausibility* of hostile comments can be used to clarify aspects of the text. If someone so egregiously misread or misremembered the story as to state that Mrs. Fletcher turned the Petrified Man in or that Fred had raped four women, these statements can be corrected. (Quite often, to encourage absolutely free discussion, I put inaccurate comments on the board—for cogitation—with a question mark appended or, later, an actual erasure, depending on the discussion.) In addition, such clarification offers a springboard to exploring real tensions within the story by turning the error and clarification into a question. By asking why it is important that Mrs. Pike and not Mrs. Fletcher turned the Petrified Man over to the authorities, obviously intended textual impressions (Mrs. Fletcher's relative fecklessness; Mrs. Pike's sharpness, untrustworthiness, selfishness) can be elicited. By asking why Fred would never have raped four women, his laziness and passiveness can be brought out and the irony of the "Petrified" Man's *action* explored.

The *hostility* of implausible comments are the least pedagogically useful and from a transactional perspective tend to indicate the student's not giving a text a fair chance. An appropriate response, when assimilation to another of the techniques mentioned seems unworkable, is to suggest that the student hold his or her hostility in abeyance until after the discussion to see whether others' comments make a difference (and then really do come back to hostile students at the end).

POSITIVE AND IMPLAUSIBLE RESPONSES

Lastly, enthusiastic but implausible comments are sometimes the most disheartening to address because a teacher's intellectual obligation to the text and his or her supportive role of the student come in conflict. A positive reaction to "Petrified Man" on the grounds of its evoking the peacefulness of hunting season is stupefying. Nevertheless, the transactional approach obligates the teacher, who is essentially a coexplorer, to attempt to trace the origins of such a response. Hypothetically, these origins may lay in the story's having been encountered in October, and the reader may have had a positive, elaborate imagining of the story's men on their fishing expedition. If the genesis of the response can be traced, a teacher can separate the personal (reading the story in October, which reminded the student of hunting) from the text (the fishing). Then the connotations of the text can be explored. In this case, the teacher could ask what hunting means to the student, perhaps attempting to elicit the plausible responses of peacefulness and escape. Then the text could be returned to to see whether the same connotations applied to fishing. They, of course, do—to an even greater extent than hunting with its connotations of brutality. Finally, the question of how fishing relates to the men in the story would bring out story elements that would put the discussion back on a track that is firmly laid on the text. Perhaps this technique elaborately coddles a shoddy reader, but the same reader may be encouraged (rather than discouraged) to read, and read carefully, and later may offer fruitful insights rather than becoming silent.

CONCLUSION

In summary, this approach to "Petrified Man" illustrates four aspects of a transactional approach. The first is the teachers' awareness of their own responses. The second is the enlargement of the teachers' initial response through participation in "discussions" by other readers so as to prepare teachers to accommodate agilely and suggest helpful organizing patterns for the many responses they will encounter in the classroom. In the case of my experience with "Petrified Man," my initial response was enlarged both through actual discussions and through reading the critical literature.[2] The third is the organization of the teacher's own responses into a pattern that will help students make sense of their own reactions. Last is the allowance of free discussion, both in terms of what is encouraged and when responses are recorded: A teacher can allow discussion responses to come as they come, using separate spaces on the board to organize them. Such a procedure begins as it only can in reality, with readers' responses; it values those (usually divergent) responses; yet it achieves at its conclusion the (tentative) wholeness and coherence of the aesthetic experience.

A last student comment on the story illustrates, I believe, how stories, given that they are intended to generate affective responses, are most objectively appreciated when those responses are identified. And Linda's comment also provides an insight into how the form of "Petrified Man" works to implicate the reader in its theme.

> I enjoyed this short story for the most part. It was amusing to me to "listen in" on the conversations between Mrs. Fletcher and Leota the beautician. The gossip that took place struck me funny in that it was so absurd and seemed very trivial. (Linda, May 1989)

The comment points to the eavesdropping that, enjoyed, consequently implicates the readers and casts them as an object of the satire on gossip. The third perspective on this story is thus truly operating here, its satire applying to every reader who enjoys the story.

---

[2]For the short story, accessing the criticism has been made relatively easy by a number of bibliographic aids. These include the Modern Language Association's annual bibliography; Jarvis A. Thurston's *Short Fiction Criticism;* and Warren S. Walker's *Twentieth-Century Short Story Explication* and its supplements.

REFERENCES

Iser, Wolfgang, *The Act of Reading: A Theory of Aesthetic Response.* Baltimore: Johns Hopkins University Press, 1978

Jones, William. M. "Welty's 'Petrified Man.'" *The Explicator* 15.4 (January 1957): Item 21.

MLA International Bibliography of Books and Articles on the Modern Languages and Literatures. New York: Modern Language Association.

Paul, R. *Critical Thinking: What Every Person Needs to Survive in a Rapidly Changing World.* Tohnert Park, CA: Sonoma State U, Center for Critical Thinking and Moral Critique, 1990.

Rosenblatt, Louise M. *Literature as Exploration.* 3d ed. New York: Noble and Noble, 1976.

Thurston, Jarvis A. et al. *Short Fiction Criticism: A Checklist of Interpretations Since 1925 of Stories and Novelettes (American, British, Continental, 1800–1958).* Denver, CO: Swallow, 1958.

Vande Kieft, Ruth, *Eudora Welty.* Boston: Twayne, 1962.

Walker, Warren S. *Twentieth-Century Short Story Explication: Interpretations, 1900–1966 Inclusive, of Short Fiction Since 1800.* 2d ed. Hamden, CT: Shoe String Press, 1968.

Welty, Eudora. *One Time, One Place: Mississippi in the Depression, A Snapshot Album.* New York: Random House, 1971.

———. "Petrified Man." *The Collected Stories of Eudora Welty.* New York: Harvest, 1982. 17–28.

10

Reader Response to Drama
Prospecting for Human Understandings and Connections

Linda Varvel

When I entered the public school classroom in 1988, I was well aware of Rosenblatt's theory of reader response and looked forward to implementing it in my classes with an expectation of exciting results. However, reality proved to be a rude awakening. In the "real" public school classroom, I was assigned 150 students; a tight sequence of novels, stories, and plays; and very little prep time. Files of former teachers and prepackaged curriculum packets for one or two of the novels were available as resources. Time constraints made working with other teachers hurried and brief, mainly efforts to achieve synchronicity in lessons and skills by the end of each semester when, in a yearlong course, the computer would scramble and reassign many students to another teacher. The seasoned handouts of tenured teachers, all neatly typed and ready for production, were intimidating.

When faced with teaching Arthur Miller's fascinating, many-layered play *The Crucible*, I was unsettled by two problems. Many students came to the literature as disadvantaged readers who genuinely needed page-to-page reinforcements to enable them to follow plot and distinguish characters, whereas other students came as defensive learners who would not read the assignment at all unless I prodded them with some kind of basic reading comprehension questions. Second, I had a predetermined length of time to cover the play and, with classes of 30 or more students, I needed some tangible control over moving them from basic conclusions about the play to more complex themes. I compromised by creating a study guide of objective questions interspersed with more subjective reader-response questions.

Because dramatic literature lends itself to oral and listening learning, I was eager to orchestrate reading the play aloud. This generated much more enthusiasm and involvement, and for that reason was rather seductive as both a learning tool and a behavioral management technique. Tenth-grade students enjoy being the "audience" as classmates interpret those scenes that are angry, judgmental, hysterical, or comic. If critical moments are noted and emphasized, the learning can become less covert.

My study guide could now be the means to explore the literature beneath the dramatic dialogue being interpreted aloud. A typical question on my first study guide was: "When the young girls are alone with Betty, what more do we find out about what happened in the woods that night?" Typical answers were: "That they were trying to talk to the dead," or "Abigail was doing something against someone's wife," or "They were doing charms and one may have danced naked." These kinds of questions stimulate active learning briefly and then just as effectively stop it. Although a study guide does help the students distinguish between Reverend Parris, John Proctor, and Thomas Putnam, it does not help students draw their own conclusions or work inward to root causes. When the more abstract questions came up, the students who were already more abstract thinkers would answer, but the concrete learners only copied them down or tuned out and waited for the next concrete question that could be answered by rote. Overwhelmed at the end of the unit, they would copy notes verbatim on the conclusions I was explaining the final day. They would then parrot them back on two or three essay questions without depth of understanding, expecting that the "objective" part of the test would save their grade. Ultimately, I had their attention, but they were engaged only at a very superficial level.

DISCOVERING DISCUSSION AND DIALOGUE TECHNIQUES IN TEACHING *THE CRUCIBLE*

For a classic play like *The Crucible* to be truly successful, students must be challenged to explore larger truths about life and draw broader philosophical analogies between the world of this particular piece of literature and life in general. So far in teaching this drama, the writing I was asking students to do was not leading to independent thinking or abstract conclusions.

The second time I taught the play, I attempted a Readers Theatre technique with cooperative learning groups of seven or eight students, which proved to be a step in the right direction. Each group was assigned to teach one act of the play by introducing the characters, summarizing the plot, dramatizing a key scene of about five or six pages, and discussing meanings or themes. Their choice of scenes was effective, and the "acting out" was lively and brought a certain degree of melodrama and humor to the sober themes. However, during the preparation week, when a number of the groups became panicked about how to teach their act effectively, I resorted to giving them some of the more traditional background sheets and study guides, mainly, I realized too late, out of my own anxiety about control and accountability. The opportunity to have each small group and then the whole class wrestle with the meaning of the play in their own reader-response style was missed. Many group presentations again focused on concrete summaries and character discussions with little examination of motivation and consequences.

However, in each of the groups, usually one person ventured into abstract conclusions about the causes and metaphorical meanings of the play that I worked to reinforce at the end of each presentation. For example, one student, Kelly, adapted the reader-response technique I modeled twice in class to her own practice of "writing to learn" about the work. In her presentation, she suggested that

> because the young girls were trying to find their identity and because Abigail was so jealous, they broke the bounds of established "proper" behavior. Unfortunately, in a society that was that afraid of nonconformist behavior, the atmosphere of judgment from God became a fearful tool, which led to a desire to place blame outside the self and a general hysteria.

Another student, Chelsea, suggested that "corruption had been building for some time; no trust existed in the community and when blame was placed, the accusations became a plague of vengeance." A third student determined that extremism was directly caused by a sense that there were absolutes of right and wrong. A fourth, Tony, actually explored the roots of such words as *solemn, remorseful, vile,* and *pretense,* relating them to the abstract causes and effects of conformity in religion. His inventiveness encouraged me to persist in relating language to abstract concepts and themes in any literary text.

The third time I taught *The Crucible,* I had the students read the play aloud, and with a sequence of open-ended questions about character and plot, we established the concrete foundation of events and complications. I then designed a series of five reader-response questions on which they were to write during the time they were viewing the modern film for the final 2 days of discussion. By noticing that almost all the students focused on two of the five questions, I discovered where the play resonated for these particular students. I then pursued a line of questioning that led to a chain of developing understandings of the play. One reader-response question of special interest was:

> After watching the relationship between Elizabeth and John Proctor evolve in the film, what do you believe true and committed love means? Examine the stages of their love from the early scenes at their farm to their final talk by the ocean.

This first question fully engaged one student in figuring out different types of love. She began to distinguish romantic love from what she called "dedicated love." When I asked her what she meant by "dedicated love," she answered that there was a difference between a love that is easy and comfortable from one that must struggle with differences in beliefs or morality. When I suggested phrases like love as obligation, love as passion, or love from the heart, students talked about how easy it was for them to fall in love, but that when they found things to argue about, it got difficult to sustain the passion. I asked them how that applied to the play. Francie said, "John made a choice that hurt Elizabeth. Then, she 'turned off' to him. This caused her to become mean to him." In writing about Elizabeth and John, another student found that to stay committed, one must forgive. The concept of isolation was mentioned, although not pursued. The students were moving toward the idea of spiritual love, yet unable to find language to clarify this concept.

The second popular question was purposely designed to focus attention on a spiritual transformation that students often miss:

> Do you think the Reverend Hale's ideas about good and evil change from the time of his arrival in Salem to the final scene? Was Hale at all heroic?

The students' first response was to ask, "Why did Hale become confused?" They decided that he saw "many good people" and "many people who were lying a little, but he could not find truly evil people." For a time, he did not know what to believe. The students made the observations that although John Proctor was a sinner, he was not an evil person, and because she told a lie to protect her sinful husband, Elizabeth was a very good woman who made the wrong choice at the wrong time. Discussion about "making mistakes" led to talking about getting at the truth and finding that good people often act in bad, even evil, ways to achieve some immediate end, yet they are not of the Devil. One student realized that when Hale saw several accused people standing their ground and proclaiming their truth, he had a strong desire to see them as private people away from village rumors and vendettas. He began to realize that some other issues were going on underneath this Devil hysteria. Another student knew that Hale's idea of evil changed throughout the play, but he could neither define evil at the beginning or end of the play nor put it in any moral or ethical context. One young man knew he admired Reverend Hale because he persisted against public pressure, but could neither find adequate language for his view nor point to particular stages of Hale's struggle. This student's main evidence was that Hale was convinced something had gone wrong in Salem and "washed his hands of it" when he could not stop the deaths.

The reader-response approach definitely encourages students to take the leap to more abstract conclusions. The next challenge they face is to link each conclusion to the concrete "moments" in the action and dialogue of the literature. By tracing and examining those connections, the students eventually learn to identify the reasoning they are using. Only then can they test it against other students' and the teacher's thinking. Because reader response is open ended, students' thinking is free to evolve and spark off some responses and build subconclusions and issues within issues. Students become confused and are forced to struggle to think their way out of the maze of their reactions and conclusions. It gives the more independent learners the incentive to mine the incidents of the play for actions and words that particularly resonate with the meanings they are getting; because this experience is lively and varied, it becomes an incentive to pursue this search more often and in more depth. When these students succeed, they become peer role models for other students in the class as well as active "teachers" and motivators for other students at the same learning level.

For the teacher, the most challenging aspect of reader-response-guided discussion is determining the scope and timing of the right question or right activity that will move the thinking up the abstraction ladder. In the preceding discussion, two techniques would have made the teaching more effective: Defining what "good and evil" mean to these particular students would have provided a richer context for the moral issues being discussed. Reading aloud the scene between John and Elizabeth Proctor and the Reverend Hale would have provided a compelling means to focus students closely on the behavior and moral choices of these three characters at a critical turning point. I needed to emphasize the fact that Reverend Hale was following his own instincts in pursuing private conferences and that this was quite radical in a Puritan theocracy at that time in history. Perhaps this would have triggered a discussion of courage. I was very close to a key link: "What compelled Hale to act in such a nonconformist manner?" This might have led to a deduction about seeking greater truth and the necessity for revolutionary actions. Or, another series of questions that I had been linking in my own mind might have enabled the students to determine the progress of Hale's spiritual transformation:

> Why was neither good nor evil absolute in Salem?
> Who wanted it to be absolute and why?
> How did Judge Danforth define good and evil?
> And finally, how did the Reverend Hale define good and evil?

A third direction for future teaching might be to articulate the difference between truly innocent and falsely innocent, which would uncover the roots of hypocrisy—another very important theme.

Reader response can potentially transform teaching in two primary ways: It changes the way a teacher structures and uses his or her knowledge, and it transforms the relationship between the teacher and students. In the traditional style, the teacher enters the classroom on a given day with certain main theme conclusions and focuses discussion on those meanings. If he or she teaches, for example, the conclusion, "Abigail's desire for revenge becomes the 'torch' for the conservatives of the town to demand that the errant believers profess a proscribed faith or 'burn at the stake,'" the teacher may communicate a seamless garment of his or her own thinking, yet leave many loose ends in the minds of students. In the reader-response style, the teacher gathers student responses and reactions to build inductively to the larger meanings in the work, constantly aware of the power of language to clarify thinking. Discussion then becomes an investigative dialogue. Teachers must discipline themselves to resist too much internal summarizing so students can actually lead and provoke each other in their own rhythm and style. The teacher must focus more intently on questions that incite and provoke more thinking rather than final conclusions and neatly resolved themes. Although the learning at times feels much less controlled and directly measurable, it is an essential step in learning as a teacher to become a facilitator and connector, a much more subtle kind of control.

The students in this last 10th-grade class were interested in true love and romantic feelings as well as in telling the truth and struggling with the consequences; these were the "keys" to their reasoning. Many students realized they were disappointed in Elizabeth and John as a couple; when I encouraged them to explore exactly why, they began to define levels of love from romantic to spiritual. In the future, I might use analogy to help them draw parallels between their disappointment with the Proctors' love and how the Puritan community as a whole was disappointed with its members, and then to look at the compassion and forgiveness that Elizabeth and John found at the same time that greed and selfishness caused the leaders of Salem to isolate and punish the members they identified as "flawed." By having a "window" on the teacher's process of moving from concrete details to conclusions and back to specifics, students will come to know and trust the teacher's abilities to guide and focus and discover that intellectual thinking is a process of trial and error that leads to clearer and more significant thinking.

When the play becomes a puzzle to be mutually explored and solved, each time the discussion becomes "stuck," the teacher reacts to it as a sign that another, deeper question needs to be solved. This feedback enables the students to wrestle with their confusion and the teacher to respond by reframing the issues and language to engage the students in another round of thinking. It requires that the teacher and the students read and reread the play, keeping essential, final meanings and dialectics more in hand as the destination of the unit. One young woman discovered she could begin to express her thinking about Abigail and all the people in Salem in terms of cruelty as opposed to kindness and caring. She clearly saw selfishness and greed as the cause of cruelty and was still looking for the root cause of human kindness.

Reader response from students, both written and spoken, is essential feedback to the teacher for diagnosing the teaching problems. Turning those problems into engaging dramatic activities unleashes more intuitive thinking skills in both teachers and students. As a teacher, I am now free to place my own unsolved questions about the work on the table for open investigation. For example:

• Part of the complexity of Miller's play comes from choice of setting. A reader response about setting would draw attention to the issue of public and private and help readers investigate important metaphorical meanings: As the hysteria in Salem accumulates, Arthur Miller repeatedly places the action of individual scenes off center, in private homes or antechambers. Why does he focus on interpersonal dynamics in such interior scenes? How are the public and private related?

• Many students confuse the three "P" characters in the written version because they grow weary of Miller's long background history narratives in the middle of Act I. As a teacher, I find that summarizing them more briefly is an improvement, but still puts students to sleep. It might be best to try a dramatic monologue. Give each of three students one of the introductory narratives and a typical costume piece. Have them design a monologue 1 minute in length in which they tell important details about that character's life as he pleads before a jury that he is a good man of Salem.

• Another helpful dramatic activity would be to focus on the interrogation of the Proctors by Reverend Hale in Act II or Hale's attempt to force Proctor to confess in Act IV. Direct two different groups to interpret the selected scene and see what differences they bring out. This would start a lively discussion about love in marriage and the religious, moral, and human issues at stake.

• A sequence of ongoing journals from a particular character's point of view might lend itself to a small group activity in which people of like minds develop testimony; each group presents one character's view of right and wrong in Salem and a final solution. The presentation and discussion would be reminiscent of the play *Roshomon*.

Invitation 10.1

Get into a character. Prepare a 1-minute monologue of any character in a drama and introduce yourself and your dilemma to your peers.

An important outcome when I use reader response is that as the teacher I have an opportunity to do more writing and thinking about the play rather than collecting and correcting half-hearted study guides and quizzes. The following is an excerpt from one of my own reader responses that led me to decide *The Crucible* needed more context if it was to be truly effective in the curriculum.

> When studying *The Crucible,* young people can relate to a personal desire for individual liberation. However, they risk staying too narrow in their focus on this theme and distorting the play's ultimate message. The deepest conflict lies within the mature, devout fabric of an established religious community. The students must see the link to the larger and much more significant act of civil disobedience that John Proctor, Rebecca Nurse, and Giles Corey undertake, which is ultimately tragic. Like Hale, circumstances force them to examine their own souls deeply and eventually to defy the communal "proclaimed faith" to remain true to the deeper principle of right and wrong within themselves. They know they are not witches and, unlike Abigail, they will not lie to escape punishment and death. They are forced to become symbols of the most evil thing in their faith, the Devil; this is the severest test. Resorting to scapegoats made the people of Salem into the very Devil they claim to fear; out of panic, they create a monster that devours the goodness within themselves and their community. Rebecca foreshadows the demise of Salem in the middle of the first Act: ". . . then let us go to God for the cause of it. [. . .] Let us rather blame ourselves. . . ." (Miller 25)
>
> Clearly, without the context of the Red scare in the 1950s, the AIDS scare in the 1980s, or hate crimes around ethnic and/or racial minorities in the 1990s, students may fail to draw critical analogies to important philosophical and social issues. When "dangerous" individuals suggest that Americans can think about communism or associate with communists, yet still be solid citizens or suggest that homosexuals have as much right to acceptance and love around disease and death as "normal" people do, battle lines can be drawn quickly. Perhaps part of our Puritan heritage is that the concept of the "Devil" has remained close to the surface of many emotional, political debates. Helping students equate the hysteria around "communism" and the "the homosexual plague" with the idea of "witchcraft" in Salem will help them see the dynamics of fear and ignorance and the difficulty of remaining rational in the face of both.

ACTING AND DRAMATIC ACTIVITIES

Death of a Salesman

After using reader-response techniques to support more traditional styles of teaching for several years, I decided to focus entirely on reader response in teaching Arthur Miller's *Death of a Salesman* to a class of 10th- and 11th-grade students. I wanted my students to gain a deeper understanding of Willy Loman's tragic struggle within the context of societal pressures and gender roles in the United States in the 1950s. Reader response in the form of two rounds of writing, 3 full days of class discussion, and a final

original playwriting project would constitute the entire grade. My main objectives were:

1. To place student response at the center of the unit.
2. To give up traditional ways of controlling in a teacher-centered
   classroom and be ready to step into the role of guide, coach, and
   facilitator.
3. To be on the lookout for clues to new pathways into the play's deep-
   est meanings for me and to monitor my students' learning more
   actively.
4. To practice new ways to adjust my teaching, encouraging:
   - Active involvement of the entire class.
   - Student ownership of conclusions.
   - Teacher ownership of the broader contexts of life and tragedy in
     literature.

Clearly, I was ready for radical change in my classroom and for reader response to be the means to that end. What follows is a record of how student
learning evolved—both in process and product, as well as a journal of my
private thoughts on the surprises, shifts, and inspiring insights it brought
about in me—as well as the tension between letting go and clinging too
tightly to my own responses as expectations for the class.

Traditionally, when teaching *Death of a Salesman*, I emphasize the conflict
between Willy and Biff as central to the meaning. I teach that Willy Loman
struggles to embody the wealthy image of success he saw in Dave Singleman
and his brother Ben, which is effortless and charismatic. Time is running
out for Willy. He harbors a secret fear that he is a failure and becomes more
obsessed with his favorite son Biff, his only hope. Biff is a tortured soul, determined to be that "golden boy" for his father, yet secretly in possession of
the family secret—that Willy Loman is a liar and a cheat. When he angrily
confronts his father about his unsuccessful meeting with Bill Oliver, Biff
takes responsibility for his part in the "family" failure in an effort to reclaim
his own goodness. He pleads: "I'm not bringing home any prizes any more,
and you're going to stop waiting for me to bring them home. [. . .] Will you
take that phony dream and burn it before something happens?" (132–33).
Willy senses deep love from Biff here, and he is inspired to one final pipe
dream for his "best boy" Biff; he runs his car off the road for the $20,000
"pot of gold."

As I designed my handouts for this class, I knew I was ready to allow the
students to prospect for their own meanings in the play and that I wanted to
be innovative in capturing and underlining the important understandings
as they emerged. I designed one handout on the philosophy of reader response to communicate clearly to the students that they were "in the pilot
seat." The questions in Round 1 were very open-ended, the Round 2 ques-

tions involved a choice between two inventive writing exercises, and the final project was a creative playwriting scene.

Invitation 10.2

Several times the author alludes to a tension between what she emphasizes—wants the students to get—and her interest in promoting full student empowerment in developing responses. Identify several points in her discussion where this tension is expressed, directly and indirectly, and how she eventually resolves her role.

Creating more open-ended questions in Round 1, such as "What went wrong in this family?" "Who holds the power?" and "Whom do you most admire in the play and why?" challenged the students to take a more definite stance and come up with a theory of how they viewed the four main characters. During our first formal discussion, many students felt that Willy put too much pressure on his boys. Nick felt: "Willy's life is not turning out the way he wanted it to. His kids are not what he built them up in his mind to become. He wanted them to be rich and successful, surrounded by women, but they are low on money, single, and out of a job." At this stage in our discussions, the students lumped both Biff and Happy together. Kevin felt that Willy struggled with "the pressure of society to act and look a certain way. In order to fill this void, he pressures his son Biff to become what he himself could not. Willy tries to live his son's life for him, causing a lot of conflict." Students had their own individual opinions about the expectation that one should be better and more successful than one actually can be or is. Norah saw Willy turning Ben's success into a pressure on himself to be as good or better. Some students seemed to empathize with feeling this pressure; others were more judgmental about putting this pressure on children.

Two students particularly identified with the way Willy had "great expectations": They believed that their "baby boomer" parents were doing the same thing. As the kids of these parents, Michelle stated that young people in the 1990s are "finding that this is not what they want; they want to find out what makes them happy . . . what is right for *them*." Another student, Charlie, discussed how his own experience with his father was similar to Happy's in the sense of being invisible compared to an older sibling. Because he identified so strongly with Happy, he had struggled more with Willy than some of the other students and observed on the first day of discussion, "Willy gives his love as a privilege instead of just parental love." The choice of the word *privilege* conveyed an intuitive understanding of the competitive atmosphere that pervaded Willy's psyche and wounded both his boys. In Round 1, the reader-response tension was definitely around the pressure

put on the boys, and I could sense many of the students resisting Willy Loman because of this narcissistic, parental pressure. Most students agreed
that Biff held the power because Willy was so obsessed with his son's success.
Therefore, whatever Biff did, felt, or said rippled through the entire family,
and the students felt that this was unfortunate.

> During this first round of discussion about *Death of a Salesman*, I realized two
> things about myself as a teacher. When I repeated a conclusion so that the stu-
> dents would "get" how important it was, my teaching suddenly felt redundant.
> Second, I began to realize that I tended to stop and emphasize a point that was
> closest to my own reader response. Perhaps because that reaction felt more
> teacher-centered, it tended to kill the liveliness of the discussion. At this early
> stage of the learning, I had to become a better listener if I was going to be a bet-
> ter facilitator.

Students went on to discuss how much power Linda had. Some felt she
was a victim and needed to demand more respect. Others felt that she did
have power. Meghan thought Linda had "hidden power. If she wasn't there,
their lives wouldn't work; they wouldn't know what to do." Gabrielle felt
Linda was responsible for giving Willy reassurance: "She is kind of the rock.
They couldn't function without her." I suggested that she was the strong
woman behind the man, to which Kevin responded that "she really didn't
want the power" because she "hasn't had to have the responsibility. It's easier to hide behind him and let him make all the big decisions; she never
really has to take any real risks because she knows no one is ever going to
really listen to her. She is always talking, but she would not feel comfortable
with the attention and the focus and responsibility." His conclusions were
quite accurate and certainly a clear reflection of many women in the 1950s.

> I was instantly aware that I did not like Kevin's conclusion. I wanted to argue
> that Linda was a victim of her time and gender rather than a willingly passive
> dependent. Trying to remain "objective" and play the "teacher," I encouraged
> students to place a 1950s template around her, but I could sense that I was de-
> fending some negative judgment about her, perhaps in me. Kevin's view made
> me realize that Linda had settled for a kind of distorted, displaced power to
> have safety and be secure.

I noticed that the class was divided: Some saw her as noble and sacrificial;
Kevin saw her as a dependent person who took the easy way out. I became
aware that the variety of reader responses to Linda's character must come directly from how these students perceive their own mother and father in
their relationship and in the world.
The students saw Willy as human mostly because he was innocent about
where he had gone wrong and why he could get no respect. They saw the entire family wanting respect, but not being able to get it because they were trying to be "too special." Scott said, "Biff was popular in school, but he flunked

out. Looks and popularity aren't enough; they are a facade, and what looked like it would work wasn't really how it worked." Kevin's thinking was crystal clear when he clarified the cause: "Willy wants to see himself in a certain way so badly, he confuses it with what he really is."

> Suddenly, I realized how strongly my own reader response as the teacher could influence my interpretation of the play. When I was 20 and a drama student, Willy was the character that held my attention. Returning to the play in my 40s, I find Biff heroic because his father's values and his father's expectations have enslaved him and because he is also trying to fix his father's life for him. I've seen his ability to start telling the truth and to claim his own life and happiness as a real victory, one that counteracts the tragedy of Willy's fall and perhaps provides some hope. Making the distinction between how much of that response is true to the text and useful in teaching accurate understandings and how much is slightly biased by my own conflicts with my father around success and money became a fruitful place for my own parallel *learning* during this unit—which was quickly becoming more complex and engaging for me as a teacher as well as for my students. What inspired me were the originality of students' thinking at this early stage and how their views were challenging my own. What made me nervous was that they blamed Willy Loman rather than felt empathy for him and seemed detached from Willy and Biff. My concern was that they would not experience the tragic impact of the play.

In designing the second round of reader-response activities, I wanted to break out of traditional thinking even further: The first option involved a creative use of quotes to identify plot structure around a main theme; the second option was even more innovative. Because my instinct was to focus on the characters' psychological dysfunction in the play, I gave the students the opportunity to take the point of view of the therapist for one of the four main characters and to write up a case study. These responses were due on our second full day of discussion. All 14 students wrote on the second option, the therapeutic model. I then gave them a choice between discussing what they had written or doing a role play based on their insights as a therapist. They chose to do the role play. I put two chairs in the center of the circle, one for the therapist and one for the client, and had all the students pull their seats in close so they could hear and participate more fully. My theater director instincts told me this would involve each of them more fully, allow me to improvise and adapt to events as they evolved, and create a kind of secure cocoon so that the two "players" felt more supported and less "on the spot."

As we began the role playing, I expected to start with Willy and then perhaps move to Biff. The students surprised me by wanting to start with Linda and then move on to Happy. They were conveying their interest in these characters as an important clue to the pattern of thinking they wanted to pursue. Role playing Linda's visit to a therapist made the class experience how needy and worried she was, yet how strong her desire was to dispel some of Willy's delusions. They realized Linda was a caretaker. When one student stated that Linda would have a hard time actually telling a stranger these things, I switched the exercise to verbalizing her inner thoughts as she sat in the therapist's chair, and I had students around the circle whisper these inner thoughts out loud. I supplied a number of them in an attempt to role model. The class then decided that she would never really go to a therapist because it would be a betrayal. Thus, they realized that she was trapped by Willy's trouble and her own desire to appear happy and without conflict. Before we moved on to Happy, I reminded them that this pressure to appear "happy and successful" was central to the 1950s. Setting up and acting out role plays can give ample opportunity for little breaks between rounds when the teacher can interject important insights and connections at a time when the students are very ready to take them in and connect them to actions and understandings.

The role play with Happy was fairly short because Gabrielle, who was playing Happy, ran out of things to say when Amanda, the therapist, asked "him" to describe his relationship with his father. Gabrielle started feeling uncomfortable that she was doing a bad job. I suggested that perhaps her being stymied was coming right out of the play and was because Happy really didn't have much of a relationship with his father. In a new way, the students realized that because of Willy's great expectations, all roads led to Biff. This brought Gabrielle to a very important conclusion that seemed to resonate with several of the students:

> It's only a failure because they see it that way. If Biff is happy in what he's doing, then he's not a failure, because he's doing what he wants, what makes him happy. It doesn't matter if he doesn't make millions of dollars. It's all in one's perspective. A person whose life is based on that, it would drive anybody crazy.

Again, the class was rejecting Willy's way of operating and feeling the frustration of both sons; they identified with Happy because he was watching from the sidelines just as they were as readers. At this point, I suggested that if the family could have changed their expectations of happiness, it might have prevented their tragic defeat, but their society didn't help them, and Willy's childhood had locked him into defeat.

> It suddenly struck me that, on some level, I was of Biff's generation, sensing that once the parents set the expectations there was no way out: You either achieved it or were a failure. Students perceived the problem as simpler than the Loman family was making it, perhaps due to 40 years of social change, the self-help movement, and therapy models for helping families, or perhaps because they are adolescents. If that was the lens they were using, how was I to help them have empathy for Willy Loman? Somehow they were not experiencing how difficult it was for Biff to speak the truth. My negative reaction, however, was overshadowed by another aspect of using this method.

In setting up and coaching these role plays that day, I began to experience my classroom as a laboratory where I could set up the experiment, watch the results, monitor and adjust the conditions. The more intuitively I used the students feedback, the more effectively I could help them understand and articulate the pathways they were finding into the central meaning of the play. The metaphorical image I kept getting was one of the play sitting on a platform in a room with many doors. The students could actually show me more complicated understandings of the play than they could ever tell me. Once I set up the role-playing format, the students wanted to focus on Linda and Happy, the two characters who did not have a voice, yet were trying to cope with the secrets they knew. The students identified with the invisible, discounted characters who, they felt, needed a voice. They also discovered that Willy needed to change his opinion of success and of his own image if the conflict within him and the family was to change. I realized that the students were ready to find solutions themselves. Writing original scenes was the perfect next step.

When I first designed the playwriting project, I struggled to find the right balance between staying true to the play and yet giving the students artistic freedom. I decided that they could rewrite the events of the play to reach the same or different outcome, but I asked that the characters of Willy, Linda, Biff, and Happy stay consistent with the personality each had in the play. I could only hope that these parameters were going to move us in the right direction and help us go deeper into the play rather than distort and modernize it.

However, by the time we actually arrived at the original scenes, I was involved in a new challenge of my own. How could I enable the students to see that Willy, although not a great man, was a good and noble man in his way, that circumstances had conspired against him, causing him to fail at achieving the American dream. Some of my students will perhaps someday realize that they, too, cannot achieve their dreams as quickly and easily as they expect. How could I help them experience compassion for a midlife problem, an inability to change learned, childhood behavior quickly enough to turn life around, something many of them will not even realize until they are away from home, earning an income and trying to love and live with their own spouse and children? Life issues in literature are complex and paradoxical, not something easily distilled and understood in three or four discussions. Now that I was resisting merely giving them the "literary" conclusions about the play, what if they failed to discover and gain an understanding of these insights? In the past, objective and essay questions gave me proof of certain concrete learning. How responsible was I for learning that was more essential, more abstract, but less immediately measurable?

Although it took us an extra week to complete the unit because rehearsing and presenting the scenes took its own time, the results were worth it. Because the class was small, each student had to act in several scenes, playing various parts. This gave them an opportunity to get inside the play from a number of perspectives and to watch the scenes play out with many different combinations of the same students, which played a key role in solving my concerns about context and empathy. Each student writer's scene was unique, yet there were some clear similarities that, I later realized, reinforced for the students some critical understandings of the Loman family.

Most of the scenes were confessional, placing Happy, Linda, and/or Biff at the center, and almost every scene was an attempt to have the family tell the truth and release pent-up hurt and anger. It was clear that Happy needed attention, Biff needed to reveal the truth about the adultery to his mother, and Linda needed to defend herself and Willy. In most cases, Happy either killed himself, pleaded with Willy, "Why can't you love me?" or became even more determined to succeed for Willy: "I'll be better than him."

Four other student scenes attempted to explore confrontation that led to real change in the dynamics of the family. Interestingly, Kevin, the young man who had described Linda as dependent and afraid of risk in our first discussion, explored the possibility of total transformation in the relationship between Willy and Linda. He acted the part of Willy in a videotape in which a female student in the class who was a good actress played both Linda and "the woman." When Linda discovered Willy with the woman in the hotel room, she went from shock to shame to grief to anger and finally stood up for herself: If the Lomans were to remain a family, she said, Willy must change. When Willy was kneeling, feeding Linda grapes in the final frame, the class's laughter revealed how surprising and "out of character" that much change would have been for a Willy and Linda of the 1950s—effectively contrasting then and now. Kevin had intuitively explored the seeds and evolution of the women's movement in showing how Linda moved from being a victim to taking power in her life.

Charlie, the student who had defined Willy's love as a privilege to be won rather than an unconditional gift, created a therapeutic outcome. His scene portrayed quite effectively the need to confront Willy about his faults and to gestalt the anger and pain between Biff and Willy around the lies and what Biff recognized as a double standard. In Charlie's scene, Biff had a very heated exchange with his father when he walked in on Willy with "the woman": "Why shouldn't I yell at a tramp like that? You yell at Mom." Biff's courageous boldness was touching because he was so frightened and awkward: "You can yell at someone that you should love and never cheat on, but you can't yell at someone that you sleep with." How, he was asking his father, could he say that Linda was so important, when he acted kinder and more protective of this "bad woman?" Linda's pain was also powerfully revealed when what she had known all along was finally brought out in the open. Charlie had her turn to Willy and plead, "It hurts, Willy, it really hurts." Willy was clearly the focus of the problem, and this student was compelled to explore deeper layers of emotional revelation.

Two other students created a confrontation between Willy and Biff that ended in reconciliation. One imaginative scene evolved into a 10-page film script in which after Linda's death 20 years later, Willy's ghost returned to haunt Biff in his happy ranch life out West. At first, Biff denied the ghost's presence, but when he was ready to listen, Willy sincerely apologized and showed a deeper knowledge and understanding of his mistakes. When Biff demanded to know why Willy had to kill himself, Willy answered:

> I was crazy! (He laughs) Trippin' on power that wasn't there. I remember that speech you made to me. I'm so proud of you about that. That was amazing! I could never've done anything like that. . . . Have I paid my dues now, Biff? Ah, Come 'ere." (They hug.)

This fully developed script came from the student Nick, who confessed on the final day of evaluations, "I can't express what I'm thinking about on a book or anything on paper so that's why I'm failing English in my other classes. I need to talk it out. I can verbally express things better than writing it. It helped to write the scene—I could do it that way." How exciting to see a student discover his own route to learning and become motivated.

As the students wrote the scenes, they discovered that even when the truth came out, it didn't necessarily solve the problem because members of the family were each trapped by their own personality. By wrestling with the conflicts, the students experienced two important aspects of the meaning of *Death of a Salesman:* These Lomans were doing a very painful dance around each other to protect a man who could not let go of a destructive dream, and they had to remain frozen in their roles to maintain the secrets. The students understood the root cause and dynamics of this dance because they saw it played out over and over again with similar results. Writing and acting in these scenes made the students directly experience the urgency and depth of each character's emotional involvement. Even "getting it out" in the 1990s mode did not provide transformation because Willy and Linda were not capable of change. As Norah said in the final evaluation session, "The play accumulated in meaning as we rehearsed, performed, and watched these scenes. I had much more feeling for Willy; he was no longer just a crazy old man." By bringing the subtext of the play—the family's unspoken frustrations and feelings—to the surface, the whole class entered into the family and felt genuine empathy.

Invitation 10.3

In writing these scenes, these readers are expressing a response to this play; in enacting them, they are extending this response interpretation. Their audience, then, is responding to these two interpretations in conjunction with their own initial responses. Prepare a journal writing in which you consider the potential response impact of these several layers of interpretation.

One of my fears had been that students would not experience Willy as a tragic hero because they would not feel what Aristotle defined as the appropriate "pity and fear" that could lead to a "catharsis." Surprisingly, working on the scenes took these students much more inside the play than merely reading it or seeing the Dustin Hoffman dramatization did. First through Happy, then through Linda and Biff, and finally through Willy, they had come full circle to discover the empathy that is critical for a tragic experience in the theater.

The final discussion and evaluation day was both exciting and stimulating. As the students eagerly circled their chairs, they demonstrated much more command and confidence around the work and were fully engaged and listening to each other and to me. I found myself becoming a recorder and a facilitator as they exchanged insights about what worked and what they thought must be kept in the unit. Here are the highlights:

1. Writing dramatic scenes, rehearsing, and watching other people's scenes helped the students both discover and express their understandings much more effectively. Norah said: "I figured out Linda better. She wanted to keep the image going. She's almost defending herself—keeping a shell. So she doesn't have to feel bad." Ellen added, "The pain didn't seem as big until we acted out the scenes."

2. Michelle was emphatic about the fact that this way of working "focused more on characters than the plot like we usually do. I liked it better." Both Kelly and Michelle agreed that by focusing on the "invisible" Happy, they understood the whole family situation better. Kelly said that watching the scenes helped her see the same thing in Willy and Ben as in Happy and Biff. When I asked her why her scene presented Linda as having an affair first, she spoke of her frustration in wanting Linda to have more power and fulfill her own desires. Time did not permit me to address an important issue that can come up using reading response. Rosenblatt would say that Kelly had had a *valued* response, but not a *valid* response to the text (Karolides 27). My quick response to her misinterpretation was that "Arthur Miller's Linda could never have had an affair because she loved Willy too much; she was more loyal and ethical than Willy was."

3. Gabrielle thought that the in-class role playing between Happy or Linda and a therapist really helped her figure out how psychological this play was and how she could begin to understand what went wrong in this family that could never be made right. She, Norah, and Amanda were adamant that it was an essential transition step to the final scene-writing project.

4. Although Kevin stated that the first round of reader-response questions, and not the role playing, was the most helpful to him, it was intriguing that given the opportunity to dramatize the most trapped character in the

play, he was able to explore quite layered, complex character motivations and dramatic styles that he could only touch on in his written reader responses. Also, in some ways the absurdity of Linda's transformation helped students realize the time warp between the 1950s and the 1990s.

5. Students unanimously agreed that having all the scenes videotaped heightened their sense of involvement and excitement, and that viewing them was an important part of discovering character and conflict.

Looking back at my objectives, I saw that by letting go of control, following my instincts, and being totally dedicated to guiding and monitoring reader response, I achieved all of my objectives. Placing reader response at the center of my teaching gave both my students and me a much more enlivening, challenging, and ultimately rewarding classroom experience. By moving out of the center of the process and placing more responsibility in the hands of my students, I became free to practice more fully the skills I do best as a teacher: listen, respond, guide, rethink, evaluate, redesign, give feedback, and summarize. Although I missed some opportunities for "teaching," I made spontaneous decisions that were more intuitive and innovative.

I discovered that my best instincts for exploring this play came directly out of my own reader response: the general question, "What went wrong in this family?", the therapy case study, the role-play guidance, and the idea that the script writing would be effective if the character traits remained consistent and the plot could change. These insights helped the students experience the tragic dimensions of Willy Loman more effectively. A more polished student performance of two or three of these scenes would give them an opportunity to memorize lines, get costumes and props, and rehearse for blocking. Videotapes of these performances would be valuable to show the next year's class and selections could become part of an ongoing resource for other teachers and students. Ideally, this unit would involve a performance of *Death of a Salesman* by a local theater ensemble or a touring company as a final enrichment activity.

A student-centered, reader-response classroom is much more fluid and varied for the teacher and ultimately more improvisatory. One case in point: The day the class began rehearsing the scenes, I brought in my own original scene between Willy and Ben, in which I emphasized the parallel to Happy and Biff that I was afraid they were missing. When I sensed the students' immediate involvement with that day's work, I held back. Sitting in on the first scene being rehearsed, I found that one student had incorporated a very similar flashback to the one I had written, and in fact, a second scene also dealt with the issue well. Identifying with Happy's invisibility and failure, they had reasoned by analogy from Happy and Biff to Willy and Ben. Identifying with Biff's visibility and pressured "win role," I had reasoned from

Biff and Happy to Ben and Willy. All routes ended at the same tragic place: enforced, false roles and lack of genuine love and intimacy.

Although my own reader response as the teacher is an excellent tool, I risk clinging too tightly to the exact pattern of my responses rather than holding a more universal, deep meaning of the play at the center of my focus and letting each teaching experience evolve. In the past, I had taught the play in terms of the fall of a modern tragic Everyman—Willy Loman. Because I had grown up in the 1950s, the daughter of a salesman who had grand expectations for the child most like him, the conflict and secret shame between Willy and Biff was a powerful doorway for me. My students went through the doorway of other characters and other struggles to discover the meaning of dreams and self-destruction for Willy and his entire family: Human beings tend to dream big in America and although such dreams fuel our lives, they are just as capable of destroying us. They are not attainable for everyone. As a teacher, I discovered again how empowering it is to allow students to trace the pattern of their own conclusions because a classic American play will not fail them or me. A wild, and sometimes chaotic, interaction of ideas between students and students, and students and teachers is the kind of intellectual training that deepens our respect for each other and enhances the learning experience.

REFERENCES

Karolides, Nicholas J. *Reader Response in the Classroom: Evoking and Interpreting Meaning in Literature.* Mahwah, NJ: Lawrence Erlbaum Associates, 1992.
Miller, Arthur. *The Crucible.* New York: The Viking Press, 1959.
———. *Death of a Salesman.* New York: The Viking Press, 1958.
Rosenblatt, Louise M. *Literature as Exploration.* 4th ed. New York: MLA, 1983.

11

Hill Climbing With Thoreau
Creating Meaningful Carryover

Mary Jo Schaars

PERIOD 7

Studying Walden—a weaving back and forth from preteaching, personalizing, associating, intellectualizing (the nitty gritty). I like a class period shaped like a hill—a gentle hill is best. The student's job is to move over it in the course of 50 minutes. A relaxed beginning—some chatter, role taking. "Attention, please," my signal to get ready: first step up the gentle slope and walking easy, still fresh.

We had been talking about Thoreau's idea that we complicate our lives with material things. On the news this morning I had heard that 79% of the affluent Americans interviewed "could not get along without" their microwaves; 49%, their VCRs; and 42%, their home computers.

Making Thoreau meaningful begins here. Rosenblatt remarks that "understanding of even one word demands a framework of ideas about man, nature, and society" (113). I believe my students have such a framework that I can tap. And then Rosenblatt suggests that nothing has much value unless the student "feels the need of it" (123). As a teacher, I am in tune to that.

"What do you suppose most rich people said they couldn't get along without?" I ask.

Responses include "a big house, fancy car, limo, butler, maid"—maybe 15 or more items are offered before the students guess "microwave." Then a bit of surprise. "We don't even have a microwave."

"How many don't have microwaves?" I ask. Only two raise their hands.

"And I'm darn proud of it," Sarah states. (Wouldn't Thoreau be pleased, I gloat.)

Yesterday we had figured out what kind of crop Thoreau wanted from the Hollowell farm, and why he went to Walden in the first place. Today we talk about morning, shams and delusions, the railroad "that rides on us," and grapple with "Time is but a stream I go a-fishing in." We center on the text now and talk about what Thoreau means in 130-plus-word sentences—the difference between morning as A.M. and morning as an attitude. We round off the top of the hill.

We each hunker down with the text. For a while all is quiet, everyone concentrating, working to meet the challenge Thoreau and I set for us. Five minutes are left. Now, the hilltop is behind us and the coast down gentle— not a thrill, just a sorting out.

"He's packed too much in the last paragraph. I can't get it." Greg slides the text away.

I smile with empathy. "I don't quite know either," I confess.

I know Greg won't go back to look now. We're done with the top of the hill for this period. Tomorrow we'll talk it over. About half the class asks for handouts on this excerpt from *Walden* to take home. Bus announcements burst forth from the PA, the bell rings, and my students go forth. I look at the empty room and take a moment to muse. I wonder if anyone will think about anything that has to do with today's discussion of Thoreau between this moment and tomorrow at class time. I'll have to ask.

A question has been recurring to me lately: How do we measure what the student goes away with? Rosenblatt comments that "the individual needs to build for himself a mental and emotional base from which to meet the fluctuating currents about him" (170). Surely, studying what Thoreau has to say should help; but of course, it won't unless there is some carryover. I decide to try a simple approach.

The following day, Period 7, we begin to climb the hill. "Attention, class." (pause) "Did any of you spend even 1 minute since class yesterday thinking about what we talked about?" I wince, expecting someone to say, "What did we do yesterday?"

Instead . . .

"I was looking around in the Sentry Theater last night—soft seats and everything. I mean, do we really need all that?" (Jeannine)

"I was just walking to my locker last period thinking about materialism. . . ." (Sarah)

"I work at Piggly Wiggly, and I always have to ask 'paper or plastic.' I hate that. Sometimes I just use paper. Last night I bagged (groceries) for someone who not only wanted plastic but bought only junk food besides." (Matt)

"I got up without an alarm clock. It was still dark . . . and I took time to eat a big breakfast." (Steve)

"My family and I talked about all the conveniences we have last night at the dinner table." (Vicki)

"Time is but the stream I go a-fishing in" (Thoreau, "Where" 193). The human intellect—we do what we can to tap the capacity of our minds.

THE PLAN: SETTING UP CAMP

In reality, the teacher is just a "fellow seeker of truth and knowledge" (Macrorie 50). How natural this is when students willingly find commitment. We begin by developing mutual trust—a satisfying balance. Students trust me to provide the text. (My responsibility is assumed and natural. They know I would not bring to them something meaningless.) I trust them to read, think and talk—together and with me.

We look at the text, associate, and personalize until the threads get properly woven into a pattern of understanding; and that understanding needs to deepen, hold, and create something new for each individual. The teacher's job is a coming around again, making sure there is pattern or design that will carry over. Thoreau says, "When any real progress is made, we unlearn and learn what we thought we knew before" (quoted in Macrorie, 188). And we can only let go and build anew if we have confidence. Camaraderie helps.

Teaching from *Walden* without personal, intellectual, and social connections? Impossible. Imagine an objective test: How much did Thoreau pay for his cabin in the woods? What years did he live there? How old was he? Thoreau did/did not purchase the Hollowell farm. Fill in the blank: "We do not ride on the _____, it rides upon us." All kinds of facts like these lie on the surface—that's automatic. Creating meaningful carryover must lie elsewhere, perhaps in the discovered ideas we drive into a corner (as Thoreau suggests life must be) and examine for "meanness" or prove "sublime."

Invitation 11.1

Consider this author's statement: "Teaching from *Walden* without personal, intellectual, and social connections? Impossible." In a journal writing, amplify its essential meaning to clarify how these factors influence the teaching and learning of nonfiction.

Where does the intellectual path of Thoreau intersect mine or theirs? That's what we seek every hill-climbing day. By juxtaposing scenes from our past, our perception of the text's words, and listening and understanding from others' experiences, we climb to larger, more pervasive meanings.

Carryover. We create carryover with journaling, grappling with our own ideas, and then comparing them with Thoreau's. We take a nature walk,

meet Henry in central Wisconsin at the age of 17, and then we leave him
when we've acquired what we can understand here and now—knowing we
will meet him again in school, while reading a newspaper, while attempting
to give meaning to living somewhere, sometime when it is important to stop
and consider.

CONSIDERING THE OBSTACLES

Creating carryover is, in fact, the major job of the teacher. First, students
need a focus, something personally and intellectually meaningful on their
level. The responsibility of the teacher is not to make sure the students
understand *Walden,* but to be sure that they can relate to it, incorporate
whatever of Thoreau's ideas they are ready for, recognize a bit of the essence
of Thoreau when they rub up against a future quote, reference, or event.
Ideally, the careful juggling of the teacher will enable each student to become confidently curious rather than turned off and frustrated. The teacher's objective must be to increase the odds that a student meeting Thoreau
again might try again, "climb" again. That is the ultimate carryover.

Look at this sentence from *Walden:*

> Let us settle ourselves, and work and wedge our feet downward through the
> mud and slush of opinion, and prejudice, and tradition and delusion, and ap-
> pearance, that alluvion which covers the globe, through Paris and London,
> through New York and Boston and Concord, through Church and State,
> through poetry and philosophy and religion, till we come to a hard bottom
> and rocks in place, which we can call *reality,* and say, This is, and no mistake;
> and then begin, having a *point d'appui,* below freshet and frost and fire, a place
> where you might found a wall or a state, or set a lamppost safely, or perhaps a
> gauge, not a Nilometer, but a Realometer, that future ages might know how
> deep a freshet of shams and appearances had gathered from time to time.
> (Thoreau, "Where" 193)

Unless one is a masochist, struggling to decipher the meaning by oneself,
age 17 in the United States, today, would certainly make Thoreau's "Real-
ometer" a Deadometer.

FITTING OUT

Thus, a couple of class periods hill climbing with Thoreau really starts on
the level—learning some connections. In my class, students never catch a
glimpse of *Walden* before they find out how they feel about materialism,
moral commitment, goals, lifestyle, and so forth. Each student fills out a
questionnaire and then we talk about the answers:

1. If you didn't have to worry about making a lot of money what occupation would you choose? Why?
2. What do you like best about autumn (spring)?
3. Are clothes and your appearance important to you?
4. What do you consider your highest achievement so far?
5. What do you consider your greatest failure?
6. Do you ever just take a walk with no destination in mind?
7. When, during a routine day, do you find yourself happiest? Most bored?
8. Do you believe you have too many, just enough, too few conveniences in your life? Explain, if necessary.
9. Would you go to jail rather than conform to a law that went against your conscience? Explain, if necessary.
10. Check one: (Explain, if necessary.)
   a. Money can buy most things I want in life.
   b. Money can buy few things I want in life.
11. Do you express your opinions even when they aren't popular? Explain.
12. Circle "A" if you agree with the statement and "D" if you disagree. Explain your answers if you feel it's necessary.

   A   D   Every person is basically good.
   A   D   I try to depend on myself and be independent.
   A   D   I want to simplify my life.
   A   D   It is possible to have a life filled with both material things and spiritual ideas.

Next we talk about transcendentalism, briefly exploring some terms: self-reliance, divine spark, intuition, reason, and others. Then we get away from the teacher centered. If the weather cooperates, we take a class period to get "A Breath of Nature"—tone up the senses. Students take a brief walk paying close attention to the smells inside and outside the building; they examine closely a small plot of ground and then a larger landscape. All their responses are written as journal entries. The following are excerpts that show a variety of honest observations:

My patch of earth is beautiful. Within, it contains three sun stripes, where a tree holds back the nurturing rays. There are two yellow flowers, each with a group of tooth edged weeds around them. One is glowing as the light shines on it. The other is shaded behind the tree. . . .

Cars go by and I hear the rumble of their engines, the sound of their jolts as they hit a bump. I suddenly hear a sharp, sawing sound, then a radio playing in the distance. I hear my classmates quietly talking as a handyman stands on a ladder and hammers on a roof panel of some sort. The trees are all different colors now. . . . They are starting to look lonely and bleak—getting ready for the white fluffs to submerge them. (Steph)

A Patch of Ground Develops a Philosophical Parallel

Sunlight makes brown grass seem almost golden. . . . Sun, like divine spark, when covered by society's shams and delusions (clouds), we (grass) become dull and lifeless. (Jennifer)

Here, the Thinking Clusters and Branches. Thoreau Would Like That

One foot of ground—. . . . The grass, once green is now dry, tan and matted together. A large green dandelion plant flattened and tinted red intertwines with the wild grass. One large yellow leaf, long fallen from a summer home, is slowly finding its way to the underground sleep of winter. . . .

A second glance takes me out of my fall-clouded head. Many green mountains exist on the backdrop of a faraway cloud, arching down out of sight. Black silhouettes also lay against the sky . . . so still . . . they seem totally unreal when I look down . . . at the street where the cars scurry by. Where to? Even stiller yet are the buildings who never say a word, not a whisper. The only sound beyond the wind on my ears is a roar of a machine; where it comes from I can't place it—it is all around me. (Lorelei)

Around school real nature is foiled by man, but that's *truth;* Thoreau would have to deal with that if he were writing today. The sounds of trucks and cars and ventilator fans and the smell of grease wafting toward us from the burger joints a quarter of a mile away make us realize how tenacious nature must be to survive man's environment. Thus Thoreau's lessons are updated and realized.

PSYCHING UP

Then, taking a step "closer" to *Walden,* we read two essays: "Death of a Pine" by Thoreau and "Seeing" by Annie Dillard. The resulting journal entries center on the literary for "Death of a Pine" and on the personal for "Seeing." In "Death of a Pine," Thoreau laments the destruction of "a noble pine," a fallen "warrior," by two men with a saw and an axe. who are described as "beavers or insects gnawing." I ask students to identify similes and metaphors and then to indicate what ideas they come away with. Most students grasp Thoreau's inferences:

Thoreau is presenting the idea that although the tree is a home for the fish hawk and hen hawk and the squirrel, nobody in town considers the tree coming down a disaster even though if two houses were ruined it would be. He also wants to point out to us that once the squirrel and hawks are accustomed to the new tree the woodcutters will ruin that house, too. One final thought: I think Thoreau is trying to present that other living things have to suffer so we can have luxuries. The lumber will be used to make luxurious, expensive (things) that aren't a necessity in life. (Jenny)

In "Seeing" Annie Dillard recounts a childhood experience where she would hide a penny on a stretch of sidewalk, then make arrows and labels, "Surprise ahead" (47), for bypassers. She hopes that finding a penny will literally "make someone's day." She goes on to compare pennies to "a healthy poverty and simplicity" and to events, easily missed in nature, like sighting a fish, a deer, or a flock of red-winged blackbirds.

After reading, students write about pennies either found or overlooked in their own lives. The excerpts reveal that students are capable of personalizing in ways that will help them to understand when they come to read *Walden*. Shelley and Trina had no concept of Thoreau's "fabulous realities" when they wrote these:

> Finding pennies in my life would be something simple like when I was taking pictures for photography. I was photographing my aunt's geese and one of the geese reached over and started smoothing another one's feathers. Almost like they were helping each other get ready for the photograph. Another one would be when I was at work I would take the food out to the table and they say, "Gosh, that was fast!" It makes you feel appreciated. . . .
>
> One of my favorite "pennies" would be when one night I was getting ready to go out and I was doing my hair, and in the mirror I saw my little sister trying to copy what I was doing.
>
> My "pennies" are just something that kind of makes you want to smile! (Shelley)

> I remember once when I was walking around in the woods, across from the creek behind my grandfather's house, I found two sheets of scrap iron. I was only about six, but every year I'd go back there to visit the scrap iron. I'd sit on the iron, because the two sheets were huge, and wonder how long they'd been there and who put them there.
>
> Anyway, about two summers ago when I was visiting my grandfather, I heard him and my dad talking about two pieces of scrap iron. My grandpa said he didn't know where he put them, but he knew he'd left two pieces of scrap iron out in the woods about 25 years ago. There was the answer to my questions. . . . But since they didn't know I'd over heard their conversation—I just went on my merry way. Those two pieces of metal are my place to go when I'm visiting my grandparents; no one else knows where they are. Those two pieces of rusted iron buried under leaves and pine needles have been mine since I was six and I wasn't about to tell them where they were. (Trina)

THE CLIMB

And *Walden* is next. We read an excerpt, "Where I Lived, and What I Lived For." Here I ask students to look at six topics: the Hollowell farm (described in the beginning), why Thoreau went to the woods to live, why he considers morning the best time of day, his objections to the ways people live, what he means by "shams and delusions are esteemed for soundest truths, while reality is fabulous," and what point we can make from the last paragraph, "Time is but the stream I go a-fishing in. . . . My head is hands and feet (to) burrow my way through these hills."

Often we read a good part of this essay out loud and talk about it as we go. I see no sense assigning this as homework. While we read together we can associate and personalize; students can announce they are bewildered and get immediate relief. My purpose is to climb gentle hills, not make mountains.

How do my students respond? They seldom respond the same way; each class reflects its own individuality—particularly because Thoreau elicits such personal reactions. Take, for example, our challenge to understand what Thoreau is talking about as he describes his experience of attempting to buy the Hollowell farm, then feeling a sense of relief when the deal falls through. It seems he reaped his rewards simply by wandering about and observing the farm, talking and thinking about it: "I found thus that I had been a rich man without any damage to my poverty" (186). Then he advises that we should "live free and uncommitted. It makes but little difference whether you are committed to a farm or the county jail" (186).

For discussion I set up the classroom beforehand by placing all the tables and chairs in a large circle so that everyone is face to face. I am part of the circle on a level with the students. The discussion goal is for the students to grasp whatever it is they are ready and able to understand from the passage. Such a general approach, at first glance, may seem an easy out for the teacher who need not "prepare" ahead of time. However it does, in fact, require much discipline (and occasionally a bit of anxiety) on my part. First, I must not allow myself too many expectations, for then I will tend to dominate and lead the talk. Second, I must realize that having no "script" will make the discussion roundabout rather than focused and direct. Therefore, I need to exercise patience and restraint. Third, I know something about my students that enters in: Many have found safety in not responding and have become, instead, passive observers; in many cases their "tuneout" encompasses not only failure to enter class discussions, but failure to "think" as well. It is only when I ask the class, "Where should we begin?" and all is silent for a few moments that students realize: "She means it. We're going to sit here until somebody says something!" At that point the more conscientious will relook at the text and someone will inevitably bring up an idea or ask a question. As much as possible I promote students talking to students. One recent group response went like this:

> KARL: It's funny. Thoreau got what he wanted by *not* buying the farm. That way he didn't have any commitment, and that's the way he wanted to live.
> CHUCK: Well, people always have dreams though, and goals.

SEAN: Yeah, but sometimes the dreams are better than the goals.

CHUCK: Maybe people ought to have a series of goals. When they reach one, then they can reach for another, and after that another.

SEAN: Man is never satisfied.

LYNN: What do you think Thoreau means when he says, "As long as possible live free and uncommitted. It makes but little difference whether you are committed to a farm or the county jail" (186)?

KARL: That's what I said. Any kind of commitment was bad to him. I mean he wasn't married, he didn't want anything.

JENNIFER: Just think, he wouldn't have family get-togethers and birthday parties for young children. . . .

AMY: . . . or girlfriends.

NATE: No job.

SEAN: But he *was* committed to nature.

KARL: He said, "As long as possible. . . ." And anyway, I don't think being committed to nature is the same as what he's talking about.

JENNIFER: I think commitment to other people is important. Like husbands and wives.

KARL: Oh, I don't! Look at all the divorces taking place today.

JENNIFER: But that doesn't mean it's not important.

KARL: Well our commitments sure aren't *forever* like it says in the marriage ceremony! I think people are much more committed to their children than to their husbands and wives.

JENNIFER: Yes, you can't just leave your kids. . . .

KARL: Sometimes in a bad divorce the parents use the kids to get back at each other in custody fights.

JENNIFER: Sure, you can always turn commitment into something bad, I suppose.

SEAN: Maybe you've got to just enjoy the trip—not set any goals.

JAMIE: Well, I think he's just a wierdo. He'd probably be a nerd. . . .

LORI: No. He'd probably commit suicide if he came back today and saw all the destruction of nature and the pollution and stuff.

JENNIFER: I still think you have to consider friends and the family. That's what my "Hollowell farm" would be.

CHUCK: I guess right now I'm committed to getting good grades and I want a good job in the future.

LYNN: What does he mean about Atlas?

SEAN: Oh, He (Atlas) did a lot of work and didn't get any pay. I guess maybe he liked what he was doing. Evidently Thoreau did too.

LYNN: This is pretty hard. How long ago did you say he lived?

In a similar discussion in another class, one student attempted to describe the place she envisioned where she would eventually live. Her description of a pristine, country manor moved us far away from "dilapidated fences" and "lichen-covered apple trees" (185). However, her sincerity sparked interest until nearly all the students had proposed their dream house. During a very animated exchange, students grappled with ideas on simplicity rather than grandeur, dreams, or reality. Although they were much more concerned with materialism than Thoreau would have wished, they were united in seeking a place to live that "fit" them individually, in which they could be relaxed and at peace; they had garnered something important to take away with them. As Rosenblatt explains:

> The teacher realistically concerned with helping his [her] students to develop a vital sense of literature cannot, then, keep his [her] eyes focused only on the literary materials he [she] is seeking to make available. He [she] must also understand the personalities who are to experience this literature. He [she] must be ready to face the fact that the student's reactions will inevitably be in terms of his [her] own temperament and background. . . . No matter how imperfect or mistaken, this will constitute the present meaning of the work for him [her], rather than anything he [she] docilely repeats about it. . . . The nature of the student's rudimentary response is, perforce, part of our teaching materials. (51)

Most student jot down notes to answer discussion questions. We read and talk for 2 days. Then, it seems as though we have absorbed what we can, and it is time to move on. When Thoreau left Walden Pond he recounts, "It seems to me that I had several more lives to live and could not spare any more time for that one" (184). So, too, when one is climbing through over 300 years of American literature in one semester (90 hours).

Invitation 11.2

Scan and review these students' responses to *Walden*. Try to separate the aesthetic from the efferent responses. Then, evaluate the author's questions as catalysts for such responses. Consider, also, how the students factor into this response equation.

THE DESCENT

We do, however, take a little time and thought about leaving before we pack up and go. Carryover continues when students are asked to reread that questionnaire they filled out before they knew Walden was anything but a bookstore in the mall. Now, after 2 days intellectualizing and developing analogies to grasp concepts, we take some time to turn inward with our new ideas. The task to compare ourselves with Thoreau on three or four topics to discover to what extent we agree or disagree.

On the initial questionnaire, students have expressed how they feel about making money, about the importance of clothes and appearance, their achievements and failures, about being self-reliant and speaking out, and about being in nature. Now, when I ask students to return to themselves, they choose a diversity of topics to consider, although most center on appearance, the simple versus complex life, and being in nature. There are as wide a variety of approaches to these topics as there are personalities, but in each case the individual associations with Thoreau's ideas can be seen — each student's fund of knowledge about the philosophy we have just been pursuing.

The Simple Versus Complex Life

I want to somewhat simplify my life, but not too much. It (would) become too dull and repetitious. . . . I also think that if you go and live all alone you limit the amount you can learn. Yes, more about yourself—the type of person you are, and also about the beauty of nature. But I think you learn from everyone. No matter if it's good or bad. There's always more to learn and the best way is through people. When you're alone, you think in one perspective and never get anyone else's opinions, just yours. (Steph)

   Too many conveniences in life—Thoreau and I think alike on this subject. Perhaps he is more against material items than I, but human beings are spoiled. We share that thought. He puts his frustration toward material items into his writings, while I have not found an outlet for these feelings. Perhaps I will choose a similar situation such as the Peace Corps or some other humanity organization. (Sarah)

   Just enough conveniences. Thoreau would strongly disagree with me on this point. Compared to him, I live a life of absolute ease. My family has a microwave, vcr, a large house, and an alarm clock that listens. Thoreau would tell me that these "conveniences" are poisoning my soul. They are keeping me away from inner peace and happiness. They take up too much of my time and become distractions. They make my life simply too complex. Ultimately, I should give up these tools of Satan and gain a life of simplicity in the wilderness. (John)

On Nature

Walking is very important to me; it matters not where or when, only why. And why is to clear my head and just think good or challenging thoughts. Destination only clutters things up, and when one gets to a certain place and it feels right, you'll turn around and go home. It's funny when your mind is free the things you can pick up on. Transcendentalism again. Thoreau would agree. . . . Freedom of the mind is very important; until one exposes oneself to it, you don't really know what you're missing. . . . I could make a pretty good transcendentalist; maybe it's just my nature, maybe it's my Mom. (Rob)

On Clothes and Appearance

I guess most teenage girls are pretty fashion conscious. I mean I'd be lying if I said I wasn't. You would have to be a pretty big person to dress in an orange polka-dot shirt and plaid bell-bottoms because you wanted to. Thoreau would

say clothes don't matter and everyone could go bucknaked for all he cared. . . .
If you've got the money and you want to look good, who cares what Thoreau
thinks. You can still be an intellectual and wear Esprit. Clothing is often a way
of expressing yourself. (Gretchen)

Our last experience with Thoreau tends toward the personal, too, although the results are published for the class. As "teacher" my duty is to
administer a test, and I choose to follow the established design, even though
evaluation is very subjective. As a result, grades, based on creativity and logical and complete support, tend to be As and Bs—deservedly, I think. The
test is an essay question, the idea originating in *Clearing the Way* by Tom Romano (156–57).

> Through the miracle of modern technology, Young Henry David Thoreau
> (same character, personality, and principles) has been transported to the pres-
> ent. He is 17 years old and living in Central Wisconsin. In an essay *describe six
> things he possesses* that reflect his personality, character, and concerns. Explain
> what each possession reveals about him. (Be sure to show an understanding of
> the man and his philosophy from our talking and reading.)

Students may use any notes or sources they wish as they write the answer
during one class period. Following is a representative sample of selected
possessions along with two excerpts of student answers. (As you can see,
some of these are almost impossible to defend. The numbers refer to the fre-
quency of selection of these items.)

Thoreau's Possessions

5 fishing gear/line and hook	antibiotics
5 sets of (3) chairs	a criminal record
8 hiking boots	1973 Pinto
16 notebook, journal, or diary	generic food
2 watch/alarm clock	2 Walkman/stereo
2 magnifying glass	gas mask
10 bike	Polaroid
9 binoculars	backpack
5 camera/telephoto lens	dog
Walden & Civil Disobedience	bland wardrobe (assorted items)
6 selection of books	2 snow shoes
2 walking shoes/tennis shoes	4 computer/typewriter
5 pencils and pens	1 cassette/tape recorder
3 canoe	2 camcorder/videocamera
3 pen and paper	bird feeder
match	hang glider
2 axe/Swiss army knife	wool blanket
bracelet of worn leather	2 sketchbook & pencil
tent/one-room shack	his own inventions

Essay Excerpts on Thoreau

And last, Thoreau would possess a boat. He could see more on a large scale in a boat. He could paddle out to the middle of a pond, lay on his back and see the birds, clouds. From the boat he could view the shores and see the trees and land animals come to drink. Since Thoreau likes the idea of the circle, I think he would really enjoy this because everything would revolve around the water. Its underground springs reach the tree's root and animals drink out of it. (Kim)

Thoreau would probably have a journal or diary to write down his daily events . . . what his inspirations were or what things were important. . . . It would tell people in the future (whoever found it) what Thoreau was thinking and what kind of person he was. It would let us know that he believed nature was a soul-searching place. "Now" should be what we're thinking of. Life should be simple and easy. We shouldn't get messed up in the hassles of bargain hunting or coupon clipping because money isn't everything. Thoreau would own a diary to write down his feelings about the hussle and bussle of today's society. (Jennifer)

Invitation 11.3

Select a short piece of nonfiction, one that potentially holds interest and value for secondary school students. It may be perceived as relating to a literary text or may have application to a composing exercise. Having identified your intended audience and purpose, plan your introduction of this piece, cognizant of the need to engage your students' attention and responses.

RECOLLECTIONS

Finally, after returning graded tests, we talk and question and hypothesize on what "things" students have selected (each student receives the list), then file the papers in notebooks and prepare for *The Crucible, The Scarlet Letter,* for *A Separate Peace* and *Go Tell It On a Mountain,* where that "spark of goodness" and life's values must be questioned time and again. Carryover can't end with a test on Friday.

One final question remains, the idea I grappled with in the beginning. What about the ultimate: literature's lifelong carryover? Rosenblatt writes, "The criterion for judging the success of any educational process must be its effect on the actual life of the student; its ultimate value depends on its assimilation into the very marrow of personality" (182). From my classroom hill climbing to Rosenblatt's pristine summit seems an immeasurable distance. Only a leap of faith allows me to think I might possibly influence my students to such a degree. It is best, I tell myself, to approach one hill at a time, giving each student the opportunity to "function at his [her] fullest emotional and intellectual capacity" (Rosenblatt 173).

Occasionally there are moments: Stu, working in the produce department at the IGA said, "Do you still teach Mark Twain's essay on Fenimore Cooper? I loved it. Could I get a copy?"

Next time I'm buying oranges I'll have to ask him about Thoreau.

REFERENCES

Dillard, Annie. "Seeing." *Literary Cavalcade* 34 (1982): 47.
Macrorie, Ken. *Uptaught.* New York: Hayden Book Company, 1970.
Romano, Tom. *Clearing the Way.* Portsmouth, NH: Heinemann, 1987.
Rosenblatt, Louise M. *Literature as Exploration.* 3d ed. New York: Noble and Noble, 1976.
Thoreau, Henry David. "Death of a Pine." *Literary Cavalcade* 34 (1982): 46.
———. "Where I Lived and What I Lived For." *Adventures in American Literature.* Classic ed. Ed. James Early. New York: Harcourt, 1973. 183–93.

12

Intensifying Transactions Through Multiple Text Exploration
A Literature Circle Approach to Novels Set in the United States During World War II

Elizabeth A. Poe

As a literature teacher, I welcome Louise Rosenblatt's theory of reader response, particularly her emphasis on the importance of a rich, satisfying transaction between reader and text. I want my students to read a novel that is interesting, holds their attention, and builds on their individual backgrounds. I want them to read a novel not just because they are required to read it, but because it speaks to them personally and aesthetically. I want them to read a novel that offers an appropriate reading challenge: One that draws them in, enables them to identify with characters or situations, and inspires them to learn about and from these connections. I want them to read a text that will make them appreciate that particular book and want to read more because this experience was enjoyable, thought provoking, and gratifying. These components comprise a rich and satisfying transaction with a text.

However, it is difficult to find one book that will offer this rich literary experience to every class member. Therefore, to provide students with increased possibilities for satisfying transactions, I present literary choices and opportunities for individual responses whenever possible. In a high school sophomore English course, I allowed students to select their reading materials from a group of thematically intertwined novels that offer an appropriate range of reading levels, a wide variety of characters, a number of different situations, and several diverse geographical settings. I hope the differences in the novels will allow students to find a book to which they can initially relate. At the same time, the books are all set in the United States during World War II and have teenage protagonists who are affected by the war. This similarity makes it possible for students to read different novels concurrently, respond to them individually, and explore them both in small groups and as a whole class.

PRELIMINARY JOURNAL EXPLORATION

To begin this exploration, students write in their journals about war in general, describing their thoughts, feelings, and associations with the concept. Then they write specifically about World War II, including all they know about this event, whatever thoughts or feelings it brings to mind, and questions they might have. I collect, read, and respond to these informal pieces of writing immediately. They help me gauge students' concepts of war and ascertain their familiarity with World War II. Sometimes students include personal information, perhaps about a relative lost or disabled in war or stories about their parents' or grandparents' activities during wartime. These personal disclosures sensitize me toward students for whom the unit may be particularly painful as well as those who may serve as future resources. I also use these entries at the end of the unit to enable students to compare and contrast their prereading and postreading thoughts. In my responses, I try to communicate that I am interested in what students have to say and sympathetic toward painful associations they may reveal.

SELECTING TEXTS

Following this preliminary activity, I introduce the six novels from which they may choose. The students understand that I hope each of them will select a personally engaging book that will provide an appropriate challenge. Being careful not to give them too much information or color their perceptions with my own opinions, I give a brief booktalk about each of the texts.

A Separate Peace, written by John Knowles, tells the story of two teenage boys who room together at a New England boarding school. One of the boys is an exceptional athlete and the other is an excellent student. Although they are best friends, there is a dark side to their relationship. *Jacob Have I Loved,* written by Katherine Paterson, is the story of twin sisters who live on Rass Island, in Chesapeake Bay. Even though they are twins, Caroline and Louise do not get along. Louise is miserable because Caroline gets all the attention. *The Chosen,* by Chaim Potok, is about two teenage boys in New York who become friends despite the fact that Reuven comes from a more liberal religious background than does Danny, making it necessary for them to attend different types of Jewish schools. They have fascinating philosophical discussions about religion and politics.

Bette Green's *Summer of My German Soldier* is the story of Patti, a Jewish girl in Arkansas, who hides an escaped German prisoner of war. This is a particularly risky undertaking because her father is already ill-disposed toward Patti and beats her at the slightest provocation. In *Red Sky at Morning,* written by Richard Bradford, teenage Joshua moves with his mother from Mobile, Alabama, to a secluded mountain village in New Mexico because his father is serving on a battleship. In New Mexico, Joshua becomes friends with white, Chicano, and Native American Indian teenagers with whom he shares several exciting adventures. *Los Alamos Light,* by Larry Bograd, is the story of Maggie who moves with her parents to Los Alamos, New Mexico, so her father can work with a group of scientists who are secretly developing the atom bomb. Maggie forms friendships with some of the other teenagers living there, but she must come to her own conclusions about the morality of what her father did.

The booktalks and passing the books around usually enable students to self-select books that are appropriately challenging and potentially engaging. Better readers generally select *The Chosen* or *A Separate Peace* and less able readers seem relieved to choose *Summer of My German Soldier* or *Jacob Have I Loved.* Middle-level readers often prefer *Red Sky at Morning* or *Los Alamos Light.* This match between reader and reading level of the text is crucial if readers are to feel equal to the task of reading the book.

Invitation 12.1

In a small group, identify a topic or theme you perceive to be potentially meaningful to a particular secondary school grade level. Then, research and select five or six novels that speak to the topic or theme. The selected works should represent a range of interests and reading levels. Exchange lists among your peers and discuss their potential for instruction.

I encourage students to change books if they do not like their original selection. Sometimes they change because a book is too difficult, or not challenging enough, or seems uninteresting. Sometimes they decide to read the same book a friend has chosen. I have never had it happen, but if a parent objected to a particular book, the student could easily switch to another book offered as part of the unit.

Once students settle on their texts, we form book groups based on the chosen texts. If more than five students in one class are reading the same book, we make two groups for that book, rather than have a group too large for effective collaboration. If only one student selects a certain book, that student may choose to work alone, change books, or try to persuade someone else to change books; no one is ever forced to read a book just for the sake of group structure, but students selecting a book no one else has chosen have always opted to create or join a group. I think they realize the advantages of sharing their responses with other class members.

EXPLORING PERSONAL RESPONSES
TO TEXTS

I tell the class we will be reading these books for exploration. I would like to leave it there, for the sake of purity, but of course they want further elaboration. I therefore explain that when they read these novels, I want them to explore their own response to the book. This might include responses to what happens in the story, what the characters are like, what the situations or people remind them of, questions they may formulate about the period, geographical setting, religious ideas, or any other thoughts or feelings the story evokes.

Their exploration might include other people's responses to the book or extend to reference resources or other literary works. They will record their responses in spiral notebooks, called *response journals,* which I will read. They will also be given opportunities to share their thoughts with members of their small group. I stress that there are no right or wrong responses, but they should aim at responses that fully articulate thoughts and feelings and explore why they responded as they did. Through the exploration of their responses, readers reflect about themselves and their connection with the text. Such introspection leads to self-awareness and understanding, the foundation of personal growth and empathy for others.

Students respond in their journals following the completion of each chapter or group of chapters if they read more than one in a sitting. They submit their journals whenever they want my feedback, which I try to provide by the following day.

As I read their entries, I make comments intended to show I have read the entry and understand its content. I compliment thoughtful entries and indicate when my own response coincides with the student's. When students respond in a manner different from my own, I thank them for providing a new perspective. If remarks indicate students are way off track, I ask questions designed to help them take a second look at the text. If students ask questions about the storyline or characters, I answer them. However, if they just say "I don't understand," I ask them to be more specific so I can help them, or I direct them to group members who may be able to clarify the confusion. For example, a student named Lisa wrote: "The characters [in *The Chosen*] use so many Jewish terms that it is hard for me to understand because I don't know the vocabulary." I wrote back: "Which terms don't you understand? Maybe someone in your group can help you figure them out. If that doesn't work, come talk to me about them." If a student's response is vague, I ask questions like: "What do you mean by this?" or "Why do you say this?" I try to help them expand and deepen their transactions with the text by inviting them to tell me more and provide specific instances or details.

When students make personal associations with the text or provide autobiographical information, I encourage them to explore the connections they have discovered. Sometimes I try to draw out these personal connections as when Lisa wrote:

> I was very upset with Danny's father when he did not allow Danny and Reuven to remain friends. I just wanted to yell and scream at him. He seemed to be ruining Danny's life because he would never talk to him, except about Talmud. And that wasn't talking. Reuven was Danny's only friend, and now that was taken away. I admired Reuven's father for helping him in understanding Danny and his family. It seemed like he could always count on his father for help whenever he was confused or needed an opinion.

Here's my response:

> I know what you mean about the two fathers. They certainly treated their sons differently. Does either of them remind you of anyone you know?

Students sometimes respond to my comments or answer my questions on the page where I asked them or in subsequent entries. I don't require them to do this, but they seem to have a natural desire to communicate their thoughts and discoveries. Lisa, for example, wrote back:

> I guess each of these two fathers reminds me a bit of my own father. He's not a stern as Danny's father, but we don't talk as much as I would like. He's supportive of me, but not as much as Reuven's father is of him. I wish he was more like Reuven's father, but I'm glad he's not as bad as Danny's father. I couldn't take that.

My response to her was "I understand," and that was the end of our correspondence on this matter. I enjoy reading and responding to journals because I can give students personal attention. It also keeps me informed as to their progress with and insights into the novels.

My responses vary in length according to the content of the entry. Often I write a brief phrase, like " thoughtful response," or "interesting reaction," or "good question." Other times I comment more extensively, especially when students express confusion or deep personal involvement. But whether my comments are brief or extensive, it does take time to read and respond to each entry. When colleagues ask me about this, I explain that I can do this because I am not spending time preparing lectures about the historical period, the author's life, or literary criticism. Nor am I using my time to create and grade quizzes, tests, and study guides. By not grading each entry, but giving each journal a holistic grade, based on whether the student responded to each section, the thoroughness of the responses, and the overall effort involved in the exploration, I optimize time and shift the focus from grades to quality of responses. Although the final journal grade is admittedly somewhat subjective, my students understand it is based on many years of experience with reading response journals.

DEVELOPING RESPONSES:
SMALL GROUP INTERACTIONS

During the weeks when students are reading the novels, they discuss them periodically in small groups. Each group determines which days will be reading days and which will be discussion days. Some days there are six small groups scattered throughout the classroom, all discussing different books. I ask each group to tell me when they plan to discuss, and I try to join them at least for part of each discussion. I do this for three reasons. First, I want to hear what the students have to say about their chosen texts. As students soon discover, I love to talk about literature and find the exchange of response exhilarating and enlightening. I join the group as another reader responder, listening to group members as they explain their responses and sharing my responses.

Second, I want to help group members expand on their responses and try to understand why they and others in their group reacted as they did. For example, a student in a group who had read *A Separate Peace* said he identified with Gene Forrester. When I asked him why, we were able to discover that he had been jealous of a friend and hoped he would fail a chemistry test. This insight elicited similar confessions from several other group members. I think we all understood Gene and our human weaknesses a little better after this discussion. In another instance, a student who had read *Jacob Have I Loved* told her group she did not like the novel. As we explored her response, it became clear that she was confused by all the crabbing terminology. Other group members were experiencing similar frustration. They decided to work on this together and devoted a good bit of time to trying to decipher the language of the waterfront.

Invitation 12.2

Select two or three of the books on your topical or thematic list (see Invitation 12.1). After each of these has been read by at least two

members of your group, conduct a discussion of the common topical
or thematic ideas to reveal how they are explored and expanded by
the books.

In both these instances I served as a facilitator. I do this by asking what the
students thought about the book so far. Then I gently probe their initial responses, which are usually "I like it" or "I don't like it," by asking them why.
I ask them to specify characters, incidents, or passages that cause them to
like or dislike the novel. I ask them if anything in the book reminds them of
themselves or people they know. I ask them what they can learn about themselves and others by reading the book. When they respond, I usually ask
them why they responded that way. I think I am successful at this because the
students sense I am genuinely interested in them and their exploration of
the text. In addition, the fact that I share my own responses and do not treat
these as the only acceptable or "right" response demonstrates that I truly
respect my students as readers with unique transactions with the text. They
know I respect the texts because I frequently suggest they return to the book
to clarity a point or find a detail that will help explain their responses.

I also facilitate their exploration of the text when I use the reader-
response technique of asking them to identify a work or passage they particularly liked and explain its appeal. The passages they select usually concern
content, such as an idea expressed by a character, but sometimes they are
descriptions of a character or place. I often select passages because I like the
flow of the words or an image created or a literary allusion and then invite
students to do the same. Our discussion of these passages enhances students' understanding of the novel as well as their appreciation for it as a
source of aesthetic enjoyment.

My third reason for joining small group discussions is so I can evaluate
students' participation in this important aspect of the unit. They know they
receive a group participation grade based on effort and attention to the task
at hand, not the quality of the discussions.

As students finish their books, they write their response to the work as a
whole. These whole-book responses give students an opportunity to synthesize their thoughts and feelings about the book, reflect on their experience
with it, and assess what they have gained from reading it. These responses
often represent some of the students' clearest, most focused writing because
they have been so intensely involved with the literary work.

From my point of view, these whole-book responses are important not
only because they provide insight into the students' transactions with the
books, but also because they function as a reality check and help me determine the appropriateness of the array of books offered for the unit. Comments like "I enjoyed this book even though I never would have picked it
up on my own because I usually hate anything that has to do with the war,"

"I learned a lot about my beliefs about war," "This was the first book I ever enjoyed reading," and "Thanks for letting us choose our books, I finally got to read a book I cared about," indicated students have had satisfying literary transactions.

EXTENDING RESPONSES:
WHOLE-CLASS DISCUSSIONS

When all the groups have finished their books and whole-book response entries, we are ready for whole-class discussions. To begin this, each group presents a panel discussion focusing on group members' responses to the book. For other class members to understand these responses, each group provides information about the book's plot, characters, literary style, or other necessary details. Then panel members basically answer the question, "What did you think about your book and why?" When the groups have finished their presentations, I ask the class if they noticed any common aspects in the novels. Eager to respond, they mention teenage friendships, jealous feelings, religious concepts, and World War II. The way these topics recur in different novels forms the basis for several days' worth of lively and provocative discussions in which students frequently make comments such as, "That's a lot like my novel because. . . ."

The theme of friendship figures in each novel and is of particular interest to most teenagers; it therefore elicits involved discussions. Whether parents should forbid friendships, as Danny's father did in *The Chosen*, is an example of a question that produces emotional discussions heavily laden with personal experiences. Students in *The Chosen* group have already shared their thoughts on this topic; now they have a larger group of peers with whom to discuss this issue. Examples of Louise's (*Jacob Have I Loved*) friendship with the elderly Captain, Patti's (*Summer of My German Soldier*) illegal relationship with Anton the POW, and Joshua's (*Red Sky at Morning*) and Maggie's (*Los Alamos Light*) friendships with teens from different racial and cultural backgrounds evoke frank discussions about benefits and potential problems when friends differ in age and personal backgrounds.

When I ask how hearing about the other books affects their exploration of their own books, students often comment that their perceptions about common themes are broadened and intensified by hearing other students' remarks. Although many of the themes are recurring, war—specifically World War II—is common to all six novels; therefore, we decide to focus our class discussion on war.

We discuss World War II and, through the various perspectives provided in each novel, we piece together information about this time period. For example, readers of *Jacob Have I Loved* tell of the sisters listening to the radio and hearing of the Japanese bombing of Pearl Harbor. Those who read *A Separate Peace* explain about 16-year-old boys preparing to enlist in the service. *Red Sky at Morning* readers recount how Joshua's father was killed in the war. Readers of *The Chosen* add information about Hitler and Zionism. Those who read *Summer of My German Soldier* inform us about German prisoners of war incarcerated in the United States. Students who read *Los Alamos Light* discuss the top-secret work of scientists who developed the atomic bomb that ended the war.

Much of what happened is difficult for students to comprehend beyond an informational level, so I ask how the war changed the daily lives of the characters in the books and how they, as readers, feel about these changes. Readers of *A Separate Peace* explain that 16-year-old Gene and Finny attended summer school so they could graduate early and join the war. However, the war came to them even before they left Devon School when older students participated in prewar physical training and school buildings were used as sewing stations for military supplies. Many conversations among boys at Devon School focused on the war, the progress of the Allied powers being of major importance to them. Most of my students are the same age as Gene and Finny, and they are firm believers that these are the best years of their lives. To think that these joyful years could be cut short and overshadowed by a war that is so far away appalls them.

In a similar vein, the war caused Louise in *Jacob Have I Loved* to work even harder and make more sacrifices for Caroline's music lessons. Louise's friend Call left Rass Island to join the Marines. Due to the war, most young men could not go to college, and it became possible for Louise to enter medical school. Louise's experience raises the issue of education for women. Class members do not have to have read this novel to have opinions on this subject. Some feel Louise benefitted from the circumstances, and others feel she was shortchanged when she had to settle for a career as a midwife instead of a doctor. Students can get rather emotional about women's rights, and I may need to remind them of the importance of listening to each other and respecting differing points of view.

Danny and Reuven in *The Chosen* spend much of their time in long philosophical discussions about the war, the Jewish people in Europe, and the state of Israel. Patti in *Summer of My German Soldier* risked the wrath of her father to harbor Anton, the German POW, and she ended up being sent to reform school for it. In *Red Sky at Morning*, not only did Joshua have to move from his home to New Mexico, but his father is killed in battle, changing Joshua's life forever. Maggie, in *Los Alamos Light*, spends much of her time wondering about the secret work of her father and his colleagues. When they test the bomb, she realizes the terrible destructive force they have created.

As the stories of these characters are told, students are horrified by the far-reaching effects of the war. They sympathize with the characters and sometimes disclose personal stories about family members during the war. They also philosophize about the bomb and the effect it has on us all. Once students understand I am interested in their thoughts on these issues, they are usually eager to discuss them. If they are hesitant or do not offer their opinions, I gently urge them by first mentioning a topic they have referred to and then asking what they think about it.

Tapping the personal level, I ask the class if the teenagers in these novels are much like them. Students generally have kindred feelings toward the teens in the novels, identifying with their desire for friendships, their problems with parents and teachers, and their questions and plans concerning the future. The students do not strongly identify with the plight of these teens during wartime (the United States was not at war when we had the discussion), but they understand how a war can make teenagers grow up faster and change their lives forever. Had we read these novels during wartime, students would undoubtedly recognize close connections with their teenage counterparts during World War II.

CULMINATING PROJECTS

The next step in our exploration of the novels entails personal response projects. Their purpose is to intensify each reader's transaction with the text. Students select a character with whom they identify, an idea that intrigues them, an image that haunts them, a scene that appeals to them, or another aspect of the text to explore in depth. They then create a project that appropriately expresses their responses to or exploration of this aspect of the novel. Students share their project with the class, explaining the relationship between the project, the novel, and their transaction with the text.

Examples of projects include charcoal drawings of characters from *Red Sky at Morning;* a board game based on *Summer of My German Soldier;* background music for *Jacob Have I Loved;* a report on Jewish religious customs by a reader of *The Chosen;* and a visit from a student's grandfather, a World War II naval captain, who discussed what Joshua's father in *Red Sky at Morning* might have experienced aboard the battleship. These projects represent emotional and intellectual responses, many of which are artistically expressed. Research for the projects involves close reading of the text and utilizing human and library resources.

Invitation 12.3

With another student who has read the same book, consider a project idea or two that you might present to your peers. Consider, further, the skills and procedures necessary to actually produce this project. Discuss with your peers these project expectations in relation to the skills and available time of "target" secondary school students.

Students generally seem to have fun presenting their projects and enjoy experiencing their classmates' creations. I ask them to write a response to the response project, and most of them say it helped them understand some part of the novel more fully. Those who did research projects on topics of personal interest, such as sibling rivalry and child abuse, say they learned not only about the characters in *Jacob Have I Loved* and *Summer of My German Soldier,* but about themselves and their families as well. Those who chose to write poetry, short stories, or sequels based on their novels often indicate they came to a closer understanding of the characters and their personal or historical situations. Many of the artistic responses are expressions of a reader's emotional reaction to the text. Some of the projects, like the board games, stay rather close to the storyline, but they may include an interpretation of characters' motivations. Although they do not use the terminology, the students almost unanimously indicate that the project has enriched their transaction with the text. Additionally, the quality of their projects and the pride the students take in them enable me to see their extended involvement with the novel and the development of their responses.

We conclude the unit by writing formal essays. Drawing from response journal entries, small group and class discussions, and new thoughts generated by the assignment, students write an essay based on their chosen novel. Although they are free to write on any aspect of their novel they like, many students choose to continue the exploration of one of the themes already identified and analyze the personal meaning this theme holds for them. It is a natural transition for book groups to become writing groups and provide peer responses and editing for each other's essays during this final stage in the exploration of the novel.

When the polished drafts of the essays are submitted, students write a final response journal entry on what they have gained through the unit. Although many students find the unit provocative and intend to further explore ideas generated by the novels or our discussions, I'll never forget the comment of one bright, but heretofore disinterested student. She said that reading *The Chosen* had inspired her to read more books by Chaim Potok and to further explore her Jewish heritage.

Comments like hers are the reasons why I use reader-response techniques whenever I facilitate literature study, be it in elementary, secondary, undergraduate, or graduate classes. Offering choices in reading materials and providing multiple means for exploring personal response make it possible for readers to have the rich, satisfying transactions that keep them reading and exploring literature.

EXTENDING IDEAS AND
INTERDISCIPLINARY CONSIDERATIONS

Since I developed this unit in the early 1980s, I have discovered many more books set in the United States (or its territories) during World War II. These titles, listed later, offer teachers and students even greater choices and can expand the geographical range of students' reading experiences. Teachers using these additional titles report, and my own observations support, that these books are successful with both middle school and high school students.

Although initially designed for a high school English course, this unit has been adapted for interdisciplinary study by social studies/language arts and social studies/history teachers who want to encourage students to expand on the responses evoked by literature with historical research about the time period. As is the case with any work of quality literature, the possibilities for exploration are myriad.

After creating this unit, I become aware of the concept of literature circles, which was being developed in the early 1980s by various educators interested in combining independent reading and collaborative literature study. The literature circle concept certainly fits the multitext approach I describe, and I embrace it wholeheartedly because it fosters reader response and nurtures readers.

REFERENCES

Bograd, Larry. *Los Alamos Light.* New York: Farrar Straus Giroux, 1983.
Bradford, Richard. *Red Sky at Morning.* New York: Lippincott, 1968.
Greene, Bette. *Summer of My German Soldier.* New York: Dial, 1973.
Knowles, John. *A Separate Peace.* New York: Macmillan, 1959.
Paterson, Katherine. *Jacob Have I Loved.* New York: Thomas Y. Crowell, 1980.
Potok, Chaim. *The Chosen.* New York: Ballantine, 1967.

ADDITIONAL SUGGESTED READINGS

Avi. *"Who Was That Masked Man, Anyway?"* New York: Orchard, 1992.
Bat-Ami, Miriam. *Two Suns in the Sky.* Chicago: Front Street/Cricket, 1999.
Cormier, Robert. *Heroes.* New York: Delacorte, 1998.
Cutler, Jane. *My Wartime Summers.* New York: Farrar Straus Giroux, 1994.
Giff, Patricia Reilly. *Lilly's Crossing.* New York: Delacorte, 1997.
Hahn, Mary Downing. *Following My Own Footsteps.* New York: Clarion, 1996.
———. *Stepping on the Cracks.* New York: Clarion, 1991.
Houston, Jeanne Wakatusuki and James D. Houston. *Farewell to Manzanar: A True Story of Japanese Americans Experience During and After World War II.* New York: Houghton Mifflin, 1972.

Levine, Ellen. *A Fence Away From Freedom: Japanese Americans and World War II*. New York: Putnam, 1995.

Levitin, Sonia. *Annie's Promise*. New York: Atheneum, 1993.

———. *Silver Days*. New York: Atheneum, 1989.

Levoy, Myron. *Alan and Naomi*. New York: Harper Collins, 1977.

Means, Florence Crandall. *The Moved-Outers*. New York: Houghton Mifflin, 1945.

Oughton, Jerrie. *The War in Georgia*. New York: Houghton Mifflin, 1997.

Platt, Randall Beth. *Honor Bright*. New York: Delacorte, 1998.

Reeder, Carolyn. *Foster's War*. New York: Scholastic, 1998.

Rinaldi, Ann. *Keep Smiling Through*. San Diego, CA: Harcourt Brace, 1996.

Rylant, Cynthia. *I Had Seen Castles*. San Diego, CA: Harcourt Brace, 1993.

Salisbury, Graham. *Under the Blood-Red Sun*. New York: Delacorte, 1994.

Thesman, Jean. *Molly Donnelly*. New York: Houghton Mifflin, 1993.

Uchida, Yoshida. *The Invisible Thread*. New York: Simon & Schuster, 1991.

———. *The Journey Home*. New York: Simon & Schuster, 1978.

13

Role-Playing Experiences
Expanding Readers'
Responses to Literature

Nicholas J. Karolides

I gaveled the class to attention, glanced around to catch the students' eyes, and announced, "The meeting of the River City School Board is called to order." Smiling slightly to acknowledge their surprise, I continued, "We're pleased to see so many of you attend this hearing about *The Catcher in the Rye,* that is, the request of a group of citizens to remove it from the curriculum of the 11th grade. I see members of the group, the Concerned Citizens for Moral Education (CCME) are sitting there (pointing) in the center of the room. There are representatives of the English Department and other teachers, grouped here to my left, and on my right there are representatives from another group, Citizens Acting to Protect the First Amendment (CAPFA).

"Now, in order to act efficiently on this challenge — the school board has a press of other business and there is urgency for the teachers — I am going to ask each group to caucus for about 20 minutes. So, if you'll go ahead and organize your presentations, we'll then be able to hear your opinions and concerns. Then we'll debate the issue."

In this manner, I set the stage for my Literature for Adolescents class to come to grips with the censorship issues surrounding *The Catcher in the Rye* as well as to consider the ideas within the book from several perspectives. With regard to the literature, my intention was twofold: to establish the range of potential responses to Holden Caulfield, concomitantly investigating the issues within his experiences and behavior through these perspectives; and to cause the students to examine their own responses, which had been discussed in a preliminary way during the previous session, so as to gain a heightened awareness of their own reading.

After the caucuses, the students as a matter of closure established their impressions in writing. An excerpt from Michael Comer's journal represents the CCME:

> When our group first got together, we tried to approach the book from the viewpoint of hyperconservative parents. We jokingly, yet deliberately, moved too far to the conservative end of the spectrum, making remarks such as: "I just don't want my little Billy reading this book" and "This book is the work of the devil." I think we had to go too far to that side of the spectrum because, as English majors, we all shared the opinion that the book should not be censored because we saw literary merit in the novel. Then, Alexandra suggested that we make a list of aspects of the novel that conservative parents would most likely attack. The list included:
>
> - language/profanity
> - homosexual episode with teacher
> - antireligion—ridiculed one of the apostles
> - shady lifestyles—drinking, prostitution
> - Holden might be looked up to by kids who read the book—dangerous because Holden is lazy and unmotivated
> - demeaning of women
> - disrespect to authority
> - death, ended up being insane (parents would say)
>
> Holly was beginning to enjoy taking on an opinion that she disagreed with, so in moments she was trying to convince the members of our small group that she was a minister and began to vehemently argue for censorship of the novel because of its anti-religious stance. The rest of us seemed to agree that we should point to the novel's glorification of Holden and his lifestyle as our reasoning.

Heather Schmidt's journal represents the direction taken by the CAPFA group:

> Immediately, the group focused on the language in the First Amendment and the rights that amendment protects for all citizens in the United States. Toni was able to write the amendment in its entirety. In planning our statement, we emphasized that youth are included in the word "all" and ought to have access to literature in the school setting, especially classic literature such as this Salinger novel. The Constitution guarantees the citizens the right to have access to material; since students are citizens, they have the rights protected by the Constitution.
>
> As a group, we certainly recognized a parent's right to monitor and select the readings his/her child would have available. We offered that option as a solution to the issue at hand—parental concern over text content, rather than censorship of the book. . . . As we arrived at these, we also planned to use

American values as our main appeal. Because America was founded by people who were seeking all kinds of freedoms, limiting freedoms, even for students, is entirely contrary to what it means to be an American. We discussed the importance of having access to information within a democratic system. I shared a John Milton quotation that supported that discussion, "To choose rightly, one must be free to choose." As a group, we maintained that young people ought to have such freedom of choice.

The task of the teachers' group was more complex, encompassing both the art and the content of the novel, as Lance Kamm's journal reveals, this excerpt focusing on the themes:

As teachers, our group decided that we must attempt to stop the "slippery slope" effect of censorship. . . . First of all, we feel that the themes that are presented are universal and artfully represented. Salinger masterfully deals with many issues that are facing our teen population today. We decided that the following are well presented and can help our students to better understand their world:

- Search for identity
- Separation from parents/transition to adulthood
- Dealing with death and loss and personal tragedy
- Isolation and crisis

Salinger deals with a subject matter that students can easily relate to and identify with. He has represented Holden as an individual who is unsure of his environment, his and other's motivations, and ultimately is unsure of himself. When read and discussed in a directed environment, students will be able to see and understand the problems that plague Holden; they will see his confusion and begin to understand the problems and difficulties that face him. The reality of Holden Caulfield may be identifiable for some students, and hopefully Holden's experience will help readers of the novel to better sort through their own problems and situations.

This scenario was played out with the meeting being called to order and opening statements from each group delivered. These were followed by debate among the participants. Comer captures the essence of this event in his journal: "By the time the groups convened for the 'hearing,' all of the other groups were questioning and cross-examining our group, but we all seemed to revel in the role of catalyst and antagonist."

The context of this activity on the surface may seem exterior to the novel, focusing tangentially through a scenario of a censorship challenge of *The Catcher in the Rye*. Indirect though it may be, it establishes dramatically the potential range of readers' responses to Holden, his language and behavior, and the issues emanating from the text. The relationship of these responses to the held values and concerns of these readers becomes immediately evident. Students, who may have read about a censorship challenge—usually presented in newspapers with minimal discussion—and have thought about the pro and con arguments, think more deeply about these positions when they take on roles of outraged parents and morally affronted clergy, of teachers defending their curriculum choice and their learning objectives, and of civil libertarians.

Within this dramatic scenario, readers' responses to the interior novel are also engaged. In projecting their role response, students offer pronouncements about Holden's behaviors and motives, his perceptions of the world. These role-engendered ideas may contrast with their personal understanding of the novel. In parrying the arguments of others in this challenge situation, the participants come to grips with their own understandings. This tension, this consciousness of contradiction, enlivens and enhances the response-development process.

The measure of success of the activity may be expressed from two angles. After the lesson, as the class was leaving, Michael Comer, who had effectively played an indignant parent, stopped to assure me that he didn't really believe the statements about the book that he had been espousing. In the subsequent journal write about the exercises and the "telling arguments," the students identified ideas they related to, often expanding on them, and cited a new idea, drawn from the discussion, that had not previously occurred to them.

The essence of the role-play scenarios, be they written or oral, is to place the respondents inside the text's situations, to create immediate connections with the characters and the issues that confront them. Such activities tend to cause readers to reach beyond their preliminary expressions of responses to the text, which may be tentative, superficial, or incomplete. They enhance "the lived-through process of building up the work under the guidance of the text" (Rosenblatt, *Reader* 69).

Taking on the role of a character encourages direct identification or an exchanged life. Such a life exchange may be provocative, causing participants to cross over into relatively unknown situations, cultures, and personas. Such attempts to become the character—feeling, thinking, behaving—heighten awareness of the individual's motivations and attitudes and of the complexity of personality. Potentially, understanding is initiated at the outset and deepened in the process. Active engagement invites thoughtfulness.

Operating here are both invention and constraint. Through their imagination and interaction, the players create the features of the scene, the expression of the characters. As with the reading process, the constraint comes from the text from which the scene and characters are drawn. The thinking and working processes are both recursive and integrative, again reminiscent of the reading process. The role players, individually and as a group, reconsider preliminary understandings, reflecting on the text's clues and boundaries, and reconfigure these through the dynamics of planning and enactment. The emerging interpretive ideas of the players cross-fertilize, the players' emotions are stirred. Decisions of language and its projection are compelling and revealing. These interactions encourage the bolstering and refining of an interpretive direction or insist on new perspectives.

A caveat: These processes are not effortless nor are the developmental stages necessarily immediate or self-generated. Students often need to be eased into playing character roles by undertaking tangential figures (i.e., personages outside the text), as in the situation just illustrated.

Identification with characters or exchanging lives with them is also not automatic. Some exchanges may be relatively comfortable when the characters, situations, or issues are familiar on the surface, as in the Norma Fox Mazer novel *Out of Control:* The female protagonist, feeling affronted and humiliated by the harassment of three male students, must come to terms with her feelings and decide on the actions she must take. Several other female characters who join her in seeking affirmation and catharsis serve as bridges for readers; the three male students and the principal are recognizable as well. Such a relatively comfortable exchange equation is not always possible. The initial evocation of the work may be shallow due to inexperience or unfamiliarity; the lived-through experience may be thwarted—even stifled—by distance, that is, by barriers raised by differences in culture, race, gender, time, or place. Readers may not be able initially to bridge the distance, which may seem chasmal, between themselves and the characters. In such instances, despite participating with the text at some level, readers may perceive themselves to be spectators, observing from the sidelines. Such a reading response might occur, for example, with Arthur Miller's *The Crucible* or Toni Morrison's *The Bluest Eye;* readers may be able to talk about the text, rather than actively experiencing it. This sense threatens depth of empathy and full cognizance.

As noted earlier, a central function of role-play scenarios is to help readers connect with characters by placing them inside the text's situations. They build bridges over the perceived chasms between readers and text. A well-conceived scenario, encouraging of thoughtfulness, will cause readers to adopt the persona of characters, becoming immersed in their personalities and situations. In my experience with this tactic, students cross the bridge and exchange lives with characters who are significantly "foreign" to themselves, taking on their personas and speaking through their struggles. In the following examples, several such exchanges are illustrated.

"HOME BURIAL" BY ROBERT FROST

> He saw her from the bottom of the stairs
> Before she saw him. She was starting down,
> Looking back over her shoulder at some fear.

She took a doubtful step and then undid it
To raise herself and look again. He spoke
Advancing toward her: 'What is it you see
From up there always—for I want to know.'

*   *   *   *

'*You*—oh, you think the talk is all. I must go—
Somewhere out of this house. How can I make you—'

'If-you-do!' She was opening the door wider.
'Where do you mean to go? First tell me that.
I'll follow and bring you back by force. I *will!*—'

Between these opening and closing lines, Frost's protagonists, wife and husband, grieving over the death of their first child, confront each other with emotional intensity. After my reading of the poem aloud—and a long pause—we discuss the impact of the poem, our reactions, and then our sense of feelings, declarations, and positions of the wife and husband.

When this discussion begins to wane but is yet incomplete, I cut it off and set up groups of four, some composed of women, some of men, and some of both. The instructions are simple: Amy runs across the road to her friend's house and into the kitchen; her friend and two other women are there. Amy, evidently distraught, expresses her agony; the three women respond. Paul (the husband), unnamed in the poem, follows but is intercepted by the husbands of the other women; they have sensed the tension. Paul responds to their queries and comments. Because my goal is to help my students internalize the feeling states of both characters—and, potentially, their own gendered responses—I assign the groups of women and half the mixed groups to role play Amy and the women; the others role play Paul and the men.

The outcomes, revealed in a postscript discussion, are intriguing. Generally, the "women" commiserate with Amy and offer advice ranging from total support, even outrage, to the need to recognize the different ways that men grieve. The "men" tend to soothe Paul's anger and provide "give-it-time-to-settle-down" advice; they seem uncertain about what can be done, somewhat mimicking the confused emotions that Paul expresses in the text.

The small group responses of the students who have switched genders elicit the most comments, particularly the men undertaking the roles of women. Although a few of the men are at relative ease, the greater number expose a sense of dismay and inability to feel (and talk) like women. The women in their groups corroborate these reactions. As group members, virtually all affirm their greater understanding of the linguistic and emotional divide in themselves as well as their increased sensitivity and empathy for the protagonists of "Home Burial."

Invitation 13.1

Consider the activities for *The Catcher in the Rye* and "Home Burial"
in relation to the expectations for the participants. What differences
do you observe? What demands does each make? How might one
type be used as a sequel for the other?

"SUMMER GIRL" BY ROBERTA HILL WHITEMAN
AND "CROW'S SUN" BY DUANE NIATUM

These short stories fit well together. They are each about young Native
Americans. Phoebe, the 16-year-old protagonist of "Summer Girl," is hired
to be a nanny for a well-to-do European-American family's three children—
until her race is discovered. Thereupon, her responsibilities with the children seem to be minimized; Phoebe sees herself treated as a servant. Comparably, 17-year-old Young Thomas of "Crow's Sun," a sailor in the Navy, has
responded to racial taunts by fighting. He is sentenced to the brig for 30
days; others involved in the fighting are not. In the brig, he experiences extreme verbal racial abuse and physical abuse from the mouth and hands of
the brig's warden.

In this scenario, I divide the students of The Native American in Literature class into two groups facing each other; the women play Phoebe; the
men play Young Thomas. The setting is a powwow that both are attending
about 6 months later. Young Thomas, in uniform, spots Phoebe standing
near the refreshment table. He strolls over and introduces himself, taking
the initiative in starting a conversation. Both are at least curious about each
other. In enacting the conversation, the players must rely on the information, attitudes, and behaviors revealed in the two texts. By causing students
to become victims of racism and to express their feelings about and reactions to this violation, my objective is to instill at least preliminary understanding of the interior feeling states and behaviors of such victims.

Without exception, each time I have used this activity, the attempts to
open the conversation have been halting, even painful. (I occasionally interrupt to offer encouragement by remarking that this hesitation is realistic
in such circumstances, as they well know.) Gradually, the players warm to the
task and begin to relate their experience in the "White world," revealing,
step by step, events and outcomes. Eventually (sometimes I step into a role
to ask a question) they talk about their emotions then and now—their feelings of being demeaned and defiled—and their sources of strength and empowerment.

The tough parts of this scenario are getting started, as noted, and grappling with inner feelings, the latter made more difficult by the racial cross-over. In this context, recapitulating the events of the insults to the psyche prepares these readers—each speaks in first person, incorporating the young Native Americans' sensibilities—for the emotional revelations. The understandings engendered by such internalization are potentially more emotionally meaningful—an aesthetic "lived-through" experience rather than only an efferent informational one. Comments made both in the postscript discussion and remarks in student journals attest to this. These students, many of whom express antagonism to taking a literature course, some of whom signal underlying biases against Native Americans, relate changes in their perceptions. As an observer, my sense is that some degree of distance between them and this "others" group has been eroded.

JOURNEY BY PATRICIA MACLACHLAN

Eleven-year-old Journey is the focus of this novel; however, his grandparents and sister, Cat, figure prominently. The children's mother has recently deserted them, their father having disappeared just after Journey's birth. Not comprehending, Journey at once longs for his mother's return but is unable to forgive her. His healing is tentative and slow. This role play, involving five elementary education students who responded to the text and portrayed their responses to the Children's Literature: Issues and Trends class, combined written and oral discourse. First, the group members discussed their evoked responses and developed their interpretations. Then, they planned their presentation: One student would narrate, briefly expressing the plot and introducing the characters; each of the others would write a letter in the role (one undertook two) of a character to another character. These were read to the class. Excerpts convey the interpretation and emotional quality, although the readers' voices were also significantly suggestive.

> Narrator: Cooper MacDougal (written by Megan A. Purfeerst)
>   Journey and Cat were left behind by their mother. Journey and Cat's father left them when they were babies. Cat seems to have accepted her mother leaving her at face value. Cat is very practical that way, just like her grandma. Journey on the other hand is struggling with the reality of it. He wants to blame someone, anyone, but his own mother.
>   Journey's mom, from what Journey and Cat have told me, is a woman who is constantly searching for something, though she never knew what. . . .

> Dear Mama and Daddy,
>   I wanted to send you this letter, Mama and Daddy, but I just couldn't mail it. I tried to explain everything before I left, but the words didn't come out right. You just didn't seem to understand why I had to leave. I couldn't take Cat and Journey with me, as I needed some time away from

all of you right now. I'll make it back home someday. Ever since I was a little girl, I've always been looking for something to happen in my life. I don't know what that will be, but I know it's not going to happen if I stay there with you. * * * *

I had to tear up all the pictures of my past life. You'll find them under my bed. As far as I'm concerned, that's all part of my past, and I don't need reminders of the past. I have to go forward with my life, as I am now doing. I'll call when I can and I won't forget to send money to Cat and Journey. Maybe they can come visit me sometime when I get settled.

> Your daughter,
> Liddie (written by Cheryl Virden)

Narrator:

Now comes Cat. She is the love of my life. She is very practical and beautiful. One day she had a photograph album that had old pictures of her mom. I thought she looked identical to her mom. But Cat informed me that she resembles her mom, but looks identical to her grandma. If you ask me, they all look alike.

Maybe what I really love about Cat is that she notices things, just like me, that other people ignore or don't see. She sees through a lot of what Journey and her grandparents do. Here is a letter that Cat might have written to her mother.

Dear Momma,

I know this letter will never get to you. You send us money but not words, no return address. I'm pretty sure that you'll never come back, but there are things I need to tell you. . . .

Grandpa is still taking pictures. Journey takes them too sometimes. Grandpa and Journey are more alike with each passing day. They take family pictures all the time. . . .

Journey wanted to know what happened to the pictures from when he was a baby. Grandpa had to tell him that you tore them up. Journey stayed in bed for two days after that. We found the pieces in the box under your bed. All those torn up pieces of pictures looked like murder to me. Journey stayed up all night trying to put them together, trying to fix everything, until he realized that it was impossible.

It's been two whole months since you left. Did you know that not all mothers know how to be a mother? Why did you leave? I hate what you have done to us.

> Cat (written by Rachel Primmer)

Narrator:

Now comes Lottie. Lottie is Journey and Cat's grandma. Lottie is a wonderful woman. She seems to know just what to say to everyone. She loves her daughter even though she has left her children. Lottie is a very practical woman. There is always an explanation for everything. I think Lottie knew that in time her daughter would leave. It was just a question of when for Lottie.

Deep down I think Lottie knew that Liddie never had the true mothering instinct, and the only way Liddie could survive was to leave.

. . . I think Lottie knew Cat would have an easier time dealing with her mother leaving than Journey would. Lottie knew Journey had to work things out for himself. Here is a letter that Lottie might have written to Journey:

Dear Journey,

I know you miss your mother—we all do. We each have our own way of dealing with her leaving. Cat keeps busy helping me in the house and garden. I try to keep busy; I read a lot and I'm learning to play Cat's flute. Grandpa takes pictures, lots of pictures, trying to capture memories and bits of time. He wants to have something to give you, some way to preserve what's important in life.

Journey, you're so young to deal with this. You were just a baby when your dad left. I doubt if you even remember much about him. Your mama changed after he left. She didn't think there was much left worth looking back on. She thought all the good things were ahead of her, waiting around the corner. She always was restless. Even in the pictures we have of her as a young girl, she seemed to look past you, into the distance. I was surprised she stayed here on the farm with us as long as she did. She seemed content when your dad was here and you two were babies. But, like I said, she changed after he left and got real restless. * * * *

As for this pregnant cat that adopted us. You know, I've said NO CATS because I like to have birds in the yard. But she came here because she needed us and I think we needed her, too. I hate to admit it, but I've gotten quite fond of her—even when she brings me her dead mice. But I thought it was kind of sneaky when Grandpa said you had already named her and then quick looked around the room for a good name. He might as well have called her Peony as Bloom. Imagine naming a cat after a vase of flowers. She seems like part of the family now. Remember when Bloom had her kittens in the box with all the picture pieces? When she started to wash them you asked, "Who taught Bloom to be a mother?" And you didn't want her to go outside after she had kittens, because you were afraid she would leave them. But she is still here.

I think Bloom helped us see that taking care of each other and loving each other is what makes us a family. You reminded me of Grandpa when you asked if you could take a family picture using the timer for the camera. You wanted us to have real smiles, the kind that shows in our eyes. And you wanted to include your friend Cooper, because he cares about you and that makes him part of your special family. Grandpa and I will always care about you and Cat. Remember that, Journey

Love,
Grandma (written by Kitty Skow)

Narrator:

Marcus is a wonderful guy. To me, Journey and Marcus are identical. . . . Marcus does a wonderful thing for Journey. Marcus starts creating a new past and future for Journey and Cat. Marcus knew Journey had a very hard time dealing with his mom tearing up the pictures, so Marcus started creating a new one. . . . Marcus takes pictures of everything. Marcus mounts the pictures on the barn wall.

But the greatest thing Marcus did was to teach Journey how to take pictures. This opened Journey's mind to different points of view that he needed to come to peace with his mom leaving. Here is a letter that Marcus might have written to Journey.

Dear Journey,

I know I often say things you don't want to hear, but it has always been my way to speak the truth as I see it. It has been hard for you and for all of us since your mother left. I wish I could help you understand why she left us. I watch you searching for clues, trying to imagine what it was like when you were younger, wanting to believe everything was happy and perfect then.

I've seen so much anger and fury in your face, and sometimes deep sadness when a letter comes from your mama with money, but no words for you and Cat. You don't always like it when I take pictures of you, but I want you to see what I see when I look at you. You said once that things look different through the camera lens, not like they are in real life. Sometimes that's true, but sometimes I think the camera shows us what is really there, even if it's different than what we expect.

Journey, do you remember the first picture you took—the one when I was playing with Cooper's baby brother? The camera moved a little so the edges of the picture were blurred and fuzzy. You thought it was a bad picture, but I think the soft edges frame that picture in a way that makes it look like a memory or a painting. A thing doesn't have to be perfect to be fine . . . things can be good enough. * * * *

I was a little surprised when your mother called last week and asked you to come for a visit. I thought you'd want to go, but you told her that a cat has come and is staying here with you forever and that the cat is a very good mother. You told me later that someday if she sent you words instead of money, maybe you would want to see her—maybe, someday. And then you said to me, "Grandpa, I told her nothing is perfect. Sometimes things are good enough." I'm proud of you for remembering that; it's a very grown-up thing to understand. * * * *

Journey, you still have a lot of people that love you and care about you. I think you realized that when you asked to take your own family picture. Remember? It was after Bloom had her kittens. It's here on the wall. You asked Cooper to be in the picture with all of us and you wanted real smiles, the kind that you can see in the eyes. The camera knows if smiles are real.

I'm glad you have a cat and kittens to take care of. You were right when you said you needed to keep her the night she came to your room. We all needed her—to take care of and to show us how important it is that we take care of each other. And I'm glad you remembered by yourself that it was me who held you on my knee and sang "Trot, Trot to Boston." I've always cared about you and I always will.

Love,
Grandpa (written by Kitty Skow)

Narrator:

And now Journey. I knew Journey from the very beginning. It was hard for me because I knew Journey needed to work through it by himself. I could see him struggling with everything. I was even with him when he was trying to put the torn pictures back together. It was then, I think, things started falling into place for Journey. He began to understand what was going on. Bloom also helped Journey with dealing with his mom. Here is a letter that Journey might have written to Marcus:

Dear Grandpa:

It's been a really long summer, but I think I've learned more as an eleven-year-old than I ever have before. I know now that it was you all along who has always really taken care of me, even when Mom was here. I thought I remembered sitting on my dad's lap playing trot-trot to Boston, but now I know that I have no memories of him, but that those earliest memories are of you. I also remember falling down in a puddle when I was little, and it was you, not Mom, that picked me up. Although I was angry that it wasn't Mama taking care of me, now I know that you were doing the best for me, always.

I remember that day in the spring when Mom left. She said she'd be back, and I wanted to believe her. I'm sorry I hit you that day, but it really hurt me that you said she *wouldn't* come back. I was so afraid you might be right. It used to bother me that you always said everything you thought. Like the first time we got an envelope from Mom. There was no return address and no note—only money. I didn't want to talk about it and I didn't want to hear about it, but you always say what's on your mind. I understand that now and I like it. I always know exactly where I stand; there are no mysteries. You tell the truth even when I don't want to hear it. There's security in that.

You understood me when nobody else did. It hurt me so much when you told me Mama had torn up all of our family pictures, but I knew you were being honest even if I didn't want to hear it. You told Grandma I had a right to the torn-up family pictures that we found later, that I could try to piece them together. I think that's when I really began to understand about the camera and the pictures.

When Cat gave you her camera, it just really annoyed me that you were constantly taking pictures. I guess everything annoyed me then. I wasn't very happy. I really didn't understand why you would want to have that camera with you always, or why the pictures were so important to you. After all, we saw each other everyday and we lived on this old farm everyday. What could those pictures show us that we didn't see all of the time? After all, the picture Cat had on her dresser of our father never told me the things I wanted to know, like "What did he think of Cat and me? Where was he? Would I know him if I saw him?" That picture you took that day you got the camera tells me a lot, though, now. Cat is laughing, Grandma is grinning, and I'm looking at you behind the camera with fury. I sure was angry at everyone and everything back then. I even asked later that day why you always took pictures. Grandma said because you had to. She brought out old pictures of the family, and when I said that she looked happy as a little girl, she said that the camera knew. That time when Cooper was over and I was playing with the camera, I said I didn't like it because what you saw through it didn't look real. You said that the camera shows us what is really there, and maybe that's why people take pictures. Although I disagreed at the time, I think I knew even then that I had seen you, a softer side of you, through the camera that I had just never taken the time to see before. I really started to understand then. There was that time later on, too, when we looked at the picture I had taken of Grandma and the cat in the garden. You said that Grandma needed the cat, and I said, "The camera knows." Grandma said once that we all do the best we can, that we all deal with things in our own ways. Cat once told me about why you like the camera so much, why you were always making us take family pictures. She said you want to give me back everything Mama took away. You want to give me family, things for me to look back on.

Thanks, Grandpa, for teaching me what family is really all about, and giving me a past to look back on.

Love,
Journey (written by Lisa L. Hyland)

These five letters reveal the repercussions of the mother's departure. They also convey the emotions of the characters, concomitantly expressing the empathy of the student writers. The class, listening to these words and the vocal tones of the readers also understood.

THANK YOU, DR. MARTIN LUTHER KING, JR. BY ELEANORA TATE

Letters are a significant role-playing medium. One of the variations I have used followed a class response discussion of *Thank You, Dr. Martin Luther King, Jr.* in the Children's Literature: Issues and Trends course. The class had responded with empathy and surprise. They were empathetic with the dilemma of the protagonist, Mary Eloise, who feels threatened by reminders of her race's heritage of slavery; they were startled into surprise, perhaps disbelieving, given their own stated sense of equality, that Mary Eloise hated "dark skin" and rejected other features of her race. Causes and effects of her attitudes had been clarified on an intellectual level.

The purpose of this writing letters with discussion scenario was to explore and expand these responses with a more emotional and personal letter. Students were asked to write a predraft of two letters; that is, letters they wanted very much to write later but only had 15 minutes to work on now, to jot down some key points. The first letter was to go to Mary Eloise out of concern for her behavior and her dilemma from any of the other characters. (The characters chosen ranged from Mary Eloise's best friend to her grandmother to her racist teacher.) The second letter was to be Mary Eloise's response to the received letter. In the interval between letters, I filled the chalkboard with proposed content of the first letters, organized by character; these were discussed. I collected the letters and, in the next class session, returned them at random so the second letter could be composed. The contents of the second letter were also recorded and discussed.

Invitation 13.2

Prepare a list of persons within and outside texts to whom readers might write letters to help create connections with and understandings of the text. Prepare a supporting list of situations that might invite such letters.

THE BRAVE BY ROBERT LIPSYTE

A sequel to *The Contender,* Lipsyte's 1967 widely read and taught novel set in Harlem, *The Brave* features Sonny Bear, an aspiring boxer from a New York state Mohawk reservation. Alfred Brooks, the contending boxer of the prequel, is a major supporting character—a sergeant on the police narcotics squad. Sonny leaves the "Res" to prove his independence and to "be somebody." In New York, immediately and innocently, he becomes involved in a narcotics operation. His troubles escalate despite warnings and support attempts from Brooks.

This scenario is staged at the height of his turmoil when Sonny faces a critical decision. The setting is a juvenile court hearing to establish his culpability, goals, and needs in relation to his "placement." Groups of four or five students are formed: Brooks and other police officers; Sonny's Uncle Jake, who has been his guardian and trainer, and other tribal representatives; the boxing commission representatives; social workers; and Sonny. Several judges preside with the task of asking probing questions to keep the hearing on track.

After a planning period, the hearing is opened, setting the stage for statements of issues, confrontations, and cross-examination. Although Sonny has supporters, the students enacting his role must establish his sense of growth and self-knowledge, defending his actions and his goals as they perceive them.

Do not expect a tidy hearing or a resolved outcome. The cross-currents of dialogue and the pulls on Sonny from several groups can become intense. Sonny may be contradictory and uncertain. However, Sonny's choices and interior rage are illuminated, including his Mohawk heritage and societal prejudice. Revealing is his struggle to find his way.

CONCLUSION

The role of the teacher in a reader-response literature classroom is, first, to encourage the readers' initial responses to the text. This first conversation or activity serves as invitation to a quest; it should pique readers' curiosity and offer the promise of discovery. Having set these expectations, the teacher formulates further discussions and activities to advance and enhance these musings. Through these, readers are guided to an awareness of details and attitudes, some of which might have been overlooked; they are brought to a keener consideration of motivations, relationships, ideas, and issues. The intention is not to solidify a class reading—the class's version of a single or "correct" interpretation—but to urge both a broader and deeper reading; that is, a more valid one.

Acknowledging the need to advance and enhance responses—which concomitantly acknowledges the probable insufficiency of only an initial or singular response session, especially for longer works—sets in motion the selection of teaching and learning strategies. As exemplified in this volume, these range from journal writing of several types to Readers Theatre, including, of course, role-play scenarios. A parallel but variant approach is described and exemplified by Peter Adams; identified as "dependent authorship," the task for students is to "*take on the role of the author,* and to write from 'inside' the world of the text" (121). In contrast to stepping inside the text as its characters, students as authors imaginatively reconstruct a gap in the text or add an episode or epilogue. It should be understood that the degree of development and refinement of these activities varies with student maturity, reading sophistication, training, and practice.

Selection of activity is made with regard to both the readers' readiness and the text's openness to applications. Care should be taken to avoid undue repetition. Teachers can anticipate resistance from some students to doing something different or to such overt activity. Also, there is a certain comfort for readers in first impressions that may be conjoined with a non-readiness to abandon the safe haven of an immature reading plateau, a relatively shallow personal reading expectation. In this context, there is resistance to rereading and further investigation, comparable to rejection of the revision process in writing.

Role-playing scenarios have the merit of breaking down or minimizing these negations. They are insistently active. As such, they draw in a wide range of students, including those who are timid, seemingly passive, in whole-class discussions. The small group orientation of the typical role play provides a less threatening venue. Also, exchanging identities seems to be appealing to students, releasing them, perhaps, from personal vulnerability. In the context of the active learning mode, role plays generally are framed in rhetorically based (as compared to rhetorically deficient) situations. Arthur Daigon defines these situations as having a logical context with a real-world applicability or orientation, an audience other than the teacher, and purposes that have "consequences beyond learning the isolated skill or fact" (4). Requisites for role playing are careful reading and imagination. The planning stage induces recursive reading behavior without the necessity of teacher assignment—rereading portions of the text, reflecting on details and reassessing characters, and exploring earlier experiences and preliminary interpretation of the text. The imagination of the participants bubbles up through these discussions, adding a dynamic quality to the enactment.

Invitation 13.3

Role plays can be made more comfortable for students and more successful for learning (i.e., enhancing and interpreting literature) with some training in oral skills. Prepare a list of such skills with ideas for teaching and practicing these. With your small group, compile a full list.

The brake on the developing scenario is the text that constrains the readers in their characterizations and the evolution of the situation and issues. Personal responses of the individual readers are weighted and balanced, one reader with another, to effect the presentation.

> There is, in fact, nothing in the recognition of the personal nature of literature that requires an acceptance of the notion that every evocation from a text is as good as every other. We need only think of our successive readings of the same text, at 15 or 30 or 50. to know that we can differentiate. Undisciplined, irrelevant, or distorted emotional responses and the lack of relevant experience or knowledge will, of course, lead to inadequate interpretations of the text. The aim is to help the student toward a more and more controlled, more and more valid, or defensible, response to the text. (Rosenblatt, *Literature* 267)

An ultimate goal, imbedded in these statements, is the examination by individual readers of their reading behavior and growth. Such study emerges from the scrutiny of the individual response in comparison to those of other readers within the cross-currents of discussion and from the contrasting of early to later interpretations. A consciousness of preconceptions or biases may emerge or a recognition of inattention to or exaggeration of certain aspects may occur. Role-playing scenarios tend to disallow or reduce passive acceptance of a point of view or a prescribed characterization and to create a consciousness of how an interpretation has been shaped and reshaped.

REFERENCES

Adams, Peter. "Writing from Reading — 'Dependent Authorship' as a Response." *Readers, Texts, Teachers*. Eds. Bill Corcoran and Emrys Evans. Upper Montclair, NJ: Boynton/Cook Publishers, 1987. 119–52.

Daigon, Arthur. "Using Adolescent Literature in the Classroom." *Wisconsin English Journal* 23 (January 1981): 4–8.

Frost, Robert. "Home Burial." *The Poems of Robert Frost*. New York: Modern Library/Random House, 1946.

Lipsyte, Robert. *The Brave*. New York: HarperCollins, 1991.

MacLachlan, Patricia. *Journey*. New York: Dell, 1991.

Mazer, Norma Fox. *Out of Control*. New York: Morrow Junior Books, 1993.

Miller, Arthur. *The Crucible*. New York: Theatre Arts, 1953.

Morrison, Toni. *The Bluest Eye*. New York: Holt, Rinehart and Winston, 1970.

Niatum, Duane. "Crow's Sun." *Talking Leaves: Contemporary Native American Short Stories*. Ed. Craig Lesley. New York: Dell, 1991. 208–16.

Rosenblatt, Louise M. *Literature as Exploration*. 5th ed. New York: Modern Language Association, 1995.

———. *The Reader, the Text, the Poem: The Transactional Theory of the Literary Work*. Carbondale: Southern Illinois University Press, 1978.

Salinger, J. D. *The Catcher in the Rye*. Boston: Little, Brown, 1951.

Tate, Eleanora E. *Thank You, Dr. Martin Luther King, Jr*. New York: Franklin Watts, 1990.

Whiteman, Roberta Hill. "Summer Girl." *Taking Leaves: Contemporary Native American Short Stories*. Ed. Craig Lesley. New York: Dell, 1991. 331–54.

14

A Writing-to-Learn/Reader-Response Approach to Teaching *Antigone*

Duane H. Roen

I must begin with a confession. When I was a senior in Clair Stein's humanities class at Baldwin-Woodville High School, Wisconsin, in the spring of 1967, we studied Sophocles' *Antigone.* By the time I had finished reading the play, I fantasized that I could save Antigone from her cursed fate if I were to marry her. Since then, every time I have read or seen or taught the play, I have had flashbacks to those romantic adolescent dreams. I also have them every time I drive by the Antigone Bookstore at the intersection of Fifth Street and Fourth Avenue in Tucson—something that happens several times each week.

I've chosen to write about *Antigone* in this chapter because my own experiences with the play suggest that it, more than most works of literature, evokes strong emotional responses in those who read or see it—responses that can serve as foundations for in-depth study of the work.

I also have chosen to offer a writing to learn (WTL) approach, as described by Anne Ruggles Gere in *Roots in the Sawdust: Writing to Learn Across the Disciplines* and by Stuart Brown, Robert Mittan, and Duane Roen in *Becoming Expert: Writing and Learning in the Disciplines.* In a nutshell, WTL approaches, as I demonstrate throughout this chapter, encourage people to use writing as a tool for learning—for making sense of the world. The focus is on learning, not on learning to write as it is in composition classrooms. Learning to write may be a by-product of writing to learn, but it is not the primary goal.

WTL strategies work especially well in conjunction with the kinds of reader-response strategies that Louise Rosenblatt offers in *Literature as Ex-*

ploration and *The Reader, the Text, the Poem* because they encourage readers to respond individually and privately *before* choosing how to respond publicly, particularly in a classroom filled with peers.

BIOPOEMS

I begin with the *biopoem,* one of the most effective and versatile of the many WTL activities available. This activity has been a mainstay at National Writing Project sites since at least 1981, but it was formally institutionalized by Gere (222) and later by Brown, Mittan, and Roen (46–50). The form looks like this:

Line 1: First name
Line 2: Four traits that describe character
Line 3: Relative of _____
Line 4: Lover of _____ (list several people or things)
Line 5: Who feels _____ (several things)
Line 6: Who needs _____ (several things)
Line 7: Who fears _____ (several things)
Line 8: Who gives _____ (several things)
Line 9: Who would like to see _____ (several things)
Line 10: Resident of _____
Line 11: Last name

When I use the biopoem, I first use it as an autobiographical poem to give students a chance to introduce themselves to everyone in the class. Of course, as I introduce the form to them, I write one about myself on the board for several reasons: (a) so they can see their teacher modeling the activity; (b) so they can get to know and feel comfortable with their teacher early in the course; and (c) so they can see their teacher struggle to produce a draft of something. The last reason is important because students often hold the myth that English teachers always write perfectly formed, complete discourse on the first attempt. My completed autobiographical poem might look like this:

Duane,
a Norwegian, a nerd, a romantic, an optimist
father of Nicholas James and Hanna Elizabeth
who loves playing shortstop, listening to *A Prairie Home Companion,* and
    restoring antique furniture
who feels sometimes overworked, often tired, but usually optimistic
who needs more time to work, to parent, and to recreate
who fears that he will outlive his children, that true success will elude him,
    and that the world's problems will persist

who gives lots of time to his students, too little to his children, and his best
    whenever he can
who would like to see all of his ancestors, an end to all suffering in the world,
    and a happy ending to the Oedipus Cycle
resident of one of the warmest cities in the United States,
Roen

Notice that I have used this opportunity to show students that I'm a lot like them; I'm not without frailties and have a full range of emotions. I've also noted that I have a particular emotional stake in *Antigone*, the play that we will soon study. On the day that we do these autobiographical poems, as many students as possible and who are willing will read their autobiographical poems to the class. And, members of the class will respond using a procedure borrowed from Peter Elbow (76–99) and modified by others, including Richard Koch and Bill Lyons. It works this way. After you've read some of your writing to your readers (or they've read it themselves), ask them first to tell you two or three things they identified with in the writing. That is, have them tell you how their experiences relate to those described in the piece of writing. Second, ask them to tell you several features of the writing that they liked. Third, have them ask questions to clarify points from your writing. Fourth, encourage them to offer suggestions for improving the writing.

It may help your readers if you go so far as to give them part of the wording for responding:

- I identify with . . .
- I like . . .
- I have these questions: . . .
- I suggest . . .

Invitation 14.1

Try, first, a biopoem of yourself for practice and, perhaps, revelation. Then, with a small group choose a character from a book you have all read that has teaching potential for you and write a biopoem of a central character. Compare your biopoems, as suggested earlier.

This procedure works successfully for training readers because it accommodates the needs of both the writers and their readers so well. The first step in the procedure, identification, allows a reader to establish a sense of community with the writer. Writers need to feel confident that everyone in the room is concerned about their and everyone else's welfare. The second step, relating approval, gives a reader a chance to reinforce the writer's sense of self-worth. This is very important because too many inexperienced writers have endured a decade or more of abusive comments aimed at their writing. Once these first two procedures have made both writers and readers feel comfortable with the transaction, the third step, the questions, will work to show writers that they may not have quite met readers' needs. It helps writers see ways of translating what Carnegie Mellon University writing scholars Linda Flower and John Hayes call "writer-based prose" (writing that meets the *writer's* needs and/or that makes sense to the writer) into "reader-based prose" (writing that also meets *readers'* needs and/or that makes sense to readers). Answering these questions helps writers understand that although readers can read words on paper, readers cannot read the writers' mind. The fourth step, asking for suggestions, if it were not preceded by the first three, would be difficult for both writers and readers; it's not always easy to either offer or accept suggestions. But because it follows the first three steps, writers and their readers trust each other enough to feel comfortable with suggestions. Incidentally, I've found that carefully guiding readers through the first three steps makes the fourth step unnecessary, especially if readers are encouraged to ask a sufficient number of questions at the third step.

I describe and explain this response procedure here because I think that it teaches students to respond to others' written and oral classroom work in a constructive, respectful way. As a result, I have found, students feel secure about offering ideas to the class. Of course, later responses are not limited to this four-step procedure, but I think that it is an important starting point for group discussion.

Once the class has begun to read *Antigone,* each student writes a biopoem for some character in the play. The poem might be biographical, or it might be autobiographical, with each student assuming the persona of a character. In either case, students usually choose the title character. A biopoem about Antigone might look like this:

Antigone,
resolved, brave, ill-fated
daughter of Oedipus and Jocasta
who loved her dead brothers, Polyneices and Eteocles, and who loves her
    sister, Ismene, and her betrothed Haemon
who feels loyalty to both of her brothers, contempt for her uncle Creon, and
    lots of sorrow
who needs a resolution to the paradoxical problem and greater reason
who fears the fate of the unburied Polyneices and the curse on her family
who gives her love freely and her life foolishly
who would like to see a family history free of curse
resident of Thebes in Greece
_____.

When this student reads this biopoem to her classmates, they can respond in all sorts of ways. They might, for example, use the aforementioned four-step procedure. Or, one of them might say something like, "My bio-poem is a lot like yours. Let me read it now." Alternatively, someone might say, "My poem is a much different portrait of Antigone. Here's how I see her." In any event, it's easy to see how this WTL activity can lead to much discussion. What's best about this exercise, and other WTL activities as well, is the way it allows individual students to respond privately to Antigone or to Creon, Ismene, Polyneices, Eteocles, or Eurydice. In contrast, by responding to literature orally without benefit of writing about it first, some students never have an opportunity to voice much of a response—because of timidity or because someone else has already said it more eloquently.

The biopoem is particularly useful in Rosenblatt's terms because "the reader must remain faithful to the text. He [she] must be alert to the clues concerning character and motive present in the text" (*Literature* 11). When students read this or another biopoem to their classmates, they can respond by pointing out how they found and used other clues. Furthermore, when several students have read their biopoems about Antigone, more and more clues are offered for consideration. Students can then debate and perhaps come to a consensus about how to interpret various clues. Then, as Rosenblatt suggests, each student "will then be led to revise or broaden his initial tentative assumptions" (*Literature* 12); however, each original biopoem still exists as a partial record of each student's thinking.

UNSENT LETTERS

Another favorite WTL activity is the unsent letter, thoroughly described in Gere (227) and in Brown, Mittan, and Roen (54–56). The name of this activity tells much about it. Each student in the class writes a letter. Students may keep their own persona to write a letter to Antigone, for example. Other students may assume the persona of Oedipus, writing to his daughter from beyond the grave. Still other students, taking the persona of Ismene, may write to her sister to try to accomplish what she could not achieve in oral pleading. Yet another group of students, keeping their own persona, may write to Sophocles to urge him to change the ending of the play because they like happy endings. Each of these letters, of course, must remain unsent because the "receivers" of them are either dead or fictional. If I had known about unsent letters when I read *Antigone* in high school, I might have written the following letter:

February 14, 1967

Antigone
The Palace of Creon
Thebes, Greece 32200

Dearest Antigone,

I love you, Antigone. I have loved you since I first met you when I read the play that Sophocles wrote about you and your family. Since then, I have not been able to sleep or eat because of my great longing for you. I want to take you away from Creon and Thebes and Greece so that you can live in happiness—a happiness that your family's curse will not allow. If you will let me marry you and take you from that wretched place, I will find a way to bury your dear brother Polyneices. I will find a way. And if I should get caught burying your brother, I will gladly face the consequences, knowing that you will live, if not in happiness, then in peace.

Please listen to me, Antigone, for I love you more than anyone else does or could—even Haemon, your betrothed. Together, you and I can put your life back in order.

With a longing heart,
Duane

Of course, 18-year-old Duane, on an emotional binge, ignores some details from the play—especially that Antigone's fate, like the fate of every descendent of Oedipus, is a horrible one that can't be altered. Still, his emotional response to the work—one that he might risk because he is secure in the privacy of writing—is a strong place to begin working on other, more intellectual considerations of the work. Moreover, my teaching experience tells me that students who take such risks in writing are often willing to share that writing with classmates if the class has the kind of supportive atmosphere that I've been describing throughout this chapter.

Unsent letters also work well because the letter form encourages writers to consider audience more carefully as they write. The act of writing the salutation in a letter helps to focus attention on the addressee—and, in this case, a particular literary character. In addition, the salutation helps the writer adopt the persona of someone actually addressing that character. Characters seem more "alive."

One extension of this activity that uses letters more fully is to encourage students to exchange letters and write replies. For example, if my student Tim assumes the persona of Haemon to write to Antigone, I will encourage Eileen, who has assumed the persona of the title character, to exchange letters with Tim. The exchanges can go on for some time, and they can lead to ever-deepening understanding of the character involved.

Of course, at times I will encourage students to share their letters and their exchanges of letters with the class; I may even duplicate some for the class. The resulting classroom discussions can be vigorous and engaging. Each "reader's contribution in the two-way, 'transactional' relationship with the text" (Rosenblatt, *Reader* ix) becomes obvious to everyone in the room because the letter form makes it so explicit. (For more on matters of audience, see Kirsch and Roen.)

JOURNAL AND LEARNING LOG WRITINGS

In addition to the activities that I've already described, I have other favorite WTL activities designed to help students respond to literature in such a way that they begin to see literature as related to human experience. Recommended as journal or learning log writings, the following activities, like those already described, enable students to read more carefully and to understand characters, events, settings, and other features of literature more fully. Here's how I word them for students:

1. If a passage or scene strikes some chord in you, stop to freewrite about it. You might start with the emotional response that the passage or scene evokes.

2. Write a hypothetical conversation that you might have with a character. You might tell that character about another character's actions or thoughts. You might warn that character about upcoming events in the novel. You might counsel the character to act in a certain way. You might tell how the character misunderstands events or characters in the novel.

3. Write a hypothetical conversation between two characters.

4. List personality traits of each character.

5. Write a letter to the author telling what you like and dislike about the literary work.

6. Place a character in a setting not found in the literary work. Describe how the character would act in that new setting. Explain why the character would act that way.

7. Pretend that you will make a film from the literary work. How would you cast the film? Where would you shoot it? What sort of shots (camera angle, distance, lens) would you use for some particular scene(s)?

8. List questions that occur to you as you read or after you have read. Bring those questions to class for discussion.

9. Does this literary work remind you of other works of literature? Or does some character or some issue remind you of others? If so, describe the similarities.

10. Write a dialogue in which you introduce a character to a friend of yours.

11. Take a special interest that you have—your major or a hobby, for example. Use some system of analysis from that special interest to analyze some feature of the literary work. This approach might easily lead directly to a critical essay, by the way.

12. Take on the persona of a character; write a diary entry.
13. Use metaphors to describe a character, setting or conflict.
14. Retell the story to a child and/or an adult who hasn't read the literary work.
15. Make a time-line for the story.
16. Rewrite the story into a soap opera.

Invitation 14.2

Select one of the suggested writings involving dialogue. After you have finished writing a dialogue, analyze your effort to establish the points of difficulty to assess learning and teaching needs for such assignments.

TOPICS FOR CLASSROOM DISCUSSION AND CRITICAL ESSAYS

To help teachers find ways to translate these pieces of writing into classroom discussion and, in some cases, critical essays, I offer the following strategies:

1. You might ask several students to read entries at the beginning of class. Those entries might serve as the basis for that day's discussion. Of course, you will need to plan to use specific kinds of entries to generate specific kinds of discussions.
2. You might ask students to do a specific kind of entry before they come to class. At the beginning of class, in a large group, you will give students very specific instructions for using the entries in small groups.
3. You might respond in writing to certain entries to help students see how the entries can lead to their critical essays. Here, of course, you may use both comments and questions.
4. You might ask questions in students' logs to encourage them to do certain kinds of additional entries.
5. You might use the last 5 minutes of class to have students synthesize the day's discussion.
6. You might ask students to write log entries to summarize or synthesize the work they did in small groups on a particular day.
7. You might ask two students to exchange logs to respond to each other's entries.

CONCLUSION

As the teacher, I try to assume several roles in the vigorous and engaging discussions that result from these discussions. First, of course, I do what I can to establish and encourage a supportive atmosphere. That is, I must be as supportive as I can by showing my interest, by offering positive feedback, by making certain that everyone in the room knows the ground rules for the discussion, and by expecting everyone else to be supportive. I also demonstrate my support by doing whatever writing my students do—especially the writing that they do in class. My second role is to become one of the learners in the class when we discuss anything. In this second role, I ask questions and offer comments just as students do. My responses are no more or less valuable than anyone else's. Of course, I have to step out of this role once in a while when discussions go awry—because someone decides to be hurtful or because someone wants to dominate the conversation. I don't have to do this very often, though.

I am convinced that WTL activities do much to enhance "aesthetic" reading, in which, as Rosenblatt asserts, "the reader's primary concern is with what happens *during* (emphasis hers) the actual reading event" (*Reader* 24). These WTL activities encourage so much self-reflective thought that they help the reader ensure that his or her *"attention is centered directly on what he [she] is living through during his [her] relationship with that particular text"* (25, her italics)—in this case, *Antigone.* The reader "fixes his [her] attention on the actual experience he [she] is living through. This permits the whole range of responses generated by the text to enter into the center of awareness, and out of these materials he [she] selects and weaves what he [she] sees as the literary work of art" (*Reader* 26–27). Writing is a powerful tool for learning because it "involves an *active reconstruction* of the knowledge or skill that is presented" to the learner (Wells 118). In this model teachers find ways to encourage students to use writing for exploring and reflecting on course content—again, in this case, *Antigone.* Students become more responsible for their learning, and they must work more diligently and think more critically. The teacher does not need to practice all of the skills of a writing teacher—very few of them in fact. The teacher also does not make curricular sacrifices. I believe, as the Soviet psychologist Lev Vygotsky did that "thought is not merely expressed in words; it comes into existence through them" (218).

Students who use their own written words to study *Antigone* and to prepare for class discussions of the play find that their thoughts about the dramatic work do come into existence through that writing. Furthermore, their written responses to the characters and events in *Antigone* give them a sense of ownership for their thoughts, for they are there, permanently, on the page, ready to be considered again and again and again.

ACKNOWLEDGMENTS

I must thank Robert Mittan and Nicholas Karolides for their comments on earlier draft versions of this chapter. I also thank Louise Rosenblatt for offering the profession, decades before anyone else did, wonderfully useful strategies for making literature come alive. We are all indebted to her.

REFERENCES

Brown, Stuart C., Robert K. Mittan, and Duane H. Roen. *Becoming Expert: Writing and Learning in the Disciplines.* Dubuque, IA: Kendall/Hunt, 1990.

Elbow, Peter. *Writing Without Teachers.* New York: Oxford University Press, 1973.

Flower, Linda, and John Hayes. "Plans That Guide the Composing Process." *Writing: The Nature, Development, and Teaching of Written Communication: Vol 2. Writing: Process, Development, and Communication.* Ed. C. H. Frederiksen and J. F. Dominic. Hillsdale, NJ: Lawrence Erlbaum Associates, 1981. 39–58.

Gere, Anne Ruggles, ed. *Roots in the Sawdust: Writing to Learn Across the Disciplines.* Urbana, IL: National Council of Teachers of English, 1985.

Kirsch, Gesa, and Duane H. Roen, eds. *A Sense of Audience in Written Communication.* Newbury Park, CA: Sage, 1990.

Koch, Richard. "Syllogisms and Superstitions: The Current State of Responding to Writing." *Language Arts* 59 (1982): 464–71.

Lyons, Bill. "Well What Do You Like About My Paper." *Iowa English Newsletter* (September, 1978): 4–5.

Rosenblatt, Louise M. *Literature as Exploration.* 4th ed. New York: Modern Language Association, 1983.

———. *The Reader, the Text, the Poem: The Transactional Theory of the Literary Work.* Carbondale: Southern Illinois University Press, 1978.

Sophocles. *Antigone. Oedipus the King and Antigone.* Trans. and Ed. Peter D. Arnott, New York: Appleton-Century-Crofts, 1960.

Vygotsky, Lev S. *Thought and Language.* 1934. Trans. Eugenia Hanfmann and Gertrude Vakar. Cambridge, MA: MIT Press, 1962.

Wells, Gordon. *The Meaning Makers: Children Learning Language and Using Language to Learn.* Portsmouth, NH: Heinemann, 1986.

Part IV

Exploring Differences:
Gender, Race, and Culture

The dynamics of personal and cultural experiences as they affect readers' transactions are the focus of the chapters in this section. The authors examine the distancing effect by gender, race, and culture and exemplify strategies that open students to texts. These strategies include an exploration of the evoked responses, a reflection on the factors and processes that influenced the reading.

The process of exploring the evoked response is itself a learning experience. It cultivates a habit of mind that is provocatively thoughtful and democratic. Classroom dynamics stimulate the expression and recognition of multiple viewpoints and cause readers to further reconsider their own knowledge, ideas, and belief structures. In this context, bridges of understanding to characters and cultures are built.

Reader-response approaches are particularly well suited to teaching feminist and multicultural literature. Teachers, who themselves may be "outsiders," need not place themselves in a position of authority, expressing the "correct" interpretation. Instead of being outsiders peering in, students may undertake to assume the persona of the character in the text. This allows those outside the gender or ethnic group depicted in the text to become momentary insiders and those inside the gender or ethnic group to validate their own experiences.

In chapter 15, Laura Quinn expresses the nature of "gendered reading" and develops comprehension of the orientation of such female and male readings in response to Susan Glaspell's "feminist" drama *Trifles*. Through class interactions and journal writing she provides opportunities for the "evolution and elaboration" of these preliminary responses. Quinn identifies two intervention strategies she uses to help students understand the gendered nature of their responses and reflect on their implications. The description of the preliminary and the evolving responses demonstrates the progressive transaction with the text engendered by such class collaboration: The responses become "more complex and less closed in their understanding."

At the center of chapter 16 is the concept of the reader as outsider. To help his students gain access to two Native American novels, David Furniss asks them to identify problems and questions they face as readers in responding to experiences far removed from their own. His focus is on opening their reactions to the text and exploring these as a means of getting closer to the events and characters. He describes a reading journal strategy accomplished in class (and two other failed attempts) that generates personal reactions revealing the students' outsider perspective. He projects the discussion of these journal entries, highlighting the focus of the students' concerns and their wide divergence of opinions. He notes that the subsequent response to the novels was closer to characters and their world—"close enough to be able to talk to other outsiders and insiders about them in a way they might not have been able to before."

By focusing on the responses of one reader, Arlette Ingram Willis, in chapter 17, examines the impact of the reading of a multicultural autobiography, Hayslip's *When Heaven and Earth Changed Places* on a second reading of O'Brien's *The Things They Carried*. All three of this reader's responses are included, illustrating meaningfully the development of an enhanced interpretation of the original text. Willis argues for the empowerment of "individuals to be socially and culturally conscious readers, writers, thinkers, listeners, and consumers of literacy." Multicultural literature serves a significant role in this regard, providing a significant historical and cultural perspective, an "alternative point of view."

Chapter 18 constitutes an analysis of a research study of a group of teachers participating in a class, Culture, Literacy and Autobiography, and a book club, the Literary Circle. Of the three case studies, one focuses on two Maya Angelou autobiographies, *I Know Why the Caged Bird Sings* and *Gather Together in My Name*, centering on reactions to race issues; the second focuses in Jill Ker Conway's *The Road From Courain*, drawing from the use of personal narratives by the readers; and the third reveals insights from teacher interviews about their learning. The authors analyze these teachers' responses both to the texts and the dialogic nature of their learning experiences and provide insights for classroom instruction.

Asserting that "Literary voices from the African Diaspora . . . bring a different lens through which African Americans and European Americans may have an opportunity to embrace a broader understanding of human nature and race issues in the Americas," in chapter 19, Linda Spears-Bunton illustrates her thesis with a class discussion of *Krik? Krak!* Her class, representing a broad spectrum of cultures, responds with surprise and dismay to this collection of nine stories of Haiti. The chapter includes bridge-making teaching tips, a bibliography, and a discussion of the social and cultural context for response.

In chapter 20, Jean E. Brown and Louise Garcia Harrison illustrate the range of responses to Theodore Roethke's "My Papa's Waltz" and discuss the influence of personal and social context on the transactions of readers. Two methods of involving students are explained—an oral brainstorming approach and a written journal activity. The discussion that follows expresses the students' recognition of multiple perspectives as well as how and why there have been varied responses.

15

Trifles as **Treason**
Coming to Consciousness
as a Gendered Reader

Laura Quinn

In *Literature as Exploration,* Louise M. Rosenblatt describes one of the aims of her reader-response approach to literature in the following manner:

> One can have no quarrel with the fact that the attitudes and ideas the reader brings to literature are the results of his past experience. Our concern is rather that if the student's superstructure of ideas is built on too narrow a base, he should be helped to gain broader and deeper insight through literature itself. That is why our emphasis has been on the interaction between the reader and the literary work. When the reader becomes aware of the dynamic nature of that interaction, he may gain some critical consciousness of the strength or weaknesses of the emotional and intellectual equipment with which he approaches literature (and life). Since we interpret the book or poem in terms of our fund of past experiences, it is equally possible and necessary that we come to reinterpret our old sense of things in the light of the new ways of thinking and feeling offered by the work of art. Only when this happens has there been a full interplay between book and reader, and hence a complete and rewarding literary experience. (126)

I find this statement of purpose to be of use to me, consistently and paradigmatically as I employ a reader-response approach in my literature classes. It is particularly applicable to the project of encouraging *gendered reading*— reading that acknowledges all of the cultural bases and biases of gender on the part of the reader—among students who have never consciously regarded themselves as gendered readers and may well resist doing so. One

way to bring students to such consciousness is to begin a literature course
with a discussion of the first statement in the Rosenblatt passage just quoted.
Generally students "have no quarrel" with the statement and are often interested in naming, listing, and writing about (in a journal assignment or an
in-class impromptu) the elements of their past experience that they believe
they bring to the reading of a literary text. The products of such an exercise,
written or oral, will, of course, contain gendered components (intersected
with race, ethnicity, and class) that the students themselves can readily identify as categories under which their past experience can be organized. The
process of situating themselves as readers sets the stage for the kind of self-
conscious and reflective reading that a reader-response approach demands.

As Rosenblatt indicates in the passage quoted, however, the situating of
oneself as a reader must be a dynamic process if learning is to take place. Indeed, the very purpose of identifying oneself as, for example, a White, male,
middle-class reader with a strong work ethic and a Christian belief system
is to be enabled to "gain some critical consciousness of the strength and
weaknesses of the emotional and intellectual equipment with which he approaches literature (and life)." What I wish to achieve in the classroom when
using a reader-response approach to a text is student understanding of both
the conditional nature of their response(s) to a text and the potential for
evolution and elaboration of those responses as a result of interaction with
the response of others, intervention by the instructor, time, reflection, and
rereading.

A large part of bringing students to consciousness as gendered readers is
sharing with them the theory of what we are doing and letting them in on
the approach. Being open about the underlying principles of the reader-
response project and presenting the project as exploratory and provisional
(a kind of working hypothesis) rather than as the definitive way in which students do and should read are ways of averting the students' suspicion of
being manipulated by a teacher with an agenda—always a risk when teaching "gender." This is why I begin my classes with the writing exercise that responds to the first line of the Louise Rosenblatt statement at the head of this
chapter—why I ask students frontally to situate themselves as readers of any
text. What I like to do next is share with them the theory about gender and
reading developed by Elizabeth Flynn in 1986, a theory that expands Rosenblatt's transactional principle to include gender relations as they are in-
flected by historical power differentials. Briefly, Flynn describes readers as
falling along a continuum from the *dominant* to the *submissive* (in terms of
the reader's relation to the text) with the (clearly desirable) *interactive* reader
falling in the middle. A dominant reader is characterized by a detachment
from the text that resists or refuses involvement. Such a reader will silence a
text by resisting both its full potential for meaning and his or her own possibilities of being transformed by the text. A submissive reader is marked by an

involvement that disables detachment and analysis, is overwhelmed by the marks on the page, and will often be able to produce little more than plot summary in response. An interactive reader exhibits a capacity for enough detachment coexisting with enough involvement to produce a meaningful transaction with the text (267–71). What is important about the continuum model here is that dominant and submissive reading responses to a text are not *disqualified* in relation to the interaction—they can, alternatively, be seen as excesses along a line that brings detachment and involvement together, in the middle, in a dialectical relation. In other words, all responses to a text (even the most hostile rejections or the most slavish entrapments) have the potential to move or be moved toward interaction.

Invitation 15.1

Consider Elizabeth Flynn's description of readers; that is, the three categories of readers that she defines. Conduct a self-analysis, identifying the types of books—or specific books—toward which you are a dominant reader, a submissive reader, or an interactive reader.

Flynn's categories of readers are not inherently gendered, a point I make to my students when introducing these categories as elements in one theory about reading. Her empirical research, however, with actual students and actual texts (Joyce's "Araby" and Hemingway's "Hills Like White Elephants," for instance) yielded some gendered results in which "men students were often closer to the extremes of domination or submission, and the women were often closer to the interactive center" (276). Our classroom use of these categories, I emphasize, is to test and, perhaps, complicate them with our own experience as a group of readers analyzing collectively our individual transactions with common texts. What I hope to produce in the classroom—and what students often find engaging in simultaneously self-reflexive and analytical ways—is a kind of anthropological investigation of ourselves as a classroom culture of readers. The same standards of interactiveness (containing both involvement and detachment) that we might ideally bring to a transaction with a text can also be brought to bear on the study of ourselves as a community of readers of a particular text.

A text that I have found particularly valuable in achieving these ends is Susan Glaspell's 1916 play, *Trifles* (or its short story version "A Jury of Her Peers"). *Trifles* raises close-to-the-bone gender issues to which any student can respond, but it also raises those issues in a problematic way that discourages (eventually if not initially) reductive readings, simplistic analyses, and premature responsive closure. It is a short and accessible text, one that can be taught so as to produce the "full interplay between book and reader" celebrated by Louise Rosenblatt.

Judith Fetterley calls *Trifles* a story about reading in which "the theory of reading proposed in it is explicitly linked to the issue of gender" (147). It is because this text is "about" gendered reading that it can be used to get students to look at and engage in gendered reading. Such reading (or the consciousness of such reading) will not take place without careful strategies on the part of the teacher. Perhaps more than any other theoretical approach to texts, the reader-response strategy works best, in my experience, when it becomes, in the classroom, both a highly permissive and a highly self-conscious approach, one that (initially) turns students loose on a text and admits almost any response as potentially interesting, at the same time, pulling back regularly and rigorously to examine variant responses, to feel for their roots, and to evaluate not their correctness or usefulness, but rather relation to text, classroom, responder, and a larger social context.

More concretely, when students claim at the start, for example (as some, mostly male students do when I teach *Trifles*) that the play is a bore, it is important and productive to credit that response with some authenticity and plausibility by posing the question (which may not be answerable until much later in the discussion but can be posed at the time of the response) of why and to whom this particular text might seem initially boring. The text may bore more men than women, the text may bore dominant readers (such readers are often bored by the texts they dominate), and, less obviously, the text may bore not only those who have been culturally programmed to resist it but also and especially those against whom the text's treason (to be discussed later) is committed. In short, boredom may be a logical defensive response that can illuminated rather than trashed in class discussion and one that can, thus, enrich the class's experience of the text.

I have taught *Trifles* repeatedly in two quite different courses; one is an introductory college literature course, and the other is an introductory interdisciplinary women's studies course. In each case I have learned that student response will be marked by gender and that my position as an unabashedly feminist woman teacher colors student discussion responses in a variety of ways, sometimes eliciting resistance or, alternatively, obedient party-line responses, sometimes creating inhibition, occasionally authorizing the exploration of new ideas. Of course, the fact that the women's studies students are generally around 80% female whereas the introductory literature class tends to be evenly divided has an important impact on the group interaction to *Trifles* and on the way in which each group interaction brings about revision or revamping of a student's initial response to the text. It is important to note here that this approach to teaching this or other texts need not, indeed should not, be limited to the college classroom. At any level at which literature is taught, students have some sense of who they are in terms of gender identity and can be encouraged to see this as an ingredient in their reading strategies.

INITIAL RESPONSES TO THE TEXT

My early (prereader response) experience with teaching Glaspell's one-act play was less than successful, largely because I did not yet know how to move students beyond their initial responses to the text. Often the first response of many male and female student readers is that the text is obsolete, a period piece. The following reading journal reaction of a male student is typical:

> As for importance, I see nothing but a play about sex roles. This had its time and place, but things are to the point where such stressings are a bit outdated.

This "that was then and this is now" dismissal (a dominant response that seeks to silence the text by establishing its obsolescence) often leads to discussions consisting of anecdotal evidence of the state of gender equality in the here and now or to extended arguments (often conducted along gender lines) as to whether women's experience "then" and "now" is appreciably different. Although such discussions are often heated and interesting, they do not always serve the purpose of developing and refining students' interaction with the text. In fact they are, I believe, a way of avoiding some of the more disturbing implications of *Trifles*.

Still, I needed to learn, as the teacher in a reader-response context, to let these discussions have some play, to let students work their way through them, rather than obeying my impulse to correct and abort such a focus. Of course, the advantage of having laid out Flynn's categories as a working hypothesis of how people read in gendered ways is that we can ask of this (and every other response) if it fits the framework of dominant/submissive/ interactive. Any such claim—and many students will see the obsolete period piece reading as a dominant reading because of its judgmental dismissal of the text—requires that the students make arguments that engage both the text as a project and the critical framework and vocabulary at hand. Students become, in effect, responding readers engaged in both the evaluation of their responses and of the critical apparatus that they've been asked to try on for size. In crucial ways, the text does not get lost in this transaction, because it is the text that we must continue to go back to as the basis for both evaluations.

The other typical initial response to *Trifles* (as recorded in reading journals or proffered in class discussion) and one that, again, is shared at least in emphasis by both male and female readers is a strong tendency to focus on the events that precede the play as what the play is "about." *Trifles* centers on solving a murder mystery—which isn't much of a mystery because all the characters believe (whether eagerly or reluctantly) that Minnie Wright killed her husband, John, by strangling him in bed in their isolated farmhouse. As official and officious male characters—the Sheriff and the County

Attorney—search for significant clues to motive and to the larger picture of the crime, tag-along women—Mrs. Hale and Mrs. Peters—are assigned the task of gathering Minnie Wright's "things" to take to her in jail. The women, in their preoccupation with domestic trifles, discover the salient clues to Minnie Wright's guilt and motive (the erratic stitching of a quilt piece, the strangled canary kept in a small ornate box) whereas the men, who don't look in the right places, are stymied. In an extraordinary act of sisterhood and solidarity, the two stolid and conventional women (one, indeed, the wife of the Sheriff) conceal the clues they find, protecting Minnie and thwarting the investigation. What takes place within the play's boundaries is a self-discovery on the part of both Mrs. Peters and Mrs. Hale (at different rates and perhaps to different degrees)—a discovery of themselves as gendered subjects whose identification with Minnie Wright makes clear to each of them that they are implicated in her crime inasmuch as they, too, have experienced the kind of anger toward men that must have precipitated her violence. The further—and truly treasonous—realization that they concur in the justice of Minnie Wright's action is what enables them to conceal evidence from "their" men.

It is not surprising that students gravitate toward the murder itself (which takes place outside of and prior to the play) rather than to the collaborative aiding and abetting on the part of "normal" characters. For one thing, students are trained by the popular mystery genre to focus on whodunit as the interesting issue in a murder story; although Minnie Wright's guilt is never questioned substantively in the play, students often want to read the text in ways that will rewrite it, exonerating Minnie. Additionally, the particular scenario is not an unfamiliar one in our culture; the rightness or wrongness of a woman murdering a cruel and abusive husband is a burning and current legal and moral issue, and it is thus natural that students will find their way to this discussion. More important though, I believe, is the possibility that the behavior of Mrs. Hale and Mrs. Peters in concealing the "trifles" (the dead bird, the erratic stitching) is potentially far more threatening and more "treasonous" to established gender relations than is the murder itself. Students (and perhaps readers generally) understandably reduce the text to the murder plot to avoid the implications of the "other crime," the one that takes place within the text's boundaries. In Flynn's terms this strategy clearly qualifies as a dominant reading, one that forecloses on the text's implications.

EVOLUTION AND ELABORATION
OF THE TEXT

There is, then, this challenge for the teacher of *Trifles:* How does one encourage a more fully interactive response to the text, one that looks not only at the other crime but also at the gendered nature of that crime and the gendered nature of responses to it, resistance to it, and fear of it. What I have learned as I have attempted to meet this challenge is that a process must be undergone in the classroom in which we must collaboratively and recursively circle in on the text's complexities.

Although class discussion is the main vehicle of this process, I have found two other strategies essential: Teacher intervention that illuminates the process at certain key points (identified and elaborated later in the chapter) is necessary, and short, written, journal-like individual responses at several different stages of the process can both get it started and get it unstuck along the way. Asking students to stop discussion at any point and to write for 5 minutes about what they are thinking of the text and of the issues under discussion at this point has many benefits: It can provide quiet students with a way into the discussion if they are asked to read their written response, it can help students "discover" what they are thinking; and, it legitimatizes the process of revising one's initial response, thereby encouraging further revision.

As the discussion leader or facilitator, I had to learn to allow the inevitable (and, for me, frustrating) discussion of both the text's obsolescence and its whodunit preliminaries to take place for a bit with minimal intervention on my part. What becomes nicely clear to astute students when this happens is that the issues in the pretext (what Minnie Wright's marriage was like and what made her murder John) undermine the claim of obsolescence. In other words, a text that leads us to argue whether spouse abuse should be a legitimate legal defense in a husband murder—an issue still not resolved in our culture—can hardly be obsolete. This realization—at which I often don't have to assist at all—forces some students to regroup and reconsider their frontal response to *Trifles,* thereby setting an important precedent for reconsideration of other responses they may have had to the text. What is important for me as teacher to do at this point is to acknowledge and recognize the process of response revision and to validate not the revised response but the act of revision itself—and also to suggest that both dominant and submissive responses can be starting points for the move toward an interactive, truly transactional reading. I point out to the class here that secondary or tertiary responses are not nullifications of initial responses, but, rather, developments of them; one of the short writing exercises that asks the students to record their present reading of the text seems appropriate here to engage their ongoing interest in the dynamism of their own reading experience.

The pretext discussion—that of the rightness or wrongness of the murder, the options that Minnie Wright had or didn't have—needs to play itself out further in most classes. The viewpoint of many male students and some strongly male-identified female readers is that murder is against the law, that no excuses can be made for it, and that John Wright's strangling of Minnie's canary does not justify her strangling of him; a man is worth more than a bird. The following prediscussion journal response is characteristic of this response:

> I sympathize with Mrs. Wright to the degree of her problem but not with the killing of her husband. I believe that was too extreme of a measure to carry out. She could've sought consolation from neighboring wives or might have gone back to her family.

The clearly opposite view (and one that appears more spontaneously in the women's studies class) is most often evinced by female readers and may fall short of condoning the murder, but sees the provocation as sufficient morally if not legally, as this female student's journal entry implies:

> The most important thing in *Trifles* is the portrayal of how women put up with a lot more than they should have to then they can't take it anymore and bust or lose control. Mrs. Wright had been pushed to the limit and she couldn't take it anymore especially when her husband killed the bird, the only thing in her life that she could identify with.

Once these two positions surface in class discussion, sharp and impatient debate can break out, producing some interesting mediating strategies on the part of (mostly) female students who are uncomfortable with conflict in general and with conflict along gender lines in particular. The three mediating strategies that I have observed repeatedly are these:

1. Students return to the period piece argument that the play reflects the attitudes of earlier, less equalitarian times: "Women seemed to not be valued or given credit for being smart, functioning parts of society [then]."

2. The mediators complain that we don't get Minnie Wright's viewpoint, only secondhand piecing together of her story: "The only information given about John Wright was through the other characters. They interpreted and gave their individual views, but who is to say that they made fair judgments?"

3. Finally, we get the argument that the community of women as represented by Mrs. Hale and Mrs. Peters failed Minnie Wright. This view comes almost exclusively from female readers: "The men were careless and logical and reasoning and careless of Mrs. Wright's house or life, and though the women were upset by the men's carelessness and they respected Mrs. Wright's house, privacy and life, they too were still intruders and 'after the fact.' They should have visited her before."

These three mitigating, and mediating responses strike me as representing a progressive transaction with the text: The first anxiously moves back to the comforting claim of the text's obsolescence, overlooking earlier discussion that effectively finished this point off; these mediators are confronting classroom conflict and tension by reasserting domination over the text's potential meaning, resisting the demands of its complexity. The second position is critique of the playwright's formal choice; it asks for a different play than the one written by Glaspell, but it has the merit of moving the discussion to the issue of why Glaspell made the choice she did to focus on Mrs. Hale and Mrs. Peters rather than on Minnie Wright. It, more than the first mediating response, opens discussion rather than closing it off. The third mediating response moves us clearly toward the play's cruces; it leads to the acknowledgment of separate, gendered spheres of activity and attitude as social phenomena. It importantly shifts the focus from Minnie Wright's guilt or innocence to the events and concerns within the play's boundaries. The students have "come to" the text and are ready to begin interaction with its complexity. It is crucial, however, that they see for themselves that the third strategy gets us farther; at this point we must step back from the substance of the discussion and engage in a critical examination of the reading strategies that have emerged. Here I generally record the reading strategies that they have generated on the blackboard (asking them to help me label the strategies; e.g., we might call the second one previously described the "different play" strategy) and ask, simply, which gives us the most to talk about. The act of evaluating their own readings, interventions, and mediation reinforces the process of ongoing response revision and, in a larger sense, includes them as members of an interpretative community from which traditional pedagogies sometimes exclude them. It also invites them to test the usefulness of Flynn's categories that ask us to examine our power relations with the text.

INTERVENTION STRATEGIES

After this collaborative effort to see where we are and how far we have come seems clear and complete to all of us, I intervene and appropriate the class discussion for a bit. I do so because I wish to describe for them what I believe they have just accomplished as readers and responders (they have sorted through a variety of responses, they have debated the text's timeliness, they have grappled with the pretext, they have tested the Flynn reading hypothesis), and to go on to put what they have done into a larger context.

The first part of my intervention relates their discussion of *Trifles* to that of other works we've read in the term. In the introductory literature class I ask them to think about the legalistic–relativistic debate over Minnie Wright's crime in light of Antigone and Creon's argument over her crime of burying her brother in *Antigone;* I also refer them to the conflict between Nora and Krogstad over the legality and morality of her act of forgery in *A Doll's House.* I give a journal assignment here that asks them to compare and contrast their responses to those three crimes and to those three debates. In the women's studies class, *Trifles* appears in an altogether different literary context, one that may include such texts as Ntozake Shange's *For Colored Girls Who Have Considered Suicide When the Rainbow is Enuf,* Marge Piercy's "For Inez Garcia," Ann Petry's "Like a Winding Sheet," and Alice Walker's *The Color Purple,* as well as sociological studies of spousal abuse. These female-focused texts clearly construct a supportive context for *Trifles,* one that enables the wronged woman's perspective to be foregrounded and validated. Here, too, I ask students to engage in journal writing that measures comparatively their responses to the legal and moral issues raised in those works. It is not to load the dice that I intertextualize *Trifles* in this manner; my goal is to nudge them into consciousness of their readerly responses to (possibly) parallel texts and to get them to bring those responses to the surface, to look at them both critically and with interest.

With such an aim still in mind, I present the second part of my intervention strategy, which is to describe to the class, briefly and broadly, Carol Gilligan's findings in *In a Different Voice: Psychological Theory and Women's Development.* I present a few of Gilligan's experimental narratives and the variant male and female responses to the moral issues raised in those narratives (e.g., should the husband whose dying wife is suffering from pain and who can't afford pain medicine steal it from the pharmacy?). Gilligan's findings, summarized briefly and generally, were that male responses tend to be legalistic, rule governed, and clearly resolved in terms of a winner and a loser. Female responses in Gilligan's study tend to be fluid, contextual, relational, and directed at somewhat fuzzier "everyone wins" kinds of resolutions. I have two goals in mind in introducing Gilligan: I want them to apply her general findings on gender-specific behavior and attitudes to the "story" in *Trifles,* and I want them to consider the extent to which the discussion they've been engaged in and the responses they have experienced individually and as a group illustrate Gilligan's observations.

An interesting phenomenon occurs every time I do this in class: Neither male nor female students question or deny that they have just acted out Gilligan's principles of differing gendered voices. They see that most of the female students have responded in a relational way to Minnie Wright's dilemma, sympathizing with the suffering that John Wright's cold, silent nature and his cruel strangling of her pet bird have caused her. They can see, as well, that the legalistic position—the one that must condemn Minnie Wright because she has violated the law, because she has disrupted the social order—has been put forward mostly by male students.

Of course there are important exceptions to this positioning by gender, and these must not be ignored in class discussion. Granting that to some female students the legalistic position is paramount whereas some male students adopt a more relational stance, we can still raise the question of whether culturally and socially constructed roles are consistent with the differences that Gilligan describes. It is also important here, I believe, to introduce some of the difficulties that other theorists of difference (including feminists) have with Gilligan's categories and research methods (such as her focus on White, middle-class individuals). Students tend to naturalize assumptions about gender very readily, and a vigilant, ongoing strategy of destabilization of assumptions needs to be undertaken, both to help them resist oversimplification of the complexities of gender as a category and to inculcate the principle of self-conscious examination of the tools of criticism that they are acquiring, even at very rudimentary levels.

At this point I ask them if they see parallels between the acts of interpretation, of "reading" the text, that they have engaged in and the investigations (both the formal one undertaken by the men in *Trifles* and the informal one that Mrs. Hale and Mrs. Peters find forced on them) of the murder scene in the play. This (admittedly leading) question is designed to get us to an understanding of what gendered reading consists of, as illustrated in a parallel manner by both the text and their own experience with it.

Students are prepared now to see their own responses to *Trifles* as marked by gender and to continue to "read" the play with this consciousness. I ask them at this point to write again, briefly and in class, about their responses to the play and to focus this time not on Minnie Wright and the murder but on Mrs. Hale and Mrs. Peters and their "crime." Generally speaking, these responses become more complex than the initial responses to the play. Of course, this complexity is overdetermined; the class discussion itself, their new consciousness of what it might mean to be a dominant or submissive reader, my introduction of Gilligan and reference to texts they've read, the factors of time, and second thoughts discovered through writing all contribute to the complexity of the advanced set of responses. Here are fairly typical female and male responses to this later writing task:

> *Female:* The women, supposedly so weak-minded and incapable of mental feats, pieced together the motives for the murder quite compactly. The men, with their rough ways and unseeing eyes, missed everything. They probably would have misunderstood the dead bird that the women barely were able to conceal. The story seems sad to me in that it shows how squashed women are in a man's world, but it also shows how women can band together, help each other, and love each other. Concealing the evidence may not have been a pure gesture of love, but it was an act that probably saved the murderer's life.

> *Male:* The Sheriff and County Attorney strike me as very simplistic in their attitudes and thinking and don't appeal to me at all. Mrs. Hale and Mrs. Peters I sort of identify with in a small way. I can see their need to be protective of "their own kind." From the beginning they have this attitude and maintain it to the end. The play shows two different opposing forces in the sexes.

What seems important to me in each of these revised responses is not that they are "politically correct" from a feminist standpoint or closer to my view of the play than some of the earlier responses were, but that they are more complex and less closed in their understanding. The female response implies (obliquely) that there may be more than one motive for the concealment of the dead bird. The male response advances this by noting that the sense of separate camps—"their own kind"—that pervades the play is important and may help to explain the actions of the two women characters. Each response seems to me to contain language that suggests that the student is coming to terms with her and his own resistance to the text and concomitant desires to "dominate" its complexities; the female student's sadness and the male student's "small way" qualification hark back to earlier, more judgmental readings that were pretransactional but that also laid the groundwork for true interaction.

Invitation 15.2

Charlotte Perkins's "The Yellow Wallpaper" has been subject to similarly variant responses as *Trifles*. Conjecture (and discuss with your peers) how these responses may shape up and why. (There are two short films of "The Yellow Wallpaper." One, the Masterpiece Theatre version, expresses a feminist interpretation; the second, a 1978 International Television Corporation production, reflects a patriarchal interpretation. If these are available, you can view and respond to these interpretations.)

CONCLUSION

It is, I believe, exceedingly difficult for students at ages 18 to 20 to acknowledge and to examine the "otherness" of men and women, not to speak of the problem of seeing that asymmetry and inequality have accompanied that otherness throughout history. (Or, as Louise Rosenblatt says in the passage that opened this chapter, "the student's superstructure of ideas is built on too narrow a base.") *Trifles*, taught in a manner that validates reader response but also sees response as a fluid, developing phenomenon, can illuminate the issue of otherness in a powerful and convincing manner and can help to make students aware of their need for a more mature and sophisticated sense of otherness than their "superstructure" allows them. Because the play is about "reading," it can also serve as a vehicle for bringing the reader-response approach into the classroom as a tool that students can use individually and collectively to make meaning from a text and to make meaning of their own experience in the interactive manner that Rosenblatt introduced to the world of literary criticism 60 years ago.

Lest I be oversanguine, however, I must acknowledge a resistance to *Trifles* on the part of (mostly) male readers—one that is difficult to overcome in the classroom transaction and that, finally, needs to be assessed analytically by the class and allowed—perhaps—to remain unresolved. (This resistance is considerably less intransigent in the women's studies class than in the introductory and mostly "mainstream" literature class.) Judith Fetterley, in her essay "Reading About Reading," sheds some light on the problem in reading *Trifles*. She argues that the play is about a text, the text of Minnie Wright's life as reflected in her "trifles," her kitchen, her quilting. Mrs. Hale is able to read this text immediately; Mrs. Peters remains a resisting reader until the dead bird is found. The men in the story are not able to read Minnie Wright's text for two reasons: First, "they literally cannot recognize it as a text because they cannot imagine that women have stories" (147–48). (This recalls to me the male student who remarked in his first written response that "[he] was . . . surprised how almost the whole play circled around the two women, Mrs. Hale and Mrs. Peters." He does not account for his surprise, but we can speculate that he assumes that the "natural" protagonists of the play would be the official male characters, the Sheriff and the County Attorney.)

Second, even if the play's men could recognize the text of Minnie Wright's life, the fact is that sometimes they will not read it (Fetterley 152), a conviction that Fetterley extends to controversies over the literary canon (the literary works that are given authority by the academy and are considered "must reads" for every student of literature) and the place (or displacement) of women's texts in it. Fetterley goes on to point out what constitutes the substantive treason in *Trifles:* Men (in *Trifles* and reading *Trifles*) cannot afford to read Minnie Wright's text because it presents "a radical challenge to the premises of men's texts, premises that men rely upon to maintain the fictions of their own identity" (153). To continue, Minnie Wright's text is "nothing less than the story of men's systematic, institutionalized, and culturally approved violence toward women, and of women's potential for retaliatory violence against men" (153). The fact that this text is highly threatening to both male and female students makes it both difficult to teach and imperative to teach. Only by teaching such treason can we hope to destabilize the cultural and political condition of male privilege.

The most radical element in *Trifles* is its thoroughly female perspective— a perspective so female that it must be kept hidden from the men in the text and from the world. In fact, as Fetterley points out, Mrs. Hale and Mrs. Peters "erase the text as they read it" (152), correcting the wayward stitching and hiding the dead bird. What is easier to get to in the women's studies class than in the mainstream literature class is the way in which this erasure is a metaphor for what has happened to many women's stories throughout literary history. The fact that women erase a woman's text to save that woman is a comment on women's lives under patriarchal constraints. It may be that *Trifles'* treason would be best understood and appreciated in a class that read it alongside *The Gulag Archipelago* and *Native Son*—texts in which, as in *Trifles,* dominance, submission, and subversion are thematized in ways that help to gloss the struggle in Glaspell's play. Gaining an understanding of how and why the oppressed characters in those texts engage in law-breaking, disruptive, subversive behavior may help to overcome some of the resistance to Mrs. Hale's and Mrs. Peters's transgressions in *Trifles.* I have not yet experimented with this kind of intertextual interaction. However, as Fetterley makes clear, it is probably the explicitly *gendered* nature of Mrs. Hale's and Mrs. Peters's behavior that raises hackles. What is, in my experience and practice (still in a highly experimental state), the best strategy for dealing with resistance to the gendered treason in *Trifles* is, simply, discussion of that resistance, in the hope that the process that Louise Rosenblatt describes in the passage that we began with will be one that continues beyond the classroom. The reader-response tools of situating oneself as a reader, of collective scrutiny and evaluation of responses, and of ongoing revision of those responses are, I believe, what we need to "reinterpret our old sense of things in the light of this new literary experience, in the light of the new ways of thinking and feeling offered by the work of art" (Rosenblatt 126).

REFERENCES

Fetterley, Judith. "Reading About Reading: 'A Jury of Her Peers.'" *Gender and Reading: Essays on Readers, Texts, and Contexts.* Eds. Elizabeth A. Flynn and Patrocinia P. Schweikert. Baltimore: Johns Hopkins University Press. 1986. 147–64.

Flynn, Elizabeth A. "Gender and Reading." *Gender and Reading: Essays on Readers, Texts, and Contexts.* Eds. Elizabeth A. Flynn and Patrocinia P. Schweikert. Baltimore: Johns Hopkins University Press. 1986. 267–88.

Gilligan, Carol. *In a Different Voice: Psychological Theory and Women's Development.* Cambridge, MA: Harvard University Press, 1982.

Glaspell, Susan. "Trifles." *Types of Drama.* Eds. Sylvan Barnett, Morton Berman, and William Burto. Boston: Little, Brown, and Company, 1985. 69–76.

Ibsen, Henrik. "A Doll's House." *Types of Drama.* Eds. Sylvan Barnett, Morton Berman, and William Burto. Boston: Little, Brown, and Company, 1985. 31–65.

Petry, Ann. "Like a Winding Sheet." *Black Writers of America.* Eds. Richard Barksdale and Kenneth Kinnamon. New York: Macmillan, 1972. 763–68.

Piercy, Marge. "For Inez Garcia." *Living in the Open.* New York: Alfred Knopf, 1976. 90–92.

Rosenblatt, Louise M. *Literature as Exploration.* 3d ed. New York: Noble and Noble, 1976.

Shange, Ntozake. *For Colored Girls Who Have Considered Suicide When the Rainbow is Enuf.* New York: Bantam Books, 1980.

Solzhenitsyn, Aleksandr. *The Gulag Archipelago, 1918–1956.* Trans. Thomas P. Whitney. New York: Harper and Row, 1974–1978.

Sophocles. "Antigone." *Oedipus the King and Antigone.* Trans. and Ed. Peter D. Arnott. New York: Appleton Century-Crofts, 1960. 61–105.
Walker, Alice. *The Color Purple.* New York: Harcourt Brace Jovanovich, 1982.
Wright, Richard. *Native Son.* New York: Perennial Library, 1968.

16

Reading and Teaching
From the Outside
Responding to Native American Literature

David W. Furniss

A number of years ago, I got a late-night panicky phone call from an acquaintance who was directing a weekend college program for adults at a local community college. She needed a guest lecturer for that weekend's session on Alice Walker's *The Color Purple:* The speaker she had lined up had just canceled. She recalled talking to me about the novel at a party one time, and thought I might be able to "come up with something." Partly out of sympathy for her predicament, and partly because I needed the money, I agreed to do it.

I immediately regretted it, and my anxiety increased almost by the hour as the weekend approached. Viewed from any angle, the situation seemed impossible. I was to deliver a lecture, a teaching technique I had never much liked as a student and had certainly never used in my years as a high school English teacher or as a graduate assistant teaching freshman composition. Worse, I was to speak to a group of working people who were giving up their precious Saturdays, clearly not an audience likely to meekly accept captivity. Still worse, I was to lecture about a novel I had read once before, for enjoyment: I had no pithy notes in the margins, no cross-references, and no underlined passages! Worst of all, I was to come before this group as a White man and pose as an authority ("lecturer" implied authority to me, anyway) on Walker's novel.

I decided to accept my limitations—in fact, to acknowledge them at the beginning of the session—and to further admit to the class that I was nervous about my role. Having done that, I asked myself a couple of opening questions, and asked them to respond as well: How is this novel different from others we've read? What do we expect when we read fiction, and to what extent does the novel fulfill those expectations?

To my surprise, that was as much structure as I needed that day. I had written several pages of notes, including other questions, answers to the questions, page numbers of important passages that I might read aloud, all prepared because I was afraid I'd get little or no response. I didn't need them. My memory of the session has faded quite a bit, but I do remember that we spent nearly 90 minutes on the opening questions. There was a wide range of reactions. Some were moved by Celie's coming of age and getting of wisdom, some were outraged at the explicitness of some of the language, some were bewildered by the jumps in time or by the mix of fiction and history. But there was also this commonality: Each of us was in some way an outsider approaching this novel. The novel held surprises for each of us and violated at least one expectation we brought to it. I can't speak for the others in that group, but this experience taught me the value of not only acknowledging but using the surprises and problems that arise from reading, that result from my experiences and preconceptions.

As I write this now, about 5 years after my "lecture" on *The Color Purple,* I find my teaching situation (to quote a common phrase in my students' essays) similar but different. At the University of Wisconsin, River Falls I teach a course titled Literature for Adolescents to juniors, seniors, and graduate students, many of them English majors, and most of them preparing to teach in elementary or secondary schools. The course is designed to acquaint students with the various genres of young adult literature, changes in the field, and issues related to adolescence and teaching adolescents.

During the semester, we read a number of novels with African American or Native American protagonists. This is an important feature of the course, first of all because young adult literature has provided a market much more accessible to minority writers than has adult, "mainstream" literature, and as such is more diverse. It is also important because, although most of my students are not members of ethnic or racial minority groups, their students may well be. Alternatively, if their students are outsiders like themselves, they should be prepared to give their students access to these texts. Finally, the university community is committed to increasing students' awareness of cultural diversity and to designing courses that reflect that diversity.

On the reading list, I have included two Native American novels: Oliver LaFarge's *Laughing Boy* and Hal Borland's *When the Legends Die.* When I was drawing up the syllabus, these two seemed to make a good pair. Although they were written nearly 40 years apart, both stories take place at roughly the same time, between 1910 and 1920. Moreover, to simplify somewhat, both address the issue of assimilation.

There are also a number of interesting and important contrasts. Borland's novel is by and large an adventure story set in Southwestern White society. Thomas Black Bull, after losing his parents, is forced to leave "the old way." After degrading attempts to "civilize" him at the agency school fail, Tom shows a talent for breaking horses that lands him in the care of a rodeo circuit gambler. He eventually becomes a famous rodeo rider, and nearly succeeds in destroying his past and himself before returning at the end of the novel to his old home in the mountains, determined to learn the "old ways" again.

Laughing Boy is a coming-of-age novel concerning a romance between the title character and Slim Girl, an orphaned girl forced, like Thomas Black Bull, to assimilate. Laughing Boy leaves his Navajo clan to live with Slim Girl. The novel's action focuses on the dilemmas each face: Laughing Boy risks ostracism from his clan if he stays with Slim Girl; she, fearing he will leave her, tries to bind him by creating a ritual involving alcohol. The novel is immersed in the Navajo culture of the period; its pace is much slower, almost meditative. Furthermore, as I said earlier, it is a romance, whereas *Legends* is an adventure full of rodeo circuit action. Thus, the novels make very different demands on their readers, despite their similarities in terms of theme and time frame.

The course is concerned with preparing students to teach, and thus is not strictly a literature course, so I do ask the class eventually to talk about how young readers might react to the text, what sorts of readers might enjoy it, and what problems young readers might encounter in reading it. However, I always begin by asking for personal responses from the class. My goal in approaching these minority novels is for us to acknowledge and put to use our "outsider" status, to identify problems and questions we face as readers in responding to experiences far removed from our own. After all, although most of the prospective teachers in my course are White and attended predominantly White secondary schools, there are many public school districts in the upper Midwest with a very diverse student population. My students, therefore, should anticipate teaching in schools very different from their own.

Moreover, as I argued earlier, even if most or all of their students are White, they should try to find ways into these novels to help their outsider students enter them. In any case, they will need to learn how to read novels like these first, before they can discuss them with their students. Thus, it is important that the course work on two levels: Students respond to the reading first, then they begin to project how young readers may respond.

Invitation 16.1

Consider the concept of "outsider" status and, its reverse, "insider" status. Identify the kinds of novels—or a particular novel or two—

for which you are an "insider." What aspects of the novel and expectations on your part create this relationship? How does it work? Who
would be "outsiders" to these works and what impact would this
have on their readership?

My approach in class is to begin with the former, asking students to respond in personal terms, to identify where their problems were in reading,
what surprised them, and how they reacted to the protagonist and other
characters. I have found the students quite willing, for the most part, to do
this in class discussions. However, I have had more difficulty getting them to
do this in writing. I elaborate on this shortly.

Attempting to generate personal responses to use as grist for class discussion, I have tried three different kinds of writing assignments, one kind for
each year I've taught the course. The first year, I required the class to keep
reading journals in which they recorded reactions of the sort described earlier or drew comparisons to other novels. Although many of the journals
were interesting, this approach didn't work well. For one thing, my teaching
schedule made it impossible to look at the journals more than three times
during the term, which made me feel rather hypocritical in asking students
to write in them diligently. I think a number of the students, deliberately or
otherwise, reacted to this contradiction: To my dismay, their entries became
shorter and less thoughtful as the term progressed rather than the reverse.
In addition, I believe that most students who have taken many writing and
education courses are "journaled out," to borrow a phrase used by one of my
students in another class, so they tend to take a rather perfunctory, "oh, this
again" approach.

The next year, I dispensed with the journals and returned to a type of
writing assignment I'd used in introductory literature classes a number of
times, asking students to write short (200–400-word) out-of-class responses
to questions I raised during class, due at the next class meeting. These are
supposed to resemble journal entries: They're informal, personal, and
nonacademic. My role was to react to them on a similar level, to respond to
them personally and informally. The only requirement was that they were
to be turned in on time. I assigned one of these in connection with the two
Native American novels. After we finished discussing *Laughing Boy,* I asked
the class to read *When the Legends Die* and write a reaction to it in which they
compared their responses to the two novels.

An odd thing happened when the students wrote their responses. Despite
my repeated assurances to them that I wanted personal reactions, in their
own voices, what I got was for the most part writing that sounded like the following two excerpts, taken from the opening paragraphs of two responses
to the assignment I already described. Bear in mind, once again, that the

great majority of the 10 out-of-class responses I assigned read very much the same way.

> The novels *Laughing Boy* and *When the Legends Die* explore the problem of the confrontation of Native American culture and white American culture in the southwestern United States in the early years of the twentieth century. Both novels portray a conflict that is unresolvable, although the Navaho culture in *Laughing Boy* remains more viable than the Ute society in *Legends*. The Indian protagonists in each need to redefine themselves in light of their experiences in the white world.

> These novels portray Native Americans as complex, unstereotyped individuals, not as the "noble savage." The major themes are survival between conflicting cultures and personal identity. There is also a universality to the novels, we all have to make choices about how to live our lives. There is also the theme of male/female love and relationships. . . . In both books there is accuracy and detail about the culture and history of the Native American, and it's from their point of view, which allows the reader to see the reasons behind the state of the American Indian today, and the limited choices they have available.

A graduate student in English education wrote the first excerpt, the second came from a senior English major. Both of them, and especially the former, show the writers to be well trained in constructing a literary analysis, learned through hours of composing dozens of five-page essays. Most intriguing, however, is not what's in these responses, but what isn't. Both of these writers did indeed compare the two works, and their pieces are admirable studies in how to use that particular rhetorical strategy. However, neither compared his or her own responses to the books, and in fact neither admitted to having a personal response of any sort, visceral, aesthetic, or otherwise. Particularly revealing is the phrase in the second piece, "allows the reader," a familiar bit of prosaic distancing from the dreaded first-person singular pronoun.

For me the most poignant piece came from another graduate student, an excellent student who was very willing to discuss her subjective responses to the readings orally. Her written response to *Laughing Boy* and *Legends*, like the first one presented earlier, is a near-perfect piece of academic architecture, including indented quotations to support generalizations about the novels' themes and styles. At the end there is this "p.s." about *Legends:* "My stomach hurt when I finished reading this book." When I read this student's response, I was torn between conflicting reactions of my own. On the one hand, I was impressed with her sophistication. For example, she was the only student in the class who noted the stylistic shift in *Legends* after Tom Black Bull is forced to join the White world. On the other, I was surprised and dismayed to see that something in the nature of the task or in this student's training had constrained this normally forthright person. She had an intense reaction to the novel but felt obliged to relay it as a brief afterthought.

In the set of 18 responses to this question, I found very few that included any personal reactions, and only three students elaborated on their feelings about the novels. Two of them were not English majors, and in fact were students who struggled throughout the term, especially with the longer essays required. Compare their opening statements with the two already quoted:

> I found that *When the Legends Die* caught my attention quicker and kept my attention. I think it tends to read easier because there is not a lot of Indian words or phrases present throughout as there is in *Laughing Boy*.

> I liked the novel *Laughing Boy* but at times it was hard to understand what was going on. For example: when the wives of one of the Navajo set his saddle outside the door it took me awhile to figure out that they had kicked him out of the house. I felt that the novel *When the Legends Die* was clearer than *Laughing Boy* in this aspect. Also the language of the Navajo is hard to follow in *Laughing Boy* and it wasn't presented as important in my estimate. When Laughing Boy was singing I skipped over the lyrics because of the language.

In addition to the sort of literary analysis and explication that the first two students wrote, the rest of the class tended to bring the terminology of the course to bear in their discussions rather than expressing personal reactions. For example, many compared the novels in terms of genre, as in this student's comment that "*Laughing Boy* is more of a romance, and *Legends* is more of an adventure." Others talked about readability, how the novels differed in terms of natural readership. One student managed to cover both the question of genre and that of audience in his first paragraph: "*Legends* is what I would consider a minority adventure story written for a younger audience (ages twelve to fifteen), while I see *Laughing Boy* as a minority historical romance aimed at an older audience (ages fifteen plus)."

Invitation 16.2

Form a literature circle with several other students. Select a novel of another culture within the United States. Respond to this novel individually in this assignment's terms, then share your responses.

Obviously, this assignment did not produce the kinds of responses that might have led us to examine our preconceptions about Native Americans, to deal with our difficulties in approaching and processing the novels and the sources of those difficulties, with the three exceptions just quoted. In particular, I wanted to pursue the fact that those two less sophisticated students found *Laughing Boy* less engaging because of its language, slow pace, and detailed accounts of rituals. I wanted to ask why they thought LaFarge includes phonetical transcribed Navajo lyrics, why he gives so much space to the conversations between characters, and the rhythms of their speech. I wanted to hear if others in the class would agree that the novels "may be confusing or boring if some of these rituals are not known," as one of the three writers quoted earlier said later in her response, to see, possibly, whether their outsider status had affected their experience or assessment of the novel.

The class discussion on the two novels that followed tended to concentrate on questions of audience and genre, not on personal response. In fact, I had noticed that, although discussions were still lively, the class had tended more and more to begin with these sorts of analytical concerns. These novels are assigned more than halfway through the term, and no doubt this increases their tendency to develop a pattern of response echoing the course terminology.

When I read the two personal reactions to the class, without identifying the writers, I finally was able to get the rest of the class to begin to articulate how they responded to the novels, and how their responses were different. Many others remarked that *Laughing Boy* made them feel like true outsiders, made them feel somewhat excluded, and talked about how that unfamiliar status felt to them. Later, a number of students told me that their initial frustration with *Laughing Boy* had changed to real sadness as a result of recognizing that the world LaFarge renders in such detail and so unapologetically was ending even as he wrote.

My experience with last year's class impelled me to change my approach yet again. I concluded that out-of-class writing for a group of experienced essay-crankers will produce writing that resembles a formal essay—thesis, supporting quotations, academic language—noting that two of the exceptions were inexperienced essay-crankers. Let me emphasize that I was pleased that so many of the students could analyze the literature in these sophisticated ways, and could write well-organized, detailed discussions of character, genre, theme, and so on. However, I felt that their previous experience in literature classes and in my own course had the effect of distancing them from the material, or more likely, of distancing them from their own transactions with it. This was something I wanted to avoid, particularly in dealing with fiction by nonmainstream authors. Many of these students, in my experience, already see themselves as far removed from the feelings expressed by characters in these novels and from the issues raised in them.

During the same school year that I was struggling to break down this distance my students were creating in their responses, I was developing another course for prospective teachers intended to encourage them to use writing to learn (WTL) techniques in their content areas. The connection between WTL and reader response is very close. In fact, I would argue that they both spring from the same principles we have come to describe as *constructivist* or *epistemic*. The transactional theory of literature, as Nicholas Karolides describes it in this collection, sees reading as a process in which readers actively construct meanings as they read, meanings that draw on their own knowledge and emotions as well as the words in the text. Constructivists say the same thing about knowledge in general: We create what we know in our transactions with the world.

WTL (see Gere 1985 and Bean 1996) stems from a long-standing recognition that writing is a particularly powerful form of learning, and particularly so when writers are truly composing rather than revising or editing their words as they write. WTL techniques often call for short, spontaneous written responses during a class setting. These responses are not graded in any formal way; in fact, the teacher may not always read them. Instead, the writing is intended to help the students think about whatever they are encountering in class that day. Because the responses are written rather than oral they allow for more reflection, a slower pace, and a permanent record that the student may build on later.

It struck me that I needed to practice in my adolescent literature class what I was preaching in my WTL course for teachers in other content areas. I needed to give the students opportunities to actually learn by writing, rather than to rehearse the kinds of learning and approaches to learning they had become accustomed to as experienced writers.

The classes' reaction when I read those two personal responses to them confirmed to me that I should take a WTL approach. Generally, I now begin each 75-minute class with a question and the students write for 10 minutes or so in response. Occasionally, I prepare them for these responses by asking them to "consider" some issue as they read, and then frame this consideration as a question the next time. The only sort of response I now assign them to write outside of class is one in which I ask them to stop in their reading and react to a particular section of the text immediately. Such a response, of course, would be difficult to write from memory in class.

These writings form a course journal consisting of some 25 entries. To begin the class discussions, I ask for volunteers to read or summarize their entries, although I encourage the former. I have found that nearly every student volunteers at least once in a while, and the rest will read if I call on them. I also write responses to my question and read them every so often. At the end of the term, I ask that students choose five to seven of their "best" entries, give them titles, and turn them in unrevised as part of their class grade (25% of the term grade). They are free to define "best" however they please.

I assigned three responses for our discussions of *Laughing Boy* and *When the Legends Die* (which we read in that order). Two of these were at-home reactions to the opening pages, chapter 1 in *Laughing Boy* and part 1 of *Legends*. The only instructions for these writings were to stop at the specified point and react to what they had read so far. These reactions could take the form of questions, a list of problems, theories as to where the novels were headed, their feelings toward the novel or the character, what they understood or what confused them so far, or anything else. The third writing was a comparative response like the one I'd assigned the previous year, this time completed in class.

I collected all three sets of responses to these novels. In this case, I was fibbing a little to the class when I told them that they could choose which entries to hand in. I had intended all along to ask for their responses to these two novels for the purposes of completing this article, although I didn't tell them this until the end of the term.

Concerning the responses to the opening sections, the students' responses to *Laughing Boy* most often revealed their outsider perspectives. I had expected this: LaFarge's novel makes few allowances for readers unfamiliar with Laughing Boy's world. As one reader put it, "*Legends* explains more of the Indian tradition to me than *Laughing Boy.*" Several readers were perplexed at the onset of *Laughing Boy*. Here are some examples:

> I am confused. Where is the story going? . . . so much seems to have happened, yet the story has gone nowhere. . . . What year is this occurring in?

> So far, I'm having a little difficulty getting into the book. It is hard for me to relate to the Indian ways of life and values and there are things I cannot understand, such as some of the expressions and language.

> I had a hard time figuring out what was going on during the ceremony in the first chapter. I'm assuming there will be more of this confusion in the rest of the book.

Most of the responses echoed these questions, although some students were more intrigued than bothered by their uncertainty, as this one was:

> I was really drawn to the book by the first chapter. . . . I felt as if I was missing something, and I desperately wanted to figure it out. . . . My overall impression of *Laughing Boy* after reading the first chapter is one of curiosity. I can't wait to finish it.

In the discussion that followed, students debated their reactions to the novel as a whole, comparing their first impressions with their feelings on completing the book. I asked them to clarify their reasons for finding it "slow," as a number did, and why some of them thought the book too "detailed" concerning customs and rituals. In fact, the class was sharply divided between those who found this detail and LaFarge's use of Navajo language and speech rhythms beautiful and those who found it boring. We spent some time discussing why LaFarge might have chosen to write the book in this way, to avoid explanations tailored for outsiders, and why some of us expect such explanations.

There was more disagreement when it came to the students' comparative responses. Among the out-of-class responses I assigned the year before, I received very few in which the writer stated a preference for one or the other books. This time, although the instructions were the same, almost all of the responses stated whether the reader liked *Laughing Boy* or *Legends* better. The class was divided almost equally, with a few more students preferring *Laughing Boy*. I was particularly interested to note that a number of those students who had found the beginning of *Laughing Boy* confusing ended up preferring it to *Legends*.

During class discussion, I was struck (as were the students) by how completely opposite the reactions often were. The written responses reveal the same deep disagreements. Note the contrasts in the following groups of statements:

- I enjoyed *Laughing Boy* because it is not as complex as *Legends*.
- The conflict in *Legends* is more obvious than the conflicts in *Laughing Boy*.
- *Legends* . . . was draggy and somewhat difficult to get through.
- *Legends* was very adventurous while *Laughing Boy* seemed to be dull.
- I found *Legends* harder to read than *Laughing Boy*. It seems to be moving slower, and is occasionally hard to follow.
- In *Laughing Boy*, the narrator got inside the minds of both Laughing Boy and Slim Girl, which made it somewhat confusing.
- There was . . . more access to the characters' thoughts in *Laughing Boy*, which helped to understand why the characters did what they did.

Many of the differences between the students' responses focused on the question of detail, and how they define "detailed." In *Laughing Boy*, the issue concerns the language, the characters' meditations and stories, and the accounts of the rituals. Some welcomed this and found it interesting, even beautiful. Others found LaFarge's approach made the novel dull or hard to penetrate. In commenting that *Legends* is more "action-packed," for instance, one reader added that "the language is much simpler to understand, with no Indian language at all."

In *Legends*, there is a great deal of detail concerning the rodeo, with sometimes lengthy descriptions of Tom's bronco rides. For some readers, this was exciting; others found it tiresome. This student found *Legends* less engaging than *Laughing Boy* for this reason. Note how she defines "detail" in this case:

> The story progressed rapidly, and was less detailed than *Legends*. *Legends* went into detailed accounts of bucking patterns and other events that did not directly or in some cases indirectly have to do with the themes presented.

Apart from the wide divergence of opinion on the two novels, the other striking feature of the written responses is their utter contrast from those my students wrote the previous year. As I hope is evident from the excerpts given here, these reactions convey much more of the students' preliminary reactions, their first transactions with the text. They aren't *crafted* statements resembling examination answers or critiques; they aren't written primarily for my eyes, as most of those earlier ones had been.

Invitation 16.3

Select an adolescent novel with a multicultural setting. What aspects of this text do you perceive as being potentially problematic for the novel's audiences? Identify several ideas you might use to create bridges of connections for your "outsider" students.

I don't mean to suggest here that all of the students who had troubles getting into the novels at first (recalling the first impressions quoted) arrived at a different view as a result of subsequent discussions. However, a number of the students did alter their thinking somewhat concerning *Laughing Boy*. As far as I can tell, Slim Girl became the protagonist in several class members' eyes. The second day of discussion, two or three stated as much: They felt Slim Girl's conflict was the central one, because it foreshadowed what would inevitably happen to Laughing Boy. They began to see that his view of the Whites (the "Americans") —as buffoons easily snookered in trading—only serves to mask the threat they represent to his culture, a threat Slim Girl perceives clearly.

For some, particularly the female students, this became a way into the novel and a way of accommodating to the difficulties of language and context they had experienced earlier. This was gratifying for me. LaFarge's novel is clearly more distancing than Borland's, which was certainly written to appeal to a mass audience. In fact, one of the things I have come to admire most about *Laughing Boy* is this sense of determined, iconoclastic resistance to popular appeal. (In spite of this, millions have read it since its publication in 1929.)

What was most gratifying was the passion with which many of the class members discussed the novels. In previous years, we had talked about the issues these books raise. Although my students are outsiders, they know enough or have heard enough to be able to talk about injustice, the tragic loss of culture and dignity forced by assimilation, and the massacres and forced migrations. Their out-of-class responses reflected on these things at length, and most were able to identify examples of these themes during class discussions.

However, I had the strong sense that, this time, the themes came through more clearly, in rawer form, perhaps, and the students were less likely to look at the novels (particularly *Laughing Boy*) as history books. This is not to say that students in earlier classes were not moved by the novels (recalling the student whose "stomach hurt"). However, I argue that this group of students, in general, got much closer to what the events in the history books really signify by getting closer to these characters and their world—close enough I like to think, to be able to talk to other outsiders and insiders about them in a way they might not have been able to before.

I recognize that my conclusions must be provisional: I'm talking about a small number of students and tasks. Nonetheless, I would argue that the more spirited and complex discussions that followed were a result of students having the opportunity to describe and clarify their reactions in a setting that discouraged their impulse to externalize their responses. They had to cope, in the case of these two novels, with first impressions and gut reactions stemming from their experiences and expectations. As one student confessed after reading the beginning of *Laughing Boy,* "I keep anticipating an act of violence, or for someone to steal his horse. I must have many stereotypes about Native Americans."

I can say that I intend to continue using short, in-class writing (or occasionally carefully limited out-of-class writing) in this class. The results were very consistent: Nearly all of the responses the students turned in at the end of the term were honest, emotive, and in their own voices. I have also come to believe in the particular value of writing as an active learning tool, to believe in writing as a way of constructing meaning, not just recording what is already in our head. When I teach the WTL course described earlier, I encounter prospective teachers who view "active learning" as something that happens as a result of oral discussion, who believe that to encourage active learning, a teacher must concentrate principally on forming good questions and practicing effective group leadership skills. Thus, when they present ideas for constructivist lessons, those ideas tend to focus on large- and small group discussion techniques. They still tend to see writing as something that occurs after the learning has taken place, rather than as a tool for encouraging learning (and more effective discussion, too). In my experience, this is just as true of those who plan to teach English as it is of those from other disciplines.

I do recognize the value of other sorts of formal writing tasks, as well as other types of journals, but my experience with this class tells me that as students progress through school, they become more and more inclined to believe that all writing assigned by a teacher must look and sound the same. After all, they are learning in most of their classes, either directly or implicitly, that they need to master academic prose to survive in an academic setting.

The best way to restrain their impulse to take an objective stance, to carefully present evidence, and to choose just the right word is to make sure they don't have enough time to do it. If they realize that they need not reveal every response to their teacher or fellow students, they may be more willing to be honest. What they will have at the end of the term is a record of responses they can sift through and choose from, responses they wrote as they read, not the night before I was scheduled to look at them: a mirror of themselves as readers, then and now.

Let me close by emphasizing my own outsider status. I did not intend (nor could I) in talking about these novels to present myself as someone who "understands" Laughing Boy or Tom Black Bull. It would be hypocritical and absurd to imply to my students that I am somehow above making judgments according to stereotype, and that my role is to show them how wrong-headed and closed-minded they are. Rather, my goal is for them to locate what they respond to in their reading what intrigues them, and what makes them yawn, and then to articulate this at first to themselves. After this, we can exchange responses in hopes of coming to some understanding of what sort of readers we are and what sort we want to be.

REFERENCES

Bean, John C. *Engaging Ideas: The Professor's Guide to Integrating Writing, Critical Thinking and Active Learning in the Classroom.* San Francisco: Jossey-Bass, 1996.
Borland, Hal. *When the Legends Die.* New York: Bantam, 1964.
Gere, Anne Ruggles, ed. *Roots in the Sawdust: Writing to Learn Across the Disciplines.* Urbana, IL: National Council of Teachers of English, 1985.
LaFarge, Oliver. *Laughing Boy.* Boston: Houghton Mifflin, 1929.
Walker, Alice. *The Color Purple.* New York: Washington Square Press, 1983.

17

Cultivating Understandings Through Reader Response
Dawn's Responses to *The Things They Carried* and *When Heaven and Earth Changed Places*

Arlette Ingram Willis

Each fall like teachers all over the country I face a brand new class of students. Each fall I wonder what we can learn and teach one another and how far along the continuum of a learning–teaching community we can move. I am a professor at a large Midwestern research university, but I try to make my classes as personal and practical as they can be in this environment by demonstrating "theory into practice" in literacy methods courses. I use reader response in my college methods course for two specific reasons. First, it allows my students the opportunity to learn about reader response from a participant's point of view, and it offers them opportunities, in a nonthreatening environment, to practice responding to readers. Second, I use reader response to multicultural literature to help my students learn more about themselves as cultural beings and as future English language arts teachers in a multicultural society (Willis "Reading").

LEARNING AND TEACHING LITERACY

I believe that one of my responsibilities is to equip my preservice teachers to function effectively in a diverse society of learners. These courses represent my interpretation and implementation of critical literacy theory and pedagogy. For me, a critically framed literacy course is one that centers on the intersection of ideology, history, culture, society, and gender in the *production* of literature. One of the goals of the course is to empower individuals to be socially and culturally conscious readers, writers, thinkers, listeners, and consumers of literacy. I share this notion with students on the first day of class and throughout the course. Another goal, briefly shared with the students at the onset (and revisited in much greater detail at the end of the semester) is my desire to create a community of mutual respect, a safe place to express ideas, and a place where learning and teaching literacy is seen as a liberatory act for social change. I use classroom activities in conjunction with reading and responding to literature to enhance self-identity; cultural awareness; and multicultural understanding, awareness, and sensitivity.

I begin to implement my theoretical position through activities the moment students enter the classroom on the first day of class. For example, students are told to rearrange the furniture, write their names on the board, introduce themselves, and answer a series of questions posted on the desk at the front of the classroom. Throughout the semester, students are encouraged to participate in the learning and teaching of the course. Moreover, activities are designed and sequenced to help move students beyond their comfort zones of insulated individual readers, writers, thinkers, listeners, and consumers as they interact with and transact with literacy. Collectively and individually, students confront their cultural identity and multicultural understandings through the activities and write about them in their journals. Some of the classroom activities include sharing a personal memory or artifact, conducting an unscientific on-campus survey of people's knowledge of multicultural terms, participation in the Horatio Alger exercise, problematization of teaching literacy in today's multicultural and multilingual classrooms, reading and responding to literary texts, and teaching and participating in literacy lessons taught by class members. The required readings include books by Atwell, Au, Freire, Rosenblatt, Smagorinsky, and Wilhelm. The recommended readings (selected in small groups, and then discussed using the jigsaw strategy) include books by Banks, Bell, Delpit, Freire and Macedo, Gates, Giovanni, Heath, Hirsch, Kotlowitz, Kozol, Kutz, Ladson-Billings, Pipher, Sanders, Schlesinger, West, and Wilson. Many of the readings for the course are written by authors whose works are underrepresented in traditional literacy methods courses. In-class readings include poetry, short stories, newspaper and journal articles, scholarly essays, and plays drawn from a broad range of authors. Students respond to this body of literature in written, spoken, dramatic, and artistic formats. Other written course requirements include an autobiography, a literacy autobiography (Britzman), a reflective journal, and literacy packet information.

READER RESPONSE

The heart of the course, however, is the reading and responding to literature for grades 6 to 12, four fifths of which is multicultural literature. Several small groups (of four to five students) are formed arbitrarily during the first few days of class. The groups can be formed according to their favorite color, animal, breakfast food, or most productive time of day. Each group selects 10 novels from a preselected list created by me that reflects the canon, local middle and high school reading lists, and a few controversial books. Small group book selections must include books written by members of each major racial group in the United States (European, African, Asian, Latina/Latino, and Native) and must include books written by men and women. We begin with literature written by European Americans because this is the literature my students are most familiar with from their earlier school experiences. I also begin with literature written by European Americans as a segue to confront issues of history, culture, society, and ideology in text before we begin reading literature written by people of color, where students bring less understanding and information about history, culture, society, and ideologies to bear. Each student is required to teach two literacy lessons (from the novels their group selects). As a group, the members create a packet of information to share with the class. (The contents of the novel packets and this process are described later in this chapter.) The purpose of the packets is twofold: to expand the background information about the novel for the group members and to serve as a resource for future use by all.

In this chapter, I attempt to describe one student's understanding of the reading-response process drawn from her responses to two novels and her critique of the process told from several different angles. I wanted students to revisit their work and articulate for me how they individually understood reader response and what influenced their response to literature.

It is not my goal to recapture every event during the semester; the entire process cannot be reinvented here. I have elected to concentrate on only a select set of responses that I believe form a reaction to the process of reader response, as articulated in the writing of one student, who I have named Dawn. I begin by offering some background information to help form a framework of the classroom context before offering excerpts from Dawn's written responses and critique of reader response. It is important to remember that Dawn's responses to literature that follow represent her thinking and writing prior to learning of the historical, cultural, and social information of each novel (supplied by other group members).

DAWN: A VERY SPECIAL PERSON

In the fall of 1996, Dawn entered my classroom along with 19 other preservice English education majors (16 undergraduates and 3 graduate students). Demographically this group was a bit more diverse than other classes: 2 African Americans, 1 Southeast Asian American, 14 European Americans, and 2 mixed race students. Students revealed early in their written assignments that they saw themselves as individuals from middle- to upper middle-class backgrounds (from rural and suburban settings). Most also revealed that they had been successful academically all of their lives. It is important that these early writings revealed that many of the European American students seldom considered their cultural identity or had interactions with others outside of their culture. In addition, few had read works written by people of color. By way of contrast, the students of color expressed in their early writings that they were very aware and proud of their cultural heritage, had multiple and varied interactions with people from many cultures, and read literature written by people of color regularly.

Reading Dawn's autobiography I found that she traced her ethnic lineage to the fourth generation and revealed a strong Germanic and Russian heritage. She wrote of her foreparents' arrival in the colonies with promises of "free passage, land, housing, freedom of religion, and the right to retain their German language and run local affairs." She also noted that her autobiography was drawn from family records and stories and myths. She revealed a strong work ethic, family devotion, and "stubborn persistence" (her words). She also shared that the women in her family moved throughout the country in search of a better quality of life, worked various jobs to help support their families, and played baseball (Bristol Bells and Paris Bloomer Girls). Her autobiography included stories of love, laughter, and sorrow.

During the first few weeks of class many of the students seemed distant and afraid of the content and structure. True, I had asked them to see themselves as a cultural being in a multicultural world. This was a difficult undertaking for many of the European American students as they resisted the thought of viewing themselves as a member of the dominant group. One very revealing moment for Dawn came early in the semester and was described in her journal. In the entry, she reflected on her participation in the Horatio Alger exercise. This is an activity in which students are asked to hold hands in a horizontal line; then, in response to a series of queries, they either step forward or backward. The activity is designed to dispel the notion of a "level playing field" and to illustrate that there are inequities that result from a consequence of birth (race, class, and gender). The activity also makes clear that inequalities and bias are real parts of people's lives. Dawn wrote about this exercise in her journal:

> I thought our example today of personal backgrounds was especially moving. At the beginning of the exercise, I stepped forward at each statement. I felt bad for stepping forward, hoped those who were stepping backward felt comfortable with the exercise. When a statement occurred (that proposed) men over women, I was left behind. That's how I felt—left behind. I was almost shocked after stepping forward for so long. I think the exercise is a constructive one for pointing out society's differences. However, it does have the ability to upset people and I am not sure I would use it in just any classroom.

I understood her response to the activity as one in which she was trying to make sense of her new consciousness about race, class, and gender issues. I also read her entry as one that tried to understand how the activity impacted her thinking and decision making as a future educator.

SMALL GROUP LITERATURE SELECTIONS

In this class, Dawn's group consisted of three undergraduate women, one graduate woman, and one undergraduate man placed together by their favorite color (blue). The group organized itself early on by devising a chart for each novel and the requirements for the novel packets. Over time their name changed from the Blue group to the Blue Birds to the Blue Bird Book Club to BBC@uiuc.edu. The students also took seriously their tasks: from designing blue book covers (complete with specially designed illustrations for each novel) to writing their responses to each novel, to preparing for their small group discussions about each novel, and to preparing their literature packets for the class. On occasion this small group's discussions were contested sites as individual members struggled with the viewpoints of others. Over time the blue group had become known for what one member called their "brutally debating" literature. Opinions among group members were often divided and voices and tempers were raised during their discussions. Dawn was an active member in each discussion, bringing with her a close reading of the text, a thoughtful analysis, and a well-written response. Her naturally quiet nature had earned her the name of "Quiet Fire." She was seen as knowledgeable, well-read, and passionate. She was also known to exhibit the "stubborn persistence" of her family that she wrote about in her autobiography.

Dawn, along with members of her group, selected the following high school novels to read: *The Things They Carried, A Lesson Before Dying, How the Garcia Girls Lost Their Accent, When Heaven and Earth Changed Places,* and *Pigs in Heaven.* I thought their selections were odd given that only one member of the group was alive during the Vietnam War and seldom have undergraduates come to class having more than a minimal understanding of this war. I found Dawn's response to her readings about the Vietnam War some of the most interesting writing she completed during the semester. I have selected her responses to two of these readings to illustrate how her responses changed over time and what she believes influenced changes in her perspective. I believe that this student's writings are the best statements of her understanding and will rely on them to help tell her story.

AN ASSIGNMENT

One of the final class assignments is to reread one novel and write a second response, discuss any differences between the first and second readings and responses, and write a critique of the process. Dawn chose to reread *The Things They Carried*. I share here excerpts from her first response, a response to an intervening novel that she identifies as critical in changing her viewpoint, her second response to *The Things They Carried,* and her critique of the process.

First Response to *The Things They Carried*

> The last paragraph of *The Things They Carried* was, for me, one of those experiences in which you are reading so intensely and so fast you forget you are reading; you are just soaking up the words and the emotions and the experiences of the page. It is as if there are no words or punctuation and you are simply thinking with the author. I was so caught up in reading *The Things They Carried* that I turned the page, only to discover that the novel was over and that they were showing me an order form. I was mad, but O'Brien need not have gone on. He ends his work powerfully by writing, ". . . and when I take a high leap into the dark and come down thirty years later, I realize it is a Tim trying to save Timmy's life with a story" (273). *The Things They Carried* is as much about war, life, and death as it is about self-discovery, self-preservation, and writing itself. What struck me most deeply about *The Things They Carried* was the sense of the personal in the work—the sense that O'Brien was writing to keep himself alive, to keep those he had loved alive, and to keep us living and thinking.
>
>   In the second story in *The Things They Carried,* I was jolted into remembering that O'Brien experienced the events of his book. While the first story, "The Things They Carried," is a third person narrative, the second story, "Love," places O'Brien in the story: he writes, "Many years after the war Jimmy Cross came to visit me at my home in Massachusetts . . ." (29). After this reference to "me," I never forgot that O'Brien was there, in the war, in the story. Sometimes I wanted to forget. In "Notes," O'Brien tells us how he came to write the story of Norman Bowker, a fellow soldier who committed suicide after returning home from Vietnam. Reading "Notes," I wanted to be able to forget that the people, the story, the events, were real. O'Brien writes that Bowker sent him a seventeen page letter prior to committing suicide; in the book, he is about to show us that letter. I hesitated at this point in my reading. I didn't want to read

the letter. It was too real and wanted to distance myself from that reality. I cannot help but think that O'Brien would have liked my reaction. He writes to experience, but he also writes so that others experience.

O'Brien's writing so that others experience his words adds a complex dimension to the work. O'Brien writes about the soldier he killed in Vietnam in detail, but in "Good Form," says that the story is "made up" and "invented" (203). In the end, I did not know if O'Brien had killed the man or simply personified his involvement in the war in this man. *The Things They Carried* contains the personal, but it is fiction. That reality was difficult for me to understand; I think it would be difficult, but not impossible, for high school students to tackle as well.

O'Brien's voice and story infuses the book; it is the book. O'Brien writes of himself: "Forty-three years old, and the war occurred half a lifetime ago, and yet the remembering makes it now. And sometimes remembering will lead to a story, which makes it forever. That's what stories are for . . . Stories are for those late hours in the night when you can't remember how you got to where you were to where you are. Stories are for eternity, when memory is erased, when there is nothing to remember except the story" (40). O'Brien says he writes to remember, to keep himself alive, to keep others alive. O'Brien writes, "But this too is true: stories can save us. I'm forty-three years old, and a writer now, and even still, right here, I keep dreaming Linda alive. And Ted Lavender, too, and Kiowa, and Kurt Lemon . . ." (255). In a story, O'Brien says, "the dead sometimes smile and sit up and return to the world" (255). O'Brien writes to return himself to the world, to keep himself in the world, and to return and keep those he has loved and lost. I deeply appreciated O'Brien's honesty, candor, and depth. In *The Things They Carried,* O'Brien not only shows us his world, but lets us enter it as well—as much as we can.

I thought *The Things They Carried* to be a powerful and remarkable book. While the many levels on which the book operates, including those of fiction–nonfiction and truth–story—may make understanding the book difficult for some students, I think discussion could help to clarify these points. In my opinion, *The Things They Carried* would be a powerful and interesting book for students to read. It caught me in its web.

SHARING WRITTEN AND ORAL RESPONSES

The day that Dawn shared her written response with her fellow group members was not unlike most others: Students enthusiastically entered the room, began informal conversations about their reading, and collated their informational packets. Everyone in Dawn's group raved about the novel and shared how it really opened their eyes and understanding to the horrors of war, and the Vietnam War in particular. The group members exchanged their written responses with a partner and wrote comments to the writer. Here is an excerpt from the comments a group member wrote to Dawn: "This story *is* powerful and interesting. I think that the line between truth and fiction is a tough one for many students and readers to handle, although discussion could help. Indeed, the stories about Vietnam might not have to be true for them to impact us."

Next, the group members shared their thoughts in a small group discussion. All group members decided that they enjoyed reading *The Things They Carried.* Some group members, however, expressed concerns about the content and doubted that they would teach the novel in its entirety. Their apprehension centered on what some considered discomforting images and language they believed inappropriate for school settings. However, all agreed that portions of the book were acceptable and could be taught.

The lesson for this book was taught by a group member who was alive during this historical period. Her instructional goals were to "encourage students to think more independently about literature and to begin to develop a strategy for their own criticism and analysis of a literary text." The lesson plan (complete with a list of supplementary materials and references) was part of the group's novel packet. Other group members were responsible for preparing the rest of the packet materials: a summary; a biography of the author, the biodata taken from Hile's (1994) *Authors and Artists for Young Adults;* and two or three book reviews (this group's selections were from Kirkus, *Booklist,* and *Publishers Weekly*). To fulfill the requirement of historical information important to understanding the novel, the group included a chronological listing of historical events surrounding the Vietnam War from 1945 to 1975. The connections between the historical events and descriptions in the novel were highlighted for readers.

Three weeks later, the group followed the same set of procedures for their reading and response to the novel *When Heaven and Earth Changed Places.* The following is Dawn's response.

Dawn's Response to *When Heaven and Earth Changed Places*

When Heaven and Earth Changed Places proved that truth creates an epic far more sweeping than fiction. I cannot even begin to encapsulate my response to this novel in two pages of concise and broken-up-into-main-idea-paragraphs. I don't even think I want to. As so many thoughts enter my mind about the book, I think I will reflect on those various thoughts in my response. Here goes . . .

My Life

I was reading *When Heaven and Earth Changed Places* in my room with my computer, stereo, books, and pictures of family around me—my things—when I realized all that I have. We don't often realize the enormity of what we have. When Hayslip visited Vietnam in 1986, only ten years ago, the country was still in disrepair and despair. And yet I sit here with my computer, books, and life full of things. I am left with the sense that I must look around me daily and thank fate or luck or God (to quote Le Ly Hayslip) for what I have. I certainly don't do it often enough.

Learning and Literature

Reading *When Heaven and Earth Changed Places* taught me more about the Vietnam War than I learned in any history class—a lesson about literature that I plan to use in my teaching. Le Ly Hayslip shows us how a young peasant girl in Ky La comes to view the war. Hayslip grew up with a father who prized his land and told her that Vietnamese independence was worth more than anything else. When the Viet Cong entered Ky La, promising independence and, at least initially, treating the villagers better than did the Republicans, Le Ly saw independence, as well as a chance to see her name on the blackboard of honor. Would I have thought any differently? I'm not sure. Why should Le Ly have seen the struggle as one of democracy versus communism? What do those words really mean anyway?

Tim O'Brien

Hayslip's perception of the war would be interesting to study in contrast with Tim O'Brien's perception in *The Things They Carried*. They both experience the war, but in much different capacities and degrees and with much different experiences and emotions.

Autobiography

Hayslip shows us the power of autobiography, of real voice. When Bon Nghe, the brother Le Ly has not seen in decades, refuses the chocolates Le Ly offers him, my heart broke with her pain and confusion at the gulf that years and distance and life had created between her and her brother, her and her family, her and Vietnam, her and all she knew.

War, Love, Loss, and Life

I am left with a profound sense of what Hayslip lost from the war. Leaving Vietnam gave her a life, but took from Ly Le her family—the touch of her mother's hand, and the smell of the land on which she stood with her father, Sau Ban, her family. She lost all she knew.

Dawn's Second Response to *The Things They Carried*

Reading Tim O'Brien's *The Things They Carried* for the second time, I was intensely confused. I did not know how to feel toward O'Brien, toward the American soldiers who fought with him in Vietnam. In my first reading of the novel, I had been awed by the enormity of O'Brien's experiences. I had read the novel with a sense of amazement of all that Vietnam was and meant. In my second reading, I was not awed, but sickened. I started to hate O'Brien and his fellow soldiers. I hated their cavalier attitudes toward a war which devastated a country and a people. I hated their trivializing of destruction. As I read on,

however, my hate turned into pity and respect. I realized that the soldiers'
seeming carelessness masked an intense struggle to keep themselves and each
other alive, both physically and mentally. I pitied a war that asked them to
struggle for their lives and souls, and I respected the strength that allowed
them to win at this struggle. In my second reading of *The Things They Carried*, I
experienced a whirlwind of emotions.

When I began reading the novel for the second time, I was shocked at my
reaction to O'Brien and his fellow soldiers. I was disgusted by their cavalier descriptions of war. O'Brien says, "The war was entirely a matter of posture and
carriage, the hump was everything, a kind of inertia, a kind of emptiness,
a dullness of desire and intellect and conscience and hope and human sensibility" (15). The war seemed to be about stomping through Vietnam, about
"[searching] the villages without knowing what to look for, not caring, kicking
over jars of rice, frisking children and old men, blowing tunnels, sometimes
setting fires and sometimes not, then forming up and moving on to the next
village, then other villages, where it would always be the same" (15). I was disgusted with these men who considered Vietnam not a country, but a land to
stomp through, a "powdery orange-red dust that covered their boots and fa-
tigues and faces" (15).

I was disgusted with these men who were in Vietnam, but seemed sheltered
from Vietnam. The men seemed to live a soldier's version of American plenty
in Vietnam. O'Brien writes, "Purely for comfort, they would throw away ra-
tions, blow their Claymores and grenades, no matter, because by nightfall the
resupply choppers would arrive with more of the same, then a day or two still
more, fresh watermelons and crates of ammunition—the resources were stun-
ning . . ." (16). While a war was going on that killed and starved thousands of
Vietnamese, American soldiers were throwing out goods. They carried Vietnamese thumbs in the same pack with cookies from home. They spoke not of
the Vietnamese, but of VC corpses, VC water buffalo, VC viruses, VC nurses,
poppa-sans, mama-sans, dinks, gooks, gook music, and gook opera. They were
ignorant of the people they fought to kill and save.

As I continued reading the novel, I realized that the American soldiers were
not wholly aggressors, but also victims. They were victims of the larger forces
of war. The American soldiers may not have starved like the Vietnamese, but
they were drafted into a war they neither understood nor accepted. They faced
war and were forced to kill. To stay sane, "they called [death] by other names,
as if to encyst and destroy the reality of death itself. They kicked corpses. They
cut off thumbs. They talked grunt lingo" (20). I believed O'Brien when he
said, "It wasn't cruelty, just stage presence. They were actors" (20). With this
awareness, my hate of the soldiers was joined with pity and respect. I pitied the
soldiers for being forced to struggle for their very lives and souls; I respected
them for engaging in such an intense struggle.

Reading *The Things They Carried* for the second time, I experienced conflicting emotions. I simultaneously hated, pitied, and respected O'Brien and
his fellow soldiers. I believe O'Brien intended his readers to feel this range of
emotions. In *The Things They Carried*, he wants us to see the destructive pur-

poselessness of war; he wants us to feel the internal horror of the soldier; he wants us to believe that we too would invent stories about the dead to stay alive. Tim O'Brien aims to show us that war is not simple, and is as much an internal battle as an external one. His message came through to me.

Dawn's Discussion

I asked the students to analyze their first and second responses and share what, in their opinion, had influenced the responses. I wanted to understand from the students' perspective what was making an impact on their thinking. I assumed, in a critically framed course, the information prepared for novel packets that described biodata, historical, cultural, and societal events and conditions would be the chief informant. Dawn's critique helps to shed light on what, for her, was of most influence in writing her second response.

> My first and second readings of *The Things They Carried* provoked markedly different responses. In my first reading of and response to the novel, I was awed by Tim O'Brien and his novel. I was awed by the sense of the personal in the work, by the sense of immediacy and urgency in his writing. I was awed and enamored by O'Brien's insistence that stories save lives. In my second response to the novel, my awe of O'Brien fell away. I read the novel and saw not the gut reality and horror of the soldiers' existence, but the injustice of their actions. I saw the American soldiers stomping through Vietnam, destroying towns and people with little thought, and then returning to base and squandering their own goods. Where was the war? Where were the Vietnamese? How could it all seem so trivial?
>
> My questioning of the soldiers' attitudes and actions in my re-reading of the novel is informed by one important fact: between my first and second readings of *The Things They Carried,* I read Le Ly Hayslip's *When Heaven and Earth Changed Places,* an autobiographical account of one Vietnamese woman's experiences and struggles with the Vietnam War. When I began re-reading *The Things They Carried,* then, I was looking at the war not through the eyes of American soldiers unjustly sent to war, but through the eyes of a Vietnamese woman who faced the war—as much as I, as an American, am able to do so. Looking at the war through a greater Vietnamese lens, I saw not the American soldiers' struggles, but their callousness and carelessness. It took my reading half the novel before I was able to abandon my hostility toward the American soldiers and open my ears to hear their thoughts and feelings. I realized that the American soldiers put up a brave front, but often were quivering inside as much as Le Ly Hayslip was. I still believe that many of the American soldiers' attitudes and actions were thoughtless, but I now see that the soldiers were struggling to stay alive. They too experienced the war and were horrified by it.
>
> Although I now have a different perspective of *The Things They Carried,* I remain awed by the novel, and both of my responses exhibit this sense of awe. However, my sense of awe no longer lies with O'Brien and the soldiers' horrific

experiences. Because of *When Heaven and Earth Changed Places,* I do not accept the American soldiers' attitudes and actions unthinkingly, but question them. Today, my awe of the novel lies with O'Brien's complex depiction of a horrific war. Having read both *The Things They Carried* and *When Heaven and Earth Changed Places,* I could no longer ethically use only *The Things They Carried* in the classroom and believe that my students were getting a rich picture of the Vietnam War. The Vietnamese are absent from O'Brien's account. Both *The Things They Carried* and *When Heaven and Earth Changed Places* would be critical and necessary for my students' understandings of the war; my classroom use of both novels would reflect that necessity.

Dawn's Critique

Dawn was able to articulate what she believed were some of the most important influences on her responses to both texts. For example, in response to Tim O'Brien's *The Things They Carried,* she wrote:

> Knowing that Tim O'Brien witnessed firsthand the realities of the Vietnam War greatly influenced my response to the novel, *The Things They Carried.* I do not think I would have considered the work as valid or authentic had O'Brien never set foot in Vietnam. Although *The Things They Carried* is fiction and O'Brien tells his readers in the novel what he has created is story-truth, his vision of and experiences in Vietnam shape the work. *The Things They Carried* could not have been written effectively by an outsider, my awe and appreciation of the novel stems from its vivid depiction of the real and the personal.

She also revealed that "Historical information concerning the Vietnam conflict shaped my response. My second response to the novel, in which I am critical of O'Brien and other American soldiers, stems from a greater awareness of the history and trials of the Vietnamese people from reading *When Heaven and Earth Changed Places.* My awareness of one Vietnamese woman's life made the war that much more real to me, and my response that much more emotional." In addition, she found the cultural information helpful to aiding her understanding. She stated, "an awareness of Vietnamese culture from *When Heaven and Earth Changed Places* made me respect the Vietnamese people and detest a war against them. O'Brien shows us that part of the American soldiers' culture was to call Vietnamese 'gooks' and 'VCs.' I was disgusted by this reality and took a more critical stance against the American soldiers because of it." Importantly, she wrote that "My second response and its differences from my first stems from my own experiences with *When Heaven and Earth Changed Places,* not my group's responses. My group may have given me a more critical in general attitude, though!"

Additionally, Dawn saw the small group reading selections and discussions as especially important in shaping her second response. Of utmost importance to her was the reading of *When Heaven and Earth Changed Places.*

She wrote, "If I had not read *When Heaven and Earth Changed Places,* I would not have looked at *The Things They Carried* from the eyes of a Vietnamese woman. My awareness of the effects of the Vietnam War on the Vietnamese contributed greatly to my shock at the American soldiers' casual attitudes and actions concerning the war." She went on to state that, "a second reading allowed me to gain greater insights to the novel. Having read the novel already, my awe of its *style* did not overshadow the soldiers' beliefs and actions. Reading the novel the second time allowed me to distance myself somewhat from a purely emotional reaction based on how the *words* on the page struck me. It allowed me to be struck in *different* ways—namely how differently American soldiers and Vietnamese peasants experienced the war."

COMMENTARY

My comments here, drawn from this entire sequence of events (student autobiography; student selection of novels; student journal writing; student written response, peer exchange, and small and large group discussion; the gathering of historical, social, and cultural background information on the novel and author; the rereading and reresponding to one novel; and the critique of the process), found each event helpful in an analysis of the range of literacy behaviors and understandings demonstrated by this preservice educator. Dawn's written responses reveal that she came to understand more clearly how writers' lives and experiences can shape their ideological viewpoints as well as confirm or disconfirm those of the reader. I believe that she realized that authors are people who help to shape ideological points of view by what they share or fail to acknowledge and share. I think Dawn learned that historical, cultural, political, and economic issues interface with everyone's life, and some are more aware of and responsive to these forces than others. She learned and connected with both novels in very different, and perhaps gendered ways. She also learned, somewhat vicariously, that there are different ways of expressing love and loss. The entire experience led her to desire to offer her future students a balanced view, one that offers more than one perspective, of the Vietnam War. I like to think of her experience, without a comprehensive examination of the historical period or a thorough understanding of the cultural, social, and economic circumstances in the lives of the U.S. soldiers or the Vietnamese, as an *informed response.* Her response was influenced, unconsciously, by her multiple readings and additional information, thus changing the quality of her response. To that end, her reading multicultural literature supported my goals for the students in the course: to develop a better understanding of the ideological, historical, sociological, and cultural contexts that nurtured and helped to produce the literature.

Invitation 17.1

Highlight the shifts in Dawn's sympathies, noting her changing impressions of the characters and people and the dynamics of the situations.

CONNECTIONS TO RESEARCH

Larry Johannessen also has found that many students who were very young or not alive during the Vietnam War, like Dawn, have begun to rethink their understanding of the period, and to consider that the many truths and distortions about the War are determined by the person telling the story. Dawn (and I) learned that one reading and one point of view of any text is not sufficient, but readers (and writers) need to engage several different texts to begin to formulate an informed response. Dawn's second reading of *The Things They Carried* was informed by several different sources of information, but none so compelling as her reading of *When Heaven and Earth Changed Places*.

I believe that Dawn's comments offer important insights into how students view the impact and import of reader response. Her writings make clear Bishop's support of the use of multicultural literature to "serve as a window into the lives and experiences different from their own and literature that serves as a mirror reflecting themselves and their cultural values, attitudes, and behaviors" (xiv, cited in Hansen-Krening & Mizokawa). For example, she notes that singular readings should be viewed as a starting place for discussions about multicultural literature and must include historical, cultural, and political information. Her conclusion is supported by research by Corcoran who found that in initial responses students often make "premature judgments of the worth of a classroom text" (21). When considering learning and teaching about multicultural literature in preservice literacy methods courses, personal responses, shared discussions, and negotiated meanings do not yield enough information about the text to allow it to be learned and taught well. As this student's responses indicate, it is important to encourage students' response to multicultural literature to move "beyond a cozy form of responsiveness" (Corcoran x). I believe that it is important that we empower students to be knowledgeable consumers of multicultural literature and encourage them to make literacy decisions that are responsible. Royster articulates this concern as "the responsibility of deciding well, not just in good faith but in good conscience, with good information and considerable thought" (152). One way to encourage students to make informed responses is to offer them alternative points of view on the same events; in this case, two different points of view on the Vietnam War by two people who had experienced it firsthand.

Much of the insight that informs this discussion was drawn from my close relationship with the students. However, I am aware of research by Fish that reveals that in academic settings readers often temper their public responses to "fit" their perceived notions of the social and cultural contexts, interpretive discourse, literary analysis, and instructor expectations. Reader-response research with college students also notes that student responses often reflect their "personality characteristics, stances, and attitudes toward reading, knowledge of social and literary conventions, and experiences in social and institutional contexts" (Beach and Hynds, 468). In addition, college students bring particular literary rhetorical and analytical orientations to text that reflect their immersion in literature. I believe that Dawn's responses were genuine and offer insights that inform praxis. I am not naive to the notion that in the context of a university graduate and undergraduate methods course on literacy I might have students who may temper their responses to "fit" what they perceive is my personal position. However, I believe that the sense of community in our classroom developed from mutual respect and trust (many of us still communicate) and this encouraged the students to see themselves as future English teachers learning the tools of the trade by experiencing the instruction they could use in their future classrooms. The students began to become responsible for their responses to literature as they began to understand how powerful reader response can be to the reader. The students' new sense of responsibility may account for their preoccupation with whether or not a novel was suitable, acceptable, teachable, or an authentic representation of cultural groups, as these issues often formed the core of whole-class discussions about literature.

Creating a sense of community and allowing small group discussions also appears to have been helpful in expanding Dawn's understanding of multiple interpretations of text. The use of unstructured groups and their freedom to frame a sense of "belongingness" appeared to nurture the expression of ideas among group members (Beach, *Literary;* Doerr, cited in Beach and Hynds). Students need to feel some sense of belongingness to be able to share in public their innermost thoughts, concerns, and fears. According to Hansen-Krening and Mizokawa, during small group discussions students often discover "their own attitudes and the influence these have on their response to literature" (183). Further they argue that, "as people begin to unearth previously unexplored assumptions they start to see beyond differences to recognize similarities between themselves and the characters in the stories they read" (183). For Dawn, this step came into focus in her response to *When Heaven and Earth Changed Places,* in her articulation of similarities and differences in her responses, and in her critique of the process.

Finally, one of the notions I find intriguing about Dawn's series of writings is that her reading of multicultural literature informed her reading of mainstream literature. This discovery adds to a growing body of research and scholarly essays that examines the use of reader response to multicultural literature (Rogers and Soter) in a variety of settings. Recent studies of the use of reader response to multicultural literature in college and university settings with preservice educators includes work by Flood, Lapp, and Vandyke; Klinger; and Willis ("Exploring"). These studies generally have focused on using reader response to multicultural literature with preservice educators to enhance self-identity, multicultural awareness, and sensitivities to the needs of students from culturally diverse backgrounds. Other studies have taken a different route by looking at how students respond to multicultural literature in natural settings (Klinger; Rogers; Royster; Spears-Bunton; Willis, "Exploring"). This area has become a thorn in the side of teacher educators who are trying both to teach and train future teachers. As Patricia Enciso points out, "multicultural literature raises questions about how we construct differences and how we enacted and continue to enact social practices related to differences" (14). Often preservice students are not interested in multicultural literature and find it difficult to read, understand, and respond to (Beach, "Research"). This latter body of research has caused some concern about the use of reader response to multicultural literature. However, as Dawn's experience points out, her rereading of mainstream literature has been greatly enhanced by her reading of multicultural literature, an unexpected but meaningful gain. It is important to note that not all theorists are in agreement. For example, critical theorists argue for the importance of acknowledging the ideological influences on the reader, writer, text, and context. They also believe that acknowledging the complex influences on the author, reader, text, and context (intertextuality) does not negate the importance of respecting individual responses to literature, the sharing of responses, the negotiation of meanings, the reflection of the reader, or the role of interdisciplinary study to help expand frameworks for understanding literature. In point of fact, many critical theorists would argue that all are necessary to understand the indeterminacy of literature in our lives.

IMPLICATIONS FOR SECONDARY SETTINGS

Many secondary English teachers use *The Things They Carried* as part of the literature in American Literature classes. Two of my three sons have read the novel as part of their high school literature assignments and one son also has read the novel in a college English course. However, their teachers have adopted a conservative stance, and neither son has been asked or required to read about the Vietnam War from the perspective of a Vietnamese person. To my knowledge their readings of *The Things They Carried* consisted of reading and responding to teacher-selected chapters. Their written responses were followed up with whole-class discussions. For example one of my son's high school assignments asked the students to read 8 of the 22 chapters and respond by writing about characterization, action, meaning of the story, and impact on their lives. My experience teaching high school students suggests that many students are capable of reading multiple viewpoints and responding to them thoughtfully.

Like Dawn, I think this is unfortunate because my sons have missed understanding another viewpoint of the Vietnam War, not a right or wrong point of view, but an alternative point of view (i.e., some recent literature anthologies now include Hayslip's autobiography). Other sources of information can also aid in expanding one's understanding of text. There is a plethora of materials on the Vietnam era that can be drawn on to form a unit about the period and the literature it has spawned. Additional sources of information can be found in documentaries, movies, fictional and non-fictional accounts, newspapers, and journals. Tim O'Brien has a Web site that some students might be interested in using to correspond directly with him. Students also can locate additional information about Le Ly Hayslip and other Vietnamese writers over the Internet.

I believe that it is the responsibility of secondary teachers to move students beyond the comfort zone of an initial response to literature and to encourage them to read more widely from a variety of literature and respond in a more informed manner, offering them multiple opportunities to read and respond. In the context of the *informed response*, I believe that multicultural literature offers students alternative points of view about history, culture, and society that challenge students and make them into more active readers, thinkers, and writers. I find especially appealing the idea the students are offered the opportunity to have some voice in their reading materials. Although it is not reasonable to have every student read independently from their own reading list, it is reasonable to allow students some decision making and responsibility.

REFERENCES

Alvarez, J. *How the Garcia Girls Lost Their Accent*. New York: Plume, 1992.

Beach, Richard. *The Literary Response Process of College Students While Reading and Discussing Three Poems*. University of Illinois. *Dissertation Abstracts International*, 34, 656A, 1972.

———. "Research on Readers' Response to Multicultural Literature." Paper presented at the annual meeting of the American Educational Research Association, New Orleans, LA, 1994.

Beach, Richard and Susan Hynds. "Research on Response to Literature." *Handbook of Reading Research*. Vol. II. Ed. R. Barr, M. Kamill, P. Mosenthal, and P. Pearson. New York: Longman, 1991. 453–89.

Bishop, Rudine Sims. *Kaleidoscope*. Urbana, IL: National Council of Teachers of English, 1994.

Britzman, D. "Cultural Myths in the Making of a Teacher: Biography and Social Structure in Teacher Education," *Harvard Educational Review* 56 (1986): 442–456.

Canto, M. *Unlearning Prejudice: Celebrating Cultural Diversity — Trainer's Manual*. Oakland, CA: University of California Agricultural Extension, 1993.

Corcoran, B. "Balancing Reader Response and Cultural Theory and Practice." *Knowledge in the Making: Challenging the Text in the Classroom*. Ed. B. Corcoran, M. Hayhoe, and G. Pradl. Portsmouth, NH: Heinemann, 1994. 13–24.

Enciso, Patricia. "Negotiating the Meaning of Difference: Talking Back to Multicultural Literature." *Reading Across Cultures: Teaching Literature in a Diverse Society*. Ed. T. Rogers and A. Soter. New York: Teachers College Press, 1997. 13–41.

Fish, Stanley. *Is There a Text in This Class? The Authority of Interpretative Communities*. Cambridge, MA: Harvard University Press, 1980.

Flood, James, Diane Lapp, and Janice VanDyke. "The Multidimensional Uses of Multicultural Literature in the Classroom." Paper presented at the annual meeting of the National Reading Conference, Charleston, SC, 1996.

Gaines, E. *A Lesson before Dying*. New York: Vintage, 1993.

Hansen-Krening, N., and D. Mizokawa. "Exploring Ethnic-Specific Literature: A Unity of Parents, Families, and Educators." *Journal of Adolescent and Adult Literacy*, 41 (1997). 180–89.

Hayslip, L. (with Jay Wurts). *When Heaven and Earth Changed Places: A Vietnamese Woman's Journey From War to Peace*. New York: Penguin, 1989.

Hile, Kevin S., ed. *Authors and Artists for Young Adults*, Vol. 12. Gale Research: 1994.

Johannessen, L. "Transforming Hearts and Mind With the Literature of the Vietnam War." *Illinois English Bulletin* 84 (Winter 1997): 3–25.

Kingsolver, B. *Pigs in Heaven*. New York: Harper Perennial, 1994.

Klinger, J. "Changing Pre-service Teachers' Attitudes Through Multicultural Literature." Paper presented at the annual meeting of the National Reading Conference, Charleston, SC, 1996.

O'Brien, T. *The Things They Carried*. Boston: Houghton Mifflin, 1990.

Rogers, T. "No Imagined Peaceful Place: A Story of Community, Texts, and Cultural Conversations in One Urban High School English Classroom." *Reading Across Cultures: Teaching Literature in a Diverse Society*. Ed. T. Rogers and A. Soter. New York: Teachers College Press, 1997. 95–115.

Rogers, T. and A. Soter. *Reading Across Cultures: Teaching Literature in a Diverse Society*. New York: Teachers College Press, 1997.

Royster, J. "Literature, Literacy, and Language." *Critical Theory and the Teaching of Literature: Politics, Curriculum, Pedagogy*. Ed. J. Slevin and A. Young. Urbana, IL: National Council of Teachers of English, 1996. 140–52.

Spears-Bunton, L. "Literature, Literacy, and Resistance to Cultural Domination." *Literacy Research, Theory, and Practice: Views from Many Perspectives. Forty-First Yearbook of the National Reading Conference*. Ed. C. Kinzer and D. Leu. Chicago: National Reading Conference, 1992.

Willis, A. "Exploring Multicultural Literature as Cultural Production." *Reading Across Cultures: Teaching Literature in a Diverse Society*. Ed. T. Rogers and A. Soter. New York: Teachers College Press, 1997. 135–60.

Willis, A. "Reading the World: Contextualizing the School Literacy Experiences of a Young African-American Male." *Harvard Educational Review* 65 (1995): 30–49.

18

Teacher Learning in Response to Autobiographical Literature

Jocelyn Glazier, Mary McVee, Susan Wallace-Cowell,
Bette Shellhorn, Susan Florio-Ruane and Taffy E. Raphael

PART 1: TEACHING TEACHERS ABOUT LITERACY AND CULTURE

Susan Florio-Ruane and Taffy E. Raphael

Despite efforts to recruit a diverse teaching force, U.S. educators remain typically young, European American, female, monolingual, and from lower and middle-income backgrounds. A recent report reveals that the past decade has actually seen an increase in the percentage of European American monolingual teachers and a decrease in teachers from racial, ethnic, and linguistic minority backgrounds (National Center for Education Statistics). In contrast, their students tend increasingly to be from linguistic minority backgrounds and lower income families. This disparity is particularly troublesome when teachers work to support language and literacy development (Cazden and Mehan).

Literacy is deeply rooted in cultural experience, and our society presents teachers with a broad and rich diversity of youngsters whose cultural experiences may differ considerably from their own. Yet, being members of the so-called "mainstream" and trained within a profession linguistically and socially homogeneous, many teachers find themselves culturally isolated. They lack awareness of the cultural foundations of literacy in their own lives and the lives of others. It is therefore difficult for them to investigate complex issues of race, culture, social class, and language diversity.

Their professional education typically does not foster in teachers a sense of culture as a dynamic process whereby people make meaning in contact with one another (McDiarmid and Price). The needs of a changing world and the current national expectations we hold for literacy and learning require us to address the continuing disparity in linguistic and cultural background between our teaching force and student population with new urgency—both by working to recruit a more diverse teaching cohort, and also by preparing the teachers currently in practice to serve more effectively pupils whose lives and language practices differ widely from their own. What follows is a description of our work toward achieving the latter.[1]

Problem Statement and Research Questions

Our project grew out of dissatisfaction with current practices in teacher education. We were dissatisfied with both the cultural education of beginning and experienced teachers and their preparation for teaching about literacy. As Burbules observes, although status quo professional education practice encourages teachers to support learning that is dialogic in nature and aimed at framing and solving complex problems, it rarely provides teachers with opportunities to experience directly such teaching and learning. In addition, teachers are encouraged to attend to "cultural diversity" in their classrooms and curriculum, yet they are not supported to consider the idea of culture. Furthermore, members of the so-called dominant culture, teachers among them, often have few opportunities to examine their own biases toward others (Ferdman, "Becoming"). They lack, in Galda's words, both "mirrors and windows" for examining the social and cultural foundations of literacy and the values and practices related to it.

Description of the Study

Within our study, we addressed the following three research questions:

1. What is the nature of the teachers' oral and written participation in book club activities?
2. How does participation influence teachers' understandings of literacy—its cultural foundations as well as the process of learning from literature?
3. How does teachers' participation inform teacher thinking about literacy curriculum and instruction?

---

[1]This project was supported by a grant from the National Council of Teachers of English awarded to Susan Florio-Ruane and Taffy E. Raphael and by the Center for Improvement of Early Reading Achievement (CIERA). CIERA is funded under the Educational Research and Development Centers Program, PR/Award Number R305R70004, as administered by the Office of Educational Research and Improvement, U.S. Department of Education. The ideas and opinions expressed in this paper do not reflect the position or endorsement of the National Council of Teachers of English or the U.S. Department of Education.

One goal of our study was to investigate the role alternative texts (ethnic autobiographies) and contexts (peer-led discussion groups) might play in improving experienced teachers' learning about literacy instruction and their understanding of the cultural foundations of literacy. This goal stemmed from contemporary expectations that teachers will innovate to improve youngsters' literacy development by making instruction more responsive and dialogic. This typically involves changes in (a) textual materials (i.e., moving from commercially prepared text excerpts as a basis for instruction to using original literature), (b) curriculum organization (such as moving from isolated instruction in reading, writing, language, and subject matter to intra- and interdisciplinary teaching), and (c) roles and contexts (i.e., the teacher moving from controlling topics and turns to assuming a supportive instructional role as students take greater responsibility for topic selection, discussion—as is the case in a reader-response orientation—and assessing their own progress).

A second goal of our study was to learn about participating teachers' own learning as they read, wrote, and talked about compelling personal literature describing cultural experiences. We were interested in teacher learning both about culture and literacy instruction. The study addressed two challenges in contemporary U.S. teacher education: the disparity in background between a largely European American teaching force and the diverse pupils it serves and the difficulty of teaching about literacy and culture in responsive, dialogic ways.

The study combined two lines of prior research. The first focuses on the use of narrative, specifically ethnic autobiography, as a resource for preservice teacher learning about culture (Florio-Ruane and deTar, "Conflict"; Florio-Ruane and deTar, *In Good*). The second focuses on the pedagogical power of reading, writing, and talking about literature in peer-led book clubs to foster youngsters' comprehension and critical thinking (McMahon and Raphael, with Goatley and Pardo). We reasoned from these lines of work that teacher-led book club discussions might provide a strategic site in which to foster and investigate teachers' own professional development.

We researched two contexts for teacher learning: a master's course called, "Culture, Literacy and Autobiography," which was created and taught by Susan Florio-Ruane, and a subsequent voluntary book club, the Literary Circle. Typical of the profession at large, and consistent with trends at our university, the experienced teachers enrolled in the course and continuing in the Literary Circle were homogeneous in many ways. All are European American, monolingual speakers of English, female, and middle income. Yet, due to our location in an industrial state capital surrounded by both suburbs and small agricultural towns, the teachers had grown up and now worked in a range of communities encompassing the rural, the suburban, and the urban.

The autobiographical texts read in the course were selected by Florio-Ruane in three pairs. Two were written by teachers who examine their own ethnic identities as part of coming to understand the diverse students they teach (Vivian Paley's *White Teacher;* Mike Rose's *Lives on the Boundary*). Two were written by immigrants who came to the United States seeking and finding greater freedom, economic resources, and educational opportunity (Eva Hoffman's *Lost in Translation;* Jill Ker Conway's *The Road from Coorain*). Two were written by the children of people who came to the United States either as slaves or economic refugees subject to racism and discrimination, for example, on the basis of first language or country of origin (Maya Angelou's *I Know Why the Caged Bird Sings;* Richard Rodriguez's *Hunger of Memory*).[2] Thus, the books provided contrasting cases of the immigrant experience, the occasion to reflect on one's background, the relation of racial or ethnic identity to one's experience of schooling, and one's sense of self as a literate person.

Within the Culture, Literacy, and Autobiography course, the book club discussions of the autobiographical texts occurred within a classroom structure modeled on the Book Club Program (see McMahon et al., *The Book Club;* Raphael et al.), a program based in sociocultural theory, emphasizing dialogic teaching with a balance between teacher-led and student-led discussion. As in reader-response theory, students' experiences of and with the text, along with the experiences they bring to the text, are critical to Book Club. The four components of Book Club—reading, writing, community share, and book clubs—were modified for use with practicing teachers. The reading component was modified from an in-class activity to one that occurred prior to the class meetings. All participants read the autobiography to be discussed that evening prior to the class.

Class began with an opening *community share,* a whole-class, teacher-led setting in which Florio-Ruane set the stage for discussion. Sometimes a related text was introduced, such as a videotape of Maya Angelou's poetry reading during the 1992 inaugural events. At other times, Florio-Ruane introduced a particular theme or issue. This was followed by all students writing in sketch books for approximately 10 minutes. The *writing activity* was designed to encourage participants to prepare for the upcoming book club discussion by revisiting notes they had taken, places in the text they had highlighted, questions that grew out of their reading, connections to other texts, and memories of personal events related thematically or topically to the book(s) read. Following the 10 minutes of individual writing and a brief break, the students convened in one of two book club groups. In these book clubs, which remained constant throughout the course, participants dis-

[2]For more information on the book selections and their rationale, see Florio-Ruane and deTar ("Conflict").

cussed the texts for the next hour, coming together for a closing *community share* to end the class session. This focused on pulling together ideas, themes, and issues that emerged in the two book club discussions.[3]

After completing the course, the participants chose to continue their book talk in a voluntary, less formal club called the Literary Circle. Although participants still read books and discussed them in monthly meetings, they did so over dinner at Susan Florio-Ruane's house. Here, the students who had been in the course discussed texts as a whole group without the more formal framing of opening community share and without a required writing component. After the first 6 months, participants began meeting in a room at a local bookstore cafe. This is the site where we have continued into our third year, meeting to talk about texts, reading more than 24 books together.

Invitation 18.1

Stretch your memory to identify the autobiographies that you have encountered as part of your education. (Substitute biographies if the list is meager.) As you recall, for what purpose(s) were these taught and what was the teaching methodology? From a learning and response perspective, how might you approach such materials differently? What role do you see for them in an English curriculum? If there were no autobiographies or biographies in your education, what is significant about this omission?

As participant observers, the six researchers worked collaboratively with teachers to read and talk about literature and document the group's meetings. We used ethnographic and sociolinguistic methods to study participants' learning as they read, wrote, and talked about compelling personal literature describing the cultural experience. The researchers collected and analyzed five kinds of data: (a) an instructor's journal detailing Florio-Ruane's observations of the class and her ongoing questions and instructional decisions, (b) field notes written by researchers immediately after each meeting, (c) audiotapes and videotapes of book discussions, (d) written texts produced by the teachers during the course, and (e) interviews with the teachers about the book club experience.

Using analytical techniques of grounded theory development including the constant comparative method (Glaser and Strauss), triangulation across the data (Gordon), and collaborative analysis of conversations (Witherall and Noddings), we identified themes within the data related to teachers'

---

[3]For more information on Book Club pedagogy, see Raphael et al.

participation. As is illustrated in the following sections, we developed case studies that describe and analyze participation and learning in the book clubs. The next section of this chapter describes the cases developed and written by the individual research assistants. The chapter concludes with some general comments on how these cases contribute to our understanding of learning to teach about culture and literacy.

PART II: A CLOSER LOOK:
THREE CASE STUDIES

Jocelyn Glazier, Mary McVee, Susan Wallace-Cowell, and Bette Shellhorn

Case 1: Unsettling Discourse:
Moving Through Silenced Topics

Jocelyn Glazier led the first study, an analysis of conversations the participants in the course and the subsequent Literary Circle had around two autobiographical works by Maya Angelou: *I Know Why the Caged Bird Sings* and *Gather Together in My Name*. Prompted by her own awareness of a lack of discussion in particular on the topic of race during the conversation of *Gather Together in My Name*, Glazier wanted to explore how this topic and other often-silenced topics were approached both in this conversation and in the earlier conversation about *I Know Why the Caged Bird Sings*. This analysis reveals participants' difficulties discussing certain topics raised in these texts, in particular those related to race, sexual assault, and social class. Both the texts themselves and the particular audience of White women contribute to the difficulty of placing these topics on the conversational floor.

Glazier began her analysis of these conversations by first identifying what conversations around these two works sounded like. Drawing on work in the area of participation strategies (Tanner; Edelsky), Glazier identified particular differences between the two conversations that took place 5 months apart. She found that the conversation of *I Know Why the Caged Bird Sings*, which took place at the beginning of the Culture, Literacy, and Autobiography course in September 1995, was reminiscent of a fishing expedition. It was as though the six participants involved in this particular book club were attempting to hook three things in conversation: each other, the text, and Maya Angelou herself. What was evident in particular was how difficult it was for participants to hook one another in conversation. Triangulating (Gordon) across participant–observer field notes, discussion transcripts, and interview data, Glazier identified the ways in which conversation that particular evening was difficult.

Topics throughout the evening's discussion were varied and unsustained, ranging from Angelou's writing style to her sense of dignity as revealed through the text. As single topics were introduced by speakers, there was little uptake by others in the group. Turns frequently did not link topically to one another. Often the same speaker would reintroduce a topic throughout the conversation as when one participant, Kate, mentioned the topic of "transitions" once at the beginning of the evening's discussion, again toward the middle, and two more times late in the conversation. Only one other participant chose to pick up on this topic when Kate raised it and this happened only once during the conversation. The lack of uptake among speakers was also revealed in how topics were discussed when brought to the floor. Often, a participant would repeat a phrase or word within her turn essentially to garner support for a particular topic. For example, in the following excerpt, in attempting to bring the topic of religion to the floor, Hannah repeats the term *belief* within her turn, saying:

1. Hannah: . . . Like the religion issue was, was really, really one that I toyed with a
2. lot when reading this book. Just because that's an important issue in my life
3. right now. And so it was really interesting to see the, like the succession of her
4. grandmother's **beliefs**[4] to her **beliefs** to you know, to her mother's **beliefs**.
5. You know, like I was looking for different things, like okay, what, what does
6. her mom feel? Like what is her mom's **beliefs** even though she leads this sort
7. of a life, yet there are times in the book when her mom says, you know, you
8. need to pray. . .

Hannah continued two turns after this one, again mentioning the topic of belief: "at times she [Maya] was . . . mocking . . . her grandmother's **belief** . . . and yet, there were other times when she would turn to that in her life." Hannah carried this topic primarily on her own. There was no repetition among speakers of the term *belief*, which would have been evidence of mutual participation (Tanner) or a coconstructed conversational floor (Edelsky). Other evidence of the challenging nature of conversation on this particular evening was revealed in the gaps evident in the discussion: There were multiple pauses throughout the 65-minute discussion, ranging from 3 to 29 seconds in length. Simply put, talk this night was challenging.

Five months and five book club discussions later, the six participants

---

[4]Transcripts were made to reflect conversation with periods, commas, and dashes to indicate pauses. Lines are numbered for ease of reference. Words highlighted for analysis and commentary are designated by boldface type.

joined their other class members during a Literary Circle meeting to discuss Angelou's second book, *Gather Together in My Name*. Within this conversation, the fishing hooks took hold; talk was sustained. Although there continued to be multiple topics of conversation, there were now many rounds of collaborative talk, where participants engaged in conversation around specific topics. As evidenced in Lines 10 through 17 in Fig. 18.1, participants collaboratively constructed sentences (i.e., Hannah's completing Taffy's sentence at Line 11 and Taffy latching onto Pam's at Line 17), indicating a higher level of rapport and joint construction of the floor. There was exten-

1.	Pam:	I don't remember her graduating from high school.
2.	Bonnie:	I don't, I don't remember it either.
3.	Hannah:	Wait, wait, wait. When she was in like San Francisco though, she was, she was going to school, remember? To that special school, the—
4.	Pam:	But wasn't that dance?
5.	Hannah:	—where that later on, the communist
6.	Pam:	But that was dance.
7.	SFR:	She couldn't get into the army because she'd gone to that school.
8.	Hannah:	Right, but that wasn't just a dance school. Wasn't it . . .
9.	Pam:	I thought it was dance.
10.	Taffy:	I thought it was, too. That it was just—
11.	Hannah:	—just only that? It wasn't a school where, like an art school—
12.	Taffy:	Well it might have been
13.	Hannah:	—where they went and that was part of the . . .
14.	Shelly:	But if she, if she was being accepted by the Army, even though she was rejected later as a candidate for officers' candidate school, wouldn't she have had a high school diploma?
15.	Hannah:	Yeah.
16.	Pam:	But I thought I remembered at the beginning of it, her saying, you know her mom said I'll keep the child at home so you can go back to school and she said no. And I, that must have been—
17.	Taffy:	—for college.
18.	Pam:	Was that?
19.	Taffy:	Must, yeah. Because I think, I mean, the Air Force you can't unless you've got a college degree, go into office, can you? But I think in the Army you can. I can't imagine that the Air Force would have required a college degree and the Army wouldn't require anything.
20.	Pam:	I imagine it must be high school.

FIG. 18.1.   Example of sustained talk about *Gather Together in My Name*.

sive repetition of phrases and words among speakers (e.g., repetition of the terms *remember* and *dance school*), tying the stream of discourse together and the participants to one another, linking "individual speakers in a conversation and in relationships" (Tannen 52). This is revealed in the collaborative development of the floor around the topic of Angelou's education, a partial transcription of which appears in Fig. 18.1.

Another indication of sustained engagement during this particular discussion is the lack of gaps between turns. During the whole 81-minute conversation, there are only two pauses in contrast to the 16 evident in the *I Know Why the Caged Bird Sings* conversation. On this night talk flowed. Participants eagerly and effectively responded to many themes within the text and to one another. One might expect and hope to see such changes over time and, noting them, not look further at this particular discussion. However, prompted by a sense that something was missing from the talk—specifically discussion of the topics of race and racism—Glazier continued her analysis.

Despite powerful differences between the two discussions—likely the result of participants' growing familiarity with one another, with the book club format, and with the reading of autobiographical texts[5]—the conversation around Angelou's second book seemed similar to the first in some ways. As mentioned, in her role of participant observer that evening, Glazier had noticed a lack of discussion in particular around the topics of race and racism, topics Angelou explores in her text. To analyze this apparent thematic gap, Glazier returned to the data from the *I Know Why the Caged Bird Sings* discussion, looking in particular at moments when topics were abruptly shifted or when conversation came to a halt. What became evident in this analysis was that there were topics around which conversation became challenging, topics of "hot lava." Like the children's game where the goal is to avoid stepping on certain rocks that are deemed hot lava, the same evasion was happening in conversation. There were topics that participants were avoiding, related to race, social class, and sexual assault.[6]

This same evasion was also evident in the *Gather Together in My Name* conversation. Like the first session, there were places on this evening when conversation seemed to take a turn, sometimes a sharp turn, away from difficult material. Sometimes on the second evening conversational turns were like those of a Sunday driver, slower and more subtle to the listener because of the fluid, collaborative nature of the talk. However, the data analysis reveals

---

[5]Work in progress by Shellhorn reveals how unfamiliarity in these areas influences the participation by course participants during the group's first book club conversation 2 weeks prior to the conversation on Angelou's *I Know Why the Caged Bird Sings*.

[6]When describing these incidents of topic avoidance, Glazier was reminded by a colleague, Christopher Clark, of this particular children's game.

that topics were approached, yet avoided on both evenings. There clearly remain alleys down which participants were reluctant to travel. In the first conversation, they simply don't. In the second, they see a stop sign, but inch forward, tempted to make the turn. Yet, they turn back. Interestingly, most often in both discussions, hot lava topics are initially placed on the floor by either Florio-Ruane, Raphael, or one of the research assistants. The examples of participants' talk in Fig. 18.2 illustrate the different forms avoidance takes in both conversations. Notice in the earlier discussion that talk on the topic of rape was fairly short and ended abruptly, turning instead to a safer topic related, perhaps ironic, to Angelou's "burying" things. In the second conversation, the transition from the topic of rape is less abrupt, occurring over multiple turns. As is described later, we followed this pattern as an indication of growing willingness on the part of participants to engage the topic in conversation and cross-checked this interpretation in extended debriefing interviews at the end of the group's first year.

Conversations about topics such as racism, sexual assault, and social class —all raised in Angelou's books—are among those difficult for these book club participants to sustain. Like the hot lava of the children's playground game, participants dash conversationally around them, leaping instead for the safety of topics such as Angelou's writing style or her own love of literacy as expressed in the text. This finding leaves us with questions about the limits and possibilities of female European American teachers' learning about difference by means of reading and discussing literature. It is likely that the texts, the particular audience, and the social context of the book club influence how far one is able to travel down roads lined with challenging topics.

With respect to audience and the topic of race, for example, it is not surprising that evasion takes place. White women in particular have learned to silence any discussion of race, an act that is perceived as acting "appropriately" and "protecting" oneself from being perceived as racist (Frankenberg; McIntosh, "White"; McIntyre). In addition, avoiding the topic of race in some ways enables Whites to maintain "White privilege" (McIntosh, *Interactive*). In regards to text and this same topic of race, it is likely that Angelou's texts present certain challenges for this particular readership. Specifically, Angelou's use of poetics—her use of humor, irony, and exaggeration, for example—can leave a White reader unsure how to respond to the injustices that Angelou confronts in her life and then writes about in her texts. When these readers arrived at topics raised within the texts, they were unsure how to engage them. To do so meant learning an alternative "discourse" (Gee) or way of speaking and thinking about oneself and others. Over time in sustained, collaborative contexts (the book club and the Literary Circle) and through the use of alternative texts (autobiographies), participants inched toward these challenging issues. Teachers began to move through these silenced topics into unsettling, but imperative, discourse.

I Know Why the Caged Bird Sings	*Gather Together in My Name*
Hannah: . . . One thing that I was . . . trying to find if there's any other time she mentioned it, after um, the, uh [rape] trial with Mr. Freeman and . . . I just thought that you know, she, she explained that episode in her life and you know, she, she didn't really talk about her feelings or anything . . . I'd like to go back and look more carefully because that was the first time I really looked, that she like came back to that issue. Whereas a lot of books could have been written, you know, like that was a big thing that happened and the whole rest of the book could have been reaction to that happening to her as a, as a child and it wasn't . . . She just chose not to write about it or to dwell on it or to . . .	**Hannah:** And she did the interview, the two things that like you could noticeably see her emotions change within her was one, when she was talking about the accident with her son . . . and the other was not the rape but that her uncles had killed the man who had raped her. She just sat there and she was like—
	Pam: She felt so much it was her own fault.
	Hannah: The thought, I mean, you could just see her, you could see her face.
	Jerri: She said, just like in her book, that her words—
Bonnie: She had a good way of just burying things and really tuning things out, I got a sense.	**Hannah:** She's like that my words had the power to kill someone . . .
	Susan FR: Did she talk about not talking after that?
Hannah: Uh huh. And I think a lot of that came probably from her grandmother. You know, I mean, the whole thing we talked about with her grandmother.	**Hannah:** Yeah, a large part of it was how she didn't talk.
	Pam: Yeah, 'cause we, I mean how long was it? . . . Wasn't it—
	Hannah: Three years or something, wasn't it?
	Jerri: Longer than that.
	Hannah: Was it?
	Jerri: It was from 7 until 13, isn't it?
	Pam: . . . I don't remember it being that long that she kept that silence . . .
	Hannah: I thought she was raped when she was 8.
	Kate: Oh man.
	Jerri: Maybe it was 8 to 13 . . .
	Kate: Now do you think part of it was because she knew that they killed? I'm trying to remember.
	Hannah: Oh yeah, absolutely. She knew because she had said something about it . . . she just knew it was her fault . . .
	Kate: That's right. She'd never tell anything.
**Both earlier and later in the conversation, when the topic of rape is introduced, it is discussed briefly and then followed by a noticeable pause before the topic shifts.	**Hannah:** It was just amazing. And the other thing . . . about the interview . . . is whenever she would go to recite her poetry, she didn't recite it, she sang it.
	Pam: She sang it.

FIG 18.2.   Examples of talk avoiding difficult topics in discussion of Maya Angelou's books.

Once within that arena, perhaps they might lead their students into it as well.[7]

As high school teachers well know, there are some topics that are easier to avoid than engage with in classroom conversations. If we can barely engage with these topics ourselves as teachers, it is no wonder that we would not choose to have our students engage with them. What this case reveals is both the difficulty and the potential of carrying these topics to the floor. Teachers may do well to first engage with these hot lava topics in circles of peers as they have come to be able to do in the Literary Circle. This engagement, however, happens only over time as participants grow more familiar with one another, with the context of the book club, and with the content of ethnic autobiography. One would expect the same to be true when prepared teachers bring these "difficult dialogues" (hooks as cited in Britzman) into the high school classroom. Students and teachers alike are quite expert at the game of hot lava. Learning and mastering a new game, something both critical and rewarding, can come only with time and practice.

Invitation 18.2

Is race as difficult a topic for secondary school students as it seems to have been for these teachers? How might the conversation about race be different in other, more diverse book groups? Again, stretch your memory to recall your reactions during secondary school and those of your peers to this topic. Discuss this issue with your peers both to assess the range of your experiences and the tactics that might be used to alleviate the closed reactions that these authors anticipate.

Engagement in conversation is expressed in many ways. One way engagement is created and sustained in conversations in our society is by means of the telling of personal narratives (Tanner). In the next case study, Mary McVee explores the role of oral narratives in facilitating and limiting conversation around multicultural texts, particularly ethnic autobiographies.

Case 2: Narratives as Sites of Connection and Disconnection

Theoretical perspectives on narrative and the self (e.g., Bruner; Polkinghorne; DiPardo) suggest that stories of personal experience are powerful ways for us to explore issues of diversity and culture in our own lives and the

---

[7]See Raphael, T. E., S. Florio-Ruane, A. Topper, K. Highfield, M. George, and B. Shellhorn (1999) for an example of ways that book club teachers are creating a book club curriculum for youngsters on the theme, "Our Storied Lives."

lives of others. Additionally, multicultural educators posit that to explore issues of culture and diversity, participants should begin with critical exploration of the self (Ferdman, "Literacy"). Discussion of ethnic autobiography
allows for opportunities to explore how individuals are positioned within
and by cultural contexts; language practices; and issues such as social class,
ethnicity, or gender. In discussions about autobiographical texts, readers
may choose to respond by sharing their own narratives. These narrative responses to text allow participants to make connections to their own life experiences (see Florio-Ruane and de Tar, "Conflict"). Given the function of
narrative in helping us explore issues of self and other, teachers and teacher
educators must then create spaces where narratives are valued and encouraged. One such space is peer-led book clubs structured around discussions
of autobiography.

The analysis presented here focuses on a book club discussion of *The
Road from Coorain* by Jill Ker Conway. McVee and others on the research team
were intrigued by how the discussion of Conway's text provided a context to
explore the role of narrative by inviting connections among participants
and exploring issues of self, culture, or diversity in life experience. In her
text, Conway depicts life on an isolated sheep station in Australia's outback
in the 1930s and 1940s. She paints a vivid portrait of the natural surroundings and the family's struggle against drought and forces of nature. Several
participants in the book club shared an agrarian background or experiences
in rural environments and told personal narratives related to their past experience. For McVee, the ties to land and the isolation of a rural environment were particularly powerful because she was raised on a ranch in east-
ern Montana where her family struggled in ways similar to Conway's. In describing her response to Conway's text, McVee wrote:

> Through Conway's vivid descriptions of the Australian flatlands and the fam-
> ily's struggle against drought, I relived my own family's struggle—against
> drought and foreclosure on bank loans. My response to Conway's story was an
> emotional one, and I felt deeply connected to the text. (November 6, 1995)

Narratives, as told by participants, provided snapshots into the lives of
participants and reflected and sustained a sense of engagement. Yet, even as
narratives appeared to foster exploration of particular topics or build thematic connections, they were problematic. Although such narrative talk appeared highly connected in terms of theme and topic, closer analysis revealed that such narratives fostered not only connection but disconnection.
This raised questions about narrative as a form of response to literature in
Book Club discussions. As a response to literature, how do oral narratives
help sustain conversation among participants? How might oral narratives
constrain conversation or limit exploration of issues among participants?

Analyzing field notes revealed two types of talk over the course of the

Segments	1	2	3	4	5	6	7	8
Themes (in chrono-logical order)	Transi-tions Jill made in her life	Jill's rela-tionship with her mother	Jill's role as author, how the text is con-structed	Hoffman & the Southern Cross (not fully devel-oped)	Exploring Jill's leav-ing Coorain	Weather (not fully devel-oped)	Respon-sibility vs. Rebellion in Jill's life	(reprise) Exploring Jill's leaving Coorain

FIG 18.3.   Themes discussed in book club on *The Road From Coorain.*

60-minute discussion. As the analysis in Figure 18.3 illustrates, the book club participants first stayed close to the text, exploring themes in the book such as transitions in Conway's life; her relationship with her mother; father–daughter relationships; land or nature versus mankind; and failure, loss, and dislocation (see Fig. 18.3).

The second half of the evening's talk revealed participants telling both brief and extended personal narratives, fostering connection with one another and the book. For example, one participant shared her experiences of living in a remote, isolated area of Africa; another shared how her husband's family lived in an isolated area of Michigan throughout the winter; and a third shared how she had felt flying over the vast deserts of Australia. A substantial amount of talk focused on two participants sharing narratives about their lives on dairy farms. After the discussion, several participants commented on how good it had been, how interactive everyone had been. In addition, in follow-up interviews, participants recalled this night of talk frequently and referred to how engaging it had been and how connected the talk was. However, closer analysis of individual responses to this conversation around *The Road From Coorain* revealed an interesting pattern.

First, where some participants seemed to be connecting, others felt disconnected. One way speakers' exclusion came about was through a gradual narrowing of topic. For example, in response to other stories that had been told about land and isolation and a question about affective ties to land, two participants, Kate and Hannah, constructed a discussion that explored the relationship between weather and farming (see Fig. 18.4).

There is a high degree of repetition within these speakers' turns as well as across them (e.g., weather, farm, rainy day, sunny day, crop). Hannah and Kate collaborated in sustaining this conversational floor (Edelsky) in other ways as well, for example, in helping to finish each others' sentences as Kate does at the end. In addition, the talk flowed quickly and smoothly. Although these features give the appearance of engaging and connected talk, few others enter this conversation. Kate and Hannah had constructed a narrowing floor that focused on weather and farmers making a living related to weather.

Others, who did not share their knowledge of farming or did not connect the topic to the book, remained silent.

Hannah: Well, I know just the, what the nature and the **weather** thing

Kate: Yeah, that affected me because being on a **farm**, what your dad is able to do and his farm hands in the course of the day has to do with the **weather**. You know and what you're gonna be able to accomplish in that day and, you know, it's all around the **weather**. The connection between nature.

Hannah: I find myself even now, you know, like being very conscious of how many **sunny days** we've had in a row.

Kate: Me too.

Hannah: And how many **rainy days** we've had in a row.

Kate: How are the farmers doing?

Hannah: It's like a constant worry of mine. . . . It's a **farm** thing to do. . . . I grew up in an area where there's a lot of **crop** farmers, too and we were dairy farmers. But I always felt like we were the lucky ones . . . even if something happened with the **crops**, we could always buy it. You know, granted it would cost more money and would be a harder year for my parents, but like those **crop** farmers. I just remember feeling so sorry for if we had a bad summer. Or even

Kate: Too much **rain**.

FIG 18.4. Narrowing of discussion by Hannah and Kate's talk about farming and weather.

At this point in the conversation, Florio-Ruane, the course instructor, commented that since some appeared to have had experiences with landscapes similar to Conway's, there could potentially be a broader discussion. She asked, "Is there a connection between [Conway's] experience and how she goes about blazing intellectual trails?" But Hannah and Kate rejected Susan's bid for the floor and continued to talk about farming. For example, Hannah replied, "I mean it's not really along those lines but . . ." and returned to talk about farms, particularly the responsibilities that farm children have. Thus the gradual narrowing of talk from narratives that foster connections across the group to narratives that narrow talk to two participants continued.

In written logs and follow-up interviews, participants demonstrated that they did not always "connect" through narratives. They also note that some stories of personal experience are more emotionally charged or entail more risk in the telling than others. Therefore, some are told, and some are not. McVee's field notes reflect her feelings of discomfort and isolation in the midst of apparent connection among the group members. She wrote,

> Although I have shared some things about my personal background, I did not share as much as I could have, nor did I share the things that were most mean-

ingful to me. I disagreed with some interpretations . . . , but I did not share my own views. . . . [One] time I felt that I held a somewhat different view [from others] was in the discussion of the weather. Both Kate and Hannah saw this as important because it determines what you can and can't do. Hannah also noted that things were different for crop farmers because dairy farmers could always buy hay and feed. There is a major difference between stockmen, crop farmers, and dairymen. The first two are wholly dependent upon the land and weather; not only does it determine when they work, but it determines their success as it did in the case of Coorain. (November 6, 1995)

As revealed here, McVee felt deeply connected to the story but disconnected in the conversation. Surface features of the conversation—repetition of phrases and words, sharing of personal narratives that thematically connected to each other and the book—indicated the connective and often harmonious nature characteristic of White, middle-class women's means of communicating (Tannen). However, on closer examination, although the narratives are highly coordinated with respect to topic, their themes and organization reflect differences in participants' background knowledge, values, point of view, and conversational role. The surface features mask the underlying sense of difference that McVee was feeling. Similarly, during the debriefing interview, Bonnie reported that despite sharing a narrative about her feelings of isolation living in Africa, she did not feel connected to either the text or the discussion regarding land. What she had connected with was Conway's intellectual journey, a topic barely touched on by the group, even after the instructor's attempt to place it on the conversational floor.

The analysis of narratives finds that telling stories can foster a sense of engagement and connection among participants around a text. Yet at the same time, narratives can constrain and limit talk, creating a feeling of disconnection. In conducting this analysis, it becomes clear that a group that initially assumed consensus gradually discovers itself to hold a range of differing, sometimes conflicting cultural experiences and values. Thus, teachers can celebrate their students' sharing of narratives but also need to be aware that there are important narratives that remain untold or that aren't allowed space on the conversational floor. Teachers need to make consistent pedagogical moves to invite additional narratives into the folds of discussion.

Case 3: "If It's So Difficult, Why Do It?": Sustained Participation and Intellectual Growth

Given the challenges participants faced in terms of sustaining topics, addressing issues of race and culture, and trying to achieve deep connections within discussions, one might ask why they would continue to participate voluntarily in the Literary Circle. In what ways might participants value their participation enough to continue? Led by Susan Wallace-Cowell, this case study explores how the book club, as a social context for learning, thinking, and knowing, may facilitate participants' intellectual development, both personal and professional. The primary data for the analysis are interviews conducted with each of the participants.

Following the first year of participation in the book club and the Literary Circle, Wallace-Cowell interviewed participants about their experiences in the book club. These interviews focused on broad themes of culture, literature, group processes, narratives, teaching, and learning. Wallace-Cowell initially cataloged and summarized each interview in close detail and added field notes and commentary throughout each catalog. In analyzing the interview catalogs, Wallace-Cowell found that literature and discussions of that literature impacted the intellectual development of participants in both their personal and professional lives. This was an interesting and surprising finding, not anticipated when the study was conceived. In addition to learning about culture and response to literature, participants were learning about themselves. The fact that the dialogue fostered by the book club and literary circle enhanced in a more general sense participants' experience of themselves as "knowers" (Belenky et al.) prompted Wallace-Cowell to think about the potential power of peer-led, conversation-based book clubs for facilitating intellectual development.

Using constant comparative method (Glaser and Strauss), drawing on the catalogs of the interviews as a starting point, Wallace-Cowell identified nine features of intellectual growth as the teachers described it (Wallace). From these broad categories, Wallace-Cowell revisited the data to refine and to further test her assumptions. A useful construct in testing and refining initial assumptions about the intellectual growth of participants was the notion of "gaining a voice" (Belenky et al.). Through continued analysis of catalogs and transcripts, three features emerged as indicators of participants' "gaining a voice"—of their developing as intellectuals: (a) they found *themselves reading, writing, and talking differently;* (b) *they were making changes in their professional* lives based on their experiences in the course and subsequent literary circle; and (c) they were reenvisioning *a future life for themselves as intellectuals.* These areas relate to different ways in which the participants were experiencing intellectual development by gaining voice.

Reading, Writing, and Talking Differently

In the book club and Literary Circle, students read, wrote, and talked in ways that were different from their previous experiences. As Hannah[8] commented, "I have a tendency to read a book because I want to read it not because I want to sit there and think about it a whole lot . . . and I think that one of the best things about book club is that I have to be more conscious about that" (Interview, July 15, 1996). Participating in the book club en-

---

[8] All participants except members of the research team are referred to by pseudonyms.

couraged her to read differently than she had in the past. This type of change in her interactions with texts was typical for participants not only around reading, but also around writing and talking. The book club and Literary Circle fostered for them new ways of thinking. For some, these new ways of thinking allowed them the opportunity to challenge themselves and others in new and exciting ways. For Jerri, this meant learning how to reassess what it meant to have an independent voice within a community. She stated,

> I used to be really bad at taking issue with anybody on saying anything. . . . I'd sit back, let people say things and walk away. But book club has actually helped me to discuss things on that level without being mean. Like deciding it's OK to do that and to say, "you know what? I'm not so sure I agree with that" and to actually state something. . . . We disagree with each other on an intellectual basis and then we go on to be friends. And I don't think before book club I could have done that. (Interview, July 15, 1996)

For Jerri, and women in general, research has shown that connection, remaining in relation to others, is important. Women will disengage intellectually to stay in relation with others (Belenky et al.; Gilligan, *Different;* Gilligan, Lyons, and Hanmer; Orenstein). Book club was an experience where Jerri learned that she could be smart and have her voice heard within a community of friends and colleagues. Again, participants were learning how to engage in and think about interactions differently. Gaining a voice involved changed perceptions of how they viewed themselves as intellectuals. This is clearly demonstrated by Hannah who remarked,

> I have always had this thing that I am not that smart. Like I'm just okay, I'm an okay student and I've always been okay. And I can't participate with doctoral students or professors. I think this was an experience that allowed me to do that [participate] and to see that I could kind of hold my own . . . and I realize that maybe I do have something to offer that's worthwhile. (Interview, July 15, 1996)

Hannah was an active contributor and was always telling stories and sharing. Still, she had doubts and needed to feel that what she had to offer was valuable. As she began to be taken seriously by the group and realized she could "hold her own," she then began to change her view of herself as an intellectual.

This analysis augments McVee's study of the discussion of *The Road From Coorain* in suggesting that participants in general appeared to be coming to understand that their opinions and ideas were worthwhile and that they did not have to agree with everyone else, particularly authority figures in the group. This type of knowing seems closely associated with Belenky et al.'s "constructed knower" who is able to listen to her own voice in coming to know, but also weigh it against outside information and values. The shift toward this type of knowing is indicative of intellectual growth: individuals are "gaining a voice" that had not previously been experienced. As Shelly remarked, "In the end I wasn't sure that I had any pat answers to anything, but I knew that I at least have been forced to consider a lot of things I had never considered before. Although I wish I had more answers, at least I knew that I would never assume things, maybe the way I had in the past" (Interview, June 24, 1996).

Professional Action

Participants were growing and changing in ways that were affecting them professionally as well as personally. Some of the teachers in the group were putting to use in their classrooms the things they were learning about themselves and their teaching. For example, Jerri created and taught a unit on culture, and Shelly started a book club with her kids, modeling her approach after her own experiences in the course and the Literary Circle. These curricular changes were a result of Jerri's and Shelly's participation in the book club. In addition, Kate talked about how a book we had read together had influenced her teaching. In *White Teacher*, Vivian Paley describes avoiding the uncomfortable topic of racism within her classroom and her attempts to shift her behavior. Kate commented, "I am more aware of when people say things. [The book] made me not be able to just try to brush over it or just say it's non-existent but maybe try to take it apart a little. Let's talk about this" (Interview, July 10, 1996). In particular, Kate introduced an artifact unit into her classroom, asking students to share with the rest of the students in the class artifacts representative of their own lives and cultural experiences. In doing so, she hoped her students would grow to value their own cultural experiences and those of others. Thus, as Glazier's conversational analyses also find, the teachers reported increased and sustained attention to hot lava topics both in their own reading and in their literacy instruction.

Participants have also engaged in different types of professional action as they attempted to engage their school community in literacy acts that could enhance everyone's intellectual environment. Not only were people enacting change in their classrooms, but they were also attempting to influence their larger professional communities. This type of professional engagement suggests an enhanced sense of themselves as intellectuals. In the case of Shelly, this meant starting a book club with other teachers in her school. The group began meeting in the spring in 1996. For Kate, this meant initiating poetry reading at her school where everyone in the school (including custodians, lunch staff, and administrators) read poetry each morning. She described:

> Part of me has tried to think a lot about how I can share what I have learned, can I somehow share with the teachers, staff that I work with. . . . I did get a poetry month going in our school. I chaired the committee and we tried to really build a community and get everyone in the building reading. The custodian read over the loud speaker, the principal. . . . It really underscored the

importance of participation in a literacy community. I became more conscious of the big picture. (Interview, July 10, 1996)

Kate went on to talk about how much she learned about the importance of participating in literacy acts. She now believes that if teachers are going to teach something like book club then they should be participating in it as well. She finds that she is really trying to encourage those around her to engage in what she's experiencing. These sorts of professional activities underscore the significance of this book club experience not only for members personally but also for their professional communities.

Future Orientation

Participants were also expressing changes in the way that they were envisioning themselves differently in the future. For example, participants talked about seeing themselves in different roles or doing different things with their lives both in and out of the classroom—things they would not have considered prior to the book club experience. As exemplified by Hannah's comment here, the new voices they were developing suggested that they were envisioning themselves in intellectual ways:

[Jill Ker Conway] was such an amazing person and she made me think about other options in my life that I maybe never would have thought about before. Now I look at what you and Mary are doing [in the doctoral program] and I think, that's feasible. I could do that . . . the whole idea that that's an option for me. That's a door that could be opened for me and that surprised me. (Interview, July 15, 1996)

According to Sadker and Sadker (1994), Hannah is typical of many women who have come to view themselves as people who can't or don't want to think about themselves as intellectuals. Yet Hannah's consideration of pursuing a doctoral degree—inherently an intellectual endeavor—suggests that she begins to see her own worth and views her ways of knowing and learning as valid. This was also the case for other participants such as Beth, who undertook doctoral studies as an outgrowth of the project. Simply stated, participants began to take themselves more seriously and this changed the way they perceived their own intellectual growth and development.

The Book Club and Literary Circle: Contexts for Learning and Development

As stated earlier in this chapter, the theoretical perspective guiding this study is a social constructivist one based on Vygotsky's ideas about learning as a social process (Vygotsky; Wertsch). Thus, the social context of the book club was central to learning and development in this project. More specifically, safety, community, and intimacy—developed only over time—seemed particularly salient for participants, who repeatedly spoke about the significance of having a group of people with whom to share ideas and safely talk about issues—an opportunity they did not have in other settings. As Kate commented, the context was,

> a place where it's safe, you know, to share your life. I know I feel much closer to the group based on their stories and their sharing. You put yourself in a vulnerable situation . . . you're willing to take more risks because other people are . . . and in a learning community that is important. (Interview, July 10, 1996)

For Kate, sharing did not initially come easily and she talked about the uneasiness of her experiences in the group. This feeling was shared by other participants and by the earlier data in this chapter suggesting that talk was not always easy, but that over time the book club context fostered the opportunity for participants to enter, sustain, and learn from this difficult conversational work.

Belenky et al. argue that women may come to know in ways that are not typically valued in schools or in the society at large so their voices often go unheard. In the book club context, perhaps ways of knowing that align more closely with these women's ways of knowing are valued, and as such the environment may have contributed to participants' enhanced experience and their desire to continue on. As suggested earlier, the book club and Literary Circle allowed these women to feel that they were able to develop their voices and that what they said and what they thought really mattered. Kate reflected this feeling when she stated, "I guess one of the feelings I had was validation . . . a real sense of community. . . . It was something I wanted to go to" (Interview, July 10, 1996). For Kate, this was a surprising revelation because she had assumed that this experience would just be "fun to get together and read books and talk." This type of shift in interest and passion highlights the importance of the book club and Literary Circle as sites for learning and growth.

PART III: BRINGING WHAT WE'VE LEARNED
TO THE HIGH SCHOOL CONTEXT

The book club context invited a different type of learning for many of the participants. Understanding participants' growth as intellectuals in their personal and professional lives helps to shed light on their continued participation despite the difficulties of engaging in "real" talk around difficult topics. The teachers are getting a great deal of personal and professional satisfaction from this experience, which surfaces in the interviews as changes in the way they see themselves as thinkers and knowers, and how they are changing their practice to reflect this experience. These insights not only help us to understand what intellectual growth might look like for this group of participants, but they also shed light on contexts that may benefit and support teachers' and students' intellectual development.

As reflected in the cases presented here, the learning that occurred within the course and subsequent Literary Circle was at once precarious and promising. Through our research, we discovered a number of things that might help high school teachers in particular as they set out to transform the learning that occurs within their classrooms, particularly the learning associated with cultural understanding and knowledge. We shifted from a traditional model of professional development that, as in classroom teaching, often treats its students as passive recipients of static, uncontested information. Book clubs encouraged discussion about compelling literature and, as such, maintained the interest of the participants, motivating them to struggle through sometimes difficult terrain. As revealed in Glazier's work, talk changed over time as participants grew more familiar with one another and with the genre of autobiography. In addition, as Wallace-Cowell reminds us, the development over time of a sense of community enabled participants to feel safe struggling through their learning both about themselves and about others. We imagine the same scenarios within the high school classroom.

Invitation 18.3

With your small group, assess the perceived outcomes of this tripartite research study by establishing guidelines for classroom applications.

As teachers work to shift the context and content of their classrooms to include reader-response discussions (i.e., book clubs) about compelling pieces of literature that may bring to the surface challenging issues often avoided in schools, they may be helped in remembering the following points. First, as was the case with the participants in our study, discussion of hot lava topics does not unfold easily but rather occurs over time and with effort. One text and one discussion will likely not be enough. Teachers must be quite purposeful in their choice of readings and in their choice of pedagogy, as was the case in the Culture, Literacy, and Autobiography course. Second, as we encourage our students to share narratives in response to text, we as teachers—working at the high school, preservice or in-service level—need to pay attention both to the narratives being told and those not being told. We should not be fooled into a sense of consensus by students' silence or by the rhythmic nature of their talk. Not everyone finds a space on the conversational floor for his or her narrative. Instead, as teachers employ reader-response-based practices, they may want to explore ways of encouraging students to share narratives (or even a single narrative) in multiple forms (i.e., verbal, written, through drawing) over more extended periods of time. Finally, as teachers, we must extend multiple opportunities for our students to feel connected to one another. Establishing and maintaining a community appears central in transforming students' literacy learning over time.

REFERENCES

Angelou, Maya. *Gather Together in My Name.* New York: Random House, 1993.
————. *I Know Why the Caged Bird Sings.* New York: Bantam, 1969.
Belenky, Mary Field, et al. *Women's Ways of Knowing: The Development of Self, Voice and Mind.* New York: Basic Books, 1986.
Britzman, Deborah. "Decentering Discourses in Teacher Education: Or, the Unleashing of Unpopular Things." *What Schools Can Do: Critical Pedagogy and Practice.* Eds. K. Weiler & C. Mitchell. Albany, NY: SUNY Press, 1992.
Bruner, Jerome. *Acts of Meaning.* Cambridge, MA: Harvard University Press, 1990.
Burbules, Nicholas. *Dialogue in Teaching: Theory and Practice.* New York: Teachers College Press, 1993.
Cazden, Courtney B., and Hugh Mehan. "Principles From Sociology and Anthropology: Context, Code, and the Classroom." *Knowledge Base for the Beginning Teacher.* Ed. M. Reynolds. Oxford, UK: Pergamon, 1989. 47–57.
Conway, Jill Ker. *The Road From Coorain.* New York: Vintage, 1989.
DiPardo, A. "Narrative Knowers, Expository Knowledge: Discourse as Dialectic." *Written Communication* 71 (1990): 59–95.
Edelsky, Carole. "Who's Got the Floor?" *Language in Society* 10 (1981): 383–421.
Ferdman, B. "Literacy and Cultural Identity." *The Harvard Educational Review* 60. 2 (1990): 181–204.
Ferdman, B. "Becoming Literate in a Multiethnic Society." *Literate Systems and Individual Lives: Perspectives on Literacy and Schooling.* Ed. E. Jennings and A. Purves. Albany, NY: SUNY Press, 1991. 95–115.
Florio-Ruane, Susan, and Julie deTar. "Conflict and Consensus in Beginning Teachers' Discussion of Ethnic Autobiography." *English Education* 27 (1995): 11–39.
Florio-Ruane, S., with Julie deTar. *In Good Company: Autobiography, Conversation and Teacher Learning About Culture and Literacy.* Mahwah, NJ: Lawrence Erlbaum Associates, in preparation.
Frankenberg, Ruth. *White Women, Race Matters: The Social Construction of Whiteness.* Minneapolis: University of Minnesota Press, 1993.
Galda, Lee. "Mirrors and Windows: Reading as Transformation." Paper presented at the International Reading Association Annual Meeting, Anaheim, CA, May 15, 1995.
Gee, James. *What Is Literacy?* (Technical Report No. 2). Brookline, MA: The Literacies Institute, Educational Development Corporation, 1989.
Gilligan, Carol. *In a Different Voice: Psychological Theory and Women's Development.* Cambridge, MA: Harvard University Press, 1982.
Gilligan, Carol, Nona P. Lyons, and Trudy J. Hanmer. *Making Connections: The Relational World of Adolescent Girls at the Emma Willard School.* Cambridge, MA: Harvard University Press, 1989.

Glaser, B. G., and B. Strauss. *The Discovery of Grounded Theory.* Chicago: Aldine, 1967.

Gordon, R. L. *Interviewing: Strategies, Techniques and Tactics.* Homewood, IL: Dorsey, 1980.

Hoffman, Eva. *Lost in Translation: A New Life in a New Language.* New York: Penguin, 1989.

McDiarmid, William and Jeremy Price. *Prospective Teachers' View of Diverse Learners: A Study of the Participants in the ABCD Project.* East Lansing, MI: National Center for Research on Teacher Education, 1990.

McIntosh, Peggy. *Interactive Phases of Curricular and Personal Re-Vision With Regard to Race* (Working Paper No. 219). Wellesley, MA: Center for Research on Women, 1990.

———. "White Privilege: Unpacking the Invisible Knapsack." *Multiculturalism, 1992.* Ed. A. Filor. New York: New York State Council of Educational Associations, 1992. 30–36.

McIntyre, Alice. *Making Meaning of Whiteness: Exploring Racial Identity With White Teachers.* Albany, NY: SUNY Press, 1997.

McMahon, S. I., T. E. Raphael with V. J. Goatley and L. S. Pardo. *The Book Club Connection: Literacy Learning and Classroom Talk.* New York: Teachers College Press, 1997.

McMahon, S., et al. *The Book Club Connection.* New York: Teachers College Press, 1997.

National Center for Educational Statistics. "Female and Far From Diverse." *The New York Times Education Life* (January 7, 1996), 22.

Orenstein, Peggy. *School Girls: Young Women, Self-Esteem and the Confidence Gap.* New York: Doubleday, 1994.

Paley, Vivian. *White Teacher.* Cambridge, MA: Harvard University Press, 1989.

Polkinghorne, Donald. "Narrative and Self-Concept." *Journal of Narrative and Life History* 1 (1991): 135–53.

Raphael, T., S. Florio-Ruane, A. Topper, K. Highfield, M. George, and B. Shellhorn. *A Network for Teacher Learning: Goals and Contexts.* Paper presented at the Annual Meeting of the American Educational Research Association, Montreal, Canada, April 20, 1999.

Raphael, Taffy E. et al. *Book Club: A Literature Based Curriculum.* Littleton, MA: Small Planet Communication, 1997.

Rodriguez, Richard. *Hunger of Memory: The Education of Richard Rodriguez.* New York: Bantam, 1982.

Rose, Mike. *Lives on the Boundary.* New York: Penguin, 1989.

Sadker, Myra and David Sadker. *Failing at Fairness: How America's Schools Cheat Girls.* New York: Charles Scribner's Sons, 1994.

Tannen, Deborah. *Talking Voices: Repetition, Dialogue, and Imagery in Conversational Discourse.* Cambridge, UK: Cambridge University Press, 1989.

Vygotsky, Lev. *Thought and Language.* Cambridge, MA: MIT Press, 1986.

Wallace-Cowell, Susan. "Exploring Teachers' Intellectual, Professional and Personal Growth: Making Private Transformations Public." Paper presented at the National Reading Conference, Charleston, SC, December 12, 1996.

Wertsch, James. *Vygotsky's Genetic Method, Vygotsky and the Social Formation of Mind.* Cambridge, MA: Harvard University Press, 1985.

Witherall, Carol A. and Nel Noddings, eds. *Stories Lives Tell: Narrative and Dialogue in Education.* New York: Teachers College Press, 1989.

19

Calypso, Jazz, Reggae, Salsa
Literature, Response,
and the African Diaspora

Linda A. Spears-Bunton

> *We spent most of yesterday telling stories. Someone says, Krik? You answer,*
> *Krak! And they say, I have many stories I could tell you, and then they go on*
> *and tell these stories to you, but mostly to themselves. Sometimes it feels like*
> *we have been at sea longer than the many years I have been on earth.*
> *The sun comes up and goes down. That is how you know it has been a*
> *whole day. I feel like we are sailing to Africa. Maybe we will go to Guinin,*
> *to live with the spirits, to be with everyone who has come and died before us.*
> *. . . They treat Haitians like dogs in the Bahamas, a woman says.*
> *To them, we are not human. Even though their music sounds like ours.*
> *Their people look like ours. Even though we had the same African fathers*
> *who probably crossed these same seas together.*
>
> —Danticat (14)

CROSSING TROUBLED SEAS:
LITERACY AND CULTURAL DIFFERENCE

Literature is a powerful way of studying the relationships among culture, readers, and response. Moreover, literature is a logical way to extend and expand literacy and to broaden the scope of reader responses. The literary experience allows the development of cross- and intercultural experiences and understandings. Literature is, in part, a representation of accumulated culture and provides us with a way of looking at how members use language to codify knowledge, determine relevance, and make connections between past heroes/sheroes and prophets and present concerns and situations. Lit-

311

erature is a powerful epistemology that defines and expresses the human predicament in cultural terms.

There are distinct differences among cultures in their expectations, needs, and uses of text-centered literacy. These differences, combined with the power relationships among groups, genders, and ideologies may be at the root of the determination of what constitutes literacy and, by extension, illiteracy. Equally important, these differences may contribute to our perceptions, understandings and behaviors toward human beings we have marked as different from ourselves. Difference may be translated as deviant depending on one's star group affiliation and the status of that group within the larger society (Turner). Star group is the point where people trace their maternity or paternity. Star group literacy is the bridge from which other literacies are built; it is the perceptual and emotional space where individuals situate themselves to examine, interpret, and explain the world.

Given this background, response to literature may be viewed as the operation of two interrelated dimensions. First is an invisible or private process that occurs while the reader is engaged in reading a given text (Applebee; Purves; Rosenblatt). Second is the expressed, or publicly articulated response to a text that is shaped—somewhat—by the readers' interpretative community such as a classroom (Fish). The *aesthetic* experience supports readers' attempts to make connections among the text, their lives, their people, and others. Living through a text, readers may come to see life just a little differently. James Baldwin (7) asserted: "If we can change the way people think about the world, even by a little, we can change the world." The text, Rosenblatt argues, must be evoked—given life—by readers connecting with their own memory as they share those of another. Reflecting on shared stories, we extend our conversations in text and talk with humanity.

The shared story responses from the African Diaspora in this text demonstrate how engaging a text can move readers toward an understanding of the complexity and richness of diverse cultural perspectives. Student responses to Edwidge Danticat's *Krik? Krak!* are used because (a) they are illustrative of aesthetic reading and cultural exchanges; (b) the lyrical beauty of the text provides an example of the kinds of literature available to students and teachers exploring the voices of "others"; and (c) these responses raised important issues, namely the relationship of curricular invisibility to social justice.

Equally important, *Krik? Krak!* is part of the story of the rewards of taking risks and asking people for their stories. Because much of this text is about stories and their capacity to move human hearts and minds, I'll share this one. Two weeks after our first meeting, Jean Pierre gave me a hardbound copy of *Krik? Krak!* and a machete. This was his response to my query, "Can you recommend a story for me that you think speaks with the spirit of your people?" "The book," Pierre said, "will let you feel the soul of my Haiti, and the machete you can use to chop your bananas or," with a teasing grin, he added, "for self-defense." *Krik? Krak!* turned out to be a gift that keeps on giving. Classroom stories and classroom responses are offered here to provide initial direction for secondary teachers who are attempting to expand their curriculums, explore differences, and enhance literacy.

This chapter argues that curriculum can play a major role in equipping students with transformed ways of thinking about the kinship among us, and a deeper understanding of the relationship of that kinship to all who share our planet. When the curriculum silences the voices of Africans in the Diaspora, it perpetuates and encourages negative-to-other attribution. The continuation of negative-to-other attribution feeds into retrogressive and hegemonic systems that have historically dominated and divided people of African descent from themselves as well as from non-African peoples. This chapter argues that the multicultural perspectives garnered from reading broadly the literature of the diverse people of the African Diaspora is a necessary process toward the acquisition of a critical literacy. Beginning with an examination of personal literary experiences, critical literacy questions taken-for-granted assumptions. Critical literacy empowers readers to read the word and the world, and to effect attitudinal and behavioral changes in individuals and communities (Freire). Critical literacy in which readers engage in the construction of meaning is quintessentially multicultural because it recognizes that transforming society into a fit place for human beings to live and grow is a noble and intractable task. The many ways of perceiving the world help us to make sense of our own stories and those of others. The stories and discussions that follow, aim to: (a) suggest that literary experiences can be a bridge over waters troubled by runaway assumptions and too-long silences, (b) present a captured portrait of literary response and culture coming together in a classroom, and (c) share some ways with bridge-making tips and a bibliography.

STORIES FROM THE CLASSROOM

Story 1: He Wore Autographed Khaki Shirt and Pants

An ebullient teacher announced, "Sewell, you got the highest grade in the class on the *Macbeth* test." "Say what," an incredulous African American female student said, leaning over Sewell's shoulder to see his paper, "that Jamaica boy got the highest grade in the whole class? He just come up in here last week, how'd he do that?" A politely smiling Sewell remained in his seat and thanked his teacher in a whisper. At the end of the day, the teacher cornered Sewell's counselor and inquired why he had been placed in a class

tracked for "average" (a pseudonym for classes comprised primarily of academically neglected working-class children of color) high school juniors.
The counselor replied simply, "Because he is fresh from Jamaica. Sometimes
we find that although a Jamaican student's school record says one grade or
another, the kid maybe has only actually gone to school for four or five
months out of the year." "Is this the case with Sewell?" the teacher asked.
"No," replied the counselor, "his record seems to be complete and his test
scores on the British system seem to be high. In fact, his parents seem to be
pretty bright folks, too, so given all of that, I put him in your class, rather
than 11–3 (the lowest junior track) or even a grade down like we usually do
when they're so fresh off the boat." "I want Sewell moved—today—to my
eleventh grade honors class." "Don't you think you're setting the kid up for
failure? Wouldn't it be better to let him prove himself, in our system for a
semester or so, and then see?" "No," responded the teacher. "When I leave
here, I am going to call his parents and let them know we have moved him
into a more appropriate English class. I am setting him up for success."
"Doggone it," the counselor responded smacking his briefcase on the desk
while irritation colored his neck, chin, and ears, "Why can't you just be satisfied, and do a good job with him where he is." To her silence he nearly
yelled, "If he fails, it's on you! Does it have to be *your* class? Now I will have to
do his whole schedule over!"

Story 2: A Rose by Any Other Name

"Oh, professor," a mature high school home economics teacher with a beautifully enunciated Jamaican accent remarked, "you can not possibly be a
Black American!" "As American as pecan (pronounced *pukon* in New Orleans) pie," said the professor, deliberately responding in the linguistic register of her native speech community. "What makes you think that?" "Why
because," the woman continued enthusiastically, "you are so knowledgeable
and so articulate and so gracious." "Really," the professor replied, "who would
you think I am; how would you call me?" "Ah," replied the woman with dramatic flourish, "a great, British Lady." "Well," the professor responded, I am
most certainly Black and American. I am also curious, please help me out
here. If you think that the person whose name is on the door and who has
titles including doctor, professor, and director of the English education program at this university can not possibly be African American, what do you
think of the African American children you teach who depend on you to
guide them toward enhanced life possibilities? Why do you teach? Why do
you want to teach English? What do you think the purpose of schooling in
a democratically organized society is?" The questions were never answered;
the home economics teacher never returned to complete her application to
the English education master's program.

Invitation 19.1

There are several kinds of stereotyping illustrated in these "stories." Complete a journal writing about these and their possible causes. How does the concept of the African Diaspora interact with these situations?

If we consider these stories, we are able to glimpse at the patterns of behaviors that can destroy students, teachers, and communities. In Story 1, we have a busy teacher to whom a new student has been assigned in the middle of the school year, in the middle of the class, in the middle of challenging reading. The teacher in this case welcomed the student, gave him a text, and promised to give him individual attention at another time. Many English teachers teach 150 or more students a day at different grade levels and different levels of accomplishment. A new immigrant, the student's introduction to the class was at best hurried. Moreover, the students in the class, as evidenced by their surprise at his test performance, held low opinions of Jamaican students. Several of them voiced opinions that the teacher must have helped him on the test to "make him feel better about being Jamaican." In this case however, the teacher acted as an advocate on behalf of the student, forcing the counselor to change his assignment and insisting that Sewell remain with her. In so doing, she accepted risk of ridicule from school administrators, colleagues, and other students.

Even so, there were several beneficiaries in the case: (a) Sewell, because his teacher took personal interest in him; (b) the teacher, because Sewell's presence, intelligence, and alienation caused the teacher to reexamine the content of her curriculum for ways to include voices from the Caribbean and create an atmosphere of respect in the class for those voices; and (c) the curriculum, because it could become more expansive when employed as an agent for creating cultural and literary bridges among the students.

The currents were not always smooth in this teacher's classroom because students quickly surmised that the works of Rosa Guy, Jamaica Kincaid, and Paule Marshall flowed into the classroom on the same tide that brought Sewell. It was clear, however, that although initial student responses were to what they defined as more work, it was work that ultimately brought all a rich harvest in increased and enhanced literacy. Sewell's shared stories of the *soucouya* (scary, night walking creatures who suck the blood of the living), *LaGahoos* (disembodied spirits who could take on different forms), and *Nansi* (same as Anansi) seemed to melt into his descriptions of waterfalls, luscious vegetation, villages, and the beaches he referred to as "back home." It is equally clear that teachers must take the initiative to include diverse cultural voices.

In the second story, a potential graduate student, intending to pay a compliment, culturally stripped a professor of her identity. Her assertion that one cannot be well spoken and intelligent and at the same time African American bespeaks the sometimes lamentable distance among peoples of the African Diaspora. That she put her foot in her mouth is far less important than the possibility that her low estimation of a group of people may translate into her expectations of the students she teaches. As a teacher, she poses a danger because her expectations may very well limit access to literacy and impede students from achieving the very attributes she admires. It is critical, therefore, that teacher preparation programs ground students broadly in literature and culture studies. Moreover, when teachers invite their students' stories, they establish a context for response in the classroom to occur; that is, one that is respectful, welcomed, and honored. Shared stories help readers navigate a course toward understanding. Stories allow us to hear humanity's many songs.

WHEN BUTTERFLIES SING: SHARING STORIES: THE TEXT AND TEACHER LITERACY

Jean Pierre's gift of Danticat's beautiful, lyrical stories captured the mind and heart of the professor. Moreover, *Krik? Krak!* and new teacher learning informed pedagogy and curriculum. The graduate adolescent literature class responding to *Krik? Krak!* had previously contained only an extract from *Amor* by turn-of-the-century Haitian author Marie Chauvet. The age and the culturally conscious authority of the narrator in *Krik? Krak!* and the eloquent simplicity of Danticat's prose made it a perfect choice for a course for preservice secondary teachers and master's-seeking university students. Moreover, the pattern of storytelling—call and response or krik and krak— is deeply rooted in the African storytelling tradition and repeated in various forms across the African Diaspora. Throughout the text, Danticat calls on the traditions of the ancestors, and simultaneously inscribes the consciousness of present generations with memories that link the present to the past.

> You hear this scraping from her. *Krik? Krak!* Pencil, paper. It sounds like someone crying . . . A thousand women urging you to speak through the blunt tip of your pencil. Kitchen poets, you call them. Ghosts like burnished branches on a flame tree. These women, they asked for your voice so that they could tell your mother in your place that yes, women like you do speak, even if they speak in a tongue that is hard to understand. Even if it's patois, dialect, Creole. . . . You have never been able to escape the pounding of a thousand other hearts that have outlived yours by thousands of years. And over the years when you have needed us, you have always cried "Krik?" and we have answered "Krak" and it has shown us that you have not forgotten us. (220–224)

Krik? Krak! is a collection of nine stories that draw readers into the world of postcolonial Haiti and traverses with them across treacherous, blood-steeped seas toward freedom. They are stories of pain, hope, fear, determination, despair, love, and the survival of the human spirit. These stories give voice to the voiceless and fill the silence created by a vacuum in the canonical construction of reality, truth, and aesthetics. It is significant that in the classroom, these stories engaged readers in powerful ways in not only the lived experiences of Danticat's characters, but also in evoking responses that tied the life experiences of the readers to the text.

THE READERS

In a class comprising students from Jamaica, Cuba, Trinidad, Belize, and America (European American and African American), students expressed surprise that, although they live in a city with a sizable Haitian population with nearly daily news reports of Haitian people either picked up in city waters, or tragically losing their lives in the attempt, none of the students had ever read a text written by a Haitian author. These are graduate students. When asked why not, they responded, "It never occurred to me . . . no one ever shared or assigned a Haitian text before this class . . . I do not have any close Haitian friends." Equally significant, students reported that they were surprised that they "didn't know how similar the stories of postcolonial Haiti were to those of their Cuban families." "It broke my heart," Isel, a Cuban American middle school teacher softly told her peers. "We never talk about them, we never help them. We think we (Cuban immigrants) are so oppressed, and yet . . . these people are so brave and so spiritual. They deserve better; they should get to stay here just like the Cubans do." "What made you feel like this; think this way?" "The Children of the Sea," Maripuli injected. "You are right there; you're with them on the boat; you can see the three cracks in the bottom. You feel with them and you feel their suffering." Nodding ascent, Isel continued: "They say that the Cubans come for political freedom, and that the Haitians only come to escape poverty." "What do you say?" "It's not true. My family in Cuba has nothing; they can barely eat. I think it is because they are black."

Isel's expressed sentiments are quite extraordinary in a city that despite its cultural, ethnic, and linguistic bounty, is sharply divided along cultural and racial lines. Moreover, in this city, there are layers and shades of color and culture designations; for example, White Hispanic, Black Hispanic (Cuba, Belize, and Brazil have both), White non-Hispanic, African American, and several others. For Isel, *Krik? Krak!* seems to have initiated the process of reevaluating her personal and cultural affiliations and the curriculum she offers to her students. "Do you think this book has anything to offer adolescents?" She reported, "I think some of the stories may be too much for middle school children. I put the book down many times during my reading, but many of them are wonderful for them . . . they are short, exquisitely crafted, and powerful. My students will enjoy them as stories and will learn, I hope, something about themselves and these wonderful neighbors we have."

Sharon, a Jamaican student, storyteller, and poet, also responded to the cultural similarities she found in *Krik? Krak!* In her journal she wrote:

> Is it not amazing, the things that various cultures share? Things that the ordinary man in the street would not think to compare. The "Krik Krak" at the beginning of a Haitian story, has the same connotation as the Jamaican "Jack man dorah, me noh choose none" at the end of a story. I really do not care what either of these phrases mean. I am just happy that we remember them.

In these excerpts we see something of the way people respond to stories, and what they respond to. The students just cited responded to the passion, pain, language, and the similarities of Danticat's stories to their own. An important aspect of the literary transaction is the cultural knowledge the reader brings to the text. To this knowledge, Sharon has added knowledge experienced in text and shared in the social context of the classroom. Isel has added her knowledge of the Caribbean exile community to the classroom and to her reading. Both readers found kinship and cause to celebrate. Students were asked, "Before this reading, what did you think or know about Haiti and Haiti's people?" Sharon responded, "You know, now that I do think about it, I'm a little ashamed to say, being Jamaican, but I really didn't think about them a'tall. When I see them on the news, I feel bad for them . . . I rant at the unfairness and the racism, but until I read this book, I didn't feel close to them . . . like I know anything about them." Kimberly, the only European American student, remarked: "I know that never again will I look at the news and not think of the love, that's for sure. I kept hoping they would somehow get together again. And the love of the people they left behind and their relatives here."

When the class was told, "Gather up your images from *Krik? Krak!;* let's hear them and write them down," the responses, "butterflies, spirit, love, a history, brutality, the way the words moved, shame, Black people killing and torturing their own, survival, desperation, beautiful, and hope," rushed out. Everyone scribbled madly trying to keep up with the flow of talk. B. J., the only African American aside from the teacher in this classroom community, noted the sound: "Hey, you all hear that? Krik? Krak! What are these . . . chalkboard or desktop stories?" "What do you think these stories are about?" asked the professor. "Survival," he responded. "And the spirit of those women from the river and the prison; it stretches across the seas," Teri added. These students seemed moved not only to respond to the text; their articulated responses suggest transformed attitudes—from indifference to kinship—from invisibility to inclusion. Moreover, these students seem to take responsibility for the continuation of their own learning and that of their students.

It would likely be naive to assume that the reading of a single text can eradicate ignorance and heal the racial and cultural divides that threaten our communities and our nation, but we can argue that conscious and consistent engagement with the voices of others provokes both feeling and thought. In this way, shared stories and our responses to them offer the possibility for long-term and lasting changes in the way we go about educating ourselves and schoolchildren. Accomplishing this, however, challenges teachers to construct contexts for reading and responding that promote literary learning and social transformation. Similarly, we are challenged to revisit the canon, not to destroy, but to build bridges and to navigate the tides that bind us.

Invitation 19.2

Select one of the stories from *Krik? Krak!* that you consider potentially useful in your classroom. How would you introduce it? How would you expand the discussion to cause a deeper response among your students?

SOCIAL AND CULTURAL CONTEXT
FOR RESPONSE: EXPLANATION/EXAMPLE

Research indicates that reader response occurs within a triad consisting of the reader, the text, and the context or environment for learning (Hickman; Langer). The sociopolitical assumptions of the classroom teacher and the curriculum are critical elements to the study and development of response. Classrooms are an ideal setting where students come into direct contact with the issues of literature, literacy, culture, and response. Classrooms should be a safe space where individuals can negotiate difference and seek resolutions to conflicts and contradictions that occur in their everyday lives.

The ability to traverse culture, class, and race is particularly pertinent in a nation founded on the principles of freedom and democracy, yet grounded in conflicting ideologies of gender, class, and the perennial American dilemma—race, often erroneously defined as skin color. Literary voices from the African Diaspora, and specifically those from outside North America, bring a different lens through which African Americans and European Americans may have an opportunity to embrace a broader understanding of human nature and race issues in the Americas; that is, the capacities to love, create, destroy, and build are universal. Resilience, compassion, and persistence are colorless, and they become multidimensional through engagement with literature.

The notion of context or instructional environment is a complex and multifaceted phenomenon that includes: (a) the curriculum in both its manifest and hidden forms, (b) the manner in which the curriculum is offered to students, (c) the type of discourse about literature that occurs and participation in the classroom discourse, (d) the method teachers use to evaluate student learning and progress, and (e) the vision and instructional purposes of the teacher. Each of these elements, either singularly or in combinations, can influence student response in powerful ways.

The student responses to *Krik? Krak!* cited earlier occurred in a learning context that has an identifiable pattern. With modifications for age of readers and composition of classes, the process has replicable elements that are independent of the ethnic and cultural makeup of the learning community. The model described herein includes the following.

- *Culturally rich reading.* The extensive required reading list (see Suggested Readings) includes voices from Africans, Native Americans, Vietnamese, various parts of the Caribbean, Pakistanis, North American Whites, Western Europeans, African Americans, Mexicans, Puerto Ricans, Chinese, and South Americans. The readings are grouped into units of instruction with a different focus. For example, Folklore and Mythology, The Spirit and Other Mysteries, Coming of Age and Other Dangerous Occupations, and Confronting Social-Isms. Within each unit of study, students select from a list of 8 to 10 themes that will be the focus of their group's project. Students understand that they do not have to conduct a formal literary analysis on the texts they read. Rather, their purpose is to gather up stories and experiences, reflect on those experiences privately and share their emergent understandings with their peers. Multicultural perspectives are not added onto the curriculum like an exotic extra. Rather, multicultural perspectives are at the core and present a foundation for integrating literature, literacy acquisition, and cultural exchanges.

- *Oral storytelling.* Student stories are invited at each class gathering. Each class begins with the teacher asking "Does anyone have a story from home about (childhood mischief, relatives, rituals, rules of behavior, etc.)?" The teacher also shares a story or recites a Brer Rabbit tale. This oral sharing typically takes only 10 minutes, yet affirms the value and authority of story, voice and readers. Laughter erupts regularly.

- *Collaborative practice: interdependent learning and teaching.* Students are required to do group projects. These projects necessitate collaboration, are conducive to small group interactions, and contribute to continued literary discussions. The process moves from individual sharing of journal entries to large group interaction with peers and teacher, and then progresses to small group interactions. This process seems to increase the depth of student analysis, that is, an examination of technical aspects of the text in addition to the reader's personal responses to the text. Student projects are shared with the entire learning community through oral presentation and copies of written materials. For example, in her examination of the setting of *Krik? Krak!*, Mariella writes, "Setting is not merely a locale, a change of scenes, but an overwhelming and powerful depiction of how the hellscape in Haiti has engulfed its inhabitants in a world of desperation, courage and flight."

• *Student and teacher journal.* Journals are required and selectively shared with the classroom community. They provide a safe first place to respond to text. Students are asked to pay attention to their feelings, note new learning, and think about teaching adolescents. Journals also provide an opportunity for personal dialogue between the student and the teacher. During class sessions, the teacher uses her journal to take notes that include paraphrasing student anecdotes, identifying key student quotes, and highlighting understandings and misunderstandings and questions raised by student discussions. Additionally, a record of class interactions is captured by a graduate student who serves as a noninteractive scribe.

• *Assessment.* Learners are involved in the assessment process at the individual and group level. For example, each group makes an assessment of the work of other groups according to criteria established by the classroom community. Further, individuals within groups make assessments of their peers' contributions to the group effort. The teacher contributes to the assessment process using notes with records of student contributions, conferences with students regarding the progress of their learning, and assessments of students' written products.

Inherent to this model is the centrality of multicultural perspectives. Inclusion and diversity are the norm. Oral storytelling connects the voices of the readers with the voices of the text. Storytelling and story sharing are instructive. They often interject humor and engender empathy; they establish an environment of conviviality that provides a foundation for a rich response to literature. Moreover, when you value your own voice and when others value your voice, then valuing the voices of others more readily follows.

SMOKING GUNS NO MORE:
THE CANON IN CULTURAL PERSPECTIVES

Speaking with the voice of those who have conquered, the canon comprises the bulk of traditional English curriculums in U.S. classrooms. The canon silences the voices of the majority of ethnic voices. As the singular or majority "text" in school curricula, it is a persuasive agent of intellectual and cultural domination, restricting all learners to a narrow and incomplete view of the world (Freire & Macedo). A recurrent observation among these students concerns the absence of non-Western European voices. Moreover, students reported that they did not realize that something was missing until they were introduced to multicultural literary experiences.

Invitation 19.3

Define the term *canon* as it applies to a literature curriculum. Then, using this definition, evaluate a current secondary school literature textbook to establish the approximate percentage distribution of canonical and other authors. Then, list authors and their texts you would want to add to your class's curriculum to augment this textbook, identifying the "voice" each represents.

Thus, even African Diasporic students and teachers may live and work in proximal neighborhoods and yet have only skewed knowledge of each other. The dissonance that exists among people of African descent serves to not only colonize students physically but encourage the practice of uncritical, ahistorical thinking. Not infrequently, inimical behaviors follow. Equally important, the traditional curriculum miseducates students (including teachers who have been students) because the absences and silences of voices from even our closest neighbors in the Caribbean suggests to novice learners that neither the people nor their stories have anything of value to say. Among teachers, this issue is critical, because teachers set the stage for the kinds of classroom interactions that will act either as a harbinger of the good news of literacy or as gatekeepers. Clearly, both the African American student and the home economics teacher cited earlier were poised to become unwitting gatekeepers and purveyors of cultural imperialism by their assumptions of Jamaican and African American inadequacy.

I have argued elsewhere (Spears-Bunton, "Colors") that teaching literature through multicultural perspectives is logical as well as eloquent if our aim is to transform classrooms, schools, society, and individual hearts and minds. Literary response offers teachers a tool to "change the way people think about the world . . . change the world" (Spears-Bunton 17). Change must be radical if it is to be transformative. Transformation makes continual personal demands on our time, our way with words, and our choices. It is a conscientiously critical and creative process. Transformation is quintessentially different from reforming what is and what has always been. Importantly, transformation necessitates an informed willingness to take risks.

Thus, challenges of reified knowledge and taken-for-granted assumptions are critical to the transformative process. Transformation seeks to change not only the shape of institutions and their attendant ritualized race, gender, and class behaviors, but also the social fabric that created those institutions and sanctioned those behaviors in the first place. Shifts in the locus of control are reasonable but seldom seamless because transformation involves the replacement of ineffective and inequitable elements in our social, political, educational, and ethical fabric with chemically different elements. These include the following: (a) a disposition to develop multiple literacies in teachers and students, (b) equitable and regular participation in literacy activities, (c) an honoring of difference and the historical and cultural experiential bounds among the people of the African Diaspora, and (d) expectations of academic success among African Diasporic students.

Guiding students through the transformative process requires inclusion in our curricula. The transformative curriculum garners expansive critical literacy intent on empowering readers to engage in respectful and scholarly discourse while reading the "word and the world" (Freire). Multicultural literature study generally, and study of the literature of the African Diaspora particularly, promotes transformation. Diverse literary experiences are necessary if schoolchildren are to be grounded in the principles of a humanely organized society. Unsilencing the voices of the African Diaspora in literature invariably leads to questions and discussions about difficult social issues such as racism and divisiveness. If future generations are to avoid replication of the destructive, negative-to-other attributions that plague our nation, communities, and schools, transformation must occur.

CURRICULAR TRANSFORMATION: RIDING THE CURRENTS OF CHANGE

There are identifiable steps that teachers may take to facilitate curricular transformation:

1. Teachers can read as a scholar and as a teacher searching for suitable class materials. Teachers can select texts that will provide the kinds of information and literary materials they are seeking for their students. It is important to carefully examine your own likes and dislikes, remembering that you are involved in educating other people's children for participation in a world that will be larger, yet smaller and more complex, than your own.

2. Teachers can solicit recommendations for books that will provide background knowledge; these should be both fiction and nonfiction.

3. Teachers can select texts that have an adolescent as a protagonist and portray characters, settings, and themes that are culturally authentic.

4. Teachers can restructure their curriculum. Chronological time ordering, for example from the planters and the Puritans typical in U.S. anthologies, encourages teachers to "cover" material without depth, and to omit all
peoples who do not fit into the historic myth and image of the United States
as an emerging, powerful, and God-fearing nation. Thematic organization
allows for coherence, depth, and breadth of meaning construction among
the community of learners. There are, of course, numerous themes that are
critical to the literature of the African Diaspora, including survival efficacy,
alienation and identity, immigration, migration, and coming of age, to name
a few. Thematic organization of literature and literacy lessons also helps
novice learners understand complex ideas by providing multiple opportunities to explore them from multiple perspectives.

5. Teachers can analyze conflicts and contradictions inherent in our con-
ceptualizations of race, culture, class, and gender from the perspectives presented by the literature of the African Diaspora. This promotes critical and
independent thinking and resolution of tensions through honest and scholarly discourse.

A curriculum infused with the literature of the African Diaspora is not a
watered-down course of study. Rather, students participate in more literary
activities than is typical, especially in U.S. public schools. A culturally infused
curriculum contains rich perspectives and meaningful depth of study as
learners engage with the texts, reflect on their reading experiences, and
then participate in ongoing discussions as a community of readers, learners,
and thinkers.

Finally, the opening of self to multiple perspectives is not a closed door or
a fixed state that is either us or them. Rather, people can come to see the
world with their own eyes and another's heart as they read, write, think, and
share lived and vicarious experiences. Ultimately, however, the disposition
underscoring the tide that welcomes multiple perspectives—for participa-
tory debate about human issues rather than a curricular filibuster—becomes a habit of heart that binds the spirit of those who seek genuine literacy for themselves and their students.

REFERENCES

Applebee, A. N. *The Child's Concept of Story.* Chicago: University of Chicago Press, 1978.
Baldwin, James. "Forward." *Daddy Was a Number Runner.* Louise Meriwether. New York: Pyramid, 1971.
Chauvet, M. "Amor." *Her True-True Name: An Anthology of Women's Writing From the Caribbean.* Ed. Pamela Mordecai and Betty Wilson. London: Heinemann, 1990. 84–89.
Danticat, Edwidge. *Krik? Krak!* New York: Soho, 1991.
Fish, Stanley. *Is There a Text in This Class?* Cambridge, MA: Harvard University Press, 1980.

Freire, Paulo. *Pedagogy of the Oppressed*. New York: Continuum, 1986.

Freire, Paulo and D. Macedo. *Literacies of Power: What Americans Are Not Allowed to Know*. Boulder, CO: Westview, 1994.

Guy, Rosa. *Friends*. New York: Bantam, 1973.

Hickman, Janet. "Everything Considered: Response to Literature in an Elementary School Setting." *Journal of Research and Development in Education*, 16. (Spring 1983): 8–13.

Kincaid, Jamaica. *Annie John*. New York: Farrar, Straus, Giroux, 1985.

Langer, J. A. "The Reading Process." *Secondary School Reading: What Research Reveals About Classroom Practice*. Ed. A. Burger and A. Robinson. Urbana, IL: National Council of Teachers of English, 1982. 39–51.

Marshall, Paule. *Brown Girl, Brownstones*. New York: Random House, 1959.

———. *The Chosen Place, the Timeless People*. New York: Vintage, 1969.

Purves, Alan C. "Evaluation and Learning in Literature." *Handbook on Formative and Summative Evaluation of Student Learning*. Ed. B. S. Bloom et al. New York: McGraw-Hill, 1971. 697–766.

Rosenblatt, Louise. *Literature as Exploration*. New York: Modern Language Association, 1983.

Spears-Bunton, Linda A. "Literature, Literacy, and Resistance to Cultural Domination." *Literacy Research and Practice: Views From Many Perspectives*. Ed. Charles Kinzer and Donald Leu. Chicago: National Reading Conference, 1992. 393–401.

———. "All the Colors of the Land: A Literacy Montage." *Teaching and Using Multicultural Literature in Grades 9–12: Moving Beyond the Canon*. Ed. Arlette Willis. Norwood, MA: Christopher-Gordon, 1998. 17–36.

Turner, V. "Social Dreams and Stories About Them." *Critical Inquiry* 7 (1980): 141–67.

SUGGESTED READING

Abrahams, R. D., ed. *African Folktales*. New York: Pantheon, 1983.

———, ed. *Afro-American Folktales: Stories From Black Traditions in the New World*. New York: Pantheon, 1985.

Adisa, O. P. *It Begins With Tears*. Portsmouth, NH: Heinemann, 1987.

Allen, Paula G., ed. *Spider Woman's Granddaughters*. New York: Fawcett Columbine, 1989.

Allende, Isabel. *The House of the Spirits*. New York: Bantam, 1986.

Alvarez, Julia. *How the Garcia Girls Lost Their Accents*. New York: Plume, 1991.

Anaya, Rudolfo. *Bless Me, Ultima*. New York: Warner, 1972.

Angelou, Maya. *The Heart of a Woman*. New York: Random House, 1981.

———. *I Know Why the Caged Bird Sings*. New York. Bantam, 1993.

Ashabranner, N. and R. Davis. *The Lion 's Whiskers and Other Ethiopian Tales*. New Haven, CT: Shoe String Press, 1997.

Augenbraum, H. and I. Stavans, eds. *Growing Up Latino: Memories and Stories*. Boston: Houghton Mifflin, 1993.

Butler, Octavia. *Parable of the Sower*. New York: Four Walls Eight Windows, 1993.

Campbell, E. and P. Frickey, eds. *The Whistling Bird: Women Writers of the Caribbean*. Boulder, CO: Ian Randle, 1998.

Carter, Alden R. *Up Country*. New York: G. P. Putnam's Sons, 1989.

Cliff, M. *The Store of a Million Items*. Boston: Houghton Mifflin, 1998.

Cofer, J. O. *An Island Like You: Stories of the Barrio*. New York: Orchard, 1995.

Danticat, Edwidge. *Krik? Krak!* New York: Soho, 1995.

Erodes, R. and A. Ortiz, eds. *American Indian Myths and Legends*. New York: Pantheon, 1984.

Garcia, Cristina. *Dreaming in Cuban*. New York: Ballantine, 1992.

Gilroy, B. *Boy-Sandwich*. Portsmouth, NH: Heinemann, 1989.

Griffin, Adele. *Rainy Season*. New York: Hyperion Paperbacks for Children, 1996.

Hamilton, Virginia. *Arilla Sun Down*. New York: Scholastic, 1976.

———. *The People Could Fly: American Black Folktales*. New York: Alfred Knopf, 1985.

Hodge, Merle. *Laetitia*. New York: Farrar, Straus, Giroux, 1993.

Hunt, Irene. *Across Five Aprils*. New York: Berkley Books, 1986.

Kincaid, Jamarca. *Lucy*. New York: Plume, 1990.

Lester, J. *Othello: A Novel*. New York: Scholastic, 1995.

Lewis, T. *Caribbean Folk Legend*. Lawrenceville, NJ: African New World Press, 1990.

Marshall, Paule. *Brown Girl, Brownstones*. New York: The Feminist Press, 1981.

Mordecai, P. and B. Wilson, eds. *Her True-True Name*. London: Heinemann, 1990.

Morrison, Toni. *Song of Solomon*. New York: Penguin, 1997.

Parks, Gordon. *A Choice of Weapons*. St. Paul: Minnesota Historical Society Press, 1986.

Roumain, Jacques. *Masters of the Dew*. Portsmouth, NH: Heinemann, 1978.

Santiago, Esmerelda. *When I Was Puerto Rican*. New York: Vintage, 1993.

Staples, Suzanne. *Shahanu: Daughter of the Wind*. New York: Random House, 1989.

Taylor, Theodore. *Sweet Friday Island*. New York: Harcourt Brace & Company, 1994.

Thomas, Joyce C. *When the Nightingale Sings*. New York: Harper Trophy, 1992.

Yep, Lawrence. *Dragon's Gate*. New York: Harper Trophy, 1993.

20

Reader Responses to Roethke's "My Papa's Waltz"
Exploring Different Perspectives

Jean E. Brown and Louise Garcia Harrison

> *The poem, then, must be thought of as an event in time. It is not an object or an ideal entity. It happens during a coming-together, a compenetration, of a reader and a text. The reader brings to the text his [her] past experience and present personality.*
>
> —Rosenblatt, *Reader* 12

The notion that reading a poem is an interactive event between the reader and the text provides a unique set of challenges for teachers in providing opportunities for students to be actively engaged in their experiences with literature. As Rosenblatt reminds us, "The personal nature of the learning process places a decided responsibility upon the teacher" (*Literature* 247). This responsibility demands that teachers aid their students to become active in their transactions with literature. This becomes especially challenging because many students have experienced literature as a "guided" exercise in which they are directed to accept an interpretation of the work. These students then have difficulty accepting the freedom to respond and interact with the text. They are frequently conditioned to seek the "correct" response as it is determined by some distant literary authority or by the more immediate classroom authority, the teacher. By providing students with opportunities to interact with the text, teachers are able to help lift the "screen" that traditionally occurs between students and their reading.

To help students begin to become more responsive to their reading, teachers need to provide literature that will offer students the opportunity to be able to identify with their experiences in reading. "My Papa's Waltz" by Theodore Roethke has proved to be a selection that always elicits adamant responses from students because it allows for the meeting of readers, armed with their range of experiences, and the text.

In this chapter, we explore the responses that our students, at all levels from high school—Grades 9 through 12—through graduate school, have had in experiencing the poem. In addition to examining the student responses, we also explore the impact that the social context has on student responses. Although the poem appears to be a simple remembrance of a childhood experience, it has a powerful effect on readers of all ages. The experience with "My Papa's Waltz" does become "an event" for readers.

My Papa's Waltz

The whiskey on your breath
Could make a small boy dizzy;
But I held on like death:
Such waltzing was not easy.

We romped until the pans
Slid from the kitchen shelf;
My mother's countenance
Could not unfrown itself.

The hand that held my wrist
Was battered on one knuckle;
At every step I missed
My right ear scraped a buckle.

You beat time on my head
With a palm caked hard by dirt,
Then waltzed me off to bed
Still clinging to your shirt.

            —Theodore Roethke

Invitation 20.1

Before reading further, complete a journal writing expressing your response to "My Papa's Waltz." To the extent that you can, indicate what in yourself and the text has led you to this preliminary response.

METHODS FOR INVOLVING STUDENTS

In teaching "My Papa's Waltz" to our students we have used two primary teaching methods: The first is a brainstorming approach; the second is a written response or journal approach, which leads to both whole group or small group discussion. While both of these approaches involves students in a different way, their responses to the poem are consistent regardless of the approach. Most of this chapter focuses on student responses obtained by using the second approach of written responses and discussion; however, brainstorming is also examined.

The brainstorming activity involves teachers using an overhead projector with a transparency of the poem. The process involves showing one line of the poem at a time, beginning with the title. Teachers then engage students in speculation about each line, generating many possible interpretations. Initially, students often speculate that the title means "a dance the father does," or "the waltz may stand for his life." As possible meanings are generated, a student recorder writes all of the responses in list form on the chalkboard. Periodically, the class stops to review the responses to decide which responses are no longer valid as they have seen more of the text. In a poem with stanzas, the end of each stanza is an appropriate place to review and eliminate responses unsupported by the text. If the students come to consensus that any response is no longer appropriate, it is eliminated from the listing. In using this approach with "My Papa's Waltz," inevitably, the students' responses fall into two broad areas: First are those that support the notion that the poem is a happy recollection of childhood, second, there are those that support a negative response to the poem.

After the whole poem is revealed, all responses are examined and the process of eliminating inappropriate responses is continued. The nature of responses to this poem creates an opportunity to have students acknowledge, if not accept, different interpretations of the poem. The method we use is to consolidate them into lists, categorizing the responses of students. Each list is examined along with the text of the poem, demonstrating that students are able to accept the responses of others while supporting their own.

The other classroom strategy that we have used with this poem is the less directive. Students are given the opportunity to write about their responses to the poem. We have students who have had limited experience responding to literature, so we begin by modeling with the whole class exploring another poem. Roethke's "Child on Top of a Greenhouse" provides an appropriate springboard. After this introductory experience, we both use a similar approach in presenting "My Papa's Waltz." First, after distributing copies of the poem, we read the poem to the class (either once or twice, depending on their experiences with responding to poetry). In this way students have the opportunity to hear the language and to begin to create images in their minds. Then we ask that students become active readers as they read it to themselves and determine, in their view, what was happening in the poem. We also ask students if the poem recounts either a pleasant or an unpleasant experience, stressing that there are no "right" answers. In most cases, the students are asked to write their responses.

Following the writing experience, students are given the opportunity to share their reactions by reading their responses either in small group discussion or during whole class discussion. Some students will choose to talk about their reactions rather than read their papers. Regardless, their responses then become a springboard for class discussion. All responses are welcomed in the discussion. Students are encouraged to relate their responses to the text as a means of helping others recognize differing views. Inherent in the process is that students recognize perspectives that are different from their own.

Writing about "My Papa's Waltz" provides students with a valuable experience. It helps them to articulate the transaction they have experienced while reading. They then realize that experiencing literature is more than an analytical dissection. As a result, their responses mirror a wide range of human emotions from joyous memory, to fond recollection, to leery anticipation, to sad remembrance, to painful identification, or to poignant and painful awareness. The range of emotions that the poem elicits confirms Boyer's argument for greater attention to literature in the secondary school curriculum: "Literature addresses the emotional part of the human experience. Literature transmits from generation to generation enduring spiritual and ethical values. As great literature speaks to all people, it must be available to all students" (97).

Most students have had a personal identification with the situation in the poem and with the young boy who is waltzed around the kitchen by his father. For those students who empathize with the boy, they react in two primary ways. For many of them, it evokes a positive remembrance of childhood play with their fathers; for a number of others the poem is evocative of unpleasant or, on occasion, painful experiences. In these types of personal responses readers relate the poem to their own lives, making a subjective connection with the young boy and his waltz. One ninth-grader exemplified, poignantly, how powerful the connection can be when she wrote:

> I remember when I was about six years old, my father had been drinking some and he pretended like I was a (sic) airplane and flow (sic) me to my bedroom to go to bed. Then he tugged (sic) me in, give (sic) me a kiss good-night and then after that night I never-ever seen (sic) him again.
>
> And this isn't a very good memory though. But when I read this poem thats (sic) what I started to remember from the past.

Other students are either unable or unwilling to empathize with the boy. These students react from a third-person perspective, being sympathetic to the situation that they generally perceive to be a difficult one. They respond

to the small boy, but they either do not or cannot relate his experience to
their own lives and experiences.

STAGES OF DEVELOPMENT
AND READER RESPONSE

By examining student responses at various stages of their development, a
number of differences in the type and perspective become obvious. Although the examples of the responses from the graduate students and undergraduate students differ greatly in syntax and linguistic sophistication
from those of the high school students, it is the range and depth of their
experiences that make the greatest difference in how they respond. These
differences reflect the fact that the high school students are closer in age
to the boy in the poem, and they are still involved in the family structure as
dependents, whereas even the traditional-aged college undergraduate has,
most often, left home and has gained a degree of independence and auton-
omy. The secondary students view the poem from a more limited point of
reference, their own experiences:

> The man I pictured was my father. He has a blue collar job, as Roethke de-
> scribes so well. When I decided to go to bed, he would not waltz me, but carry
> me piggyback up the stairs to my room, read me a story, and wish me good-
> night. Although my mother would say we made too much noise in a playful
> way, I still had fun.

For this reader, the poem provides the event in which he is able to think
back on a pleasant memory, and the description of the mother's reaction
added authenticity to the response because his mother, too, had commented about the rough-housing, although in a "playful way." Such a response by younger students seems to be directly influenced by their current,
ongoing relationship with their fathers. For older students, their perspective
of the family has expanded and changed; distance has an impact on their
view of the poem. This difference becomes even more pronounced for non-
traditional undergraduate students or graduate students who have families
of their own. The following response from a secondary English teacher who
was working on a master of arts in teaching degree illustrates the contrasting
impact that experiences have on her response to the poem.

> We danced a lot for years. Even today, I feel that only men over sixty are worth
> dancing with. We were so silly that Mother did her adult frown at us kids and
> (at) Dad, with a youngster on each shoe. We'd giggle and laugh and fall into a
> heap—but always to very good music. Later, ages 10–16, he'd teach me (to)
> foxtrot and waltz and polka and I would teach him American Bandstand
> dances—it was magic, and I still remember, and I always will. Now Oedipus is
> dead and I "understand" Dad—but the memory is still golden.

The perspective of time has helped the second reader to view her experience and her whole relationship with her father from a more objective perspective. Implicit in this response is the recognition that while she and her father have had difficulties over the years, there is still that special memory of time shared and differences put aside. Interesting in the passage is also the ongoing and changing nature of the dancing ritual that she experienced with her father.

Experience also leads readers to understand reactions that may be based on biases. One undergraduate who is also a grandmother realized that her first reading of the poem led her to make assumptions about the degree of "drunkenness" of the father.

> As I reread the poem, I realized that it didn't say that the father was intoxicated, only that his breath smelled of whiskey. When we read, we often assume things that relate to our own biases. This poem portrays the sense of a healthy, loving relationship between father and son. Unfortunately, my past experience with drunken fathers and stepfathers has negatively influenced my opinions of fathers in general and drunken fathers in particular.

The level of development of this student allowed her to look beyond her obvious negative experiences, respond to the text itself, and acknowledge the merit of the relationship that she recognized in the poem.

PERSONAL AND NONPERSONAL
STUDENT RESPONSES

Students who view the poem from a positive perspective seem to respond to the poem holistically. They are influenced by their total impression of the experience they have with the text. The following response from a 10th-grader illustrates this type of response:

> I find the "Waltz" to be an exciting and pleasant memory from a young child's life and one that I can relate to. I believe that most children have such experiences as these. With me, my father would give us what he called, "the Treatment." Though it sounds bad, he would simply tickle us. We would usually laugh until we cried, but as small children we were always doing whatever possible to dare my father to tickle us.

This student and others see the waltz as a happy remembrance because they are able to respond to the poem through positive experiences with their fathers. The romping between the boy in the poem and his father triggered a parallel experience that the students had with their fathers. For some older students it sometimes reminds them of experiences that their children are having:

> I can picture the romping and identify with it. We do the same at our house (minus the whiskey). It reminds me of how my husband and I will either pick

up one of our children and do a fast dance around the room or have them stand on our feet and frolic around. I guess it goes even further back to when I danced on my father's feet. Like the boy in the poem, you get a feeling for timing and rhythm that way.

This undergraduate student describes the continuity of a happy family tradition filled with warmth and love. She has chosen to relate to her children as her father related to her.

One ninth-grader compares the boy's experience with his own, demonstrating that "each reader brings to the transaction not only specific past life and literary history, not only a repertory of internalized 'codes,' but also a very active present, with all its preoccupations, anxieties, questions, and aspirations" (Rosenblatt, *Reader* 144).

This poem does not remind me of anything or does not bring me to a memory of me (sic) and my father. Me (sic) and my father enjoy watching funny movies on TV or HBO, and we get along very well. The poem is about a boy who probably has a great relationship with his father and who would show his emotions, give a lot of affection to his father.

Although this student seems to have a positive relationship with his own father, he recognizes that something is missing. For him the poem provides a vicarious recognition that there is a warmth and affection between the boy in the poem and his father that the reader longs to have. His response to the poem accomplishes what Aleksandr Solzhenitsyn in his 1972 Nobel Acceptance Speech discusses as the inherent value of literature: "can overcome man's unfortunate trait of learning only through his own experience . . . recreating in the flesh what another has experienced, and allowing it to be acquired as one's own" (93).

Although these students are able to respond from a positive viewpoint, the poem is an unpleasant or even frightening experience for many students. Most of them cite specific experiences from their own childhoods as indicative of how the boy must have felt about the waltz. These students use an analytical approach. They usually cite specific language from the poem to support their negative responses, such as:

whiskey
dizzy
held on like death
waltzing was not easy
countenance could not unfrown itself
battered
scraped a buckle
beat time
still clinging to your shirt

Certainly, in isolation these words and phrases do have negative connotations. For these students, the words and phrases fit together to paint a picture of an unhappy experience in which the young boy is subjected to the whims of his inebriated father.

> Most of the feelings were negative ones associated with alcoholism in my immediate family. I felt a sadness for the boy because I can relate very well to the "whiskey on your breath" and the mother's frown.

For one undergraduate student, a woman in her late 30s, a mother of three who had returned to school after being divorced, the poem evoked a specific unhappy memory:

> The poem made me mad. It was just like when my former husband would come home and roughhouse with the kids and get them so riled up that they couldn't get to sleep. He was only there for the fun and I had to do all the dirty work. The kids thought he was the big hero and I was the villain. I could really relate to the mother in the poem.

Her experiences provided her with the insight to recognize and to empathize with the forgotten person in the poem, the mother. From her account, she also felt that she was reduced to the role of the enemy while she tried to maintain order in the family. Another student expressed the impact of the language when he said: "I couldn't get into the poem. The first line, talking about the whiskey, reminded me so much of my dad that I couldn't read any more of it." This type of response or overreaction to the poem appears to be the result of the process Rosenblatt describes as when a reader "projected on the text elements of his past experience not relevant to it, and which are not susceptible of coherent incorporation into it" (*Reader* 11). For this student the past experience was so unpleasant that the student was unable to entertain any possible involvement with the poem.

Many students, who have studied literature as an academic exercise in which they seek the correct interpretation, have a difficult time establishing a transactional relationship with their reading. The following response by a ninth-grader sees the poem positively; however, he does not interact on a personal level. Although his insights are perceptive, he does not engage directly with the poem:

> I liked this poem because it presented closeness of a boy and his father. The poem hints that the man is a hard worker and spends time with the boy whenever he can. At least, that was my first reaction.
>
> The poem was constructed neatly and the rhyme gave it an added emotion of innocence or joy.
>
> And it shows how secure the boy feels in his father's arms, which may have been why the author chose to write the poem in a rhyming fashion.

His response is a good example of this type of reaction, more likely to be sympathetic rather than empathetic to the text. He made the assumption that the boy had a good relationship with his father and that interpretation colored his whole reaction to the poem.

SOCIAL CONTEXT

Over the years, students have responded to the boy remembering the smell of whiskey on his father's breath, but recently the attitudes of college and graduate students more often assume that he is drunk during the waltz and his "drunkenness" is the product of alcoholism rather than a singular experience. Certainly the public awareness of alcoholism has increased in recent years. Public service announcements in the media, organizations like Mothers Against Drunk Driving, and cautions from the medical establishment have all led to a heightened awareness of the potential problems of drinking. The only reference to drinking is in the poem's first line. The text does not support nor does it deny the assumptions of alcoholism or even drunkenness. Interestingly, whereas today's secondary students are more conscious of the "whiskey on your breath" than students were when we first used the poem 17 years ago, they are also less judgmental and less likely to assume a drinking problem than the older students. There is a matter-of-fact acceptance by these students, even if they assume that the father was drunk during the waltz. One ninth-grader expressed this attitude:

> I think that the father was probably drunk, and that is why they're dancing. I know my father wouldn't have danced with me unless he was drunk (which didn't happen very often).

His attitude of acceptance is typical of many of the younger readers. The drinking is reality to be recognized but not necessarily judged. The extreme example of the acceptance of drinking among the secondary students was illustrated by the ninth-grader whose response to the poem was beyond the text as he related an experience he had drinking at a party and returning home drunk himself and getting grounded by his stepmother. Again this example is of an irrelevant experience stifling a student's ability to interact with the text.

The impact of social change—family structure—is evident as an influence on how some secondary students respond to the poem. The number of students from single-parent homes is significantly different now than it was when even the undergraduate students were growing up. Some students whose parents are divorced were unable to interact with the poem from their own personal experience because they had never "frolicked" with their fathers. Several of the students translated the experience to an uncle who danced with them, whereas another was reminded of experiences with a friend's father. An additional implication of the single-parent home was described by one of the undergraduate students:

Poems like this make me really sad because they remind of what I missed when I was a kid. My dad was killed in Viet Nam when I was only two, so I never knew him. I would have been glad even if he did smell of whiskey once in a while. Just to have known him. . . .

The influence of current social concerns manifests itself in another significant way in the interpretation of the poem. Although some students have traditionally viewed the poem as an unpleasant experience, the interpretation of abuse is a recent development. The attention to abuse evokes powerful emotional responses; there are words that have special connotations when they are used in this context ("battered," "scraped a buckle," and "beat time"). The word *battered* has gained a whole new meaning than it had when Roethke wrote the poem. But readers respond from the perspective of their times and to those expressions that are familiar. For today's reader, the term battered has a strong emotional impact. It is interesting that a frequently used expression such as "beat time" in this context evokes a negative response from some readers.

Additionally, the spectre of violence in society is identified by several students who assumed that the "battered knuckle" indicated that the father was involved in a fight when he stopped for the drink. Others made an even more startling assumption: The knuckles were battered when Papa hit the boy or his mother. Several students even expressed concern that the boy was endangered while dancing.

On the other hand, other students from families where the father is a blue-collar worker frequently assumed that he hurt his hand because he is a laborer. A 10th-grader said: "I think that the boy's father was a hard working man that is involved in some sort of manual labor because of his battered knuckle and palm caked with dirt."

Invitation 20.2

The concept of potential multiple responses to a text (vs. the idea of one correct answer) is central to the transactional theory of response. Select another poem or a short story (e.g., Robinson Jeffers' "The Bloody Sire" or Ernest Hemingway's "The Killers") and write a personal response, followed then, by a small group discussion. In addition to comparing your responses, consider the personal, textual, and social factors that conditioned your responses.

DIVERSITY OF OPINION

I love this poem, have always loved it, because of its technical excellence—its rhythm, its imagery, its mingling of pleasure and pain. Will I condemn the father because he is drunk and hurts the son unknowingly? No—and Roethke didn't either. Papa just was.

The evidence that the poem evokes a range of student responses is well documented by the examples that we have examined. They reflect the reader's experiences, life situation, and culture in relation to the text. As teachers recognize the potential that a text provides for diverse reactions, they will view the diversity of student responses as an indication that the process of making the connection between the reader and the text is coming to fruition. In this process one of the central areas of discussion is on the differences in interpretation among the students. The teacher's role is not to attempt to find ways to reconcile differing opinions, but rather to help students to accept and to honor attitudes different from theirs. These responses are broadly either personal or nonpersonal and those students who have personal responses react either positively or negatively to their experience reading the poem. The discussion then moves to an exploration of *how* and *why* there have been these variations.

By using both the brainstorming and the written response and discussion approaches, students are encouraged to express their reactions in a supportive, accepting environment. In this process students freely exchange their responses. Students are neither expected to come to a common attitude nor to adapt their transactions to conform to any other responses. The sharing of student reactions either as they read their responses or through the class discussion is conducive to building a sense of community within the classroom. In this environment, students are willing to disclose very personal reactions. It is the nature of this poem and the type of intense transactions that the students have with it that helps to establish this supportive classroom climate. This feeling of community, in turn, stimulates the students' willingness to hear differing attitudes and to acknowledge another perspective. The honesty, candor, and openness of this experience serves to make students more respectful of their peers, the diversity of their lives, and the differences of their opinions.

Rosenblatt explains that the reader "may learn indirectly about others' experiences with the text; he [she] may come to see that his [her] own was confused or impoverished, and he [she] may then be stimulated to call forth from the text a better poem. But this he [she] must do him[her]self, and only what he [she] him[her]self experiences in relation to the text is— again let us underline—*for him* [her], the work" (*Reader* 105). Therefore, through class discussion we can provide enriched opportunities for students to explore their experiences with the text so they may choose to reexamine their responses.

The experiences that we, as teachers, have had in using "My Papa's Waltz" with students at all levels, affirm that responding to literature can be an "event" that speaks, often poignantly, to their lives and perspectives rather than an academic exercise in which they seek correct interpretations. This type of personal connection with literature provides readers of all ages with opportunities to be active participants in their relationship with the text.

REFERENCES

Boyer, Ernest L. *High School: A Report on Secondary Education in America.* New York: Harper & Row, 1983.

Roethke, Theodore. "My Papa's Waltz." *The Pocket Book of Modern Verse.* Ed. Oscar Williams. New York: Pocket Books, 1972. 433.

Rosenblatt, Louise M. *Literature as Exploration.* 4th ed. New York: Modern Language Association, 1983.

———. *The Reader, the Text, the Poem: The Transactional Theory of the Literary Work.* Carbondale; Southern Illinois University Press, 1978.

Solzhenitsyn, Aleksandr. *Nobel Lecture.* New York: Farrar, Straus and Giroux, 1972.

Glossary
Key Concepts and Strategies

Aesthetic stance.   The approach of a reader toward a text that focuses attention on her or his senses and feelings in the experiencing of the text; that is, what is being lived through *during* the reading event. Aesthetic responses are personal and unique because private language nuances come into play along with personal associations, attitudes, and values. Refer to *Efferent stance; Stance.* (chaps. 1, 5, 6, 13, 14, 16, 18)

Affective fallacy.   The assertion that rejects biographical and social factors in shaping the meaning of texts, in accordance with the tenets of New Criticism. Also rejected is the reader's emotional response in shaping meaning. (chap. 1)

Biographical criticism.   Based on the view that the literary work is primarily a reflection of the author's life, personality, and times, this critical approach assumes the text can be interpreted in terms of the author's intention. (chap. 1)

Biopoem.   A structured autobiographical poem with a designated number of lines that can be varied to suit individual purpose. Each line has a lead and a specified number of words to indicate how it is to be completed. (chap. 14)

Cultural theory of response.   In this approach, theorists examine the way readers are socialized to respond; that is, the shaping of responses by cultural rules, attitudes, and values, as well as larger cultural, historical contexts. (chaps. 1, 16–19)

Dialogue journal.   Refer to *Journal, response.* (chap. 6)

Efferent stance.   The approach of a reader toward a text that focuses attention on the denotative definition of words, on their public meanings. The reading is impersonal, removed from emotional involvement. The purpose of efferent reading is the ideas, the information or instruction to be learned or acted upon after the reading event. Refer to *Aesthetic stance; Stance.* (chaps. 1, 5, 13)

Experiential theory of Response. Refer to *Reader response criticism.* (chap. 1)

Expressive writing. Personal writing that expresses the feelings or examines the ideas of the writer. Often the writer explores or discovers aspects of the self or clarifies the relationship of self to the world. Expressive writing may take various forms, but it tends toward the informal. (chap. 4)

Feminist criticism. An approach to literature that takes into account the image of women characters in texts, the place of women writers in the literary canon, and the unique responses of female readers to texts as contrasted to those of male readers. In the assumption that the reader (i.e., gender) is significant in establishing meaning, feminist criticism falls within the reader-response context. (chaps. 1, 9, 15, 17)

Gendered reading. Terminology used to suggest the impact of the gender of a reader on her or his response to and interpretation of a text. Refer to *Feminist criticism.* (chaps. 5, 15, 17)

Historical criticism. The critical approach involving the study of historical materials; that is, the history of literary periods, movements, and culture, to understand the literary document. (chaps. 1, 17)

Imaginative writing. Writing that creates or re-creates experience, rather than explains it, that uses language to evoke emotions and experiences in others. Imaginative writing includes drama and narratives—fables, tales, short stories, novels, poetry, and others. (chaps. 4, 13)

Intentional fallacy. The assertion that negates references to evidence outside a text to establish the interpretation of that text. Such evidence might include statements by the author that express her or his intentions —purpose, meaning—or information about the author's life, beliefs, and times. In the first instance, the author's intentions may not be borne out in the text. Further, the text must speak for itself to its audience. (chap. 1)

Journal, response. When used with literature, the purpose of this writing activity is to engage or elicit the reader's personal response to a text. It is intended as a process response, a reflection of spontaneous feelings and attitudes. There are several names and formats for such journals, including reading journal, learning log, and dialogue journal. The last involves a written dialogue between two readers responding to a text, perhaps two students or a student and a teacher. (chaps. 1, 7, 8, 11–19)

Learning log. Refer to *Journal, response.*

Marxist criticism. An approach to literary criticism that is based on the economic and cultural theory of Karl Marx. Such critics examine the ideological background of the authors and the expression of social realism in the text. To the extent that the reader is significant in establishing meaning, Marxist criticism falls within the reader-response context. (chap. 1)

New criticism. Literary criticism that is based on the primacy of the text. The literary work is perceived as an object, autonomous from the world. The text is examined objectively with close analysis of the internal interrelationships, such linguistic relationships as word interactions, figures of speech and symbols, and the central theme. The author—intentions and biography—and social factors are rejected; the reader is depersonalized. (chaps. 1, 3, 4, 6)

Plausibility. Comparable to the term *validity,* this suggests the probability of an interpretation reflecting elements of a text, being coherent and inclusive of its various features and language subtleties. *Implausibility* suggests the opposite; that is, a response that is or tends to be outside the text. Refer to *Validity.* (chaps. 1, 8, 9)

Prereading. An activity conducted before a text is read or before it is discussed to prepare the readers for the text or the discussion. Such exercises tend to help students and readers to connect their personal experiences with those of the text or help them to activate and begin to shape their experiential response to the text. (chaps. 2, 7–9, 11, 20)

Psychological criticism. This term is applied to two avenues of criticism, one focusing critical attention on the text to analyze the psyche of the author, the other encompassing aspects of the reader's psychological response, defined later.

Psychological theories of response. In this approach, the focus of attention is on the reader, that is, the reader's cognitive or subconscious processes in response to a text. Readers' responses are shaped by their level of intellectual development and cognitive abilities as well as subconscious focus. An extension, psychoanalytical theories of responses, focuses on subconscious fantasy themes in the shaping of readers' experiences. (chap. 1)

Reader-response approach. The application of reader-response criticism. Teachers establish a classroom climate using appropriate language, stance, processes, and procedures to encourage the active role of the reader with the text; readers use the concepts embodied by the theory as they process their reading. Refer to *Reader response criticism; Stance.* (chaps. 1–20)

Reader-response criticism. That body of criticism that focuses on the reader in relation to the text as differentiated from other critical theories that ignore or reject the reader. There is an array of critical positions referred to by this terminology that are generally differentiated by their orientation toward the reader, the text, or the reader and text. By invoking the role of the reader as active re-creator of the text, reader-response criticism recognizes the validity of more than one interpretation, thus rejecting the notion of a single determinate meaning of a text. Refer to *Subjective criticism; Transactional theory*. (chaps. 1, 8, 17)

Reader-response diagram. An exercise designed to help students reflect on their transaction with the text. Each reader is asked to identify characteristics, attitudes, or ideas of herself or himself along with aspects of the text that might have affected the transaction. (chap. 8)

Readers Theatre. An activity using a script that involves rendering a literary work orally with some—usually minimal—movement and character interaction. The presentation may be staged but without props. (chap. 7)

Reading event. A reading occasion; that is, an act of reading that occurs at a particular moment to an individual reader in the context of a particular situation or environment. (chap. 1)

Role-play activity. An activity in which readers are asked to take on the persona of a character (or in some way relate or respond to a character), enacting a "frame" of the character's life situation within or extending from the text. This activity might be oral, written, or a combination (e.g., creating a monologue, dialogue, or conversation; writing a diary, log entry, letter, or advertisement). (chaps. 1, 10, 13, 14)

Selective attention. In a reading context, this term refers to the reader's process of selecting certain features of the text to relate to and certain subtleties of language and relationships to focus on or minimize. Consciously or unconsciously, the reader processes the text according to her or his dominant reader stance and interest, and is influenced by individual language and life experiences. The process is dynamic in the sense of response to individual elements and in the evolving of responses—the shifting and changing, the building and restructuring that occurs as the reader proceeds through the text. Refer to *Stance; Transactional theory*. (chaps. 1 and 17)

Simulation exercise game. Refer to *Role-play activity*.

Social theory of response. In this approach, the focus of attention is on the social dynamics of sharing responses. It is inclusive of social constructivist theory and the dialogue theory, among others. (chaps. 1, 17)

Stance. The approach that a reader adopts toward the reading of a text; that is, to what the reader consciously or unconsciously directs her or his attention. A continuum of response possibilities (stances) exist from the predominantly aesthetic to the predominantly efferent and in between. The same text may be read in either direction, toward the efferent or toward the aesthetic, by different readers or by the same reader at different times. Refer to *Aesthetic stance; Efferent stance.* (chaps. 1, 4)

Structural criticism. The focus of structural critics is on the operative structure of a literary work. This approach identifies and analyzes the conventions that characterize and differentiate the different forms (e.g., genre and subgenre) as well as the elements of the text, such as narrative structure and characterization. (chap. 1)

Subjective criticism. Primacy is given to the reader in this reader-response position. Meaning emerges from the readers; they create texts as expressions of their individual "identity themes" or to produce self-understanding. The focus is on the reader's response experience and its interpretation. The concept of the objective text is rejected. (chap. 1)

Textual theory of response. Refer to *New criticism.*

Transaction. This term as it is applied in a reading context establishes the dynamic relationship of reader and text in which they go beyond merely affecting one another; each conditions and is conditioned by the other. The term *transaction* is differentiated from *interaction,* which suggests two discrete elements acting on each other. Refer to *Transactional theory.* (chaps. 1, 3, 5, 6, 8, 9, 12, 15–17, 19, 20)

Transactional theory. The theoretical approach within the reader-response spectrum that insists that the reader and the text are mutually essential elements of a reading event. The text acts as a catalyst or stimulus for the reader, activating aspects of her or his personality and experience, as well as a guide or constraint during the reading process. The reader responds to the text as influenced by these aspects and the immediate situation, selecting features and nuances of language and relationships according to these internal and external factors. Refer to *Selective attention.* (chaps. 1, 2, 5, 6, 8, 9, 12)

Unsent letter. Refer to *Simulation exercise game.* (chaps. 13, 14)

Validity. A term denoting the appropriateness of a reading—interpretation—as measured against the constraints of the text. An out-of-context response or a strongly skewed response may be said to be an invalid or a less valid transaction with the text. This is not intended to suggest that there is a single correct interpretation or meaning of a literary work. Refer to *Plausibility.* See Chapters 1, 2, 6)

Writing to learn. The use of writing as a tool for learning rather than for learning to write. It places emphasis on the writing process rather than on completion of a product. Frequently, it uses the short writing activities often associated with prewriting and prereading. (chaps. 13, 14, 16)

Bibliography

Representative selections of the following bibliography are annotated. In addition to books expressing reader-response theory and pedagogy, several recent titles expressing alternative theories are included for purposes of comparison.

BOOKS

Anderson, Philip, and Gregory Rubano. *Enhancing Aesthetic Reading and Response.* Urbana, IL: National Council of Teachers of English, 1991.

Appleyard, J. A. *Becoming a Reader: The Experience of Fiction From Adolescence to Adulthood.* New York: Cambridge University Press, 1990.

Beach, Richard. *A Teacher's Introduction to Reader-Response Theories.* Urbana, IL: National Council of Teachers of English, 1993.

Beach, Richard, Judith Green, Michael Kamil, and Timothy Shanahan, eds. *Multicultural Perspectives on Literary Research.* Urbana, IL: National Conference on Research in English/National Council of Teachers of English, 1992.

Beach, Richard, and James Marshall. *Teaching Literature in the Secondary School.* San Diego, CA: Harcourt Brace Jovanovich, 1990.

Bettelheim, Bruno. *The Uses of Enchantment: The Meaning and Importance of Fairy Tales.* New York: Knopf, 1976.

Bleich, David. *Readings and Feelings: An Introduction to Subjective Criticism.* Urbana, IL: National Council of Teachers of English, 1975.
    Bleich's stated aim is "to demonstrate that literature exists altogether on the basis of the subjective re-creation of the reader." He illustrates and

analyzes levels of response to text—perception, the affective, and the associative. Further, Bleich discusses subjective interpretation as a communal act and provides suggestions for applying his ideas in the classroom.

———. *Subjective Criticism.* Baltimore: John Hopkins University Press, 1978.
Bleich asserts the power of individual readers to create and control interpretation of texts. He projects a three-stage reading process: subjective response, resymbolization (i.e., the reader's desire and thrust toward explanation or interpretation), and negotiation with a community of readers to develop new knowledge. By stating that having an interpretation is not possible in "isolation from a community," Bleich seems to undermine his basic premise.

Boyum, Joy Gould. *Double Exposure: Fiction Into Film.* New York: New American Library, 1985.

Burke, Kenneth. *The Philosophy of Literary Form.* New York: Vintage, 1957.

Cain, William E. *The Crisis in Criticism: Theory, Literature, and Reform in English Studies.* Baltimore: Johns Hopkins University Press, 1984.
An extended discussion of New Criticism, followed by a review of the "state of criticism" in the 20th century.

Clifford, John, ed. *The Experience of Reading: Louise Rosenblatt and Reader Response Theory.* Portsmouth, NH: Boynton/Cook, 1991.
Rosenblatt's transactional (reader response) theory is explored in the context of both criticism and pedagogy. Essay topics include: promoting the values of democracy, feminism, teacher–student relationships, bridging pedagogy and theory, and modes of reading.

Cooper, Charles C., ed. *Researching Response to Literature and the Teaching of Literature: Points of Departure.* Norwood, NJ: Ablex, 1984.

Corcoran, Bill, and Emrys Evans, eds. *Readers, Texts, Teachers.* Upper Montclair, NJ: Boynton/Cook, 1987.
Revising the basis for teaching literature and encouraging the experience of literature are the foci of this anthology. The chapters, after two on theoretical and historical background, provide classroom, reader-response practices. Four of these are concerned with writing, others with types of mental activity and methods of developing responses.

Corcoran, B., M. Hayhoe, and Gordon Pradl, eds. *Knowledge in the Making: Challenging the Text in the Classroom.* Portsmouth, NH: Heinemann, 1994.

Culler, Jonathan. *Structural Poetics: Structuralism, Linguistics, and the Study of Literature.* Ithaca, NY: Cornell University Press, 1975.

Daniels, Harvey. *Literature Circles: Voice and Choice in the Student-Centered Classroom.* York, ME: Stenhouse Publishers, 1994.

Eagleton, Terry. *Literary Theory: An Introduction*. Minneapolis: University of Minnesota Press, 1983.

> Literary theories of the 20th century—with some prefatory historical background—are defined and discussed. Eagleton further expresses the limitations of these theories from a social political (Marxist criticism) perspective.

Eco, Umberto. *The Limits of Interpretation*. Bloomington: Indiana University Press, 1990.

> In this collection, Eco discusses aspects of interpretive theory and applies his thinking to a variety of materials. He proposes a "moderate" position: Although acknowledging the concept of multiple readings of a text, he asserts that some reader-response critics overdominate the text, that "it is possible to reach an agreement, if not about meanings that a text encourages, at least about those that a text discourages" (45).

———. *The Role of the Reader: Explorations in the Semiotics of Texts*. Bloomington: Indiana University Press, 1979.

Farrell, Edmund J., and James R. Squire, eds. *Transactions With Literature: A Fifty-Year Perspective*. Urbana, IL: National Council of Teachers of English, 1990.

> These essays, commemorating the 50th anniversary of the publication of *Literature as Exploration*, explore books for young people over that time span, the classroom tradition, and the research tradition. A retrospective essay by Rosenblatt and an extended bibliography round out the book.

Fetterly, Judith. *The Resisting Reader: A Feminist Approach to American Fiction*. Bloomington: Indiana University Press, 1978.

Fish, Stanley. *Is There a Text in This Class?* Cambridge, MA: Harvard University Press, 1980.

> In the early essays of this collection, the reader is identified as "the self-sufficient repository of meaning" in opposition to the text. Later, Fish advances the concept of the interpretive community, which supersedes both the reader and the text. A reader, as a "product" of a community, interprets meaning from a text as enabled by that community; interpretations will vary accordingly. Communities are defined by such aspects as culture, situation, context, perspective, and interpretive strategies.

Flynn, Elizabeth A., and Patrocinio P. Schweikart, eds. *Gender and Reading: Essays on Reader, Texts and Contexts*. Baltimore: Johns Hopkins University Press, 1986.

Freund, Elizabeth. *The Return of the Reader: Reader Response Criticism*. New York: Methuen, 1987.

Greene, Gayle, and Coppelia Kahn. *Making a Difference: Feminist Literary Criticism*. New York: Methuen, 1986.

Harris, Wendell V. *Interpretive Acts: In Search of Meaning.* New York: Oxford University Press, 1988.

Hernadi, Paul, ed. *What Is Criticism?* Bloomington: Indiana University Press, 1981.

Holland, Norman. *The Dynamic of Literary Response.* New York: Oxford University Press, 1968.

———. *Five Readers Reading.* New Haven, CT: Yale University Press, 1975.
Identified as subjective/psychological criticism. This study of the detailed responses of five readers to the same texts reveals, according to Holland, that "the way one puts a story together derives from the structures in the mind one brings to the story" (39). Although acknowledging that readers "draw on" textural features, Holland focuses on their "identity themes" as the source of meaning.

———. *Poems in Persons: An Introduction to the Psychoanalysis of Literature.* New York: Norton, 1973.

Iser, Wolfgang. *The Act of Reader: A Theory of Aesthetic Response.* Baltimore: Johns Hopkins University Press, 1978.
Identified as a "reception" theorist, Iser acknowledges the active role of the reader—"the reader is present in the text" (118)—and the potential for more than one interpretation of a text. His discussion relates how the strategies of the text guide or direct the reader who fills in gaps, textual indeterminacies. It seems that the features of the text control the meaning, giving it, ultimately greater prominence.

———. *The Implied Reader: Patterns of Communication in Prose Fiction From Bunyan to Beckett.* Baltimore: Johns Hopkins University Press, 1974

Karolides, Nicholas J., ed. *Reader Response in Elementary Classrooms: Quest and Discovery.* Mahwah, NJ: Lawrence Erlbaum Associates, 1997.

Kintgen, E. R. *The Perception of Poetry.* Bloomington: Indiana University Press, 1983.

Langer, Judith A., ed. *Literature Instruction: A Focus on Student Response.* Urbana, IL: National Council of Teachers of English, 1992.

Mailloux, Steven. *Interpretive Conventions: The Reader in the Study of American Fiction.* Ithaca, NY: Cornell University Press, 1982.
Mailloux compares and analyzes five theories of reader-response criticism: the subjectivism (psychological), phenomenology (intersubjective), and structuralism (social). He proceeds to develop a social reading model that is "temporal and convention-based." Interpretive conventions are defined as "shared ways of making sense of reality . . . communal procedures for making intelligible the world, behavior, communication and literary texts" (149).

Many, Joyce, and Carole Cox, eds. *Reader Stance and Literary Understanding: Exploring the Theories, Research and Practice.* Norwood, NJ: Ablex, 1992.

Marshall, James. *Patterns of Discourse in Classroom Discussions of Literature.* Albany, NY: SUNY at Albany, The Center for the Learning and Teaching of Literature, 1989.

Milner, Joseph O., and Lucy F. Milner, eds. *Passages to Literature: Essays on Teaching in Australia, Canada, England, the United States, and Wales.* Urbana, IL: National Council of Teachers of English, 1989.

Moran, Charles, and Elizabeth F. Penfield, eds. *Conversations: Contemporary Critical Theory and the Teaching of English.* Urbana, IL: National Council of Teachers of English, 1990.

Probst, Robert E. *Response and Analysis: Teaching Literature in Junior and Senior High School.* Portsmouth, NH: Boynton/Cook, 1988.
    Teaching literature through the transactional model of reader-response criticism is the center of this text. Its concepts inform discussions of, for example, classroom strategies, text selection, the literature curriculum, and evaluation.

Purves, Alan, Theresa Rogers, and Anna O. Soter. *How Porcupines Make Love: Notes on a Response-Centered Curriculum.* 2d ed. New York: Longman, 1990.
    Literature instruction and curriculum development are the two foci of this text. Discussions of the response-centered curriculum and the roles of the teacher are followed by explanation and illustration of teaching strategies: discussion, use of visuals, oral activities, and written activities. Concluding chapters are concerned with assignments and examinations.

Purves, Alan C., and Richard Beach. *Literature and the Reader: Research in Response to Literature, Reading Interests and the Teaching of Literature.* Urbana, IL: National Council of Teachers of English, 1972.

Rogers, Theresa, and Anna O. Soter. *Reading Across Cultures: Teaching Literature in a Diverse Society.* New York: Teachers College Press, 1997.

Rosenblatt, Louise M. *Literature as Exploration.* 5th ed. New York: Modern Language Association, 1995.
    Identified as the first to establish the importance of the reader in creating meaning, Rosenblatt discusses the nature of the literary experience, asserting the relationship of reader and text in evoking a "poem." The influence of persona, social, and cultural aspects is expressed. Significant implications for teaching are drawn, underlying themes being the development of humanistic concerns and democratic values and practices.

———. *The Reader, the Text, the Poem: The Transactional Theory of the Literary Work.* 2nd ed. Carbondale: Southern Illinois University Press, 1992.
    The focus of this work is theoretical. Rosenblatt enunciates fully the transactional nature of the reading process, exploring in detail the

"poem as event" and the "evoking of a poem." She expresses the efferent–aesthetic continuum and the "openness and constraint" of the text, that is, the factor of validity. The text concludes with a discussion of response and interpretation for all readers in relation to criticism.

Scholes, Robert. *Textual Power: Literary Theory and the Teaching of English*. New Haven, CT: Yale University Press, 1985.

Scholes acknowledges the role of the reader, eschewing the New Critical approach. However, he concentrates on the power of the text. Establishing three related skills—reading, interpretation, and criticism—he illustrates their teaching and argues for a curriculum of textual studies, that is, textual knowledge and skill. In his final chapter, he contests Stanley Fish's concept of interpretive communities.

Selden, Raman. *Practicing Theory and Reading Literature*. Lexington: University Press of Kentucky, 1989.

Short, Kathy, and Kathryn Pierce, eds. *Talking About Books*. Portsmouth, NH: Heinemann, 1990.

Showalter, Elaine, ed. *Speaking of Gender*. New York: Routledge, 1989.

Slatoff, Walter J. *With Respect to Readers: Dimensions of Literary Response*. Ithaca, NY: Cornell University Press, 1970.

The varieties of involvement as shaped by individual differences among readers are explored, and divergent responses in relation to the guidance and limitation of the text are detailed. Slatoff expresses the need to go beyond the seeking of commonalities among responses, that is, to reflect on and discuss the differences as well. A general discussion of pedagogical implications concludes the book.

Squire, James R., ed. *Response to Literature*. Champaign, IL: National Council of Teachers of English, 1968.

Suleiman, Susan R., and Inge Crosman, eds. *The Reader in the Text: Essays on Audience and Interpretation*. Princeton, NJ: Princeton University Press, 1980.

This anthology focuses on reading and the reader, its primary aim being "to explore fundamental questions about the status—be it semiotic, sociological, hermeneutic, subjective—of audience in relation to the artistic text" (vii). The introductory essay discusses six varieties of audience-oriented criticism. An extensive bibliography is included.

Thompson, Jack. *Understanding Teenagers' Reading: Reading Processes and the Teaching of Literature*. Melbourne: Methuen Australia (New York: Nichols Publishing), 1987.

Tompkins, Jane P., ed. *Reader Response Criticism: From Formalism to Post-Structuralism*. Baltimore: Johns Hopkins University Press, 1980.

A clear overview of the major theoretical positions within the body of reader-response criticism. The collected essays are arranged logically to show relationships among the positions but also to pattern the focus on text orientation through reader plus text to reader domination. The closing chapter provides a historical "shape of literary response."

Vine, H. and M. A. Faust. *Situating Readers: Students Making Meaning of Literature.* Urbana, IL: National Council of Teachers of English, 1993.

Willinsky, John. *The Triumph of Literature/The Fate of Literacy.* New York: Teachers College Press, 1991.

Worton, Michael, and Judeth Still, eds. *Intertextuality: Theories and Practice.* Manchester, UK: Manchester University Press, 1990.

ARTICLES

Adams, Peter. "Writing From Reading: Dependent Authorship as a Response." *Readers, Texts, Teachers.* Ed. Bill Corcoran and Emrys Evans. Upper Montclair, NJ: Boynton/Cook, 1987. 119–52.

Allen, Carolyn. "Louise Rosenblatt and Theories of Reader Response." *Reader* 20 (Fall 1988): 32–39.

Anderson, Philip M. "The Past Is Now: Approaches to the Secondary School Literature Curriculum." *English Journal* 75.8 (December 1986): 19–22.

Athanases, Steven. "Developing a Classroom Community of Interpreters." *English Journal* 77.1 (January 1988): 45–48.

Beach, Richard. "New Directions in Research on Response to Literature." *Transactions With Literature.* Ed. Edmund J. Farrell and James R. Squire. Urbana, IL: National Council of Teachers of English, 1990. 65–77.

Beach, Richard, and Linda Wendler. "Developmental Differences in Response to a Story." *Research in the Teaching of English* 21 (1987): 286–97.
   This study compared the inferences of readers from four class levels (secondary and college) about characters' acts, perceptions, and goals. Readers' cognitive development, social cognition, and self-concepts significantly affected their focus.

Beach, Richard, and Susan Hynds. "Research on Response to Literature." *Handbook on Response to Literature,* Vol. II. Ed. Rebecca Barr, et al. White Plains, NY: Longman, 1991. 453–89.

Beehler, Sharon A. "Close vs. Closed Reading: Interpreting the Clues." *English Journal* 77.6 (October 1988): 39–43.

Black, Stephen A. "On Reading Psychoanalytically." *College English* 39.3 (November 1977): 267–74.

Blake, Robert W., and Anna Lunn. "Responding to Poetry: High School Students Read Poetry." *English Journal* 75.2 (February 1986): 68–73.
   Report of a study of what five untrained high school students do as they process a new poem.

Bleich, David. "The Subjective Character of Critical Interpretation." *College English* 36.7 (March 1975): 739–755.
    Projects the dynamics of the subjective response, denying the objective text. Bleich contrasts his position with that of Holland.

Cai, Mingshui. "Reader Response Theory and the Politics of Multicultural Literature." *Reading Across Cultures: Teaching Literature in a Diverse Society.* Ed. Theresa Rogers and Anna O. Soter. New York: Teachers College Press, 1997. 199–212.

Carey, Robert F. "The Reader, the Text, the Response: Literary Theory and Reading Research." *English Quarterly* 18.3 (Fall 1985): 17–23.

Chase, Nancy D., and Cynthia R. Hynd. "Reader Response: An Alternative Way to Teach Students to Think About the Text." *Journal of Reading* 30 (1987): 530–40.

Clifford, John. "A Response Pedagogy for Noncanonical Literature.: *Reader* 15 (Spring 1986): 48–61.

———. "Transactional Teaching and the Literary Experience." *English Journal* 68.9 (December 1979): 36–39.
    Presents a philosophy of teaching literature founded on Rosenblatt's transactional theory.

Connor, John W., and Irene Chalmers-Neubauer. "Mrs. Schuster Adopts Discussion: A Four-Week Experiment in a English Classroom." *English Education* 21.1 (February 1989): 30–38.

Corcoran, Bill. "Spiders, Surgeons, and Anxious Aliens: Three Classroom Allies." *English Journal* 77.1 (January 1988): 39–44.
    Three clusters of classroom strategies are presented, responding to three features: readers, texts, and cultural contexts.

Cox, Carole, and Joyce Many. "Toward an Understanding of the Aesthetic Response in Literature. *Language Arts* 69.1 (January 1992): 28–33.

Crosman, R. "Do Readers Make Meaning." *The Reader in the Text: Essays on Audience and Interpretation.* Ed. S. R. Sulleman and I. Crosman. Princeton, NJ: Princeton University Press, 1980. 149–64.

Cullinan, Bernice E., Kathy T. Harwood, and Lee Galda. "The Reader and the Story: Comprehension and Responses." *Journal of Research and Development in Education* 163 (1983): 29–38.

Culp, Mary Beth. "Literature's Influence of Young Adult Attitudes, Values, and Behavior, 1975–1984." *English Journal* 74.8 (December 1985): 31–35.
    Report of a study to ascertain the influence of literature based upon the responses of the readers themselves.

Dasenbrock, Reed Way. "Do We Write the Text We Read?" *College English* 53.1 (1991): 7–18.

DeMott, Benjamin. "Learning How to Imagine a Poem." *English Education* 22.2 (May 1988): 71–87.

Dilworth, Collett B. "The Reader as Poet: A Strategy for Creative Reading." *English Journal* 66.2 (February 1977): 43–47.

Dionisio, Marie. "Responding to Literary Elements Through Mini-Lessons and Dialogue Journals." *English Journal* 80.1 (January 1991): 40–44.

Duke, Charles R. "The Case of the Divorced Reader." *English Journal* 66.2 (February 1977): 33–36.
    The negative effect on readers of distancing the text is contrasted to personal response experiences.

———. "Tapping the Power of Personal Response to Poetry." *Journal of Reading* 33 (1990): 442–47.

Earthman, Elise A. "Creating the Virtual Work: Readers' Processes in Understanding Literary Texts." *Research in the Teaching of English* 26 (December 1992): 351–84.
    Compares college freshmen to graduate students in their interaction with and creation of meaning of literary texts.

Eeds, Maryann, and Deborah Wells. "Grand Conversations: An Exploration of Meaning Construction in Literature Study Groups." *Research in the Teaching of English* 23 (1989): 4–29.
    The way readers and teachers build meaning together is expressed and illustrated in this study. Teacher behavior as it influences these "conversations" is described.

Evans, Emrys. "Readers Re-Creating Texts." *Readers, Texts, Teachers.* Ed. Bill Corcoran and Emrys Evans. Upper Montclair, NJ: Boynton/Cook, 1987: 22–40.

Fairbanks, Colleen M. "Reading Students: Texts in Contexts." *English Education* 27 (February 1995): 40–52.

Fillion, Bryant. "Reading as Inquiry: An Approach to Literature Learning." *English Journal* 70.1 (January 1981): 39–45.

Flood, James, and Diane Lapp. "A Reader-Response Approach to the Teaching of Literature." *Reading Research and Instruction* 27.4 (Summer 1988): 61–66.
    Proposes a design for an instructional process for response-based teaching.

Florio-Ruane, Susan. "The Future Teachers' Autobiography Club: Preparing Educators to Support Literacy Learning in Culturally Diverse Classrooms." *English Education* 26 (February 1994): 52–66.

Florio-Ruane, Susan, and Julie deTan. "Conflict and Consensus in Teacher

Candidates' Discussion of Ethnic Biography." *English Education* 27 (February 1995): 11–39.

Flynn, Elizabeth A. "Composing Responses to Literary Texts: A Process Approach." *College Composition and Communication* 34 (1983): 342–48.

Flynn illustrates the process of responding to literary text, moving from "expressive" or "writer-based writing"—relating texts to their own experience to "reader-based writing"—that is, *about* literary texts, reflecting analysis. Journal writing is used in the initial stage.

———. "Gender and Reading." *College English* 45 (1983): 236–253.

A comparison of the attitudes, strategies, and interpretations of men and women to the same stories.

Fowler, Lois Josephs, and Kathleen McCormick. "The Expectant Reader in Theory and Practice." *English Journal* 75.6 (October 1986): 45–47.

Galda, Lee. "A Longitudinal Study of the Spectator Stance as a Function of Age and Genre." *Research in the Teaching of English* 24 (1990): 261–78.

The movement of students toward a spectator stance, that is "to evaluate more broadly, to savor feelings, and to contemplate forms," is documented according to grade level. Also revealed is the impact of genre on the response process.

Galda, Lee. "Research in Response to Literature." *Journal of Research and Development in Education* 16.3 (1983): 1–7.

Gilles, Carol. "Reading, Writing, and Talking: Using Literature Study Groups." *English Journal* 78.1 (January 1989): 39–41.

Golden, Joanne, and John Guthrie. "Convergence and Divergence in Reader Response to Literature." *Reading Research Quarterly* 21 (Fall 1986): 408–21.

Graham, Joan, and Robert E. Probst. "Eliciting Responses to Literature." *Kentucky English Journal* 31.1 (Fall 1982): 30–46.

Greco, Norma. "Recreating the Literary Text: Practice and Theory." *English Journal* 79.6 (November 1990): 41–46.

Hancock, Marjorie R. "Exploring the Meaning-Making Process Through the Content of Literature Response Journals: A Case Study Investigation." *Research in the Teaching of English* 27 (December 1993): 335–68.

Henly, Carollyn P. "Reader-Response Theory as Antidote to Controversy: Teaching *The Bluest Eye*." *English Journal* 82 (March 1993): 14–19.

Hoffner, Cynthia, and Joanne Cantor. "Perceiving and Responding to Mass Media Characters." *Responding to the Screen: Reception and Reaction Processes.* Ed. Jennings Bryant and Dolf Zillman. Hillsdale, NJ: Lawrence Erlbaum Associates, 1991. 61–102.

Hunt, Russell, A. "Toward a Process-Intervention Model in Literature Teaching." *College English* 44 (1982): 345–57.

Hynds, Susan. "Bringing Life to Literature and Literature to Life: Social Constructs and Contexts of Four Adolescent Readers." *Research in the Teaching of Literature* 23 (1987): 30–61.

   Two questions are explored in this study: How students bring social-cognitive processes to reading and what contextual factors in and outside the classroom appear to influence readers' connections between literature and life.

———. "Interpersonal Cognitive Complexity and the Literary Processes of Adolescent Readers." *Research in the Teaching of English* 19 (1985): 386–402.

   This study examines the degree to which interpersonal cognitive complexity affects readers in their perceptions of characters as well as story comprehension, response preferences, and literary attitudes.

Jacobsen, Mary. "Looking for Literary Space: The Willing Suspension of Disbelief Revisited." *Research in the Teaching of English* 16 (1982): 21–38.

   The author's students describe their experiences while reading a short story. What they contribute to the reading and what might block their responses are discussed.

Karolides, Nicholas J. "Challenging Old Habits of Mind: Revisiting Reader's Stance." *The New Advocate* 11.2 (Spring 1997): 161–69.

   Stance has significance for readers and teachers. Discussed in this article are the underpinnings of the concept of stance within the framework of the reading process and the recognized role of the reader in that process. The choice-making activity of the reader is explored in conjunction with the role of the text in stimulating and conditioning the reader.

Langer, Judith A. "The Process of Understanding: Reading for Literary and Informative Purposes." *Research in the Teaching of English* 24 (1990): 229–60.

   The meaning-making processes of middle and senior high school students are described. Four stances that are taken toward texts are explored, revealing that the focus of readers' concerns in each stance differs. Characteristics of readers' approaches to reading for literary and information purposes are differentiated.

———. "Thinking and Doing Literature." *English Journal* 87 (February 1998): 16–23.

Lee, Valerie. "Responses of White Students to Ethnic Literature: One Teacher's Experience." *Reader: Essays in Reader-Oriented Theory, Criticism, and Pedagogy* 15 (1986): 24–33.

Leitch, Vincent B. "A Primer of Recent Critical Theories." *College English* 39 (1977): 138–52.

Lewis, Cynthia. "The Social Drama of Literature Discussions in a Fifth/

Sixth-Grade Classroom." *Research in the Teaching of Literature* 31 (May 1997): 163–204.

This investigation of the social contexts and interactions of students in peer-led discussions of literature reveals the impact of power and status on the discussions and the interpretation of literature.

Lindberg, Barbara. "Teaching Literature: The Process Approach." *Journal of Reading* 31 (1988): 732–735.

Lundberg, Patricia L. "Dialogically Feminized Reading: A Critique of Reader-Response Criticism." *Reader: Essays in Reader-Oriented Theory, Criticism, and Pedagogy* 22 (1989): 9 37.

Machet, Myrna. "The Effects of Socio-cultural Values on Adolescents' Responses to Literature." *Journal of Reading* 35.5 (1992): 356–62.

Mandel, Barrett J. Text and Context in the Teaching of English." *English Journal* 68.9 (December 1979): 40–44.

Expresses the limitations of teacher-dominated "contexts" and offers an alternative approach.

Martin, Bruce K. "Teaching Literature as Experience." *College English* 51 (1989). 377–85.

McCormick, Kathleen. "Theory in the Reader: Bleich, Holland, and Beyond." *College English* 47 (1985): 836–50.

Alternatives to the purely spontaneous response statements within a reader-centered course are offered and discussed.

Muldoon, Phyllis A. "Challenging Students to Think: Shaping Questions, Building Community." *English Journal* 79.4 (April 1990): 34–40.

Myers, Kris. "Twenty (Better) Questions." *English Journal* 77.1 (January 1988): 64–65.

Nystrand, Martin, Adam Gamoran, and Mary Jo Heck. "Using Small Groups for Response to and Thinking About Literature." *English Journal* 82 (January 1993): 14–22.

Peterson, Bruce T. "Writing About Responses: A Unified Model of Reading, Interpretation, and Composition." *College English* 44 (1982): 459–68.

Petrosky, Anthony R. "From Story to Essay: Reading and Writing." *College Composition and Communication* 33 (1982): 19–36.

Petrosky draws the connections between reading, responses to literature, and composing. They share similar processes, "rooted in the individual's knowledge and feelings and characterized by the fundamental act of making meaning." The reading-response journal is used to generate responses.

Pradl, Gordon M. "Close Encounters of the First Kind: Teaching the Poem at the Point of Utterance." *English Journal* 76.2 (February 1987): 66–69.

Pritchard, Ruie Jane. "Developing Writing Prompts for Reader Response and Analysis." *English Journal* 82 (March 1993): 24–32.

Probst, Robert E. "Adolescent Literature and the Curriculum." *English Journal* 76.3 (March 1987): 26–30.

———. "Dialogue With a Text." *English Journal* 77.1 (January 1988): 32–38.
      Projects criteria for successful dialogue with a text along with sample questions for various foci.

———. "*Literature as Exploration* and the Classroom." *Transactions With Literature.* Ed. Edmund J. Farrell and James R. Squire. Urbana, IL: National Council of Teachers of English, 1990. 27–37.

———. "Mom, Wolfgang, and Me: Adolescent Literature, Critical Theory, and the English Classroom." *English Journal* 75.6 (October 1986): 33–39.
      The assumptions of New Critical literature instruction are questioned; reader-response concepts are promoted as is the appropriateness of adolescent literature.

———. "Response-Based Teaching of Literature." *English Journal* 70.7 (November 1981): 43–47.

———. "Three Relationships in the Teaching of Literature." *English Journal* 75.1 (January 1986): 60–68.
      The three relationships—reader and text, among readers, and between texts—are examined as to their assumptions and classroom implications.

———. "Transactional Theory in the Teaching of Literature." *Journal of Reading* 31 (1988): 378–81.

Purves, Alan C. "Putting Readers in Their Places: Some Alternatives to Cloning Stanley Fish." *College English* 42 (1980): 228–36.

Rabin, Sydell. "Literature Study Groups: Teachers, Texts, and Readers." *English Journal* 79.6 (November 1990): 47–51.

Reed, Susan D. "Logs: Keeping an Open Mind." *English Journal* 77.2 (February 1988): 52–56.

Reissman, Rose C. "Leaving Out to Pull In: Using Reader Response to Teach Multicultural Literature." *English Journal* 83 (February 1994): 20–23.

Roemer, Majorie G. "Which Reader's Response?" *College English* 49 (1987): 911–21.
      A classroom situation in which contrasting responses emerge serves as a vehicle for exploring the effects to such openness in the classroom and the attitudes and behaviors of teachers.

Rogers, Theresa. "Exploring a Socio-Cognitive Perspective on the Interpretive Processes of Junior High School Students." *English Quarterly* 20.3 (Fall 1987): 218–30.

Compares the effect of social context on interpretation in two types of discussion: question–answer and response centered.

Rosenblatt, Louise M. "The Acid Text in Teaching Literature." *English Journal* 45.2 (February 1956): 66–74.

―――. "The Aesthetic Transaction." *The Journal of Aesthetic Education* 20.4 (Witinter 1986): 122–128.

The aesthetic stance is discussed as it may be adopted by a reader, but also as it applies to other arts. Implications for curricula and classroom methods are suggested.

―――. "Continuing the Conversation: A Clarification." *Research in the Teaching of English* 29 (October 1995): 349–54.

―――. "The Literary Transaction: Evocation and Response." *Theory Into Practice* 21.4 (Autumn 1982): 268–77.

―――. "A Performing Art." *English Journal* 55 (1966): 999–1005.

―――. "The Poem as Event." *College English* 26 (1964): 123–28.

Rosenblatt counterposes her sense of the reader's role in "making" the poem against that of New Critics.

―――. "Toward a Transactional Theory of Reading." *Journal of Reading Behavior.* 1.1 (Winter 1969): 31–49.

―――. "The Transactional Theory: Against Dualisms." *College English* 55.4 (1993): 377–86.

―――. "The Transactional Theory of Reading and Writing." *Theoretical Models and Processes of Reading.* Ed. R. R. Ruddell, M. R. Ruddell, and H. Singer. 4th ed. Newark, DE: International Reading Association, 1994. 1059–1092.

―――. "Viewpoints: Transaction Versus Interaction—A Terminological Rescue Operation." *Research in the Teaching of English* 19 (1985): 96–107.

The distinction between the usages of *transaction* and *interaction* in defining or describing the reading act or reading event is clarified. Aspects of Rosenblatt's theoretical position are incorporated.

―――. "What Facts Does This Poem Teach You?" *Language Arts* 57 (1980): 386–94.

The reader's activities in making meaning from texts are differentiated according to the focus of attention, the reader's adopted stance. The efferent and aesthetic modes are described.

―――. "Writing and Reading: The Transactional Theory. *Reader: Essays in Reader-Oriented Theory, Criticism, and Pedagogy* 20 (Fall 1988): 7–31.

Compares the reading transaction with the writing transaction, expressing parallelisms and differences. Aspects of theory are incorporated as well as discussion of the writer as reader.

Rouse, John. "An Erotics of Teaching." *College English* 45 (1983): 535–48.
In the context of exploring the factor of personal relationships between students and teacher, Rouse contrasts the assumptions and learnings of the theoretical approaches of Holland, Bleich, and Rosenblatt as well as the potential differences in personal relations.

Sampson, Gloria P., and Nancy Carlman. "A Hierarchy of Student Responses to Literature." *English Journal* 71.1 (January 1982): 54–57.

Schaars, Mary Jo. "Teaching *My Antonia* With Guidance From Rosenblatt." *English Journal* 77.1 (January 1988): 54–58.

Schade, Lisa. "Demystifying the Text: Literary Criticism in the High School Classroom." *English Journal* 85 (March 1996): 26–31.

Schull, Ellen. "The Reader, the Text, the Poem—and the Film." *English Journal* 78.8 (December 1989): 53–57.

Senger, Heinz, and B. M. Lynn Archer. "Exploring *Sounder:* The Novel, the Screenplay, and the Film." *English Journal* 78.8 (December 1989): 48–52.

Sheridan, Daniel. "Changing Business as Usual: Reader Response in the Classroom." *College English* 53 (November 1991): 804–14.

Squire, James R. "The Current Crisis in Literary Education." *English Journal* 74.8 (December 1985): 18–21.

Tanenbaum, Miles. "1984: A Confessional Reading and Teaching Approach." *English Journal* 78.4 (April 1989): 31–34.

Tanner, Stephen L. "Education by Criticism." *English Journal* 75.6 (October 1986): 22–26.
Tanner presents an exercise in which critically opposing views are discussed, promoting both awareness of multiple views and the recognition of the student's own voice.

Weaver, Constance. "Parallels Between New Paradigms in Science and in Reading and Literary Theories: An Essay Review." *Research in the Teaching of English* 19 (1985): 298–316.
Key concepts from scientific disciplines and current reading and literary theory are compared, illustrating that they share an emphasis on "organicism and process, specifically the process of transaction between interdependent entities."

Webb, Agnes J. "Transactions With Literary Texts: Conversations in Classrooms." *English Journal* 71.3 (March 1982): 56–60.

White, Brian. "Assuming Nothing: A Pre-Methods Diagnostic in the Teaching of Literature." *English Education* 27 (December 1995): 221–39.

Whitin, Phyllis E. "Exploring Visual Response to Literature." *Research in the Teaching of English* 30 (February 1996): 114–40.

Wilentz, Gay. "Toward a Diaspora Literature: Black Women Writers From Africa, the Caribbean, and the United States." *College English* 54 (1992): 385–405.

Wyman, Linda. "Faking Out the Darkness: Trudell's 'The Jump Shooter'." *English Journal* 76.6 (October 1987): 89–91.
   Illustrates a class's aesthetic experience with a poem.

Zaharias, Jane A. "The Effects of Genre and Tone on Undergraduate Students' Preferred Patterns of Response to Two Short Stories and Two Poems." *Research in the Teaching of Literature* 20 (1986): 56–68.

———. "Literature Anthologies in the U.S.: Impediments to Good Teaching Practice." *English Journal* 78.6 (October 1989): 22–27.
   Discusses the tasks that textbooks assign in relation to general principles based on current theory. Exemplary activities are presented.

Zancanella, Don. "Teachers Reading/Readers Teaching: Five Teachers' Personal Approaches to Literature and Their Teaching of Literature." *Research in the Teaching of English* 25 (1991): 5–32.

Author Index

Subject Index

A

"Acting out," *see* Readers Theater; Role-play activity
Active learning, 266
Activity selection, 21–22, 120, 221
Adolescent readers, 207
    reader-response theory and, 123–124
Adolescents, and text selection, 124–127, 193–194
Aesthetic experience, 9–10, 78, 214, 233, 259, 312
Affective fallacy, 18
African Diaspora, 312, 322–324
African Diaspora literature, 312, 319, 323, 324
African Diaspora students and teachers, 312, 322, 323
Alternative "discourse," 296
Alternative points of view, offering students, 282–283
Analytical writing, 61
Antigone, 225, 227–230, 233, 247
Arguing among students, 52, 84–86, 273
Argumentative essay, overemphasis on, 61, 62
Assessment
    at individual and group level, 321
    student self-assessment, 289, 321
Assimilation, *see* Native American novels
Associations to text, 65, *see also* Memories evoked by text
Author
    intention, 18
    reader having same feelings as, 47
    role(s), 11–12
    in shaping meaning, 18

    taking on, *see* "Dependent authorship"
"Authority" of reader, 15, 60

B

Biases, becoming aware of, 223, 266, 332, *see also* Multicultural literature
Biographical factors, 18
Biographical-historical vantage point of teaching, 18
Bipoems, 226–229
"Black Walnuts," 50, 51
Book Club Program, 192, 290, 295, 298, 299, 304–306
    as context for learning and development, 306–308
Boring, finding literature, 242, 263, 264
Brainstorming, 328–329
The Brave, 220–221
"Breakings," 49, 50

C

Canon, 321–323
Carryover, 181, 191
    creating meaningful, 181–182, 191–192
The Catcher in the Rye, 207–209
Characters
    empathy for and identification with, 125, 211, 219, *see also* Bipoems
    liking *vs.* disliking, 154